POINT–COUNTERPOINT

Readings in American Government

Sixth Edition

Herbert M. Levine

St. Martin's Press   New York

For Albert, Philippe, and the late Louise Boudreau

Sponsoring editor: Beth A. Gillett
Development editor: Susan Cottenden
Manager, Publishing services: Emily Berleth
Associate editor, Publishing services: Meryl Gross
Production supervisor: Scott Lavelle
Project management: Pine Tree Composition
Cover design: Lucy Krikorian

For information, write:
St. Martin's Press, Inc.
175 Fifth Avenue
New York, NY 10010

ISBN: 0–312–14987–5

Acknowledgments

Acknowledgments and copyrights are continued at the back of the book on page 388, which constitute an extension of the copyright page.

It is a violation of the law to reproduce these selections by any means whatsoever without the written permission of the copyright holder.

Thurgood Marshall, "The Constitution: Past and Present." Speech at the Annual Seminar of the San Francisco Patent and Trademark Law Association, Maui, Hawaii, May 6, 1987. Notes have been omitted.

William Bradford Reynolds, "The Wisdom of the Framers." Speech at the Vanderbilt University Reunion 1987 Celebration Luncheon, University Club, Nashville, Tennessee, May 23, 1987.

Kirk Cox, prepared statement for U.S. Cong., House of Representatives. *The Perspective of State and Local Governments and the Impact of Federal Regulation.* Hearing before the Committee on the Budget, 104th Cong., 1st Sess., 1995, pp. 87–89.

John G. Kester, "Forever Federal." *Washingtonian* 31, no. 3 (December 1995): 47–48, 51. Permission of the author.

William J. Murray, *Let Us Pray: A Plea for Prayer in Our Schools* (New York: William Morrow & Co., 1995), pp. 187–202. Copyright © by 1995 Gospel Films, Inc. As adapted from William J. Murray, "Q: Does America Need a Constitutional Amendment to Protect School Prayer? Yes: Restore Free-Speech Rights to Local Communities." *Insight on the News* 11, no. 32 (August 21, 1995): 18, 20–21. Reprinted by permission of William Morrow & Co.

Rabbi A. James Rudin, testimony before the Subcommittee on the Constitution of the House Committee on the Judiciary, 104th Cong., 2d Sess., July 23, 1996.

Ernest van den Haag, "Pornography and the Law." *The Heritage Lectures*, no. 111. Reprinted with permission of The Heritage Foundation.

Barry W. Lynn, "Pornography and Liberty." Reprinted by permission.

J. Michael Echevarria, "Reflections on O.J. and the Gas Chamber." *San Diego Law Review* 32, no. 2 (Spring 1995): 491–534. © 1995 San Diego Law Review Association. Footnotes have been omitted.

James C. Anders, "The Case for the Death Penalty." Reprinted by permission.

Louis Michael Seidman, "Criminal Procedure as the Servant of Politics." *Constitutional Commentary* 12, no. 2 (Summer 1995): 207–11. Copyright © 1995 by Constitutional Commentary.

William T. Pizzi, "Punishment and Procedure: A Different View of the American Criminal Justice System." *Constitutional Commentary* 13, no. 1 (Spring 1996): 55–70. Copyright © 1996 by Constitutional Commentary. Footnotes have been omitted.

Contents

Preface

NEW TO THE SIXTH EDITION

The sixth edition of *Point-Counterpoint* is heavily revised from the fifth edition. New to the sixth edition are thirteen debates: school prayer (Chapter 3), constitutional protections for accused criminals (Chapter 6), English as the official language of the United States (Chapter 8), the meaning of voting and elections (Chapter 9), campaign finance reform (Chapter 10), the Electoral College (Chapter 11), media bias (Chapter 12), the War Powers Act (Chapter 14), the confirmation process (Chapter 16), removal of a federal judge (Chapter 18), decriminalization of drugs (Chapter 20), global warming (Chapter 21), and U.S. interests in the United Nations (Chapter 22). Some of these issues appeared in earlier editions of *Point-Counterpoint*, but here many of the readings are new. In addition, there are updated readings on federalism (Chapter 2), the death penalty (Chapter 5), affirmative action (Chapter 7), congressional term limits (Chapter 13), the bureaucracy (Chapter 15), and gun control (Chapter 19). The sixth edition of *Point-Counterpoint* is supported by an online Instructor's Manual. This manual contains at least ten suggested lecture topics for the instructor and five student assignments to accompany each debate issue as well as a general introduction to using the debate format. You will find the site on the Web at:

http://www.smpcollege.com/point_counter

THE RATIONALE FOR *POINT–COUNTERPOINT*

The debate tradition in the United States is as old as the Republic itself. Soon after the colonists achieved independence from British rule, they debated issues as fundamental as slavery, tariffs, and the policy of the United States toward the French Revolution. Some debates in U.S. history — Lincoln-Douglas and Kennedy-Nixon — have become part of the national memory, even if misremembered or embellished.

It is with this tradition in mind that *Point-Counterpoint* has been developed. The text is a collection of readings that present contending sides of important issues in U.S. government. It is designed to contribute to a democratic tradition where vigorous controversy is regarded as both proper and desirable.

The selections deal with the basic structure of the U.S. political system, civil liberties and civil rights, political participation, the power of government policy makers, and the direction of public policy. The format of the book encourages critical thinking. Part and chapter introductions provide important background information and a synopsis of the major points in each selection. For each debate question, one "Yes" response and one "No" response are given. "Questions for Discussion" follow each debate to help students formulate their own answers to the debate question. If both conflicting views on an issue seem convincing, students can then turn to the "Suggested Readings," which provide general background information as well as pro and con arguments.

Three cautionary points are in order. First, issues can rarely be broken down into a neat classification such as liberal or conservative, In this regard, it is often the case that some of the most meaningful controversy goes on among advocates of the same political philosophy.

Second, space limitations and the format of the book dictate that only two views — "Yes" and "No" — are given for each question. More often than not, other answers could be presented, such as "Yes, but ... ," "No, but ... ," or even "Maybe." In the process of debate, refinements can be developed. This yes-no approach, however, should provide a start toward understanding problems of U.S. government.

Third, the book does not present a single ideological perspective. As a whole, it does not take a side on the issues but presents, instead, many views. If there is an ideological commitment, it is implicit in the nature of the format: a commitment to vigorous debate as befits the democratic tradition.

ACKNOWLEDGMENTS

I am indebted to numerous people in the academic and publishing communities who helped me at various stages in the writing and production of this edition of *Point-Counterpoint*. The editorial consultants for the book offered superb suggestions and insights, including proposals for different debate topics and stylistic changes. Specifically, I want to acknowledge the following consultants for St. Martin's Press: John Francis Burke, University of Houston-Downtown; M. Jeffrey Colbert, University of North Carolina, Greensboro; John Coleman, University of Wisconsin-Madison; Art English, University of Arkansas at Little Rock; John J. Kennedy, The Pennsylvania State University-Allentown; Robert W. Langran, Villanova University; Lauri H. McNown, University of Colorado at Boulder; and Noelle H. Norton, University of San Diego.

I am indebted to Ann Hofstra Grogg, who copyedited the manuscript with her usual extraordinary skill. I also want to thank Beth A. Gillett, the sponsoring editor; and Susan Cottenden, the development editor, for their thoughtful assistance.

Herbert M. Levine

Part I

Foundations of the United States

Political System

I n 1987 the United States celebrated the two hundredth anniversary of the Constitution by drawing attention to the basic institutions and practices of the nation's political system. Political officials, leaders of private associations, and writers assessed anew the fundamental assumptions under which the U.S. political system was established; they examined how a system designed for a largely agrarian society consisting of thirteen eastern seaboard states had evolved over two centuries to meet the needs of a postindustrial society that spans a continent.

These observers often evaluated how well or how poorly the United States was living up to the ideas professed by the Framers of the Constitution. Whether positive or negative in their assessments, they focused on social, economic, and political institutions.

Those who looked favorably at the development of the past two centuries often drew attention to a number of features: the rise in the nation's standard of living; the integration of groups from diverse ethnic, religious, and racial backgrounds into a "melting pot" in which these groups could live in peace; the resilience of the Constitution in adapting to change; the expansion of democratic practices to include ever larger numbers of people; the competition of political parties for electoral success; the freedoms accorded to U.S. citizens in expressing ideas, protesting peacefully, and responding to accusations in the criminal justice system; and the promotion of the common defense.

Those who were critical of the developments of the past two centuries pointed to different facts to justify their negative conclusions: the great disparity in assets, in which less than 10 percent of the U.S. population controls 90 percent of the nation's wealth; the long history of discrimination against African Americans, Hispanics, and Native Americans; the use of the Constitution by the dominant economic groups to prevent or delay social or economic change; the practical means used by government to prevent or slow down the participation of lower-income groups in the political process; the limitation of choice resulting from a two-party rather than a multiparty political system; the use by government of infiltration and disruption tactics to undermine groups holding ideas perceived to be threatening; the failure of the criminal justice system to give all defendants an equal chance regardless of wealth and background; and the use of military force and secret operations in influencing nations abroad, such as in Indochina in the 1960s and 1970s and in Nicaragua in the 1980s.

The views of contending sides assessing the U.S. political system raise the most fundamental issues underlying that system. This part considers two of these issues: the role of the Framers in creating a "more perfect Union" — and how perfect was and is that Union — and the future of federalism.

Chapter 1

Has the Wisdom of the Framers of the Constitution in Promoting a "More Perfect Union" Been Overrated?

The Constitution establishes the ground rules governing the political system of the United States. What the Framers believed and how they acted at the Constitutional Convention at Philadelphia in 1787 raise questions about the effect these rules may have had on political behavior thereafter.

Historians disagree sharply about the Framers of the Constitution. Characterizations of delegates to the Constitutional Convention range from self-serving men of prominence seeking to promote the interests of their own economic class to pragmatic leaders encompassing profound differences of economic interest and political philosophy.

The basic facts about the Constitution, however, are generally accepted. The Articles of Confederation, presented in Congress in 1776 but not finally ratified by all the states until 1781, established a league of friendship among the states rather than a national government. The period under the Articles was marked by widespread debt, Shays's Rebellion (a revolt of poor Massachusetts farmers), economic decay, and an inability to negotiate commercial treaties. In 1786 a Constitutional Convention was called to revise the Articles; it met in Philadelphia from May through September 1787. Most of the delegates were young, politically experienced, financially comfortable, and afraid of the common people, whom they called "the mob." Although they shared some assumptions about government and society, they disagreed profoundly about what should and should not be included in the document they were drafting.

Despite the celebration of the Framers at many civic occasions during the Constitution's bicentennial year, some observers, like the late Supreme Court Justice Thurgood Marshall, think the wisdom of the Framers of the Constitution has been overrated. Marshall was the first African American appointed to the Supreme Court. Earlier in his career, he was an attorney with the National Association for the Advancement of Colored People (NAACP), and he argued major civil rights cases in the courts.

In a speech sparked by commemorations of the bicentennial, Marshall faults the Framers for producing a defective document that allowed for the perpetuation of slavery and denied African Americans and women the right to vote. He contends that developments *after* the writing of the Constitution created a more promising basis for justice and equality than did the accomplishments of the Framers. He emphasizes the adoption of the Fourteenth Amendment ensuring protection of life, liberty, and property of all persons against deprivations without due process and guaranteeing the equal protection of the laws. Credit for change, Marshall says, should go to the people who passed amendments and laws that sought to promote liberty for *all* people of the United States. Marshall celebrates the Constitution as a living document, evolving through amendments and judicial interpretation.

Marshall's speech prompted a direct response by William Bradford Reynolds, at that time the assistant attorney general in the Civil Rights Division of the Justice Department. Reynolds was a controversial figure in the Reagan administration because of his actions on civil rights matters. A number of civil rights leaders criticized him for his opposition to affirmative action and voting rights legislation. Reynold's supporters defended him as a proponent of real racial equality.

In a speech delivered at Vanderbilt University, Reynolds argues that the Framers deserve the respect accorded to them in the bicentennial celebrations. Accepting Marshall's evaluation that the original Constitution was flawed, Reynolds still asserts that the Constitution marked "the greatest advance for human liberty in the entire history of mankind, then or since." Indeed, Reynolds continues, the constitutional system of divided governmental authority and separated government power eventually allowed African Americans to secure liberty. He notes that much blame for the low status of African Americans in the United States should go not to the Framers but rather to those justices who failed to follow the terms of the Constitution and the laws of the land.

 YES

Has the Wisdom of the Framers of the Constitution in Promoting a "More Perfect Union" Been Overrated?

THURGOOD MARSHALL

The Constitution: Past and Present

Nineteen eighty-seven marks the 200th anniversary of the United States Constitution. A Commission has been established to coordinate the celebration. The official meetings, essay contests, and festivities have begun.

The planned commemoration will span three years, and I am told 1987 is "dedicated to the memory of the Founders and the document they drafted in Philadelphia." We are to "recall the achievements of our Founders and the knowledge and experience that inspired them, the nature of the government they established, its origins, its character, and its ends, and the rights and privileges of citizenship, as well as its attendant responsibilities."

Like many anniversary celebrations, the plan for 1987 takes particular events and holds them up as the source of all the very best that has followed. Patriotic feelings will surely swell, prompting proud proclamations of the wisdom, foresight, and sense of justice shared by the Framers and reflected in a written document now yellowed with age. This is unfortunate — not the patriotism itself, but the tendency for the celebration to oversimplify, and overlook the many other events that have been instrumental to our achievements as a nation. The focus of this celebration invites a complacent belief that the vision of those who debated and compromised in Philadelphia yielded the "more perfect Union" it is said we now enjoy.

I cannot accept this invitation, for I do not believe that the meaning of the Constitution was forever "fixed" at the Philadelphia Convention. Nor do I find the wisdom, foresight, and sense of justice exhibited by the Framers particularly profound. To the contrary, the government they devised was defective from the start, requiring several amendments, a civil war, and momentous social transformation to attain the system of constitutional government, and its respect for the individual freedoms and human rights, we hold as fundamental today. When contemporary Americans cite "The Constitution," they invoke a concept that is vastly different from what the Framers barely began to construct two centuries ago.

For a sense of the evolving nature of the Constitution we need look no further than the first three words of the document's preamble: "We the People." When the Founding Fathers used this phrase in 1787, they did not have in mind the majority of America's citizens. "We the People" included, in the words of the Framers, "the whole Number of free Persons." On a matter so basic as the right to vote, for example, Negro slaves were excluded, although they were counted for representational purposes — at three-fifths each. Women did not gain the right to vote for over a hundred and thirty years.

These omissions were intentional. The record of the Framers' debates on the slave question is especially clear: The Southern States acceded to the demands of the New England States for giving Congress broad power to regulate commerce, in exchange for the right to continue the slave trade. The economic interests of the regions coalesced: New Englanders engaged in the "carrying trade" would profit from transporting slaves from Africa as well as goods produced in America by slave labor. The perpetuation of slavery ensured the primary source of wealth in the Southern States.

Despite this clear understanding of the role slavery would play in the new republic, use of the words "slaves" and "slavery" was carefully avoided in the original document. Political representation in the lower House of Congress was to be based on the population of "free Persons" in each State, plus three-fifths of all "other Persons." Moral principles against slavery, for those who had them, were compromised, with no explanation of the conflicting principles for which the American Revolutionary War had ostensibly been fought:

the self-evident truths "that all men are created equal, that they are endowed by their Creator with certain unalienable Rights, that among these are Life, Liberty and the pursuit of Happiness."

It was not the first such compromise. Even these ringing phrases from the Declaration of Independence are filled with irony, for an early draft of what became that Declaration assailed the King of England for suppressing legislative attempts to end the slave trade and for encouraging slave rebellions. The final draft adopted in 1776 did not contain this criticism. And so again at the Constitutional Convention eloquent objections to the institution of slavery went unheeded, and its opponents eventually consented to a document which laid a foundation for the tragic events that were to follow.

Pennsylvania's Gouverneur Morris provides an example. He opposed slavery and the counting of slaves in determining the basis for representation in Congress. At the Convention he objected that

> the inhabitant of Georgia [or] South Carolina who goes to the coast of Africa, and in defiance of the most sacred laws of humanity tears away his fellow creatures from their dearest connections and damns them to the most cruel bondages, shall have more votes in a Government instituted for protection of the rights of mankind, than the Citizen of Pennsylvania or New Jersey who views with a laudable horror, so nefarious a practice.

And yet Gouverneur Morris eventually accepted the three-fifths accommodation. In fact, he wrote the final draft of the Constitution, the very document the bicentennial will commemorate.

As a result of compromise, the right of the Southern States to continue importing slaves was extended, officially, at least until 1808. We know that it actually lasted a good deal longer, as the Framers possessed no monopoly on the ability to trade moral principles for self-interest. But they nevertheless set an unfortunate example. Slaves could be imported, if the commercial interests of the North were protected. To make the compromise even more palatable, customs duties would be imposed at up to ten dollars per slave as a means of raising public revenues.

No doubt it will be said, when the unpleasant truth of the history of slavery in America is mentioned during this bicentennial year, that the Constitution was a product of its times, and embodied a compromise which, under other circumstances, would not have been made. But the effects of the Framers' compromise have remained for generations. They arose from the contradiction between guaranteeing liberty and justice to all, and denying both to Negroes.

The original intent of the phrase, "We the People," was far too clear for any ameliorating construction. Writing for the Supreme Court in 1857, Chief Justice Taney penned the following passage in the *Dred Scott* case, on the issue whether, in the eyes of the Framers, slaves were "constituent members of the sovereignty," and were to be included among "We the People":

We think they are not, and that they are not included, and were not intended to be included. . . . They had for more than a century before
been regarded as beings of an inferior order, and altogether unfit to associate with the white race . . . ; and so far inferior, that they had no rights
which the white man was bound to respect; and that the negro might
justly and lawfully be reduced to slavery for his benefit. . . . [A]ccord-
ingly, a negro of the African race was regarded . . . as an article of property, and held, and bought and sold as such. . . . [N]o one seems to have
doubted the correctness of the prevailing opinion of the time.

And so, nearly seven decades after the Constitutional Convention, the
Supreme Court reaffirmed the prevailing opinion of the Framers regarding the
rights of Negroes in America. It took a bloody civil war before the Thirteenth
Amendment could be adopted to abolish slavery, though not the consequences slavery would have for future Americans.

While the Union survived the civil war, the Constitution did not. In its place
arose a new, more promising basis for justice and equality, the Fourteenth
Amendment, ensuring protection of the life, liberty, and property of *all* persons against deprivations without due process, and guaranteeing equal protection of the laws. And yet almost another century would pass before any significant recognition was obtained of the rights of black Americans to share
equally even in such basic opportunities as education, housing, and employment, and to have their votes counted, and counted equally. In the meantime,
blacks joined America's military to fight its wars and invested untold hours
working in its factories and on its farms, contributing to the development of
this country's magnificent wealth and waiting to share in its prosperity.

What is striking is the role legal principles have played throughout America's history in determining the condition of Negroes. They were enslaved by
law, emancipated by law, disenfranchised and segregated by law; and, finally,
they have begun to win equality by law. Along the way, new constitutional
principles have emerged to meet the challenges of a changing society. The
progress has been dramatic, and it will continue.

The men who gathered in Philadelphia in 1787 could not have envisioned
these changes. They could not have imagined, nor would they have accepted,
that the document they were drafting would one day be construed by a Supreme Court to which had been appointed a woman and the descendent of an
African slave. "We the People" no longer enslave, but the credit does not belong
to the Framers. It belongs to those who refused to acquiesce in outdated notions
of "liberty," "justice," and "equality," and who strived to better them.

And so we must be careful, when focusing on the events which took place
in Philadelphia two centuries ago, that we not overlook the momentous
events which followed, and thereby lose our proper sense of perspective. Otherwise, the odds are that for many Americans the bicentennial celebration will
be little more than a blind pilgrimage to the shrine of the original document
now stored in a vault in the National Archives. If we seek, instead, a sensitive

understanding of the Constitution's inherent defects, and its promising evolution through 200 years of history, the celebration of the "Miracle at Philadelphia" will, in my view, be a far more meaningful and humbling experience. We will see that the true miracle was not the birth of the Constitution, but its life, a life nurtured through two turbulent centuries of our own making, and a life embodying much good fortune that was not.

Thus, in this bicentennial year, we may not all participate in the festivities with flag-waving fervor. Some may more quietly commemorate the suffering, struggle, and sacrifice that have triumphed over much of what was wrong with the original document, and observe the anniversary with hopes not realized and promises not fulfilled. I plan to celebrate the bicentennial of the Constitution as a living document, including the Bill of Rights and the other amendments protecting individual freedoms and human rights.

Has the Wisdom of the Framers of the Constitution in Promoting a "More Perfect Union" Been Overrated?

WILLIAM BRADFORD REYNOLDS
The Wisdom of the Framers

Let me start with the observation that I regard myself to be most privileged to be a public servant at a time when we celebrate the 200th Anniversary of the Constitution — a magnificent document that has, in my view, no equal in history and every reason to be feted. It is by now no revelation that the Framers would be aghast at the size and reach of government today; but they would also be enormously proud of how much of their legacy has endured. The vitality of the original Constitution, and its various amendments, is reflected by its ability to withstand spirited debate over its content and meaning, a process that thankfully has been taking place with more and more enthusiasm in town meetings and forums all around the country, involving students, public officials, and citizens of every variety in evaluating how well our Constitution has served us over the past two centuries. I find it remarkable — and an enormous tribute to the Constitution — that in every instance about which I have read, these gatherings have been hard-pressed to think of ways in which to improve it in any meaningful manner.

That is not to say that the original Constitution of 1787 was flawless. And in our celebration of the document, we must not overlook its flaws and our long and painful struggles to correct them.

If there was any tendency to do so, it was no doubt corrected a few weeks ago when Justice Thurgood Marshall spoke in Hawaii on the Constitution's Bicentennial celebration. Whatever degree of disagreement one might have with Justice Marshall's comments, he has invigorated the debate on the meaning and vitality of constitutional principles in a focused way that can only serve to underscore the importance of the document itself and why it is so deserving of this Bicentennial celebration.

In recounting his remarks, I will rely on Justice Marshall's own words. He began by warning against what he called the "tendency for the celebration to oversimplify" the adoption and meaning of the Constitution of 1787 and to "overlook the many other events that have been instrumental to our achievements as a nation" — events that, as he explains, included the Civil War and the amendments added to the Constitution in its wake. Thus, he rejected what he described as a complacent belief that the "vision of those who debated and compromised in Philadelphia yielded the 'more perfect Union' it is said we now enjoy." Justice Marshall remarked further that he does not believe — and I quote — that "the meaning of the Constitution was forever 'fixed' at the Philadelphia Convention"; nor does he find "the wisdom, foresight, and sense of justice exhibited by the Framers particularly profound." The government the Framers of 1787 devised, he declared, "was defective from the start, requiring several amendments, a civil war, and momentous social transformation to attain the system of constitutional government, and its respect for the individual freedoms and human rights, we hold as fundamental today."

More specifically, Justice Marshall faulted the original Constitution because, as he put it, the Framers "did not have in mind the majority of America's citizens." The Preamble's "We the People," the Justice said, included only whites. Justice Marshall observes that the Constitution tacitly addressed the slavery issue in two ways: in Article I, section 2, by counting "other Persons" as three-fifths of "free Persons" for purposes of Congressional representation; and in Article I, section 9, by protecting the authority of states to continue importing slaves until 1808. Because the original Constitution was defective in this manner, Justice Marshall holds that "while the Union survived the civil war, the Constitution did not." Taking its place, he said, was "a new, more promising basis for justice and equality, the Fourteenth Amendment, ensuring protection of the life, liberty, and property of *all* persons against deprivations without due process, and guaranteeing equal protection of the laws." For Justice Marshall, it is this new Constitution that we should celebrate; not the old one, which contains "outdated notions of 'liberty,' 'justice,' and 'equality.' " Thus, Justice Marshall declines to participate in the festivities with "flag-waving fervor," but rather plans to celebrate the Bicentennial of the Constitution as a "living document, including the Bill of Rights and the other amendments protecting individual freedoms and human rights."

Justice Marshall chose to focus almost exclusively on the most tragic aspects of the American experience, but he is absolutely right to remind us of them. For the Constitution was intended to be the culmination of a great struggle for the natural rights of men — a philosophy whose cornerstone is the absolute guarantee of equality under the law. When the Framers sought to protect in the Constitution the fundamental rights of man but failed to guarantee explicitly those rights to every individual, they introduced a self-contradiction that preordained struggles and conflicts we continue to confront today.

I am concerned, however, that what Justice Marshall has encouraged is far more than a simple mid-course correction in our celebration of the Constitution. It is one thing to be reminded of the compromise on slavery during the making of the Constitution. It is quite another, however, to encourage the view that there are two constitutions, the one of 1787, the other consisting of the Bill of Rights and the Fourteenth Amendment; that the old one is so thoroughly defective that it did not survive the Civil War, and that the new one alone is worthy of celebration. Certainly, we ought to understand and appreciate the original Constitution in light of its weaknesses as well as its considerable strengths. But in the process, we ought to respectfully decline the invitation to consign it to the dustbin of history. That is a judgment as wrong as any on the other side of the ledger that uncritically praises the document of 1787. We indeed need what Justice Marshall called for — a "proper sense of perspective."

Notwithstanding its very serious flaws, the Constitution in its original form constituted the greatest advance for human liberty in the entire history of mankind, then or since. Indeed, it was only by preserving our underlying *constitutional system* — one of divided governmental authority and separated government powers — that blacks could enjoy the fruits of liberty once that self-contradiction I alluded to was corrected.

Fresh from the experience of subjugation under the British crown on [the] one hand, and the failure of the Articles of Confederation on the other, the Framers understood that there is an interdependent relationship between fundamental rights and the structure and powers of government. Thus, they crafted a government of limited powers, grounded in natural law principles and deriving its authority from the consent of the governed. They designed a system to protect individual rights through a balance and separation of governmental powers, which would forever ensure that the new national government would not exceed its enumerated powers. Not the least of these checks against governmental invasion of individual rights was the creation in Article III of an independent judiciary as a guardian of constitutional values.

Many of the Framers were not satisfied to protect individual rights merely by limiting the power of national government; they insisted upon a Bill of Rights to safeguard explicitly those rights they deemed most fundamental. Although the Bill of Rights was separately adopted, it would be [an] error to view the original Constitution apart from the first ten amendments, for the Framers agreed from the outset that the rights enumerated in the Bill of Rights were the object of government to protect. Beyond setting forth specific rights essential to a free people, the Framers established in the Ninth and Tenth Amendments a decentralized federal structure to more fully secure the free exercise of individual rights and self-government.

This was the basic structure of government the Framers deemed necessary to vindicate the principles of the American Revolution as set forth in the Declaration of Independence; and that, in my view, is the unique and remarkable achievement we celebrate today. But in celebrating the triumph of the Constitution, I am in full agreement that we must not overlook those parts of the constitutional experiment that were not noble and which, fortunately, have long since been corrected. Indeed, the experience of the Framers' compromise on the issue of "equality under law" provides us with important lessons even today.

From our historical vantage point, there is certainly no excuse for the original Constitution's failure to repudiate slavery. In making this deal with the devil — and departing from the absolute principle of "equality under law" — the Framers undermined the moral legitimacy of the Constitution.

But we ought to recognize that on this issue the Framers were faced with a Hobson's choice. The Constitution required unanimous ratification by the states, and at least two of the states refused to consent unless the slave trade was protected. James Wilson explained the dilemma: "Under the present Confederation, the states may admit the importation of slaves as long as they please; but by this article, after the year 1808, the Congress will have power to prohibit such importation. . . . I consider this as laying the foundation for banishing slavery out of this country." We know now that this hope was far too optimistic; and indeed, it would take the Civil War to rid the nation of that evil institution.

But even as the Framers were acceding to this compromise, they were sowing the seeds for the expansion of freedom to all individuals when circumstances would permit. James Wilson, for example, emphasized that "the term *slave* was not *admitted* in this *Constitution.*" Instead, the term "Person" was used, suggesting that when the slaves became "free Persons," they would be entitled to all the rights appertaining to free individuals.

Indeed, many abolitionist leaders argued that the Constitution, by its omission of any mention of slavery, did not tolerate slavery. Noting that the Constitution nowhere mentions the word "slave," Frederick Douglass declared that "[i]n that instrument, I hold there is neither warrant, license, nor sanction of the hateful thing." Yet such arguments were tragically unheeded by the United States Supreme Court in the *Dred Scott* decision, which provided succor to the notion that there are justifications for exceptions to the principle of "equality under law" — a notion that despite its sordid origins has not been totally erased to this day.

Indeed, the *Dred Scott* decision illustrates that a significant part of the responsibility for our failure to make good on the principle of "equality under law" can and should be assigned less to shortcomings in the original Constitution — as Justice Marshall would have us believe — but to those who sat where Justice Marshall now sits, charged with interpreting that document.

Justice Marshall apparently believes that the original flaws in the Constitution dictated the result in *Dred Scott.* I am more inclined toward the view of my colleagues at the Department of Justice, Charles J. Cooper and Nelson

Lund, who argue that Chief Justice Taney's constitutional interpretation was "loose, disingenuous, and result-oriented." Justice Curtis' dissent sounded a warning over this type of judicial interpretation unattached to constitutional moorings that is as compelling now as it was 125 years ago:

> Political reasons have not the requisite certainty to afford rules of interpretation. They are different in different men. They are different in the same men at different times. And when a strict interpretation of the Constitution, according to the fixed rules which govern the interpretation of laws, is abandoned, and the theoretical opinions of individuals are allowed to control its meaning, we no longer have a Constitution; we are under the government of individual men, who for the time being have power to declare what the Constitution is, according to their own views of what it ought to mean.

The judiciary's tragic failure to follow the terms of the Constitution did not occur in this one instance only. Indeed, the Civil War amendments and civil rights legislation passed in that era were in the next several decades emptied of meaning by the Supreme Court in decision after decision. In *Plessy v. Ferguson,* to cite but one example, the Court once again stepped in and, over the lone, brilliant dissent of the elder Justice Harlan, shamefully sacrificed the principle of "equality under law."

I daresay that had the Court fully honored its mandate under the original Constitution in *Dred Scott,* or under the Fourteenth Amendment in *Plessy v. Ferguson,* we could well have escaped much of the racial strife and social divisiveness that Justice Marshall lays at the doorstep of the Constitution itself. Indeed, the tragic legacy of those decisions — the deadening consequences that so regularly flow from a compromise (no matter how well intended) of the principle of "equality under law" — provides a sobering lesson for the present Court as it struggles with similar issues involving race and gender discrimination. These are issues that no less so than in an earlier era leave hanging in the balance the overarching question of whether the liberating promise of the Constitution, as originally understood and subsequently articulated in explicit terms by ratification of the Civil War amendments, will or will not be fulfilled for all Americans.

Justice Marshall, I would respectfully submit, too casually brushes so weighty a concern to one side in contending that the Constitution did not survive the Civil War. One would think that this assertion would at least invite from some quarter the obvious questions: Did separation of powers survive the Civil War? Did the executive branch and the Congress? Did, indeed, the institution of judicial review?

I must admit to quite a different reading of history, one that has an abiding appreciation of the fact that our Constitution did survive so cataclysmic an upheaval as the Civil War. In all too many instances of internal strife among a People, one form of subjugation is ultimately replaced by another. But the Civil War produced a far different (indeed unique) result: its consequence was to more perfectly secure and extend to all Americans — through the Thirteenth, Fourteenth, and Fifteenth Amendments — the blessings of liberty as set forth in the Declaration of Independence, blessings of liberty that had already been secured for other Americans in the original Constitution and Bill of Rights. It is revisionist history of the worst sort to suggest that the Fourteenth Amendment created a black constitutional slate on which judges could write their own personalized definition of equality or fundamental rights. The Civil War Amendments were a logical extension of what had come before: they represented *evolutionary*, not *revolutionary* change.

To be sure, the Fourteenth Amendment does offer support for Justice Marshall's claim that the Constitution is "a living document," but only in the sense that the Constitution itself provides a mechanism — namely, the amendment process — to reflect changing social realities. Indeed, this orderly process for constitutional "evolution" is a part of the original Constitution's genius, for it provides a mechanism to correct flaws while safeguarding the essential integrity of our constitutional structure. But the existence of this mechanism — coupled with the system of checks and balances among the three branches of the federal government and the strong endorsement of federalism principles embodied in the Tenth Amendment — makes it abundantly clear that the Framers gave no license to judges (members of the Branch regarded, to borrow from Alexander Hamilton, as the "least dangerous" of the three) to construe constitutional provisions as they see fit.

There is good reason for all this confluence of restraints on judicial activism. The Constitution is not a mass of fungible, abstract principles whose meaning varies with time; rather, it comprises a broad societal consensus on certain fundamental, absolute principles necessary for the protection of individual liberty. The Framers believed that these constitutional values should not be lightly disturbed or set aside. Accordingly, the Constitution was structured so as to require that any change reflect the broadest expression of societal consensus.

This does not leave the Supreme Court or lower federal courts unable to apply the Constitution to circumstances never contemplated by the Framers. But the Judges are not free to disengage from our constitutional moorings in furtherance of their own social agendas; they are not free to determine that the constitutional principles themselves are unwise or obsolete.

Indeed, the very premise on which rests the notion that the Constitution as originally framed has no relevance today is fatally flawed. For the fact remains that the core structure upon which the Constitution was based — a government of limited powers, federalism, separation of powers, protection of fundamental individual rights — has proven in the past two centuries far superior to any other governmental system in protecting human freedoms. And where proponents of change have successfully secured the broad consensus necessary to amend the Constitution, they have expanded and perfected those protections. But judicial activism as an illegitimate substitute for the amendment process can only jeopardize our fundamental freedoms by denigrating the structural underpinnings vital to their survival.

Justice Marshall's contrary thesis is gerry-built on a regrettable overstate-ment of perceived flaws in the Constitution without so much as a passing ref-erence to the qualities that have endured for the past two hundred years: a governmental structure that has withstood the test of time, weathered turbu-lent conflicts, and proven itself to be the greatest engine for individual free-dom in the history of mankind. That remarkable accomplishment is certainly worth the celebration it is receiving, and much, much more.

Let us not be content with less than a complete appreciation for this docu-ment on which our Republic stands. Let us accept Justice Marshall's invitation to explore fully the lessons of the past two centuries. But let us decline his in-vitation to break the Constitution into two, and to reject the document of 1787 and accept only that which followed the Civil War. We are under a Constitu-tion; it is the original Constitution together with its twenty-six amendments that we must seek to understand and uphold. Let us never forget that the Constitution is in its entirety the Supreme Law of the Land, and all of the branches — the executive, legislative, and judicial — are subordinate to it. We must embrace the Constitution as a whole: not uncritically, but not unlovingly either. Our task, in this Bicentennial year, should be that of loving critics. For our Constitution has provided this great nation of ours with a charter for lib-erty and government that has enabled us to move ever closer to that "more perfect Union" the Framers envisioned.

In conclusion, it is fitting that I call on the words of former Chief Justice Warren Burger, the Chairman of the Bicentennial Commission. He said it best when he remarked that the Constitution "isn't perfect, but it's the best thing in the world." Our Constitution embodies the American spirit, the American Dream, and America's doctrinal commitment to civil rights — those funda-mental rights we all hold equally as American citizens. For this reason, I re-spectfully part company with Justice Marshall in my view that it is indeed our Constitution as framed two centuries ago, and amended thereafter from time to time, that stands tall today as "the source of all the very best that has fol-lowed." Let us not hesitate to celebrate.

Questions for Discussion

1. How did the political system adopted by the United States in the late eigh-teenth century compare to the political systems in other countries during the same period in terms of ensuring individual freedom?
2. What would have been the consequences to the political development of the United States had the Framers included provisions outlawing slavery and granting political equality for African Americans?
3. What were the assumptions of the Framers about the relationship between individuals and the government?

4. What effect did the constitutional prescription to divide power between a central government and the states and between the different branches of the central government have on the condition of African Americans?
5. What evidence can you supply to accept or reject the proposition that the Constitution did not survive the Civil War?
6. What impact should the intent of the Framers have on Supreme Court justices in deciding cases today? What are the reasons for your answer?

Suggested Readings

Beard, Charles A. *An Economic Interpretation of the Constitution of the United States.* New York: Free Press, 1913. (Originally published New York: Macmillan, 1913.)

Farrand, Max, ed. *The Records of the Federal Convention of 1787,* rev. ed. 4 vols. New Haven, Conn.: Yale Univ. Press, 1966.

Goldwin, Robert A. *Why Blacks, Women, and Jews Are Not Mentioned in the Constitution and Other Unorthodox Views.* Washington, D.C.: American Enterprise Institute for Public Policy Research, 1990.

Hamilton, Alexander, James Madison, and John Jay. *The Federalist Papers,* edited by Clinton Rossiter. New York: New American Library, 1961.

Ketcham, Ralph, ed. *The Anti-Federalist Papers and the Constitutional Convention Debates.* New York: New American Library, 1986.

———. *Framed for Posterity: The Enduring Philosophy of the Constitution.* Lawrence: Univ. Press of Kansas, 1993.

Lazare, Daniel. *The Frozen Republic: How the Constitution Is Paralyzing Democracy.* New York: Harcourt Brace, 1996.

Loury, Glenn C. "'Matters of Color': Blacks and the Constitutional Order." *Public Interest,* no. 86 (Winter 1987): 109–123.

McDonald, Forrest. *We the People: Economic Origins of the Constitution.* New Brunswick, N.J.: Transaction Publishers, 1992. (Originally published Chicago: Univ. of Chicago Press, 1958.)

Mee, Charles L., Jr. *The Genius of the People.* New York: Harper & Row, 1987.

Morris, Richard B. *Witnesses at the Creation: Hamilton, Madison, Jay and the Constitution.* New York: New American Library, 1986.

Ollman, Bertell, and Jonathan Birnbaum, eds. *The United States Constitution: 200 Years of Anti-Federalist, Abolitionist, Feminist, Muckraking, Progressive, and Especially Socialist Criticism.* New York: New York Univ. Press, 1990.

Rakove, Jack M. *Original Meanings: Politics and Ideas in the Making of the Constitution.* New York: Knopf, 1996.

Chapter 2

Should Power Be Transferred from the Federal Government to the States?

An understanding of the federal system today requires an examination of what federalism is, why it was established, and how it has evolved. Federalism is a system of government under which power is distributed between central and regional authorities in a way that provides each with important power and functions. The United States is but one of many federal systems around the world. Canada, India, and Germany are examples of nations that have federal systems. In the United States the central authority is known as the federal government, and the regional authorities are the state governments.

Federalism is a structural feature not necessarily coterminous with democracy. A federal system divides power. A unitary system, in contrast, concentrates power. In a unitary system power is controlled by the central authorities, as it is, for example, in Great Britain and France. In Great Britain, regional governing authorities are created, abolished, or re-arranged by the central government at Westminster. In the federal system of the United States, however, state governments cannot be so restructured. No state boundary can be changed by the government in Washington, D.C., acting on its own authority. (An exception occurred during the Civil War when the state of West Virginia was created out of Virginia.)

A federal system was adopted in 1787 because a unitary structure would have been unacceptable to the people of the United States, who had strong loyalties to their states. In addition, the Framers of the Constitution wanted a government that would be stronger than the one existing under the Articles of Confederation, but they feared a central government that was too powerful. The federal system allowed for a compromise between those who favored a strong central government and those who supported a weak central government.

The central government was given some exclusive powers (e.g., to coin money and to establish tariffs). The states and federal government shared some powers (e.g., to tax and to spend money). The Tenth Amendment to the Constitution provides that "the powers not delegated to the United States by the Constitution, nor prohibited by it to the States, are reserved to the States respectively, or to the people."

The Constitution is not so clear about where the powers of the central government end. Two centuries of conflict over states' rights followed its ratification. In general, the trend was away from states' rights and toward national supremacy, until the past few decades. Since the administration of President Richard Nixon, however, state power has received new emphasis. The Nixon administration launched a program of New Federalism in which revenue sharing was the central feature. As finally enacted in the Nixon administration, revenue sharing provided a general grant to states and localities to be used as they saw fit, but with certain restrictions. The Nixon administration also devised block grants, in which the federal government provided funds to state and local governments for use in general policy areas rather than targeted to specific purposes. These grants gave states increased flexibility. President Ronald Reagan's New Federalism slowed down the rate of increase in funding grants and promoted grants to state governments rather than local governments.

The Republican victory in midterm elections of 1994 reinvigorated the policy of transferring power from the federal government to the states. Republicans also held thirty governorships, including nine out of the ten largest states, a dominance that made it additionally desirable for the Republican Congress to transfer power to the states.

The key elements of the Republican program were devolution of power from the federal government to the states, block grants, and an end to unfunded mandates — federal laws requiring the states and localities to perform certain tasks or meet certain standards but not supplying funds for doing so. Supporters argued that devolution would return power to the people, make government more efficient, and increase the flexibility of state and local authorities. In 1995, Congress passed, and President Bill Clinton signed, the Unfunded Mandates Reform Act requiring a point of order vote on bills imposing more than $50 million in implementation costs to states or localities not reimbursed by the federal government. While the law may slow down the pace of unfunded mandates, it does not repeal existing mandates, nor does it furnish funds for existing underfunded mandates. Clinton also encouraged the trend toward transferring power to the states by granting waivers from federal regulations that allowed states to experiment in welfare reform. And in 1996 he signed a bill that transferred power over many welfare programs from the federal government to the states and gave the states vast discretion in the use of block grant funds.

Supreme Court decisions also returned power to the states. In 1995, in *United States v. Lopez,* the Supreme Court reversed sixty years of increasing federal power under the Constitution's Commerce Clause, which grants Congress the power to regulate interstate and foreign commerce. In its 5–4 decision, the Court declared unconstitutional the Gun-Free School Zone Act, which prohibited firearms near schools, on the grounds that Congress had not shown that the possession of a firearm near an education building would disrupt interstate commerce. Regulating guns in and around schools, said the Court, was the responsibility of the states, not the federal government.[1]

Sorting out the division of power between the federal government and the states is a continuing issue. In a prepared statement before the

House Budget Committee, Kirk Cox, a member of the Virginia House of Delegates, argues that many federal programs are not necessary, justified, or efficient. He calls for additional block grants and an end to federal mandates. He justifies his position by making these points:

1. State governments have proven they can deliver more service for less money.
2. State governments are leading the way in innovating programs, such as privatization and collections from "deadbeat dads."
3. Unlike state governments, the federal government spends unnecessary funds for pork-barrel projects — local programs that have no national significance.
4. The states are laboratories of democracy. By experimenting with different approaches, states can adopt the most effective ways of doing things.
5. States are ready to accept the challenge of taking over responsibilities from the federal government.
6. State governments are closer to the people than is the federal government.

Washington attorney John G. Kester argues that a system in which state governments wield great power is a pipe dream. He contends:

1. States want only rights — not responsibilities.
2. States will not play a central role in domestic affairs so long as Washington has confiscated the tax base.
3. The United States has a national economy.
4. States have allowed the federal government to deal with social problems.
5. The United States is a homogenized country. It is not as diverse as it was before World War II.
6. The United States is a mobile society.
7. People are not as loyal to their states as they were in the nineteenth century.
8. New immigrants to the United States have little reason for developing a sense of attachment to a particular state.
9. Americans are modernists; few look to the past for guidance.
10. State bureaucracies are not noticeably more efficient than federal bureaucracies.

NOTE

1. *United States v. Lopez*, 115 S. Ct. 1624 (1995).

Should Power Be Transferred from the Federal Government to the States?

KIRK COX

Power to the States

In the broadest possible sense, block grants should be used to restore State powers that have been inappropriately assumed by the Federal Government. This should be accomplished as part of a conscious strategy to balance the Federal budget by 2002. Let me suggest an outline of such a process. There are three fundamental steps.

First, there should be a comprehensive review of Federal programs in relation to State and local governments. Each program should be examined to determine whether or not the Federal Government has the authority under the Constitution, and whether the Federal Government is best suited to accomplish our goals and objectives. In most cases, I believe that an objective analysis will find that a Federal role is not necessary, justified, or efficient. These programs should be devolved.

Second, with respect to programs that should be devolved, Congress should establish block grant programs immediately. These block grants should be as functionally broad as feasible. At a minimum, block grants should encompass broad program functions, such as education, transportation, health and human services, and so on.

And, perhaps most importantly, virtually all Federal mandates should be removed as an element of the block grant program. These mandates dramatically increase costs while substantially reducing services.

Let me also emphasize the importance of providing block grants directly to State governments, to be administered consistently with the existing mechanisms of State laws and constitutions. All local governments are creations of the State. It is not appropriate for the Federal Government to skip over the States to establish relationships with local governments. We have already paid substantially for such inappropriate arrangements, through overlapping programs, duplication, and even lobbying before Congress that pits the interests of State governments against those of local governments.

State governments have proven they can deliver more service for less money. Federal programs have been particularly costly. Centralization of power at the Federal level has resulted in waste, duplication, and contradiction as the Federal Government has intruded into functions that are also handled by State and local governments.

Yet State and local governments have been forced to spend more than they would have if they had spent taxes raised directly from their own citizens. States and localities, like people, are more careful with their own money than with other people's money.

For example, the Congressional Budget Office has confirmed that local governments routinely spend more to construct federally funded wastewater treatment plants than they spend to construct the same locally funded wastewater treatment plants. In the final analysis, we should all remember that Federal money is not other people's money, it is *the* people's money.

There is considerable potential for improving the cost effectiveness of federally funded programs. State and local governments have taken the lead in implementing strategies that improve government efficiency.

From privatization to right-sizing, State governments are leading the way. Take my home State for instance. In Virginia we are actively pursuing privatization in a whole host of areas from transportation to corrections to child support collections.

Let's look at just one example: Deadbeat dads are a serious problem. To increase collections we are experimenting with privatizing collections. Private collection companies were allowed to compete with their public counterparts. The results are dramatic.

A private company collects over 11 percent more a month from deadbeat dads than their government counterparts, and at substantially less cost. The direct cost for government collections was $7.03 per case. The direct cost for the private company was $5.77 per case.

And best of all, customer service increased. The private company offered 24 phone lines — the State office had 5 phone lines. Further, the private office was open 11 hours more a week than the government offices. The private offices were open on Saturday and provided child care. All this for less money.

And then there's pork. The Federal Government grants billions of dollars annually to State and local governments for pork-barrel projects. By definition, pork-barrel projects have no national significance. Moreover, State and local taxpayers are generally unlikely to consider such programs important enough to finance themselves.

Further, the States are laboratories of democracy. By experimenting with different approaches, the most effective public policy approaches can be identified, and copied by other States.

Just last week, Virginia's Gov. George Allen signed into law the most revolutionary welfare reform program in the Nation. It features a real work requirement, a two-year benefit limit, and a cutoff of aid for additional children.

I can't help but note that the welfare reform movement currently sweeping the Nation began in the States and is still being led by the States. Virginia was able to build on the efforts of Wisconsin and Illinois, and now other States will be able to build on Virginia's example. That is why we call the States laboratories of democracy.

Federal policies that hamstring our efforts and unnecessarily increase public costs are unwise. Indeed they are unconscionable.

Government at all levels must become more efficient. America's private sector has been restructuring and reengineering for some time. This has not occurred simply because of a desire to become more efficient; it has rather occurred because restructuring was required to survive in an increasingly competitive market. Government, too, must be restructured—it must be restructured because our present method of operation threatens the living standards of future generations. Devolution of programs to the States, through block grants, is an important component of this long overdue restructuring.

I am happy to report that the States, and their local units of government, are up to the challenge—we are prepared to do our part—but we must be freed to perform. Immediate and comprehensive relief from Federal mandates is an absolute necessity.

I want to make sure that we have not been misunderstood. We are not here today to suggest to you that State and local governments are more virtuous than the Federal Government. They are not. Nor are the State and local governments necessarily more competent than the Federal Government.

But they are closer to the people, and that makes all the difference in the world. Their closeness simply permits them to be more reflective of the public will, and provides incentives for them to spend the tax money they collect from their citizens more effectively. Moreover, it is easier for the people to effect changes through the electoral process where government is closer to the people. Greater accountability is naturally and necessarily associated with government that is closer to the people.

So, in summary, here is what I am proposing:

Congress should devolve substantial powers to the States that are not appropriately the responsibility of the Federal Government; and Congress should use a broad block grant mechanism to return funding responsibility to the States over a seven-year period. At the same time, Federal tax rates should be reduced.

We as a nation have strayed from our democratic ideals. Government has become too remote, too wasteful, and too expensive. It is time to reverse course and return government to the people. All of us hope that Congress will take effective action to return powers to the States, to restore the balance envisioned in the Tenth Amendment of the Constitution of the United States.

Should Power Be Transferred from the Federal Government to the States?

JOHN G. KESTER
Forever Federal

There is a loud buzz about reallocating power away from Washington and back to the states — something most Republicans claim to favor. Gurus sell books on the virtues of decentralization, local decision-making, and neighborliness. Judgment day for Washington is forecast.

Not so fast. Meaningful federalism — the classical concept of states that actually behave like sovereign governments with real power — is an idea with a past brighter than its future.

Some of the anti-Washington talk stems from the successful conclusion of the Cold War. It ended big central government's most tolerable excuse for being: defense from foreign military force. A federal government busy guarding you from missiles can't be all bad. One focused on taking your money to give to someone else seems less legitimate.

Some decentralization is possible, and perhaps along with it some shrinking of hyperactive government. But restoring the states to anything like real sovereigns, with noticeably different laws and unique customs, is a notion that crested at Gettysburg on July 3, 1863. And although many Americans hope for curbs on federal spending, few want simply to substitute state bureaucracies for federal in running their lives.

Always the federal government has held two unbeatable ways to expand — provided that the voters who select the Congress wanted it to do so.

First, the Constitution makes federal laws supreme over any state laws to the contrary. Until 1913, that power was restrained by having U.S. senators chosen by state legislatures.

Starting in the 1930s, the federal government decided it could regulate practically everything to make life better. The Supreme Court by 1937 decided to give up and let it try. The court turned its own energy to interpreting general clauses in the Constitution as tight limits on state laws. All Congress needs is some constitutional handle to legislate, and state laws must give way.

Second, that stick of federal supremacy is backed up by the carrot of federal grants. Grants can have conditions that Washington otherwise would lack power to order. Let us feds pay for part of that new school — as long as its curriculum adds the programs the national government wants. The Supreme Court doesn't worry; in 1987 it held that Congress could use the highway pork barrel to dictate the minimum age a state set for beer drinking.

23

So with legal restrictions on federal power gone except for occasional extreme cases, any real restoration of state power would have to come from the voters themselves, with an assist if the Supreme Court ever decided to loosen its supervision of state laws, including touchy issues like abortion and school prayer.

Real federalism in the United States — a twenty-first century in which state governments wield great power — is a pipe dream. Here is why.

STATES ARE GREEDY

The dirty little secret of states' rights is that the states want only rights — not responsibilities. Justice Sandra Day O'Connor wrote in 1992 that the Constitution did not convert the states into "regional offices nor administrative agencies of the Federal Government." But the states themselves don't seem to agree. Often they look like caricatures of welfare mothers: They look for regular handouts from federal officials, they don't say thank you, they expect to be bailed out of their problems — in short, they exhibit all the passive cunning of classic dependent behavior.

The states have not been turning away those federally funded grants, which add up to a quarter-trillion dollars a year. Even let's-run-against-Washington governors like California's Pete Wilson or Virginia's George Allen do not hesitate to ask the nation's taxpayers to pick up their earthquake and hurricane bills. Many state officials complain about the strings attached to federal education grants, but only a handful decline the money.

State irritation about distasteful conditions has brought the current block-grant frenzy. This old Republican favorite — bundles of federal money given to the states without strings — began as Richard Nixon's "revenue sharing" and was revived in Reagan's "new federalism." The 1970s notion was that the federal government was so rolling in tax revenue that it would send extra dollars back to the states (but not to the taxpayers, except when Congress under Reagan actually cut taxes).

Unclear then and unclear now is why federal money should be handed out to state governments, or anyone else, without careful regulation of how it is to be spent. The best answer may be that the regulatory red tape and bureaucracy that Democrats persistently write into federal aid is an even worse alternative.

Still, why should the federal government tax people to give money to the states at all? If the states need funds, they have their own power to tax. And if for its own activities the federal government does not need all the revenues it takes in, why are the taxes it collects so high?

Do not, however, count on Congress to forgo the pleasure of giving away money. No one said it better than FDR [Franklin D. Roosevelt] crony Harry Hopkins: "We will spend and spend, and tax and tax, and elect and elect." And state politicians are not competing to raise state taxes to pay for what the states want to spend.

FEDERAL TAXES ARE VERY HIGH

In a federal system in which the states really mattered, the significant taxes that people pay would be levied by the states. The big checks in April would be addressed to Annapolis or Richmond, not the IRS [Internal Revenue Service].

For a century and a half, that was so; for the first hundred years, except during the Civil War, the federal government was financed entirely by the tariff and a few excises, and until the Sixteenth Amendment in 1913, it could not tax incomes. The federal income tax affected scarcely anyone until the New Deal, and did not bite ordinary people until money was needed to fight World War II.

Since then, there have been no peace dividends, just federal programs that expand to meet and exceed revenue. Congress and lobbyists have never failed to discover reasons why federal taxes must stay stratospheric.

So for two generations now, the tax structure has been inverted. Federal taxes, which now go principally to pay off interest groups (agribusinesses, shipbuilders, retired people, government employees), are the big portion of the tax burden. State income taxes, though no longer trivial, are puny in comparison — not what one would expect if the principal functions of government were carried out by states. Local functions like schools and police rely on local property taxes, plus some conditional federal handouts.

As long as the federal government's voracious income tax vacuums up most of the country's tax revenue, there is little left for the states. States will not play a central role in domestic affairs as long as Washington has confiscated the tax base.

WE HAVE A NATIONAL ECONOMY

States have trouble maintaining autonomy when each is part of a larger economic unit, where goods and capital and workers move freely about. More economic integration means reduced sovereignty. (That is NAFTA's [North American Free Trade Agreement] downside, as Ross Perot and Pat Buchanan with purple prose tried to point out, while ignoring its advantages.)

The United States is a free-trade zone without state border guards. If a state cuts taxes and welfare benefits, it will wind up with businesses and taxpayers. If it adopts generous welfare or medical programs, eager recipients will be moving in.

Perhaps up to some point states should not have to bear the competitive cost of their social policies. Their helplessness to control who lives there is a reason to keep the federal government involved, at least by setting some minimum national standards. Otherwise, few states would dare provide social benefits much above the average, lest they attract too many takers.

STATES ARE LETHARGIC

A Herblock cartoon not long ago pictured a leering figure of "Congress" hand-ing a horse collar and harness to a naïf labeled "States and Cities," asking him to pull a huge cartload of baggage. The burdens being handed over were called:

- "Welfare Costs"
- "Crime Prevention"
- "Emergency Relief"
- "Health Costs"
- "Increased Local Spending Responsibilities"

Anyone who looked at that cartoon when the Constitution was drafted, or even 30 or 40 years ago, would not have understood it. Each item on the list, as-suming such matters concerned government at all, was almost entirely a con-cern of local mayors and city councils. Only in extraordinary emergencies would even state governors and legislatures get involved, much less the federal government, whose main tasks were national defense, foreign affairs, the tariff, coinage, and keeping out of the way of business. Who else but "states and cities," grandfather would have asked, would Herblock expect to handle such responsibilities — assuming that these were governmental responsibilities at all?

As late as Kennedy's administration, it was still possible for Congress to debate whether a particular issue was appropriate for the federal government to ad-dress. By the end of Johnson's, the only issue was how much government money was needed. That social problems are federal problems had become assumed.

State governments display the Patty Hearst syndrome. They have been sub-jected to federal coercion for so long that now they depend on it, and forget what self-government means. For a pathetic exhibit, look at your state income-tax form. Little effort is made by Maryland, Virginia, or other sup-posed sovereigns to decide what is income, how incomes should be taxed, or to build a tax structure reflecting local judgments. Instead, state legislatures simply adopt whatever rules Congress decides for the current year, make a handful of adjustments, and apply a percentage rate. Basic decisions of social policy, which any tax code is full of, are decided not in Richmond or Annapo-lis, but on Capitol Hill.

The taxpayer's form-filling is made simpler. But if something as basic as tax structure is to be designed elsewhere, what are state legislatures for?

WE HAVE A HOMOGENIZED COUNTRY

A real federalist system presupposes diversity. There may be a national interest in drivers staying on the right side of the highway from coast to coast, but the speed limit in Wyoming is quite a different call. States with real power would have different definitions of crimes, and even different choices as to whether particular behavior is criminal. Some would enact local preferences on many subjects into law, while others would remain permissive. Differing legal codes and customs would reflect the differences in the attitudes of their citizens.

Before World War II, and even into the 1960s before the civil-rights acts, there were distinct local cultures in this country, which a simple automobile trip could reveal. Now they are blotted out — first by radio and then television, by national control of schools, by cheap air travel. That is not all bad. The career of federalism — more aggressively described as states' rights — suffered for two centuries from becoming entangled with, first, the cause of southern slavery, and then its follow-up of racial segregation. Baggage like that could make any political theory look disreputable.

WE HAVE A MOBILE SOCIETY

Scarcely anyone born in this country has chosen to become a citizen of some other country, and then another, and then another. Yet Americans change their state citizenship almost without thinking. To them the issues in moving are jobs or real estate, not emigration to a strange land. If they feel pangs about moving, these usually relate to what a particular community is like, not the nature of its state government.

The willingness to pull up stakes is nothing new; it is how the West was won. This is a country with cheap transportation and an economy that moves workers around, so that it is not unusual for a person to live in four or five states in a lifetime. And most Americans are not looking for surprises when they travel from one state to another. Ask the people at McDonald's and every hotel chain from Super Eight to Four Seasons.

LOYALTY

When secession came, Robert E. Lee followed his first allegiance: to Virginia. The regiments that fought the Civil War, on both sides, were enlisted under state banners. Now, even the national guards of each state, successors of the state militias, have long been federally funded and supervised.

Except in some corners of the South and on a few football weekends, states no longer mean much emotionally to most of their citizens. Such people do not feel great pain when states' rights are slighted by the feds.

NEW AMERICANS

The flood of immigrants to the United States over the past two decades makes federalism an even less likely bet. These new faces, who quickly become voters, have little reason for attachment to a particular state. Consider Quebec, whose citizens of French descent would have seceded from Canada in October [1995] but for the decisive votes of national-minded newcomers.

To expect more than a few immigrants to become attached to what surely seems a mere political subdivision of the country they joined is unrealistic, particularly when dysfunctional public schools will not teach history to their children. It is not likely that new inhabitants will go to great pains for states that are abstractions — particularly states that may be theirs only for the moment.

MODERNISM

Federalism is not going to prevail based on nostalgia. Reverence for the past has never been this country's strong suit, and the current generation is a little vague about events before, say, 1992. Our commander-in-chief, indeed, on this summer's [1995] V-J Day anniversary, recalled that Japan had surrendered on "the aircraft carrier *Missouri*." People like that don't ponder in awe political arrangements designed in the good old days.

STATE GOVERNMENTS AREN'T SO GREAT

Republicans are correct that many citizens are tired of the things the federal government does. But one cannot assume that the states are the level of government that people miss. Where people want more decision-making power, and less outside interference, is in their cities and communities. The local level is where hope lies for doing something constructive about education and public safety, and it is locally that individuals can make their views felt.

State governments, by federal pressure and funds, often now are simply clones of the federal bureaucracy, though sometimes staffed with less talent. Federal domestic programs always have demanded paperwork and compliance with regulations. So state governments have grown departments to do so, and even added a few forms and regulations of their own — for which, in turn, local school districts and police departments have to hire employees who can speak and write bureaucratese. State bureaucracies are not noticeably more efficient than federal. If you think the U.S. Postal Service is bad, spend an hour or two (you seldom can spend less) at the Virginia Department of Motor Vehicles.

There is a widespread concern that the federal government has overreached, and now intrudes too far into local affairs. By setting up programs and issuing mandates, it can displace the lower levels of government from their own responsibilities.

To political scientists, decentralization may be an attractive way of channeling political participation, and to economists an efficient prod for governmental responsiveness to regional needs. But the need to decentralize does not mean that Americans are ready for states that are really governments.

There are many cleavages in today's society, but regionalism is not a big one. Emotionally, this is a country of Americans. The political theory of federalism is not going to sell to people whose hearts do not feel state allegiance.

Nor is there any reason to encourage regional differences, which states' rights promote, as if they were good. Countries get torn up by such things. The United States already has racial and ethnic frictions that need to be healed.

It is unwise for a country to try to govern local matters from Washington. But it would be folly for a country to encourage significant divisions. Ask the prime minister of Canada, or the former president of the former Yugoslavia.

Much can be done to detach federal tentacles from local affairs. But the states aren't going to handle the biggest domestic decisions, because the people don't expect them to.

Questions for Discussion

1. Which is closer to the people: the state or the federal government? Why?
2. What criteria can be used in evaluating whether a policy area properly belongs to the states or to the federal government?
3. What can the federal government do today to strengthen state governments?
4. Should the federal government strengthen state governments? What are the reasons for your answer?
5. What are the advantages and disadvantages of the United States becoming a unitary system?
6. Which groups would benefit and which would be hurt if the federal government gave more power to the states? What are the reasons for your answer?

Suggested Readings

Apple. R. W., Jr. "You Say You Want a Devolution." *New York Times*, January 29, 1995, sec. IV, pp. 1, 5.

Berger, Raoul. *Federalism: The Founders' Design.* Norman: Univ. of Oklahoma Press, 1987.

Bryce, James. *The American Commonwealth*. New York: Macmillan, 1889. Vol. 1, chaps. 29–30.

Cook, Gareth G. "Devolution Chic." *Washington Monthly* 27, no. 4 (April 1995): 9–16.

DiIulio, John J., and Donald F. Kettl. *Fine Print: The Contract with America, Devolution, and the Administrative Realities of American Federalism*. Washington, D.C.: Center for Public Management, Brookings Institution, 1995.

Dionne, E. J., Jr. "The New, New Federalism." *Washington Post*, March 7, 1995, p. A17.

Goldberg, Lenny. "Come the Devolution." *American Prospect*, no. 24 (Winter 1996): 66–71.

Kelly, Kevin, and Richard A. Melcher. "Power to the States." *Business Week*, no. 3436 (August 7, 1995): 48–54, 56.

Kinsley, Michael. "The Case against the States." *Time* 145, no. 2 (January 16, 1995): 78.

Pear, Robert. "Source of State Power Is Pulled from Ashes." *New York Times*, April 16, 1995, p. A16.

Peterson, Paul E. *The Price of Federalism*. Washington, D.C.: Brookings Institution, 1995.

Shapiro, David L. *Federalism: A Dialogue*. Evanston, Ill.: Northwestern Univ. Press, 1995.

U.S. Cong., House of Representatives. *Hearing on Block Grant/Consolidation Overview*. Hearing before the Subcommittee on Oversight and Investigations of the Committee on Economic and Educational Opportunities, 104th Cong., 1st Sess., 1995.

——, House of Representatives. *Impact of Federal Regulation on State and Local Governments*. Hearing before the Committee on the Budget, 104th Cong., 1st Sess., 1995.

——, House of Representatives. *The Perspective of State and Local Governments and the Impact of Federal Regulation*. Hearing before the Committee on the Budget, 104th Cong., 1st Sess., 1995.

——, Senate. *Federal Mandates on State and Local Governments*. Hearing before the Committee on Governmental Affairs, 103d Cong., 1st Sess., 1993.

——, Senate. *Federal Mandate Reform Legislation*. Hearing before the Committee on Governmental Affairs, 103d Cong., 2d Sess., 1994.

——, Senate. *S.1 — Unfunded Mandates*. Joint Hearing before the Committee on Governmental Affairs and the Committee on the Budget, 104th Cong., 1st Sess., 1995.

Verhovek, Sam Howe. "With Power Shift, State Lawmakers See New Demands." *New York Times*, September 24, 1995, pp. 1, 24.

Part II

Civil Liberties and Civil Rights

P olitical systems make rules that are binding upon their members. But political systems differ in the amount of freedom permitted to citizens. In twentieth-century totalitarian dictatorships, the state imposed severe restrictions on individual liberty. Not only was it concerned with what people did, but it sought to mold people's minds to a government-approved way of thinking.

Modern democracies permit a large amount of individual freedom. As a modern democracy, the U.S. government accepts the principle of civil liberties, recognizing that individuals have freedoms the government cannot take away. Among these are freedom of speech, freedom of the press, freedom of assembly, and freedom of religion. The Constitution as originally written in 1787 contains some protections for the individual against the encroachment of government, but the most important are set forth in the first ten amendments to the Constitution, known as the Bill of Rights and adopted in 1791. They are also found in federal government laws and court decisions, as well as in state constitutions and laws.

As the arbiter in constitutional disputes between the government and the individual, the Supreme Court is often at the center of the storm when it tries to determine whether government has overstepped the bounds and illegally violated the liberties sanctioned by the Constitution. And so, the Court has decided issues such as whether the government can force a person whose religion forbids worship of graven images to salute the flag (it cannot) and whether the government can ban obscene books, magazines, motion pictures, or television programs (it can).

The Court's decisions on privacy have been particularly controversial. Privacy is the right to determine one's personal affairs without government interference and without required disclosure of information about oneself. The Constitution does not specifically mention a right of privacy. The Court, however, decided that such a right can be inferred from the First, Fourth, Fifth, Ninth, and Fourteenth Amendments to the Constitution. The right of privacy has been a consideration in the Court's decisions allowing for the right of a woman to have an abortion under certain conditions. And it is now central to cases involving fetal rights.

Court decisions on freedom of speech issues have also been very controversial. The Court has often supported the rights of unpopular groups, such as Nazis and communists, to make speeches advocating their political ideas. It has at times also set limits on speech.

As a nation of immigrants, the United States has a more diverse population than many modern democracies. Its citizens have a variety of religious, racial, and ethnic backgrounds. In addition to promoting civil liberties, the U.S. government is committed to protecting civil rights — those rights that assure minority group equality before the law.

As the speech by Thurgood Marshall in Chapter 1 indicates, the record of civil rights protection for African Americans has been a sorry one. Brought to the New World as slaves, African Americans were not granted U.S. citizenship until after the Civil War. And even after the adoption of the Thirteenth, Fourteenth, and Fifteenth Amendments, which eliminated slavery and gave legal and political rights to former enslaved people, those rights were often denied in practice until the 1960s.

Although the formal barriers to civil rights have largely fallen, many African Americans believe that the nation still does not adequately promote genuine equality. They point to discrimination in employment, housing, and professional advancement as examples of unfinished business.

Part II deals with five issues of civil liberties and civil rights: the place of prayer in public schools, government controls on pornography, the sentence of the death penalty, constitutional protections against accused criminals, and affirmative action as a remedy for discrimination.

Chapter 3

Should a School Prayer Amendment Be Adopted?

The American people have a strong religious faith. According to Norman Redlich, former dean of New York University law school, as a percentage of the population, "There are more members of organized churches in the United States than any other country in the world."[1] But Americans practice different religious faiths. To protect religious freedom, the constitutional system upholds the separation of church and state. The First Amendment to the Constitution states: "Congress shall make no law respecting an establishment of religion, or prohibiting the free exercise thereof."

Where the line is drawn between what government can or cannot do in matters of religion has long been controversial. Even when the Constitution was submitted to the states for ratification, Anti-Federalists complained that the word "God" did not appear in the document. Nor did the word "Christian" appear, although the country was composed mostly of people who were Christians.

Congress begins each day with a prayer, and the Supreme Court starts each session with a prayer. Since 1863, the currency of the United States carries the words, "In God We Trust." And in 1954, the Pledge of Allegiance was changed to include the words "under God." A long-term practice in public schools was the recitation of prayers at the beginning of the school day and at assemblies. In 1962, however, the Supreme Court held in *Engel v. Vitale* that a New York State law giving school officials the option of mandating a daily prayer was unconstitutional. In 1963, the Court invalidated laws in Pennsylvania and Maryland that compelled daily Bible reading and prayer in public schools.[2]

These court decisions received widespread opposition. Nearly every year since 1962, a constitutional amendment that would allow for prayer in public schools has been proposed in Congress. At no time, however, has Congress been able to marshal the two-thirds vote necessary to submit the amendment to the states for ratification. A number of states have adopted legislation requiring moments of silence at the beginning of the school day, which are permitted so long as they are not used as a means for organized prayer. Some states allow individual school districts to decide about whether to require moments of silence. And school prayer continues to have majority support in opinion polls.

Those who favor prayer in public schools often argue that government has become hostile to religion and that it discriminates against students who wish to practice their faith either through prayers or studies. They also feel that many of the social problems that the nation faces, such as drug abuse, violence, and pregnancy of unmarried teens, are the consequence of a lack of religious values. Those who argue against prayer in the public schools fear that permitting government-sanctioned prayer in public schools would be unfair to nonbelievers and a violation of the Establishment Clause of the First Amendment. They also say that there are many opportunities for young people to practice their religious faith and that social problems cannot be blamed on a failure to have state-sanctioned prayer in the public schools.

When the Republicans won control of Congress in 1994, those who favored school prayer felt they now had an opportunity to get a school prayer amendment passed and submitted to the states. A number of Republican candidates had endorsed such an amendment, and Newt Gingrich, the Speaker of the House, favored it as well. Several House Republicans introduced amendments dealing with religion. Representative Ernest J. Istook of Oklahoma proposed a Religious Liberties Amendment, which allows for student-led prayers but bans compulsory prayer. The proposed amendment states:

> To secure the people's right to acknowledge God according to the dictates of conscience: Nothing in this Constitution shall prohibit acknowledgments of the religious heritage, beliefs, or traditions of the people, or prohibit student-sponsored prayer in public schools. Neither the United States nor any State shall compose any official prayer or compel joining in prayer, or discriminate against religious expression or belief.[3]

President Bill Clinton indicated his views on religion and the First Amendment in a directive dated July 12, 1995. He said that the First Amendment "does not convert our schools into religion-free zones." He declared that the Constitution permits and protects a great degree of religious expression in public schools. According to the president, permissible religious practices are the following: individual private prayer, group prayer by students on school grounds but outside the classroom, bringing a Bible to school or writing a book report on a religious work, and announcements by religious clubs on school bulletin boards or public address systems. Not permitted, however, are teacher-led prayers in classrooms or the proselytizing of religion.[4] The president ordered the government to distribute the guidelines explaining the kinds of religious expression permitted in public schools under current law.

The case for school prayer is made by William J. Murray, head of a school prayer interest group who once, influenced by his atheist mother Madalyn Murray O'Hair, objected to school prayer and Bible reading. Murray first clarifies that a school prayer amendment should not mandate prayer in the schools but should permit it if students choose to initiate it and the school district accommodates it. He also indicates that the amendment should not reverse the Supreme Court decision banning government-mandated school prayer. He contends:

1. It is possible that some children might feel discomfort during school prayer. But student discomfort or the fear of peer pressure is not necessarily more important than issues of free speech and prevailing community values.
2. Not every student believes the same thing. The differences between students on religious matters should enrich the educational experience.
3. Minority viewpoints must, of course be protected, but they would no longer hold the majority hostage.
4. The government would not establish its own brand of "orthodox" religion but would allow communities to set their own standards.
5. By affirming our central religious heritage, we will combat the secularism that will destroy us.

Testifying before the Subcommittee on the Constitution of the House Committee on the Judiciary, Rabbi A. James Rudin opposes a constitutional amendment allowing school prayer. Speaking on behalf of the American Jewish Committee (AJC), a group concerned with Jewish and religious matters, he makes the following points:

1. Prayers and Bible readings in public schools and in other public settings are bitterly divisive.
2. Nondenominational prayers in public schools insult the religious sensitivities of millions of Americans.
3. The Supreme Court has held that students may still pray in and out of school. Consequently, no school prayer amendment is needed.
4. A school prayer amendment would place the weight of the government behind religious expression. As a result, the independence of religions would be in jeopardy.
5. Core beliefs and religious convictions cannot be established by majority vote.
6. A school prayer amendment conflicts with the principles established by the Framers of the Constitution.

NOTES

1. Quoted in Laurie Goodstein, "Religious Freedom Amendment Pressed; Conservatives Cite Need at Hill Hearing," *Washington Post*, June 9, 1995, p. A12.
2. *Engel v. Vitale,* 307 U.S. 421 (1962); *School District of Abington Township v. Schempp,* 374 U.S. 203 (1963).

3. For a discussion and text of the amendments, see Bill Broadway, "Religion-Schism over School Prayer; Two GOP-Proposed Constitutional Amendments Reflect Split in Conservative Thinking," *Washington Post*, December 2, 1995, p. B7.

4. See Todd S. Purdum, "President Defends a Place for Religion in the Schools," *New York Times*, July 13, 1995, pp. A1, B10.

☑ *YES*

Should a School Prayer Amendment Be Adopted?

WILLIAM J. MURRAY

Let Us Pray

Recent Supreme Court decisions have gone well beyond giving privilege to secularism; they suggest an actual hostility toward religion. With hindsight we can see that the secularization of our schools has done great harm. No one can claim any longer that change is not needed.

Several draft constitutional amendments have been written to restore our First Amendment rights and put religion on equal footing with secularism. With the support of House Speaker Newt Gingrich, Rep. Ernest Istook, an Oklahoma Republican, is expected to introduce a final draft of a school-prayer amendment in Congress early in September.

Several important observations need to be made about what is an acceptable amendment.

First, it cannot mandate prayer in schools, but should permit it if students choose to initiate it and the school district accommodates it.

Second, the amendment should be worded to limit the power of government, primarily the federal government, so that the Constitution no longer may be used by the Supreme Court or other courts to prohibit prayer by private citizens. Students and local school boards should have the right not to have classroom prayer, but officials should not be able to cite First Amendment or federal-court decisions to support a ban on prayer. Conversely, districts that choose to allow voluntary prayer should be free of federal interference.

Third, the proposed amendment should not reverse the Supreme Court's various decisions banning government-mandated prayer and Bible reading. Most Americans, including Christians, do not want government dictating religious exercises of any kind. The amendment must not support state-sponsored religion but rejects the idea that a "wall of separation" must be erected to equate separation of church and state with separation of religious speech from public life.

Fourth, the amendment should make clear that the government does not necessarily sponsor or endorse everything it allows. Schools and judges often mistake accommodation for endorsement. The idea that student-led prayer is inherently coercive is wrong. As Justice Sandra Day O'Connor has argued, there is a crucial difference between *government* speech endorsing religion and *private* speech endorsing religion, which the free-speech and free-exercise clauses protect.

Fifth, it should not be a "moment of silence" amendment. The Constitution already protects our right to engage in silent prayer anywhere. The amendment should permit a local board to adopt a moment-of-silence policy or to institute a voluntary program of oral prayer.

Sixth, the amendment should seek to restore lost rights. The intent of the amendment is to reinstate and protect the liberty of America's public-school students to initiate or lead in prayer or other religious expressions.

Many people have stated that an amendment is not necessary. Barry W. Lynn argued in a January issue of the *Congressional Digest* that prayer is a strictly private affair; consequently, there can be no law prohibiting it. However, Lynn's article misses the point: Prayer is equally a social as well as a private act and exists for the community as well as the individual. Though Congress has members of many faiths (and of no faith), it opens with prayer on a daily basis; it is a communal gesture.

Perhaps the most persistent argument employed against a constitutional amendment is that it will institute a regime of coercion. This is the issue raised by President Clinton, whose initial reaction to a proposed school-prayer amendment was: "I have always thought that the question was, when does voluntary prayer really become coercive to people who have different religious views from those who are in the majority? . . . I want to see what the details are. I certainly wouldn't rule it out; it depends on what it says." A reasonable answer, but under pressure he soon retracted the statement. Making a 180-degree turn, he called any such amendment "inherently coercive." His first response was far more balanced — it really does depend on what it says, and the proposed drafts are not inherently coercive.

It is argued frequently that because children are so susceptible to peer pressure, no school prayer really could be voluntary. Joe Loconte writes in *Policy Review* for Winter 1995: "It is one thing for members of Congress to begin a legislative session with prayer or for the Supreme Court to open with 'God save the United States and this honorable court.' But it's quite another thing for a minor, who has no choice but to be in school, who is there without her parents, who perhaps already is having trouble fitting in."

It *is* possible that some children might feel discomfort during school prayer. But schools cannot ensure the comfort of every student in every circumstance. Some students feel discomfort because they cannot pray, carry a Bible to school or speak openly about their religious convictions. The issue of school prayer exists in a context of competing values. Student discomfort or the fear of peer pressure is not necessarily more important than issues of free speech and prevailing community values. Students would not necessarily be asked to "acknowledge or ignore" the practice of voluntary prayer. Nonparticipating students, by the very act of nonparticipation, affirm their constitutional right to be different. This is the essence of toleration. Toleration assumes difference; there is no toleration in the absence of conviction.

Not every student believes the same thing. The differences between students should enrich the educational experience. Abstention need not mark students for ridicule. Nonparticipating students create the opportunity for the discussion of different religious or nonreligious viewpoints. Expression of religious convictions of any kind are currently excluded. The amendment should not establish a national standard for schools. Local school districts should be empowered to work out their own solutions. Homogeneous communities may have programs that are quite different from heterogeneous communities. There is no obligation on the part of any school district to do anything under the proposed amendments.

Every one of the proposed amendments imposes a restriction on the federal government, not local schools. Communities would be empowered to exercise their own judgment. It is a simple tradeoff: federal power for local control.

Some critics of an amendment suggest that it would institute a tyranny of the majority. Of course, minority viewpoints must be protected, but not to the point of discrimination against the majority. Every citizen has basic rights that are inviolable. Any hint of coercion would be wrong. But this is a religious-freedoms amendment. It does not provide any mechanism for coercion; it *prevents* the federal government from coercing schools into a uniform secularism — or religious doctrine. In 1960, I was the only student who objected to prayer and Bible reading at Baltimore's Woodbourne Junior High School, yet the entire school was made to conform to my wishes as a result of the Supreme Court's 1963 decision outlawing voluntary prayer in public schools. The principle can be taken too far; the minority can hold the majority hostage.

The issue for many religious people is whether they have the right to control education in their own communities. Bobby Clanton, a school-prayer activist from Mississippi, argues that the majority of students in his state are conservative Christians and should have the right to decide whether and how to pray in public schools. In a *New York Times* article he said, "We're tired of yielding to a tiny minority." While the minority should be protected, the majority should rule.

Some evangelical critics imply that prayer must conform to a particular doctrinal standard — their standard — or there should be no prayer at all. "The same parents who press for prayer in the South would be outraged by Buddhist meditation in Hawaii or readings from the Book of Mormon in Utah," according to Os Guinness, an evangelical writer. Yet if parents in Mississippi had the right to set standards in their own community, most of them would be glad that other communities had the same right. They are smart enough to understand that freedom is reciprocal.

Loconte also objects to school prayer on the basis that it implies a state endorsement of religion: "If 'student-led' prayers become a routine part of public education, they could revive a mutated version of civil religion in the schools. Many evangelicals view civil religion as a threat to religious freedom, because in its worst forms it allows the government to establish its own brand of 'orthodox' religion, by which it judges other expressions of faith."

There would be no uniform civil religion if the federal government had no control of religious expression in schools. First Amendment guarantees are not compromised; they are strengthened. Local control establishes policy-making at the district level. Without an amendment, the federal government will maintain its existing ideological hegemony on schools. We already have the equivalent of an "orthodox" state religion: secularism.

I understand the concern of Americans who fear government involvement in religion. As a teenager, I shared my mother's loathing of religion. As an adult, I came to understand the vital role of religion in the life of this nation. I abandoned my atheism for a life of faith. I was not mature enough in 1963 to understand the comprehensive nature of the changes taking place in our nation. I did not realize that my mother, Madalyn Murray O'Hair, was just a foot soldier in the war between the secular and the sacred. I knew of her involvement with communism and her deep personal anger, but I did not recognize the larger social forces at work. The world is different now. Communism is dead, but secularism is vital and alive. Though it was much more subtle and hidden, secularism was at the heart of the moral crisis that destroyed the Soviet empire from the inside out. Is our democratic capitalism immune to the same disease? Can our schools survive their own moral crisis?

Unlike England, Germany or Japan, America does not have a common heritage. We are many different colors, nationalities and ethnic backgrounds. What will bind us together if not a common belief in God? If we abandon our central religious heritage, as my mother and others desire, what will be the bond that holds our nation together? The common thread that binds us as a people is the belief that we are indeed one nation under God. Belief in God is the safety net of democracy, without which we surely will perish.

 NO

Should a School Prayer Amendment Be Adopted?

RABBI A. JAMES RUDIN
The Case against School Prayer

The proposals for a constitutional amendment on religion — variously proffered as a "Religious Equality," "Religious Liberties," and "Religious Freedom" amendment — have one unifying element. Any of them would effectively repeal the No Establishment Clause of the First Amendment, the mere suggestion of which sets off alarm bells for millions of Americans, including the membership of the AJC [American Jewish Committee].

While I will specifically allude to Rep. [Dick] Armey's "Religious Freedom" initiative — better termed a "Religious Establishment" amendment — please understand that the concerns I will raise apply to the other initiatives as well. . . .

Prayers and Bible readings in public schools and in other public settings are bitterly divisive. The passage of the proposed amendment would cause ugly sectarian strife throughout America.

The United States is a multi-religious and multi-ethnic nation. What kind of prayer or Scriptural reading is appropriate when the students are not only Christian and Jewish (in all their myriad forms), but are also followers of Islam, Buddhism, Hinduism, American Indian tribal faiths, or are of no religious tradition?

Public schools have problems aplenty these days, and must not become battlegrounds in political and religious power games. Today's crop of second graders and all other public school students in America would become cannon fodder in the warfare that is currently being waged by some politicians and clergy. Indeed, I have the feeling that school prayer advocates have not carefully examined what the imposition of such prayers actually means in the real and complex world of public education.

In an obvious attempt to avoid the constitutional issues, there are calls for something called "non-denominational" prayers in our public schools. Such watered down devotionals are spiritual pablum that blatantly insult the religious sensibilities of millions of Americans, including myself, who make authentic prayer a central part of their lives.

But, more to the point, there can be no such thing as "non-denominational" prayer because there is no such thing as religion in general anymore than there is language in general. Every expression of faith must include elements of some specific creed or beliefs, however generalized, which by their very nature will therefore exclude those who do not share the precepts expressed.

It is ironic that, at a time when we hear so much of the need "to get the government off our backs," we are faced with a campaign for prayers and Bible readings in public schools, schools that are supported by the taxes of all Americans. Putting the intrusive and invasive weight of "government prayers" upon the backs of little children makes no sense.

And there are repeated fervent cries "to put God back into the classroom" through the device of providing for verbal prayer during the school day. But God dwells everywhere, and God's presence cannot be defined, invented, limited, or curtailed by humans. The Bible made that clear with the awesome verse that "God will be whatever God will be."

Public schools and buildings as well as public spaces are not, it must be remembered, houses of worship or family homes. The latter institutions are the proper places for authentic religious expressions, teachings, and rituals.

All of these considerations, and more, underlay the landmark cases of more than thirty years ago in which the Supreme Court ruled that the First Amendment bars government from either composing prayers or sponsoring prayers for American school children to recite.

These rulings, it should be remembered, were limited to governmental involvement. Thus, public school students need no constitutional amendment to permit them to pray. Students can and do pray quietly any time they wish. They can pray vocally in a group as long as school routine is not disrupted and other students are not interfered with. It is perfectly legal for children to engage in voluntary prayer in the cafeteria, the classroom, the gymnasium, and the playground. There is nothing in any Supreme Court ruling to the contrary. Indeed, the American Jewish Committee and virtually all other advocates for strong church-state separation believe that this right of religious expression is an essential aspect of religious liberty.

In addition, under the Federal Equal Access Act of 1984, student religious clubs in secondary schools abound, and provide a constitutionally permissible opportunity for devotional Bible reading, as well as group prayer, during noninstructional time. Parents for whom it is important that their own children pray while in the public school are, of course, free to direct them accordingly. . . .

And when there are cases in which school officials, including school boards, have improperly prohibited students from exercising these rights — "horror stories," as it were — adequate legal remedies exist. The Rutherford Institute, a legal advocacy organization for the "religious right," correctly notes that ". . . many cases can be solved with a strong and professional letter from an attorney, a legal memorandum from our office, or a phone call. . . ." Clearly, a new constitutional amendment is not needed or even desirable to deal with such instances.

While the proposed amendments to the Constitution would do nothing to add to, or further protect the free-exercise rights of students, they would have the effect of placing the weight of the government behind religious expression. Thus, the "Religious Freedom" amendment, by broadly asserting that the government shall not "discriminate against any person, on account of religious belief, expression, or exercise," eliminates the line between private and public religious expression that has been crucial in determining when the government is acting in a coercive fashion or otherwise unacceptably entangling itself with religion.

Sometimes private religious speech may be tantamount to government action because it is so couched in the context of state sponsorship as to leave the impression of government endorsement. That is one reason why the oft-touted alternative of having a majority of students in a class, or on a football team, or at a graduation ceremony decide what prayers will be said — as opposed to a school official — simply does not resolve the constitutional infirmities that the courts have found in school-sponsored prayer. And, of course, there is another crucial consideration. The right to engage in voluntary prayer does not include the right to have a captive audience listen — or, in effect, to coerce other students to participate. The First Amendment currently has the sensitivity and flexibility to respond to such situations; the proposed amendment would obliterate that capability.

In addition to the importation of sectarian symbols, prayers, and rituals into the public realm, the proposed "Religious Freedom" amendment would open the floodgates of the public treasury to religious groups. The taxes collected from Americans of various religious beliefs and of no religious creed would be used to support religious institutions in their most narrowly and pervasively sectarian activities.

This proposed use of tax money to advance religion would violate the consciences of taxpayers who rightfully expect the government to remain neutral toward religion. The government should not be allowed, much less required, to use our tax money to promote religious activities, whether they are sponsored by Baptists, Jews, members of the Nation of Islam, or Branch Davidians.

But, perhaps even more crucially, government funding for religion inevitably creates entangling church-state alliances and weakens religion's autonomy. With government money comes government restrictions. Religious organizations that receive public funds would be subject to intrusive government regulation, accounting, and monitoring. Have we forgotten the old adage that "Whoever takes the King's pence also takes the King and his men?"

Moreover, government simply cannot fund the multitude of religious groups in our country. It would have to make agonizing, divisive, and political choices about which religions get government subsidies. This would spur unhealthy competition among faith groups and enmesh religion in the inevitable political horsetrading that accompanies entitlement decisions. All too often, only majority religions would prevail.

To be sure, the debate over a "Religious Freedom" amendment graphically illustrates the desperate hunger for values that is a major element of the contemporary American scene, and the desire of many to respect authentic religious voices as part of that scene. Unfortunately, an amendment that permits public school prayers and the use of public money for sectarian purposes will not effectively address these concerns. It will only make things worse; much worse.

Our ultimate values, our core beliefs, our religious convictions cannot be established by majority vote, by partisan platforms, by political compromises. Quite the contrary, they can only be demeaned and diminished by the intrusion of the state into the sacred realm of the spirit.

Some proponents of the amendment charge that the principle of church-state separation is a late twentieth century political invention that is new or alien to the American democratic society. But just the opposite is true.

As a direct result of the religious strife in Europe, especially the Thirty Years War and the Inquisition in Spain and Portugal, as well as the excesses committed both in Great Britain and in the American colonies against religious dissenters and minorities in the seventeenth and eighteenth centuries, the Framers of the Constitution of the United States, especially James Madison who later became the fourth American President, took great care to provide specific guarantees for religious freedom and liberty.

The concluding clause of Article VI of the Constitution reads: "No religious Test shall ever be required as a Qualification to any office or public Trust under the United States." Immediately following the Constitution's ratification in 1787, ten Amendments were added, constituting the "Bill of Rights." The First Amendment deals in part with religion:

> Congress shall make no law respecting an establishment of religion, or prohibiting the free exercise thereof; or abridging the freedom of speech, or of the press; or the right of the people peaceably to assemble, and to petition the Government for a redress of grievances.

The unique American contribution to religious freedom is crystallized in the two key provisions of the First Amendment: no establishment of religion by the state and the free exercise of religion. These Religion Clauses mean that no branch of government — federal, state, or local — can grant preferential favors to a particular religion, nor can the government officially disapprove of any religion. The First Amendment also guarantees that we can freely practice or not practice our religion free of government control, favoritism, or discrimination. Government must be neutral in matters of faith. . . .

In contrast to the right of students to engage in voluntary, noncoercive religious expression, a constitutional amendment would create new rights, rights of government officials and students, with implicit governmental sanction, to impose prayer on other parents' children, whether these other parents or children may want this or not. And this is not to mention the raids by religious institutions on the public treasury that the amendment would sanction, a raid in which the most powerful and populous denominations would have the upper hand.

It is essential to recall that, even if a majority of Americans were to favor restoring organized school prayer or subventing religious institutions, the Bill of Rights, in general, and the First Amendment, in particular, are antimajoritarian — that is, their provisions are intended to protect the rights of minorities and dissenters by placing certain matters, like religion, outside the reach of majorities. And these same principles apply in all institutions of government to which citizens come in the expectation that they will not be made to feel like outsiders in their own home. The state has a responsibility to remain religion-neutral in the public schools, military bases, and courtrooms that it maintains. As Congressman Melvin Watt (D.-N.C.) said during the hearing of this Subcommittee in Washington on June 8: "If everything that was in the Constitution was done by a simple majority, then I guess you would have a Constitution that was based on protecting the rights of the majority." That is not the Constitution we now enjoy and cherish. "Each for himself — and God for us all — said the elephant as he started to dance among the chickens" is hardly the American constitutional way.

The "Religious Freedom" amendment would deceptively nullify the No Establishment Clause while cloaking the demise of this core principle of American freedom in the disguise of "religious freedom," when the freedom ostensibly sought already exists. Indeed, recent Supreme Court decisions reaffirm the robust protection provided by the First Amendment for religious expression in public places. To the extent that such expression is stifled improperly, these situations can and should be dealt with by measures well short of the drastic remedy of amending the Bill of Rights—with education the most significant such avenue. We at AJC which, as I have noted, has always strongly supported free expression of religion by people of all faiths, are ready, willing, and able to assist in such endeavors.

But there is no need, for the very first time in our history, to amend the First Amendment to allow prayer in public schools or to protect other forms of religious expression. That provision is the preeminent safeguard of freedom of conscience for all that has allowed this nation, more than any other, to avoid the tragic religious conflicts that have afflicted people in other lands and do so even today. In 1785, we were warned by James Madison "to take alarm at the first experiment on our liberties." No experiment should be viewed with greater alarm than any proposal to amend the First Amendment of the Bill of Rights, which has served us so well. . . .

I strongly urge this Subcommittee on the Constitution to reject all attempts to weaken our traditional constitutional guarantees of religious liberty and freedom. Such a commitment coming from the United States Congress would provide welcome assurances that our remarkable heritage of religious liberty, pluralism, and church-state separation will be safely passed to future generations of Americans.

And let those later generations say of us that we responded to the challenges of our day. Let them say that we remembered our history and our traditions. Let them say that we actively worked together to protect and enhance the sacred trust that was preserved for us.

Questions for Discussion

1. Is the practice of saying a prayer at the beginning of each day in Congress a violation of the First Amendment? What are the reasons for your answer?
2. Is there a relationship between the Supreme Court's decision on school prayer since 1962 and the emergence of major social problems in America? What are the reasons for your answer?
3. Is the fact that the majority of the American people favor prayer in public schools sufficient evidence for adopting a constitutional amendment for school prayer? What are the reasons for your answer?
4. Students who do not wish to recite the Pledge of Allegiance to the flag in the public schools need not do so, but the pledge is recited nonetheless. Should not school prayer be treated the same? What are the reasons for your answer?
5. What would be the effect of the adoption of a constitutional amendment for school prayers on other religious practices in the public schools?

Suggested Readings

Alley, Robert S. *School Prayer: The Court, the Congress, and the First Amendment.* Buffalo, N.Y.: Prometheus Books, 1994.

Davis, Derek H. "Editorial: A Commentary on the Proposed 'Equality/Liberties' Amendment." *Journal of Church and State* 38, no. 1 (Winter 1996): 5–23.

Durham, James R. *Secular Darkness: Religious Right Involvement in Texas Public Education.* New York: P. Lang, 1995.

Fenwick, Lynda Beck. *Should the Children Pray?: A Historical, Judicial, and Political Examination of Public School Prayer.* Waco, Tex.: Markham Press Fund of Baylor Univ. Press, 1989.

Horan, Kathleen. "Pray in School? Pray to Whom?" *New York Times*, September 9, 1995, p. 19.

Kramnick, Isaac, and Laurence Moore. *The Godless Constitution: The Case against Religious Correctness.* New York: W. W. Norton, 1996.

Laconte, Joe. "Lead Us Not into Temptation." *Policy Review*, no. 71 (Winter 1995): 24–31.

Lynn, Barry, Marc D. Stern, and Oliver S. Thomas. *The Basic ACLU Guide to Religious Rights*, 2d ed. Carbondale: Southern Illinois Univ. Press, 1995.

Murray, William J. *Let Us Pray: A Plea for Prayer in Our Schools.* New York: William Morrow & Co., 1995.

O'Hair, Madalyn Murray. *An Atheist Epic: The Complete Unexpurgated Story of How Bible and Prayer Were Removed from the Public Schools.* Austin, Tex.: American Atheist Press, 1989.

"Prayer in Public Schools: Pros & Cons." *Congressional Digest* 74, no. 1 (January 1995): entire issue.

Purdum, Todd S. "President Defends a Place for Religion in the Schools." *New York Times*, July 13, 1995, pp. A1, B10.

Sikorski, Robert, ed. *Prayer in the Public Schools and the Constitution.* New York: Garland, 1993.

Chapter 4

Should Government Impose Stricter Regulations on Pornography?

Americans have been inundated with graphic materials of a sexually explicit nature, including film, videos, telephones lines, and the Internet. The fact that the American people spend billions of dollars for such items demonstrates the popularity of what critics used to call "smut." But a growing chorus of voices is calling for increased government regulation of sexually explicit material.

Any discussion of the permissibility of sexually explicit material requires a definition of the terms "obscenity" and "pornography." "Obscenity" is a legal term for written or photographic materials of a sexual or violent nature. "Pornography" is a broader term, referring to material designed to be sexually arousing. The terms are often used interchangeably, however. In the United States the courts have determined that obscene materials are not protected under the First Amendment and can be banned by government.

Historically, government agencies have taken steps to keep material regarded as obscene away from the public. But what the government has regarded as obscene has varied over time. A few prominent works of twentieth-century literature — including books by Henry Miller and D. H. Lawrence — could not be sold in the United States for many years after they were published because they were characterized as obscene. Magazines, movies, and hard-core videos have also been suppressed when found to be obscene.

Even when there is agreement about the desirability of curbing obscenity, a continuing problem is determining whether a particular work is obscene. The mere fact that sex and violence are depicted in a particular work is not sufficient to find it obscene from a legal point of view. Some people who are opposed to the sale or display of any works depicting graphic scenes of sex and violence are not interested in legal niceties, however, and just want to censor any works they do not like. But the courts have had to grapple with the problem of applying standards to distinguish obscene work from materials protected by the First Amendment.

The battle over obscenity is a continuing one and has produced some unusual political alliances of conservatives and liberals. Traditionally in the United States, criticism of pornography has come from conservative sources, particularly religious groups. They regard pornography as corrupting traditional values of respect for women and the sanctity of marriage and the family.

The conservative critique was exemplified during the Reagan administration by the establishment of a commission under the jurisdiction of Attorney General Edwin Meese III to investigate the impact of pornography on society. The commission's report concluded that there was a direct relationship between pornography and violence. In 1986, the federal government set up a special section in the Criminal Division of the Justice Department to aid the prosecution of pornography.

But conservatives have found support for regulating pornography from some feminists, most notably Catharine A. MacKinnon and Andrea Dworkin. While generally regarded as liberals, they find common cause with conservatives on this issue. They condemn pornography because they feel that it causes harm to women, encouraging exploitation and rape. They favor legislation allowing the victims of pornography (such as women who have been raped) to collect civil damages from the people who create or sell pornographic material that may have prompted the rape.

Although most feminists agree that pornography demeans women, many — if not most of them — feel that government involvement in this area is a violation of the First Amendment. In this view, they share the opinion of most liberals that any censorship is dangerous to freedom of speech. Liberals worry that antiobscenity legislation will only stifle ideas.

The debate that follows features a traditional conservative-liberal division on the issue. Ernest van den Haag, former professor of jurisprudence and public policy at Fordham University in New York City, argues from a conservative perspective in defense of legislating against pornography. Speaking before the Heritage Foundation, a conservative think tank, he contends:

1. Pornography reduces males and females simply to bearers of impersonal sensations of pleasure and pain; in short, it dehumanizes people. In this way, the empathy that restrains us ultimately from sadism and nonconsensual acts is eliminated.
2. Pornography lacks artistic value.
3. It undermines the social bond on which human association — from family to nation — must depend.
4. The First Amendment does not protect pornography.
5. Distinctions can be made between pornography and literature.
6. Regulating pornography is not the beginning of a police state.

Testifying before a congressional committee considering new initiatives to regulate pornography, Barry W. Lynn, as legislative counsel for the American Civil Liberties Union (ACLU), argues against further restrictions. He contends:

1. Pornography cannot be objectively defined.
2. Pornography — unlike obscenity — is protected by the First Amendment and should not be abridged.
3. New antipornography legislation would threaten the livelihood not only of distributors who deal only in sexually explicit films but of every owner of a major bookstore chain.
4. Antipornography laws would impose a "chilling effect" on literature or art.
5. Pornography is speech and not an act or a practice.
6. Pornography is not a central cause of sex discrimination.
7. The fact that pornography asserts an often repugnant world view graphically or persuasively does not place it in a special category distinct from literature.
8. The evidence is not conclusive that most pornography is an incitement to violence against women.

Lynn argues that there are ways to fight pornography other than to ban it or regulate it severely. In his view, the ultimate answer to the existence of offensive images must be the production of "affirmative" alternative images.

 ✓ *YES*

*Should Government Impose Stricter Regulations
on Pornography?*

ERNEST VAN DEN HAAG

Pornography and the Law

The Meese Commission report on pornography was released last year [1986] and is now old hat. Perhaps this is a good time to examine with some detachment the question on which it sought to shed light: Should we continue to outlaw pornography while, in effect, tolerating it? Should we legalize it? Or should we find a method of outlawing it effectively?

For those who wish to legalize pornography the answer is simple. Whether or not pornography is distasteful or morally harmful, it affects only those who buy it. The government is not in charge of their morals. It is part of one's freedom to make choices that are harmful to oneself or disapproved by others. Those offended by pornography can readily refrain. There is no need for the law to protect them; no one compels them to see X-rated movies or buy pornographic magazines. Legitimate questions about advertising, public visibility, and access by children are marginal and could be solved by such measures as plain wrappers and inconspicuous signs.

RIDICULE BY "CIVIL LIBERTARIANS"

Surely the people who want to legalize pornography are right if, as they contend, pornography does no harm to those who do not volunteer to buy it. This is the question the Meese Commission addressed. The Commission has been ridiculed by all the usual "civil libertarians." However, if one actually looks at its report, one finds that the Commission did quite reasonable work in trying to answer the question it focused on: Does pornography lead to crime? If it does, obviously it harms persons who did not volunteer for the harm. They are entitled to protection, provided that protection is consistent with constitutional principles.

The Commission decided that pornography, particularly sado-masochistic pornography, stimulates, to say the least, sex crimes. One can argue about this. There is a chicken and egg problem. Does the prospective rapist consume pornography because he independently is a prospective rapist, or is it the pornography which causes, or stimulates, a disposition to rape that did not preexist or was minor? Which comes first? However, there seems to be little doubt that a disposition to commit sex crimes may be strengthened or activated by pornography, which appears to legitimize them and to weaken internal restraints.

CHANGING SEXUAL MORES

The general evidence strongly suggests that crime can be stimulated by communications, ideas and sensations aroused by movies or books. Few sayings are as silly as the *dictum* attributed to Jimmy Walker (the late New York mayor) to the effect that "No girl has ever been seduced by a book." Books do not seduce directly any more than whiskey does. But they help. After all, even if one discounts the "sexual revolution," one cannot deny that sexual mores have changed over time, owing not to changes in biology, but to changed ideas and sentiments that infect people and lead them to action. Books such as the Bible or *Das Kapital* influence people's actions because of the ideas they expound. Pornography, which is bereft of ideas, influences people because of the sensations and attitudes it stimulates. It is consumed for the sake of these sensations as drugs are and may influence actions analogously.

But pornography is not the only thing that may lead to sex crime, and certainly it does so only sometimes. Many people consume it without being led to crime. Others become criminals without pornography. Further, alcohol too may lead to crime, or TV violence — indeed myriad things. We cannot outlaw everything, not even every communication, that sometimes leads to crime. Why then outlaw pornography?

EXPLOITS SEX

If the Meese Commission conclusion — let's prohibit pornography because it may lead to crime — does not quite follow from its evidence, the idea of some feminists, that pornography is a male conspiracy against females to exploit them, and foster, or help, violence against them, is even less well founded. Pornography exploits sex, not females. The criminal effects are not intended, let alone conspired for. Women are accidental. Pornographers would be just as willing to present pictures of males as of females if there were a market for them. There isn't, except for male homosexuals, who indeed are catered to by pornographers. Most females — be it for cultural, psychological, or biological reasons — do not seem to want to consume pornography. Actually males, who spend good money for the stuff, are more, not less, exploited than the females who earn it. At any rate, I can't see exploitation (a cloudy concept to begin with, meaning not much more than "I don't like it"), since both buyers and sellers volunteer and both have alternatives. They do what they want to do; they are not compelled to do it. Exploitation without compulsion is hard to figure out.[1]

O.K., forget about the feminists. Why should we punish the sale of pornography? (Nobody advocates prior restraint censorship, which is a pseudo-issue.) The Meese Commission reason, that it may lead to crime, is not sufficient. Are there other reasons? I believe there are. The social damage pornography does is greater, yet more diffuse than indicated by individual crimes. Just as chemical pollution may erode stones, statues, and buildings, so pornography erodes civility and our social institutions.

AVOIDING ART AND HUMANITY

By definition, pornography deindividualizes and dehumanizes sexual acts. By eliminating the contexts it reduces males and females simply to bearers of impersonal sensations of pleasure and pain. This dehumanization eliminates the empathy that restrains us ultimately from sadism and non-consensual acts. The cliche-language and the stereotyped situations of characters not characterized, except sexually, are defining characteristics of pornography. The pornographer avoids distraction from the masturbatory fantasy by avoiding art and humanity. Art may "cancel lust" (as Santayana thought) or sublimate it. The pornographer desublimates it. Those who resort to pornographic fantasies habitually are people who are ungratified by others (for endogenous or external reasons). They seek gratification in using others, in inflicting pain (sometimes in suffering it), at least in their fantasy. In this respect, *The Story of O,* which, itself pornographic, also depicts the rather self-defeating outcome of pornographic fantasy, is paradigmatic.

In a sense, pornographic and finally sadistic literature is anti-human. Were it directed against a specific human group — e.g. Jews or blacks — the same liberal ideologues who now oppose outlawing pornography might advocate prohibiting it. Should we find a little black or Jewish girl tortured to death and her death agony taped by her murderers,[2] and should we find the murderers imbued with sadistic anti-Semitic or anti-black literature, most liberals would advocate that the circulation of such literature be prohibited. Why should humanity as such be less protected than any of the specific groups that compose it? That the sexualized hate articulated is directed against people in general, rather than against only Jews or Negroes, makes it no less dangerous; on the contrary: it makes it as dangerous to more people.

WITHOUT ARTISTIC VALUE

But shouldn't an adult be able to control himself and read or see, without enacting, what he knows to be wrong or, at least, illegal? Perhaps he should. But we are not dealing with a homogeneous group called grown-ups, nor is it possible in the modern American environment to limit anything to adults. Children and adolescents are not supervised enough. Further, the authority of their supervisors has been diminished too much to make effective supervision possible. As for grown-ups, many are far from the self-restrained healthy type envisaged by democratic theory. They may easily be given a last, or first, push by the materials I would like to see prohibited.

Now, if these materials had artistic, indeed any but pornographic value, we would have to weigh the loss against the importance of avoiding their deleterious influence. We may even be ready to sacrifice some probable victims for the sake of this value. But pornographic "literature" is without literary value. It is printed, but it is not literature. Else it cannot be defined as pornography. Hence there is nothing to be lost by restricting it, and much to be gained.

AFFECTS THE QUALITY OF LIFE

Self-restrained and controlled individuals exist and function in an environment which fosters reasonable conduct. But few such individuals will be created, and they will function less well, in an environment where they receive little social support, where sadistic acts are openly held up as models and sadistic fantasies are sold to any purchaser. To be sure, a virtuous man will not commit adultery. But a wise wife will avoid situations where the possibility is alluring and the opportunity available. Why must society lead its members into temptation and then punish them when they do what they were tempted to do? But more than individual cases are at issue.

Pornography affects the quality of our lives. It depreciates emotional ties and individual relationships in favor of fungible ones, in which physical pleasure is, in principle, separated from any emotional or even personal relationships. Yet, without "emotional ties which hold the group together," according to Freud there is "the cessation of all feelings of consideration" and therewith social disintegration and crime. "Emotional ties" are systematically depreciated by pornography.

EROSION OF THE SOCIAL BOND

Thus pornography undermines the social bond on which human association — from family to nation — must depend. It is this social bond which deters most of us, most of the time, from using our neighbors as we please, without regard to their own preferences. We are taught, and most of us learn, to perceive others as ends in themselves and not merely as means to our pleasure. This learning is the basis of society. Yet it is precarious. We need to be socialized continuously. Pornography undermines the internal restraints on which society must depend and which the criminal law with its sanctions can reinforce but not create. This seems quite enough to limit pornography (we will never succeed in doing more). No need (or possibility) to prove a direct and unavoidable relationship to crime. Such a direct causal relationship is likely occasionally, perhaps often. But it is largely beside the point when compared to the erosion of the social bond.

I prefer to live in a society in which public invitations to do without love in individual relationships, to regress to an infantile level of sexuality, stripped of emotion, are not consistently extended. Such invitations are all too likely to be tempting. We all are vulnerable to regression. After all, each of us developed laboriously and with much social effort from anti-social infants into acceptable adults. Invitations to regression should not be socially endorsed. Wherefore the case for prohibition of obscenity seems to be quite strong regardless of whether pornography can be shown to be among the many causes of crime.

PORNOGRAPHY NOT PROTECTED

Interstate commerce in pornography is already illegal under federal statutes, and intrastate pornography is illegal in most states. As interpreted by the Supreme Court the First Amendment does not protect pornography, defined as that which:

1. taken as whole predominantly appeals to the prurient interest (a morbid interest in sex); and

2. lacks serious literary, scientific, artistic, or political value (i.e., does not predominantly offer new ideas or aesthetic experiences); and
3. describes sexual conduct in ways judged to be patently offensive by the standards of the community in which the material is sold.

These legal criteria are rather porous. For instance, the depiction of intercourse with animals may be legal, since it may not appeal to the prurient interest of the average person. The depiction of excretion may be legal, since it may not appeal to the prurient interest of the average person either. The standards of the local community are vague (and costly to ascertain), unless the jury is taken to mean the community. The court could have been more concrete and specific.

CAMOUFLAGE AND PRETENSE

Further, present law requires that the material at issue be considered "as a whole" to determine whether it "predominantly" appeals to the prurient interest. This makes perfect sense for, say, novels, works meant to be taken as a whole, but no sense for periodicals, which, by definition, consist of independent articles or pictures. Why should it not be sufficient if some pictures, or other contributions, to a periodical are obscene, even if the rest consists of non-obscene essays? The non-obscene material usually serves as camouflage or pretense. For a movie, if more than 5 percent of its running time is devoted to images which, taken in isolation, would be regarded as obscene, the movie should be so regarded.

Traditionally pornography has not been thought to be protected by the First Amendment. The idea that the First Amendment licenses pornographers, though widespread, is quite recent. It has no legal basis. Further the First Amendment prohibits only abridging freedom of speech and of the press. Yet current interpretations have led the courts to conclude that the First Amendment protects "expression" (such as nude dancing) as well. Although expression, dancing is certainly not speech, let alone print. Nothing in the First Amendment protects speechless expression, such as music or dance, or for that matter, pictures.

Thus, in accordance with the First Amendment, legislatures cannot abridge the communication of information or of ideas. But pornography as defined by the courts is bereft of either. Legislatures can constitutionally allow pornography or nude dancing, but they need not. The legal question is not, can we prohibit pornography? (The answer is yes.) What is in dispute in each case is only: Is this material obscene according to the legal definition given above?[3]

EXPLICIT VISUAL DEPICTIONS

Of course there will be doubtful cases — but no more so than in other areas of the law. Courts exist to decide doubtful cases and can do so in this area as well as in any other. Standards of obscenity vary over time. Yet at any time there are standards discoverable by the courts. There is no great difficulty in discerning them — as lawyers are aware, though they often pretend otherwise. Yet, although often professing to be unable to distinguish obscene from non-obscene material, lawyers do not expose their genitals in court. They must have some knowledge of prevailing standards.

Depiction of the nude body, even in alluring poses, is no longer regarded as offensive. Nor is explicit prose. Visual depictions that focus on the genitals — rather than to merely include them — are. Detailed and explicit visual depictions of genital actions, including copulation, masturbation, and depiction of genital arousal, are prurient and offensive. So are prurient depictions which make public what traditionally has been private and intimate.

MAKING DISTINCTIONS

The perception of pornographic qualities in any work depends on literary or aesthetic criticism. Therefore, some argue, it is a matter of opinion. In court, serious critics often behave as though they believed criticism to be a matter of opinion. But why be a critic — and teach in universities — if it involves no more than uttering capricious and arbitrary opinions? If criticism cannot tell pornography from literature, what can it tell us? Of course, critics may disagree; so do other witnesses, including psychiatrists and handwriting experts. The decision is up to the courts; the literary witnesses only have the obligation to testify truthfully as to what is, or is not, pornography.

Some of the critics who claim that they cannot make the distinction do not wish to, because they regard pornography as legitimate; others fear that censorship of pornography may be extended to actual literature. Whatever the merits of such views (I don't see any), they do not justify testifying that the distinction cannot be made. A witness is not entitled to deny that he saw what he did see, simply to save the accused from a punishment he dislikes. A critic who is really incapable of distinguishing pornography from literature certainly has no business being one; a critic who is capable of making the distinction has no business testifying that he is not.

200 YEARS OF OUTLAWING OBSCENITY

Oh yes, there is one bugaboo: A "police state," it is feared, may develop from prohibiting the sale of pornography and punishing violators. That argument is not too plausible. To begin with, America did not become a "police state" although obscenity has been punished for the last 200 years. Not a single instance is known, throughout history, of a police state, or a dictatorship, developing by prohibiting obscenity, or even by censoring it, or by censoring anything else. It is the other way around. Once you have a police state, censorship follows. A police state cannot continue without it. But no democracy has ever become a police state by using the criminal law to restrain obscenity.

The Weimar Republic in Germany was not replaced by Nazism because it did. It did not. Once Hitler was in power, he used it to abolish all freedom and to institute censorship.

NOTES

1. Depiction of females merely as sexual objects, expressions of hostility or contempt for them, and depictions of sadistic humiliation, are sometimes called "exploitation." If not exploitative, pornography of this sort is certainly antisocial. One may favor prohibition for this reason as much as for the sake of women.

2. This was done by the "Moor murderers" in England.

3. There are the usual ancillary questions: Was it offered for sale? Was it properly seized? But they need not detain us.

 N O

Should Government Impose Stricter Regulations on Pornography?

BARRY W. LYNN
Pornography and Liberty

We live in a country where the equality of men and women is neither generally portrayed nor routinely practiced. It is also a nation in which there is persistent violence against women by men who resent their achievements and the challenges they present to a male-dominated society. Against this volatile backdrop it is possible to reach for drastic proposals, including ones which could erode vital constitutional guarantees. One such flawed avenue is the new effort to curb sexually explicit material by creating broad new civil remedies so that individuals offended by it may hinder its use, sale, and distribution.

Many of the witnesses who have appeared during your previous two days of hearings, and several here today, have called for new legislative initiatives to regulate "pornography," which they erroneously assert can be objectively defined. They have made claims which would allegedly permit "pornography," now protected by the Constitution, to be excised from First Amendment protection just as "obscenity" and "child pornography" have been.[1]

Unfortunately, this approach blurs critical distinctions between advocacy and action and between cause and symptom, distinctions which must be retained in order to preserve important First Amendment guarantees. It is clearly contrary to the guarantees of free speech and a free press, because it ultimately rests on the constitutionally-forbidden premise that governments can be parties to the suppression of offensive ideas and images.

The recently adopted Indianapolis ordinance which has been embraced by several witnesses makes actionable "the graphic sexually explicit subordination of women, whether in pictures or in words" if it also includes one or more specific elements, including, for example, the portrayal of women "as sexual objects . . . who enjoy humiliation" or the presentation of women "through postures of servility . . . or display." Such language as "presented as sexual objects" lacks intrinsic or objective meaning. It either requires inquiry into the motive of the producer or allows even the most sensitive viewer's characterization to be the ultimate determination.

(The ACLU [American Civil Liberties Union] has filed an *amicus* brief in the case challenging the facial constitutionality of the Indianapolis ordinance. This is not a hearing on that ordinance *per se.* However, it is important to note that any approach to regulation of sexually explicit material which seeks to cover material not included within the Supreme Court's definition of "obscenity" in *Miller v. California,* 413 U.S. 15 [1973] or its description of "child pornography" in *United States v. Ferber* 458 U.S. 747 [1982] will face insurmountable constitutional "over-breadth" and "vagueness" problems.)

These phrases can in fact be construed by reasonable people to cover vast amounts of literature, art, and popular culture in today's marketplace. Novels by Norman Mailer, Erica Jong and John Irving, sex education "self-help" books, much "erotic" and even religious art of Eastern and Western cultures, and popular music videos could clearly be included. Likewise, many of the highest grossing films of 1984, including *Indiana Jones, Tightrope,* and *Purple Rain,* all contain sufficient graphic thematic messages about subordination of women to result in legal actions. It would not be simply the proprietor of the "Adam and Eve" bookstore who would have to wonder whether a court would find some of his sales items "pornographic"; it would be every movie exhibitor and every owner of a major bookstore chain.

That problem is the essence of a "chilling effect" — that persons will not write, or photograph, or sell because they do not want to risk that some particularly sensitive or particularly zealous individual will decide that their product is covered by the statutory language. Creating broad individual civil causes of action, particularly ones which allow injunctions against continued distribution, will lead to "self-censorship." This can have as drastic an effect on the free flow of ideas as direct government censorship.

THE ALLEGED EFFECTS OF PORNOGRAPHY

The underpinning of new efforts to control "pornography" is that recently discovered and newly articulated factors take the material outside the scope of the First Amendment. However, the new framing of the argument against pornography, combined with the varieties of empirical research data, still meets no test ever articulated by the Supreme Court which would allow the state directly or its citizens indirectly to suppress this sexually explicit material.

The so-called "findings" section of the Indianapolis ordinance and other proposals notes that "Pornography is a discriminatory *practice* based on sex which denies women equal opportunities in society. Pornography is *central* in creating and maintaining sex as a basis for discrimination. . . . The bigotry and contempt it promotes, with the acts of *aggression it fosters,* harm women's opportunities for equality of rights . . ." (emphasis added). Many previous witnesses have made statements suggesting agreement with this analysis. However, these conclusions are unsupported by the actual evidence available.

Pornography as a "Practice"

Pornography includes words and pictures. It is "speech," not an act or a practice. The parallels between certain racist activity and pornography drawn by some pornography critics are inappropriate. Racial segregation is an "act" and it can be prohibited in spite of First Amendment claims of a "right of association." However, racist speech by the American Nazi Party or the Ku Klux Klan which may, implicitly or explicitly, urge segregation cannot be barred (*Collin v. Smith* 578 F.2d 1197 [7th Cir. 1978], *cert. denied* 439 U.S. 916 [1978]).

Even the vilest and most graphic sexist or racist speech is not transformed into action because of the intensity with which its critics detest it or the success it demonstrates in getting others to accede to its viewpoint. It is important to guarantee as a "civil right" that no person is denied a job, an education, or entry to a public facility on the basis of race or sex. This is true whether the decision to discriminate is based on listening to well-reasoned academic discourse, reading "hate literature," or watching old movies containing negative stereotypes. However, our "civil rights" laws do not, and may not, insulate individuals from the repugnant speech of others which urges the denial of such opportunities.

Pornography as a Central Cause of Sex Discrimination

Another "finding" is that pornography is "central" to maintenance of women's inequality. The "centrality" of pornography as a source of inequality is not empirically supportable. Unless one works in an adult bookstore, graphic, sexually explicit "pornography" is not a major source of sensory input for many people. However, if all that critics define as "pornography" were to dis-appear tomorrow, and it had *in fact* been central to subordination, the central position would then be taken up by other images from comic books, cartoon shows, jean advertising, television situation comedies, and dozens of other sources which assault our eyes and ears on a regular basis. Precisely the same arguments that undergird the efforts to eliminate graphic sexual images showing the subordination of women would then be applicable to a variety of remaining images which cast women in a demeaning light.

It may be popular to start the process of eliminating negative views of women by proceeding against graphic sexual images, since allies in such an effort could include those persons who see the issue simply as one of "indecency." However, there is no logical reason to stop there, given the vastly greater number of persons who are exposed to the concept of "subordination" in other, "non-explicit" media. Once we accept the premise upon which this "pornography" regulation is based — the eradication of contemptuous images — there is nowhere to stop the regulatory process.

In fact, once the decision to suppress "negative" portrayals is made, it is only a short trip to mandating "positive" portrayals. As Justice Brennan noted in his dissent in *Paris Adult Theatre I v. Slaton* 413 U.S. 49 (1973):

> For if a state may, in an effort to maintain or create a moral tone, prescribe what its citizens cannot read or cannot see, then it would seem to follow that in pursuit of that same objective a state could decree that its citizens must read certain books or must view certain films.

The sexually explicit messages labeled "pornographic" have not been demonstrated to be central to any discriminatory practices. However, even if such evidence was present, it would not dispose of the guarantees of the First Amendment.

Pornography as Behavioral Stimulus, Not Advocacy

There is also the claim that pornography is somehow different than other cultural expressions because it is not "speech." Professor Catharine MacKinnon, the co-author of several proposed anti-pornography ordinances, noted in the *amicus* brief she prepared in the Indianapolis case, that "unlike the 'literature' of other inequalities, pornography works as a behavioral conditioner, reinforcer and stimulus, not as idea or advocacy."

That assertion is simply incorrect. Sexually explicit material may communicate that the activity depicted is pleasurable and appropriate. It is often a rejection of ascetic lifestyles, rational analysis, and prudence. Women's studies professor Ann Barr Snitow notes that it promotes "the joys of passivity, of helpless abandon, of response without responsibility. . . ." According to *Vil-*

lage Voice writer Ellen Willis the meaning of sexually explicit material is highly individual and complex:

> Sex in this culture has been so deeply politicized that it is impossible to make clear-cut distinctions between "authentic" sexual impulses and those conditioned by patriarchy. Between, say, *Ulysses* at one end and *Snuff* at the other, erotica/pornography conveys all sorts of mixed messages that elicit complicated and private responses.[2]

Of course, it also may communicate a more sinister message, that women do, or should, gain pleasure solely from subordination to men. Repulsive as that construct may be, it is a political philosophy which has been dominant in most civilizations since the beginning of human history. It is clearly an "idea" and much pornography serves as a tool for its advocacy.

Similarly, virtually all printed and visual material seeks not only to communicate ideas, but also to act as a "behavioral conditioner, reinforcer, and stimulus." Books and movies frequently: (1) teach people to view an issue in a certain way ("behavioral conditioner"), (2) legitimatize particular ways of thinking ("reinforcer"), or (3) urge people to act in accord with the images presented by the author ("stimulus"). The fact that pornography asserts an often repugnant world-view graphically or persuasively does not place it in a special category from other literature.

The Supreme Court recognized this in *Cohen v. California* 403 U.S. 1526 (1970), where it assessed the impact of Cohen entering the trial court wearing a jacket emblazoned with the words "Fuck the Draft."

> [M]uch linguistic expression serves a dual communicative function: it conveys not only ideas capable of relatively precise, detached explication, but otherwise unexpressible emotions as well. In fact, words are often chosen as much for their emotive as their cognitive force. We cannot sanction the view that the Constitution, while solicitous of the cognitive content of individual speech, has little or no regard for that emotive function which, practically speaking, may often be the more important element of the overall message sought to be communicated. . . .

There is yet another dimension of this false "stimulus-advocacy" dichotomy. A number of commentators have criticized the new effort to regulate pornography as an effort to totally rationalize human sexuality. Historian Alice Echols has lamented the rejection by some feminists of "the notion that fantasy is the repository of our ambivalent and conflictual feelings," which she says leads to "a highly mechanistic and behavioristic analysis that conflates fantasy with reality and pornography with violence."[3] Indeed, it is as dangerous for the state, directly or indirectly, to police fantasies as to police politics.

Pornography as a Cause of Sexual Violence

Finally, much has been claimed about new data purporting to demonstrate a causal connection between certain types of pornography and sexual violence against women. Unfortunately, there is little recognition of distinctions between "causes" and "symptoms" in much of this discussion. This error is compounded by drawing unwarranted implications from the evidence.

For example, at a previous hearing several researchers reported findings that in a sample of "serial murderers," 81 percent noted a "high interest" in pornography and that in another sample of persons arrested for various forms of child exploitation, all had at least some "pornography" (from *Playboy* on down) in their homes. However, the presence of two phenomena, criminal activity and pornography, does not necessarily demonstrate a causal connection between them; it is at least as likely to demonstrate that persons with certain abusive personalities are attracted to both crime and use of pornography.

It is also possible to misdirect the outrage against specific instances of sexual violence. It is undeniable that there are examples of media portrayals of sexual violence whose elements are replicated almost identically by persons during the commission of a criminal act. These occurrences do not permit broad intrusions into First Amendment rights, even if it were demonstrated that *but for* the media portrayals, no crime would have occurred (something which has not been proven in any case). Certainly, the results of psychological experiments on male college students which demonstrate only that some tend to react temporarily more aggressively under laboratory conditions after seeing "aggressive-erotic" films provides no basis for suppressing speech.[4] As Kate Ellis notes in "Pornography and the Feminist Imagination": "In all of these studies a single stimulus and response is being made to stand in for a long conditioning process."

The First Amendment may not be suspended because an image or an idea causes the most susceptible or most malleable person who hears it or sees it to behave in an anti-social manner. This was recognized by the Supreme Court in *Roth v. United States* 354 U.S. 476 (1957). An uncomfortable volume of previous testimony before this subcommittee suggests a return to this "most susceptible" standard. It is carried to its greatest extremes in some ordinance language permitting injunctions against the future distribution of a specific book or film if it can be linked to one act of violence.

An even more direct argument is that pornography is a form of "incitement" to violence against women. However, even sexually explicit material which implicitly advocates the subordination of women does not urge that viewers commit criminal activity. In the event that some piece of literature did urge criminal activity its possible suppression would be measured on the basis of well-established constitutional principles.

Supreme Court decisions on speech which allegedly incites listeners to criminal acts make it clear that mere speculative damage is insufficient to suppress speech and that only if there is a close and demonstrable causal nexus between speech and violence may speech be barred. This is the "clear and present" danger standard announced first in *Schenck v. United States* 249 U.S. 47 (1919). The Court has subsequently ruled that not even "advocacy" of "revenge" against public officials by Ku Klux Klan members carrying guns, *Brandenburg v. Ohio* 395 U.S. 444 (1969), or student revolutionaries' threat to "take the fucking street later," *Hess v. Indiana* 414 U.S. 105 (1973), could be suppressed. A violent criminal act was not likely to be the direct and imminent result of the speech in these cases. A review of the data on "incitement" to violence against women by pornography demonstrates nothing to meet the *Brandenburg* standard.

WHAT CAN BE DONE?

It is important to use the means of communication available to make it clear that remedies already exist for some of the conduct which has been previously described at your hearings. There has, for example, been testimony in regard to husbands forcing their spouses into sexual activity, described in "pornography," which they did not desire. That constitutes rape in most jurisdictions. The ACLU has been actively supporting elimination of "spouse" immunity in rape cases in those states where it still exists. We would not minimize the problem of getting prosecutors to charge in such cases, but that is no excuse for not empowering the public with the knowledge that such actions can be taken.

Similarly, at previous hearings, Ms. Linda Marchiano testified regarding her physical coercion into the production of the film *Deep Throat.* It appears that the statute of limitations has run, precluding any criminal prosecution. Assuming the facts as she reported, however, she would seem to retain the possibility of civil actions without need for new ordinances or federal intervention.[5]

Privacy-related torts which could already cover Ms. Marchiano's situation include "public disclosure of private facts" (since there was the intimate portrayal of sexual activity), placing one in a "false light in the public eye" (since she could argue that the film gave the false impression that she was enjoying what was actually repugnant coerced activity) or "wrongful appropriation" (her unwanted activity was photographed and appropriated by the perpetrators of a crime for commercial advantage).

Damages or even injunctive relief could certainly be sought in such individual cases, but depending upon the precise facts elicited, First Amendment limitations on such actions could also arise. The ACLU is exploring whether narrow legislation covering such coerced activities would be consistent with such constitutional concerns.

Obviously, this would be costly litigation, with substantial attendant problems of proof. However, any action brought under an Indianapolis-type statute would be similarly expensive, since there could be no statutory presumption of coercion in regard to all women appearing in pornography.

In addition, in a society which has the regard for openness and tolerance found in the United States, the ultimate answer to the existence of offensive images must be the production of "affirmative" alternative images. It means the replacement of images of female subordination with images of equality and authority. The First Amendment was designed to protect the "marketplace of ideas" because of a deeply rooted belief that when ideas and images compete (even if they begin in "unequal" status), the "true" and "accurate" have the best chance to prevail.

No one could seriously suggest that women have an equal "voice" in institutions in the United States. On the other hand, there has already been a historically unprecedented increase in the number of women's voices speaking in every academic field, from law to medicine to theology, and in every artistic endeavor. Those are the sources for the positive views of women which will help shape the future.

In addition to the creation of alternative images, it is certainly constitutionally acceptable to work to create a "negative image" for pornography: to urge that our society would be healthier without it, to critique its moral and aesthetic value, and to urge its disuse by all persons.

CONCLUSION

It is unfortunate when the issues raised by the Indianapolis ordinance are couched as ones of "women's rights" versus "civil liberties." It is clearly possible to protect and enhance both. There is a right to be free from sexual coercion; however, there is no similar right to be free from offensive and insulting images. There may be instances where genuine constitutional claims will clash, where, for example, the constitutional right of privacy runs squarely into the free press guarantees of the First Amendment. The ACLU would be happy to review any statutory language in these delicate areas.

NOTES

1. "Obscenity" has been defined by the Supreme Court as requiring proof of three crucial elements: (1) that it appeals to the "prurient interest" as judged by the average person applying contemporary community standards; (b) that it describes or depicts, in a patently offensive way, specific sexual conduct defined by statute; (c) that, as a whole, it lacks serious literary, artistic, political, or scientific value. The ACLU believes this standard violates the First Amendment. However, "pornography" definitions would restrict even more material since there are no "average person" or "lacking value" tests.

2. "Feminism, Moralism, and Pornography," in *Powers of Desire: The Politics of Sexuality,* eds. Ann Snitow, Christine Stansell, and Sharon Thompson (New York: Monthly Review Press, 1983), p. 463.

3. "The New Feminism of Yin and Yang" in *Powers of Desire,* p. 448.

4. See, for example, Edward Donnerstein and Leonard Berkowitz, "Victim Reactions in Aggressive Erotic Films As a Factor in Violence against Women," *Journal of Personality and Social Psychology,* Vol. 41, No. 4 (1981), pp. 710–724.

5. The ACLU believes that some of these causes of actions, particularly when applied to a broad range of facts, may be inconsistent with the First Amendment.

Questions for Discussion

1. What criteria would you use in determining whether a particular work is art or pornography?
2. Should the regulation of child pornography be considered in any way different from the regulation of other forms of pornography? What are the reasons for your answer?
3. Is the regulation of pornography consistent with the First Amendment? What are the reasons for your answer?
4. What effect would a scientific finding determining conclusively that pornography increases the likelihood of violence against women have on your view of the subject?
5. What effect would new antipornography legislation have on writers, artists, and bookstore owners? What are the reasons for your answer?

Suggested Readings

Baird, Robert M., and Stuart E. Rosenbaum, eds. *Pornography: Private Right or Public Menace?* Buffalo, N.Y.: Prometheus Books, 1991.

Irving, John. "Pornography and the New Puritans." *New York Times Book Review,* March 29, 1992, pp. 1, 24–25, 27. *See also* "Pornography and the New Puritans: Letters from Andrea Dworkin and Others." *New York Times Book Review,* May 3, 1992, pp. 15–16.

MacKinnon, Catharine A. "Pornography As Defamation and Discrimination." *Boston University Law Review* 71, no. 4 (July 1991): 793–815.

———. "Pornography, Civil Rights, and Speech." *Harvard Civil Rights–Civil Liberties Law Review* 20, no. 1 (Winter 1985): 1–70.

McElroy, Wendy. *XXX: A Woman's Right to Pornography.* New York: St. Martin's Press, 1995.

Russell, Diana E. H., ed. *Making Violence Sexy: Feminist Views on Pornography.* New York: Teachers College, Columbia Univ., 1993.

Stoller, Robert J. *Porn: Myths for the Twentieth Century.* New Haven, Conn.: Yale Univ. Press, 1991.

Strossen, Nadine. *Defending Pornography: Free Speech, Sex, and the Fight for Women's Rights.* New York: Scribner's, 1995.

Sunstein, Cass R. "Porn on the Fourth of July." *New Republic* 212, nos. 2 and 3 (January 9–16, 1995): 42–45.

"Symposium: The Sex Panic: Women, Censorship and 'Pornography.'" *New York Law School Law Review* 38, nos. 1–4 (1993): entire issue.

Wolfson, Nicholas. "Eroticism, Obscenity, Pornography, and Free Speech." *Brooklyn Law Review* 60, no. 3 (Fall 1994): 1037–1067.

Chapter 5

Should the Death Penalty Be Abolished?

The Eighth Amendment to the Constitution forbids "cruel and unusual punishments" but does not specify what makes a punishment cruel or unusual. When the Bill of Rights was adopted, the death penalty, or capital punishment, as it is called, was not considered cruel or unusual. But particularly since the nineteenth century, there has been continuing controversy about the morality of capital punishment, not only in the United States but throughout the world. The global trend has been away from capital punishment. Today the United States is the only Western industrial country that allows the death penalty.

The death penalty has been brought before the Supreme Court on a number of occasions. In 1972, the Supreme Court decided in *Furman v. Georgia* to bar the death penalty as it was imposed under statutes at the time, objecting to the randomness of procedures.[1] As a result of the decision, most state legislatures enacted new laws complying with the *Furman* decision so that capital punishment could still be used as a punishment for major violent crimes.

The Supreme Court again considered capital punishment in 1976 in *Gregg v. Georgia.* In that case and in four related cases it accepted the constitutionality of the death penalty under certain conditions.[2]

The death penalty is under continuous legal challenge. One related issue the Supreme Court considered involved racism. In 1987, the Court rejected a challenge that capital punishment was more likely to be inflicted on African American defendants than whites and therefore violated the Equal Protection Clause of the Fourteenth Amendment.[3]

The death penalty is also under consideration in the executive and legislative branches. In the late 1980s and 1990s, political leaders sought to be "tough on criminals" by making punishments more severe: expanding the coverage of existing criminal laws, making it more difficult for prisoners to get parole, and strengthening capital punishment laws. Advocates of capital punishment also objected to the long time between sentencing and execution. Between 1976, when the death penalty was reinstated, until August 1996, only 337 of the 5,000 death sentences in the United States were carried out. About 3,000 inmates currently are on death row. Many may die from natural causes while awaiting execution.

The slow progress of appeals through the court system is the principal reason for the delay. To speed the process, Congress directed in the Antiterrorism and Effective Death Penalty Act of 1996 that prisoners be barred from filing a second writ of habeas corpus unless a three-judge appeals court panel approves. (A habeas corpus writ orders a state to produce a prisoner before the court so that the inmate can make his or her case.)

This decision cannot be appealed. In addition, the statute expands the federal death penalty to more than fifty crimes. The law was enacted in response to outrage at the bombing of the World Trade Center and the Oklahoma City federal building. In 1996, the Supreme Court unanimously upheld the provision of the antiterrorism law restricting habeas corpus petitions.[4]

As of 1996, twelve states and the District of Columbia ban capital punishment. In New York State, as governors successively from 1976 to 1994, Hugh Carey and Mario Cuomo vetoed legislative bills to reintroduce the death penalty. But when Republican George Pataki became governor in 1995, he signed a bill to reintroduce capital punishment. Death penalty legislation has been introduced in Wisconsin and Iowa.

The death penalty became a subject of popular discussion when former football star O. J. Simpson was charged with the murder of his wife Nicole, and her friend, Ron Goldman, in 1994. The prosecutor agreed not to ask for the death penalty. Eventually, however, Simpson was acquitted. Law professor J. Michael Echevarria argues against the death penalty in light of the O. J. Simpson case. Written before Simpson was acquitted, the article contends:

1. Capital punishment has no deterrent value. In fact, the evidence seems to indicate that capital punishment actually tends to increase the homicide rate.
2. The safety of the community can be equally protected by the provision for life imprisonment without possibility of parole.
3. The death penalty sought on retributive grounds is often arbitrary in application.
4. Innocent persons, especially the poor who cannot afford adequate trial counsel, are sometimes wrongly sentenced to death.

James C. Anders, an attorney in South Carolina, argues for the death penalty. Speaking before the Senate Judiciary Committee, he contends:

1. Capital punishment is a deterrent to violent crime.
2. Capital punishment satisfies society's compelling desire to see justice done.
3. The death penalty is a sentence sanctioned by law and implemented only after exhaustive criminal proceedings through the courts. In no way can it be equated with murder.
4. To say that some people are put to death while others who commit similar offenses are not is no argument against the death penalty, since the same argument could be used against subjecting any criminal to penalties.

5. The criminal justice system in the United States is so sophisticated that it is unlikely that an innocent person will be executed.
6. Because prisoners escape or are paroled or furloughed, sentences other than the death penalty offer no real assurance that these criminals will not commit violent crimes again.

NOTES

1. *Furman v. Georgia*, 498 U.S. 238 (1972).
2. *Gregg v. Georgia*, 428 U.S. 153 (1976).
3. *McCleskey v. Kemp*, Supreme Court docket no. 84-6811 (April 22, 1987).
4. *Felker v. Turpin*, 116 S. Ct. 2533 (1996).

☑ *YES*

Should the Death Penalty Be Abolished?

J. MICHAEL ECHEVARRIA
Reflections on O. J. and the Gas Chamber

Instead of saying, as we always have, that the death penalty is first of all a necessity, and afterwards that it is advisable not to talk about it, we should first speak of what the death penalty really is, and only then decide if, being what it is, it is necessary.

— Albert Camus

Picture this: On Monday morning, June 13, 1994, the former wife of a national sports celebrity is found murdered in front of her Brentwood, California townhouse. Along with her body is also found the corpse of a 25-year-old male friend. The scene is described by police officers as among the most gruesome they have ever viewed. The ex-wife is nearly decapitated and the state of the male corpse provides evidence of a fierce struggle. The scene is drenched in blood. Six days later the sports celebrity is charged with double homicide. Under California law, a double homicide constitutes an "aggravating circumstance" entitling the prosecution to seek the death penalty. The celebrity, who has an estimated net worth of more than ten million dollars, hires a battery of world renowned attorneys, forensic experts, and investigators.

Within weeks, experts conclude that the celebrity will probably not face the possibility of the gas chamber because of his celebrity status and because the victim is his spouse. Less than three months after the celebrity is charged with the crimes, the prosecution announces that although the state contends that the brutal murders were premeditated, the state shall not seek the death penalty. No specific reasons are given by the prosecution for its decision.

Now picture this: An African-American male murders a white female. The evidence against him is highly circumstantial — there are no eyewitnesses. The defendant, who cannot afford an attorney, is represented by an over-worked public defender. The death penalty is sought by the state because of, among other reasons, the "quality" of the victim. After a short trial, a verdict is returned. The defendant is sentenced to death.

O. J. Simpson is lucky. During the same period when prosecutors considered whether to seek the death penalty against Simpson, 2,812 people in this country were sitting on death row. Most were poor, many were black, and many were guilty of murdering whites. It is likely, nay, inevitable, that some of these people were not guilty of the crime for which they had been sentenced. Some of these people will be executed. Are their deaths necessary? Beneficial? Justifiable?

Three rationales are often advanced in justification of the continued imposition of the death penalty: (1) deterrence, (2) safety, and (3) retribution.

Empirical data concerning the death penalty's deterrent value shows that the justification is dubious at best. Far more studies show that capital punishment empirically has no deterrent value when compared to studies that reach the opposite conclusion. In fact, the evidence seems to indicate that capital punishment actually tends to increase the homicide rate. With respect to the murders of Nicole Simpson and Ronald Goldman, it is unlikely that the death penalty, which was on the statute books in California at the time, had a deterrent effect on the murderer. It apparently did not enter the calculus of the decision-maker with a sufficient gravity to change the ultimate decision. Would deterrence be proved, however, if the rich and powerful were subject to capital punishment's force? Who can say? It is clear, however, that the question will never be answered because the penalty is unlikely to be imposed, given its legal requirements, on a person who can afford to hire exemplary legal counsel.

Capital punishment's safety justification also lacks merit. Of course, if a murderer is executed, he no longer poses a threat to the safety of the community. However, our safety can be equally protected by the provision for life imprisonment without possibility of parole. Furthermore, the public safety argument has little merit in cases like *People v. Simpson.* In that case, prosecutors claim that the defendant acted out of jealousy. This is an implicit acknowledgement that the potential victims were not the public-at-large, but the object of his wrath — his ex-wife.

Given that there is no good evidence that the death penalty serves a deterrent function and given that the safety function can be equally served with a less drastic measure, the only true justification that remains is retribution. In recent years there has been much debate as to the legitimacy of retributive justice. However, in the context of the Simpson case, capital punishment justifications based on retributive theory come under closer scrutiny. The public's lack of desire for retribution most likely influenced the prosecution's decision to not seek the death penalty against Simpson. As a result, the Simpson case exemplifies the arbitrary nature of the death penalty when it is sought on retributive grounds. In any event, even if retribution is a legitimate interest, capital punishment is still not warranted.

A number of studies (anecdotal and otherwise) indicate that innocent persons have been sentenced to death. This is hardly surprising for a number of reasons. First, capital punishment must ordinarily be premised on a finding of first-degree homicide (that is, premeditated murder). Because the crime ordinarily involves a great degree of secrecy and stealth, convictions are often based on circumstantial evidence. As a result, a first-degree murder conviction presents a greater possibility of error than other crimes in which the miscreant does not as actively plan out and conceal his crime. It is thus inevitable that a certain percent of innocent people will be convicted of first degree murder, especially where the victim is a sympathetic person and the defendant is unpopular. Additionally, given the class-based nature of the system many first-degree homicide defendants are inadequately served by their trial counsel. Unlike Simpson, most defendants simply cannot afford to present to a jury numerous alternative scenarios of the crime. Potential "reasonable doubts" only exist to the extent they are presented at trial. Moreover, even where it is indisputable that the defendant committed the act, absolute culpability can never be firmly established because of the *mens rea* requirement (especially in light of emerging medical and biological evidence vitiating the notion of free will).

The question thus becomes: Should we impose a perfect (that is to say, irreversible) penalty in the context of an imperfect (that is to say, error-prone) system? More specifically: Given that it is inevitable that innocent people will be condemned to death, is there a legitimate purpose being served by killing an innocent person? If it could be proven that the death penalty was necessary for deterrence or safety, arguably a (weak) argument could be advanced. But given that the only rationale that survives its retribution, it is hard to justify the continued existence of capital punishment. . . .

Should the Death Penalty Be Abolished?

JAMES C. ANDERS
The Case for the Death Penalty

There are in this world a number of extremely wicked people, disposed to get what they want by force or fraud, with complete indifference to the interests of others, and in ways which are totally inconsistent with the existence of civilized society.

— James Fitzjames Stephen

What is society to do with these people? I believe that in certain cases, the death penalty can be shown to be the only rational and realistic punishment for an unspeakable crime. But before embarking on a discussion on the merits of the death penalty, a fundamental philosophical question must be answered. What is the purpose of punishment? Harmonious coexistence among people in any society is dependent upon the advancement of mutually agreed upon goals for the good of the whole society. Obviously, the most basic right a citizen has is the right to be secure in his person, the right to be safe from physical or economic harm from another. Laws to protect citizens and advance the harmony of society are founded upon these principles. To enforce these laws, created in the best interest of society as a whole, there has to be a deterrent for a breach of the law. Therefore, deterrence is the first aim of a system on punishment.

Deterrence is only one side of the punishment coin, however. An equally fundamental reason to punish lies in society's compelling desire to see justice done. Punishment expresses the emotions of the society wronged, the anger and outrage felt, and it solidifies and reinforces the goals, values and norms of acceptable behavior in the society. Punishment is justified purely on the ground that wrongdoing merits punishment, and that it is morally fitting that one who does wrong suffers, and suffers in proportion to his wrongdoing.

Consider the facts of a 1977 case from my jurisdiction. Codefendants Shaw, Roach and Mahaffey spent the morning of October 29th drinking and shooting up drugs. That afternoon the three decided to, in Mahaffey's words, "see if we could find a girl to rape." They drove to a nearby baseball field where they spotted a car parked with two teenagers inside. They robbed and killed the young man on the spot. The girl was carried to a dirt road a short distance away where she was repeatedly raped and sodomized over a period of hours. When they finished with her, they forced her to place her head in a circle they

71

had drawn in the dirt, and they executed her. Later that evening, Shaw returned by himself and sexually mutilated the girl's body.

The deterrent effect of the death penalty is the favorite criticism of the opponents of capital punishment. The social scientists' studies have been mixed at best and there is no authoritative consensus on whether or not the death penalty deters anyone from committing a crime. Threats of punishment cannot and are not meant to deter everybody all of the time. They are meant to deter most people most of the time.

The threatened punishment must be carried out — otherwise the threats are reduced to bluffs and become incredible and therefore ineffective.

— Ernest van den Haag

Therefore, the death penalty can only be a deterrent if it is meted out with a reasonable degree of consistency. The deterrent effect lies in the knowledge of the citizenry that it will more likely than not be carried out if the named crime is committed.

Even if one is not fully convinced of the deterrent effect of the death penalty, he or she would surely choose the certainty of the convicted criminal's death by execution over the possibility of the deaths of new victims. These new deaths could either be deterred by the execution, or prevented by the executed criminal's obvious incapacity. Simply put, one should opt to execute a man convicted of having caused the death of others than to put the lives of innocents at risk if there is a chance their deaths could be prevented by the deterrent effect.

Death penalty opponents argue that if life is sacred (as, presumably, we all believe) then the murderer's life, too, is sacred and for the State to punish him by execution is barbaric and causes the State to bend to the murderer's level. The only similarity between the unjustified taking of an innocent life and the carrying out of a convicted murderer's execution is the end result — death. The death penalty is a legal sentence, enacted by the legislatures of various states which presumably reflect their constituents' desires. It is a penalty that can finally be carried out only after a trial where the defendant is afforded all of his constitutional rights, and the lengthy appellate process has been exhausted. It is a penalty that has been sanctioned by the United States Supreme Court, a majority of whose members have said, regardless of their personal feelings, that the death penalty is a constitutionally valid punishment. How then can its invocation be compared to the senseless, irrational murder of an innocent victim who is afforded no rights, and is tried and convicted by his murderer for the crime of being in the wrong place at the wrong time? Legal execution and murder are no more comparable than driving a car and knowingly driving a stolen car. Although the physical act of driving either is the same, the two acts are separated by the crime involved in the latter, and that makes all the difference.

Death penalty opponents are also troubled by the studies that purport to show that the death penalty is applied capriciously, that it discriminates racially and economically. They cite these studies as justification for eliminating the penalty. Notice that they are not claiming that some innocent person may be executed, but, rather, that not all the guilty are executed. Assuming that premise for the sake of argument, is that a rational reason to abolish the death penalty? Is the fact that some guilty persons escape punishment sufficient to let all guilty persons escape it? If it is then, in practice, penalties never could be applied if we insisted that they cannot be inflicted on any guilty persons unless we are able to make sure that they are equally applied to all other guilty persons. There is no more merit in persuading the courts to let all capital defendants go because some escaped penalties than it is to say let all burglars go because some have escaped detection and imprisonment. If discrimination exists in the application of the death penalty, then the remedy is statutory reform to minimize or abolish the discrimination, not the abolition of the penalty itself.

The capricious/discriminatory complaint seems by and large to be an abolitionist sham. The abolitionists would oppose the death penalty if it could be meted out without any discretion, if it were mandatory under certain conditions. They would oppose it in a homogeneous country without racial discrimination. It is the death penalty itself, not its possible maldistribution that the abolitionists oppose. Opponents rarely raise the objection that an innocent person might be sent to the electric chair. With the sophistication of the criminal justice system today, the likelihood of convicting, let alone executing, an innocent man is all but nil. But there is another more subtle reason abolitionists no longer advance the "innocent man proposition" as a justification for their opposition to the penalty and that is because this argument too would be a sham. Death penalty opponents would rid the world of the death penalty for everyone, including the admittedly guilty.

To defend the death penalty should not lead to one's being labeled "cold," "blood-thirsty" or "barbaric." A person who commits capital murder simply cannot and should not expect to be given a pat on the back and told to "go and sin no more." If the death penalty can deter one murder of an innocent life or if it can make a statement to the community about what will and will not be tolerated, then it is justified.

Opponents of the death penalty advocate the life sentence in prison as a viable alternative to execution. My experiences lead me to believe that life imprisonment is not a satisfactory means of dealing with the most horrid of criminals. Early release programs, furloughs, and escapes combine to place a shockingly high number of convicted murderers back on the streets in record time. Hardly a day goes by when one cannot pick up a newspaper and read a gruesome account of the crimes committed by a now liberated "lifer." But that is not the worst of it. Consider the plight of the victims' families, forced to re-live the nightmare again and again each time a parole hearing is scheduled. Year after year they endure the uncertainty and agony while waiting on the decision of the parole board. Will this be the year the man who turned their lives upside down will be released to live out his life, perhaps to put another family through the same nightmare?

The life without parole sentence is no solution either. First the possibility of escape cannot be completely eliminated, even in the most secure of institutions. For example, convicted triple murderer and death row inmate Fred Kornahrens escaped with a ploy so simple it caught prison officials completely by surprise. During a body search prior to being transported to court, Kornahrens concealed a key between his index and middle fingers. When handcuffed, he simply uncuffed himself and made good his escape. Given enough time, I am certain Fred Kornahrens could escape again. Second, the life without parole sentence places a tremendous burden on prison administrators. Faced with controlling inmates who have already received the worst punishment society can mete out, they can only throw their hands up in frustration. Lastly, the true lifer is not only capable of continuing to murder, but may actually be more likely to do so. Every prison in the country has its own stories of the lifer who killed another inmate over a cigarette or a piece of chicken. In my home state this scenario was taken one step farther when disenchanted crime victim Tony Cimo hired convicted mass murderer Donald "Pee Wee" Gaskins to kill an-other convicted murderer Rudolph Tyner, the slayer of Cimo's parents. Pee Wee Gaskins is a perfect example of why life imprisonment is never going to be an acceptable alternative to the death penalty and why the death penalty for murder by a federal prisoner serving a life term is a viable proposal.

I recently prosecuted a capital case involving the murder of a state highway patrolman. Trooper George Radford was brutally beaten and executed with his own weapon over a $218 ticket. All Trooper Radford did was show his murderer the same consideration and courtesy he exhibited to all every day on duty. Rather than handcuffing the defendant, Warren Manning, whom he had ticketed for driving under suspension, Trooper Radford allowed him to remain unhand-cuffed for the twenty minute ride to the police station so that he would be more comfortable. Manning surprised Trooper Radford halfway there and callously murdered him. Law enforcement personnel deserve the additional protection and security the death penalty affords them. The scores of highway patrolmen who travelled to Camden, South Carolina for the sentencing of Warren Manning show exactly how important the death penalty issue is to them.

Based on the foregoing analysis, the death penalty takes on special signifi-cance in deterrence and punishment of federal law violations. Serious prob-lems exist in American society on a large scale basis or threaten to grow to such a basis. As discussed above, the benefits of deterrence and social justice on crimes such as murder, murder for hire and attempts to assassinate the President are obvious under the death penalty.

Drug-related murders are on the rise and the death penalty could be particularly effective in combating this murder-for-profit trend. Law enforcement officers who are often required to work undercover in the drug community would be protected to a degree under the deterrence effect of the death penalty. In order to support President Bush's plan to combat the drug problem nationally and internationally, it seems obvious that drug kingpins should know that they are subject to the death penalty. What group of individuals create more chaos and death than these?

Other heinous crimes which pose a threat of great magnitude are those of terrorism. Crimes such as explosions, air piracy, mailing bombs and taking hostages, all where death results, very simply and obviously demand the strongest punishment and deterrent the law can impose. The effects of terrorism are so potentially great and devastating that the death penalty is the only conceivable punishment. The death penalty is not merely an alternative but a necessity for dealing with these large scale national problems.

One leading proponent of the death penalty, E. van den Haag, wrote "never to execute a wrongdoer, regardless of how depraved his acts, is to proclaim that no act can be so irredeemably vicious as to deserve death." In the question of deterrence this principle is exacerbated by a special group of sane murderers who, knowing that they will not be executed, will not hesitate to kill again. If opponents of the death penalty admit that there is a reasonable probability that such wrongdoers will murder again and/or attempt to murder again, and still insist they would never approve of capital punishment, I would conclude that they are indifferent to the lives of the human beings doomed to be the victims of the unexecuted criminals. "Charity for all human beings must not deprive us of our common sense," [said] Hugo Adam Bedau. To those who could not impose the death penalty under any circumstances, van den Haag attributed what he called "a failure of nerve," a feeling that they themselves are incapable of rationally and justly making a life and death decision and that, therefore, everyone else is equally unqualified to decide life or death.

Such a view grossly and tragically underestimates our system of justice. I have always been impressed with the intelligence, compassion and common sense jurors display. Jurors really are the "conscience of the community." That is more than just a phrase lawyers bandy about in closing arguments. I have seen how seriously jurors take their oath to decide the issues, based on the law, regardless of their personal prejudices, and biases. The juries and the courts can evade decisions on life and death only by giving up paramount duties: those of serving justice, securing the lives of citizens and vindicating the norms that society holds inviolable. Justice requires that the punishment be proportional to the gravity of the crime. The death penalty comes closest to meeting this supreme standard while still falling short because those criminals sentenced to execution still had the luxury of choosing their fate when their victims did not.

Questions for Discussion

1. How would you evaluate whether capital punishment serves as a deterrent to murder?
2. How could you determine whether the death penalty is an instrument of racial oppression?
3. What role should family members of a murdered victim play in influencing a sentence involving the death penalty?
4. If the death penalty is acceptable, in what kinds of cases should it be applied? Why?
5. What effect would public executions have on violent crimes?
6. What role does possible arbitrariness of capital punishment sentences play in your evaluation of this issue?

Suggested Readings

Baird, Robert M., and Stuart E. Rosenbaum, eds. *Punishment and the Death Penalty: The Current Debate.* Amherst, N.Y.: Prometheus Books, 1995.

Bedau, Hugo Adam, ed. *The Death Penalty in America: Current Controversies.* New York: Oxford Univ. Press, 1996.

Berns, Walter. *For Capital Punishment: Crime and the Morality of the Death Penalty.* Lanham, Md.: University Press of America, 1991.

Black, Charles L., Jr. *Capital Punishment: The Inevitability of Caprice and Mistake,* 2d ed. New York: Norton, 1981.

Costanzo, Mark, and Lawrence T. White, eds. "The Death Penalty in the United States." *Journal of Social Issues* 50, no. 2 (Summer 1994): entire issue.

Haines, Herbert H. *Against Capital Punishment: The Anti-Death Penalty Movement in America, 1972–1994.* New York: Oxford Univ. Press, 1996.

Hood, Roger G. *The Death Penalty: A World-Wide Perspective,* 2d ed. New York: Oxford Univ. Press, 1996.

Koosed, Margery B., ed. *Capital Punishment.* 3 vols. New York: Garland, 1996.

Kozinski, Alex, and Sean Gallagher, "Death: The Ultimate Run-On Sentence." *Case Western Reserve Law Review* 46, no. 1 (Fall 1995): 1–23.

Kuntz, Tom. "Killings, Legal and Otherwise, around the U.S." *New York Times,* December 4, 1994, sec IV, p. 3.

Prejean, Helen. *Dead Man Walking: An Eyewitness Account of the Death Penalty in the United States.* New York: Vintage, 1994.

Romano, Lois. "With Death, Hope That Life Goes On." *Washington Post,* August 8, 1996, pp. A1, A18–A19.

Sellin, Johan Thorsten. *The Penalty of Death.* Beverly Hills, Calif.: Sage, 1980.

U.S. Cong., Senate. *Innocence and the Death Penalty.* Hearing before the Committee on the Judiciary, 103d Cong., 1st Sess., 1993.

Van den Haag, Ernest, and John P. Conrad. *The Death Penalty: A Debate.* New York: Plenum Press, 1983.

Worsnop, Richard L. "Death Penalty Debate." *CQ Researcher* 5, no. 9 (March 10, 1995): 193–216.

Chapter 6

Have the Constitutional Protections for Accused Criminals Become So Weakened As to Deny the Accused Fundamental Rights?

Organizers of a symposium in the summer 1995 issue of *Constitutional Commentary*, a publication of the University of Minnesota Law School, invited participants "to identify the stupidest, most mistaken, most deleterious, or their least favorite clause of the Constitution."[1] Contributors to the symposium responded — some humorously, others seriously — on various provisions. Among the more serious contributions, law professor Louis Michael Seidman argues: "The Constitution is mostly good for providing a platform external from our ordinary politics from which current arrangements can be criticized." He laments this view because he feels that constitutional law should serve as a corrective to ordinary politics and becomes corrupt when it becomes the servant of politics.

Seidman notes that the United States has the most elaborate and detailed constitutional protections for criminal defendants of any country in the world as well as the second highest incarceration rate in the world.[2] In his view, constitutional protections supposed to make the prosecution more difficult actually make the prosecution's job easier. He specifically points to weakening of the Fourth, Fifth, and Sixth Amendments that deal with such matters as searches and seizures, self-incrimination, due process, and criminal court procedures.

Seidman makes a number of specific charges:

1. *Miranda* warnings, which inform suspects of their rights during questioning and which police are required to read, have not reduced the rate at which suspects confess.
2. The poor quality of criminal defense work means that counsel now serves primarily as a barrier to the defendant's participation in his own trial.
3. Judges have virtually gone out of the business of policing the voluntary character of confessions and sanction the kinds of coercive tactics that would have led to the suppression of evidence a half century ago.
4. Courts have been tolerant of inadequate counsel for the defense.
5. Habeas corpus has been weakened as a protection for the defense.

Seidman notes that although crime rates have remained static and even declined slightly in recent years, the rate of incarceration has skyrocketed. The increased rate of incarceration is not caused by an increase in crime. Instead, people perceive that crime is out of control and that ever more severe punishment is necessary to deal with it. The criminal procedure amendments have done nothing to change this pressure for severe punishment.

Law professor William T. Pizzi takes issue in a direct response to Professor Seidman's article. He notes:

1. Incarceration rates are not a fair measure of how harshly particular defendants are actually sentenced, nor do they show that the criminal justice system is repressive and unjust. Incarceration figures do not take into account societal factors in criminal activity.
2. On a comparative basis, civil law countries and common law countries with much lower incarceration rates grant defendants far fewer protections than defendants receive in American courts. For example, *Miranda* offers far more protections to a suspect in the United States than are available to a suspect in England.
3. It is not an accident that a country with a system of criminal procedure that is the most complicated and the most expensive in the Western world, and a trial system that is not very reliable, would also turn out to have a system that threatens, and sometimes inflicts, punishments that are harsh compared to those in other countries. There is a synergy between procedure and punishment such that extremes in one encourage extremes in the other and vice versa.

NOTES

1. Sanford Levinson and William N. Eskridge Jr., "Constitutional Stupidities: A Symposium," *Constitutional Commentary* 12, no. 2 (Summer 1995): 140.

2. Since Professor Seidman's article was published, the incarceration ranking of the United States has changed. The United States now has the highest incarceration rate in the world.

Have the Constitutional Protections for Accused Criminals Become So Weakened As to Deny the Accused Fundamental Rights?

LOUIS MICHAEL SEIDMAN
Criminal Procedure As the Servant of Politics

Any assessment of what the Constitution is bad at must be grounded in a theory of what it is good for. So let me begin with a brief statement of such a theory: The Constitution is mostly good for providing a platform external from our ordinary politics from which current arrangements can be criticized.

This theory does not entail the view that all that matters is criticism. Any sensible political system requires legitimation as well as destabilization. The theory merely asserts that our ordinary political processes already provide very powerful legitimation. We do not need *constitutional law* to endorse results that our existing political system has already endorsed.

Nor does the theory entail the view that constitutional law necessarily privileges change. Political systems need to change, but they also need to maintain continuity. Although the Constitution can promote change, it can also appropriately entrench the status quo by providing a platform to criticize proposals for change.

The theory *does* entail the view that a constitutional provision that does no more than make us more satisfied with outcomes that already satisfy us is not accomplishing anything worthwhile. This is so because constitutional law should serve as a corrective to ordinary politics, and, so, is corrupted when it becomes the servant of politics.

If one shares my view of what the Constitution is good for, it follows, I think, that it is quite bad at dealing with problems of criminal procedure. If the Constitution were doing its job, it would obstruct and destabilize our political impulses concerning crime control. Yet today, the Fourth, Fifth and Sixth Amendments function mostly to make us satisfied with a state of affairs that should trouble us deeply.

Here are two facts about American criminal law: The United States has the most elaborate and detailed constitutional protections for criminal defendants of any country in the world. The United States also has the second highest incarceration rate of any country in the world.[1]

The relationship between these two facts (if, indeed, there is one at all) is controversial. Some critics of the Fourth, Fifth, and Sixth Amendments argue that they stymie effective law enforcement, thereby encouraging crime and requiring a high incarceration rate. Although this connection is theoretically possible, it is quite implausible. The best data available suggest that criminal procedure protections are doing very little to obstruct successful prosecutions.

For example, a tiny percentage of criminal cases are lost or "no papered" because of Fourth Amendment problems.[2] Virtually every empirical study of the impact of *Miranda* suggests that it has not reduced the rate at which suspects confess.[3] The poor quality of criminal defense work has led some distinguished commentators to conclude that counsel now serves primarily as a barrier to the defendant's participation in his own trial.[4]

In contrast, some defenders of the Constitution's criminal procedure provisions argue that incarceration rates would be even higher if these protections were unavailable. This claim is similarly implausible. By now, the Fourth Amendment is so riddled with exceptions and limitations that it rarely prevents the police from pursuing any reasonable crime control tactic.[5] Although the Supreme Court continues to insist on the ritualistic reading of *Miranda* warnings, judges have virtually gone out of the business of actually policing the voluntariness of confessions and regularly sanction the sort of coercive tactics that would have led to the suppression of evidence a half century ago.[6] The courts have been satisfied with formal rules requiring the presence of counsel in the courtroom, while tolerating actual courtroom performances that make a mockery of the formal protections.[7] And even when a defendant can demonstrate that the prosecution has violated minimal Fourth, Fifth, and Sixth Amendment protections, the recent evisceration of habeas corpus means that there may be no court available to entertain her claim.[8]

It seems unlikely, then, that the criminal procedure amendments have either exacerbated our crime problem or provided an effective bulwark against police and prosecutorial overreaching. A third possibility is more plausible: constitutional protections intended to make prosecution more difficult instead serve [to] make the prosecutor's job easier.

This reversal of the historic mission of the criminal procedure amendments functions on both the individual and the global level. In individual cases, criminal procedure protections make the punishment we inflict on criminal defendants seem more acceptable. Although the amendments do little to make the prosecutor's job harder, people commonly believe that they obstruct the prosecution of dangerous criminals. Some doubt and ambivalence that might otherwise accompany the use of violent and coercive sanctions are thereby dissipated.

On the global level, criminal procedure protections serve to redirect and exacerbate the popular anger about crime. While crime rates have remained static and even declined slightly in recent years,[9] the rate of incarceration has skyrocketed.[10] There is no easy way to demonstrate that the crime rate would not be higher if we had incarcerated fewer people, but, at a minimum, these statistics demonstrate that the increased rate of incarceration is not caused by an increase in crime. Instead, it seems to be fed by the public *perception* that crime is out of control and that still more draconian punishments are necessary to deal with it.

Popular misconceptions about criminal procedure protections feed this perception. Because people believe that "legal technicalities" set large numbers of guilty and dangerous criminals free, they think that too many miscreants are escaping punishment. Because they believe that the problem could be brought under control if only the "legal technicalities" were changed, they fail to focus on the bankruptcy of mass-incarceration as a crime fighting strategy.

In the United States today, over one million people are imprisoned, the largest number in our history and the second largest percentage in the world.[11] One out of every 193 adult Americans is behind bars, and the total inmate population is roughly equivalent to that of the city of Pheonix.[12] Despite the absence of any evidence that these extreme measures have helped to control crime, political pressures grow for still more prisons, longer sentences, and more executions.

The criminal procedure amendments have done nothing to slow this decline into barbarism. Instead, they have contributed to an atmosphere that promotes acceptance of a situation that ought to shock us.

NOTES

1. As of June, 1994, there were 1,012,851 men and women incarcerated in state and federal prisons. See *State and Federal Prison Population Tops One Million,* Department of Justice Press Release, October 27, 1994. The United States is now behind only Russia in incarceration rates. It has an incarceration rate more than four times that of Canada, more than five times that of England and Wales, and fourteen times that of Japan. See Steven A. Holmes, "Ranks of Inmates Reach One Million in a 2-Decade Rise," *New York Times,* (October 28, 1994), p. 1.

2. In the course of an opinion arguing that the exclusionary rule imposes unacceptable costs, Justice White was forced to concede that "[m]any . . . researchers have concluded that the impact of the exclusionary rule is insubstantial." *United States v. Leon,* 468 U.S. 897, 908, n. 6 (1984). A General Accounting Office study showed that in federal criminal prosecutions, 0.4 percent of cases were not prosecuted because of illegal search problems. Evidence was excluded in 1 3 percent of cases studied, and only 0.7 percent of those resulted in acquittals or dismissals. Report of the Comptroller General of the United States, Impact of the Exclusionary Rule on Federal Criminal Prosecutions (1979), 8–14. Studies of state prosecutions yield similar data. See National Institute of Justice, *Criminal Justice Research Report—The Effects of the Exclusionary Rule: A Study in California* (1983), 1; Thomas Y. Davies, "A Hard Look at What We Know (and Still Need to Learn) About the 'Costs' of the Exclusionary Rule: The NIJ Study and Other Studies of 'Lost' Arrests," *American Bar Foundation Research Journal* (1983): 611.

3. For a good summary of the empirical evidence, see Stephen J. Schulhofer, "Reconsidering *Miranda,*" *University of Chicago Law Review* 54 (1987): 435, 455–461.

4. See Lloyd Weinreb, *Denial of Justice: Criminal Process in the United States* (1977), 112. Cf. Stephen J. Schulhofer and David D. Friedman, "Rethinking Indigent Defense: Promoting Effective Representation through Consumer Sovereignty and Freedom of Choice for All Criminal Defendants," *American Criminal Law Review* 31 (1993): 73, 86. ("[I]f the Chief Defender values attorneys for their ability to move cases quickly and to persuade reluctant defendants to plead guilty, the accused might be better off making his own, poorly informed choice.")

5. In many contexts, the Court has refused "to transfer from politically accountable officials . . . the decision as to which among reasonable alternative law enforcement techniques should be employed to deal with a serious public danger," and concluded that "the choice among such reasonable alternatives remains with the government officials who have a unique understanding of, and a responsibility for, limited public resources." *Michigan Dept. of State Police v. Sitz,* 496 U.S. 444, 453–54 (1990). The modern Court has declined to treat "probable cause" as a fixed and rigid requirement that the police must meet before privacy is invaded. Instead, it is a "practical, nontechnical conception," *Brinegar v. United States,* 338 U.S. 160, 176 (1949), that is "not readily, or even usefully, reduced to a neat set of legal rules." *Illinois v. Gates,* 462 U.S. 213, 232 (1983). The Court has insisted that the expertise of the officer at the scene be taken into account, *United States v. Oritz,*

422 U.S. 891, 897 (1975), and that he not be shackled by post hoc judicial second guessing. *Illinois v. Gates,* 462 U.S. 213, 238 (1983). Even if the police act without probable cause, they need not fear the exclusion of evidence if they reasonably rely on a warrant, see *United States v. Leon,* 468 U.S. 897 (1984), and the warrant and probable cause requirements themselves are riddled with exceptions. See e.g., *New York v. Burger,* 482 U.S. 691 (1987) (exception for administrative searches); *California v. Acevedo,* 500 U.S. 565 (1991) (exception for automobiles); *Skinner v. Railway Labor Executives' Assn.,* 489 U.S. 602 (1989) (exception for "special needs").

6. In the quarter century since *Miranda,* the Court has reversed only two convictions on the ground that post-*Miranda* custodial interrogation produced an involuntary statement, compared with twenty-three Supreme Court reversals on voluntariness grounds in the comparable time period immediately preceding *Miranda.* See Louis Michael Seidman, *"Brown* and *Miranda,"* California Law Review 80 (1992): 673, 744–745, nn. 239, 240.

7. See *Strickland v. Washington,* 466 U.S. 668, 689 (1984) (judicial review of counsel's performance should be "highly deferential" and "indulge a strong presumption that counsel's conduct falls within the wide range of reasonable professional assistance").

8. See, e.g., *Coleman v. Thompson,* 501 U.S. 722 (1991) (habeas unavailable after procedural default); *Teague v. Lane,* 489 U.S. 288 (1989) ("new rules" generally unenforceable on habeas); *Stone v. Powell,* 428 U.S. 465 (1976) (Fourth Amendment exclusionary rule generally unenforceable on habeas).

9. The most recent data, from 1993, indicate that the crime rate fell by 3 percent from the previous year, the second consecutive year of decline. The violent crime rate showed an annual decline of 2 percent. See Federal Bureau of Investigation, *Crime in the United States, 1993: Uniform Crime Reports* (1993), 11.

10. For the first six months of 1994, while the crime rate was declining, the number of prisoners grew by nearly 40,000, the equivalent of 1,500 per week. In the last decade, the United States prison population has doubled on a per capita basis. See *State and Federal Prison Population Tops One Million,* United States Department of Justice Press Release, October 27, 1994.

11. Ibid.

12. See Pierre Thomas, "U.S. Prison Population, Continuing Rapid Growth since '80s, Surpasses 1 Million, *Washington Post,* October 28, 1994, p. 3.

Have the Constitutional Protections for Accused Criminals Become So Weakened As to Deny the Accused Fundamental Rights?

WILLIAM T. PIZZI

Punishment and Procedure: A Different View of the American Criminal Justice System

In a recent issue of this journal, Professor Michael Seidman notes that while we have "the most elaborate and detailed constitutional protections for criminal defendants of any country in the world," we also have "the second highest incarceration rate of any country in the world." From these premises, he goes on to argue that our constitutional protections, which he views as "intended to make prosecution more difficult," have been so weakened that instead they "serve [to] make the prosecutor's job easier." He complains that "the Fourth Amendment is so riddled with exceptions and limitations that it rarely prevents the police from pursuing any reasonable crime control tactic"; that "judges have virtually gone out of the business of actually policing the voluntariness of confessions and regularly sanction the sort of coercive tactics that would have led to the suppression of evidence a half century ago"; and that courts tolerate courtroom performances by counsel "that make a mockery of the formal protections [of the Sixth Amendment]."

The picture that Professor Seidman draws of a barbaric system in which constitutional protections are not nearly as strong as they ought to be if they are to protect defendants from such a system might not seem the meat for a response. After all, his picture of the system was tossed off with broad brush strokes in a brief essay. But two reasons compel me to respond to Professor Seidman's picture of the system. The first is that this picture of a system of brutal unfairness is common in law review writing and is often used to justify extreme positions on legal issues. Consider, for example, an essay by Professor David Luban, entitled "Are Criminal Defenders Different?", in which he argued that a more aggressive level of advocacy is justified in criminal cases than is appropriate in civil cases because our criminal justice system is so unfair. Like Professor Seidman, Professor Luban claimed that prosecutors "enjoy overwhelming procedural advantages" over the defense in the American criminal justice system. Again, like Professor Seidman, he considers the American criminal justice system to be overwhelmingly harsh in its sentencing of defendants. For Professor Luban, proof of the harshness of the system lies in the fact that we have "the dubious distinction of having a higher percentage of our population under lock and key than any nation in the world, including the pre-Glasnost Soviet Union, post-Tiananmen Square China, and pre-deKlerk South Africa." He goes on to ask, "Is this 'political abuse'? I believe that it is."

My second reason for responding to Professor Seidman is that he offers this picture of a system that is terribly unfair to defendants at a time when broad segments of the public are angry at the system for exactly the opposite reason. Statement after statement from victims complains angrily that the criminal justice system cares about little except the rights of defendants and systematically ignores the interests of victims or the broader public. These complaints are backed up by public opinion polls that show that the public has little confidence in the criminal justice system and very low respect for lawyers in general. In the wake of recent high publicity cases, one wonders if public confidence in the system might not sink to even lower levels.

Because I believe that the picture offered by Professor Seidman is inaccurate, I want to criticize that view of the system and offer a different view, in which punishment and procedure are synergistically related. Readers can decide which view of the system is more accurate, understanding of course that both pictures are painted with broad strokes. But even if readers disagree with the view of the system I will put forward, they will at least better understand the public anger directed at the system, because my view of the system is much closer to the views of the system offered by victims and others outside the system than it is to the picture presented by Professor Seidman.

A PRELIMINARY MATTER: JUDGING A SYSTEM BY ITS INCARCERATION RATES

Both Professors Seidman and Luban make dramatic use of the high incarceration rate in the United States when compared with other Western countries. In 1993 the United States had an incarceration rate of 519 citizens per 100,000. This is roughly ten and a half times that of the Netherlands (49), eight times that of Norway (62), six times that of Germany (80) and France (84), and five and a half times that of England/Wales (93). But while these statistics are sad and disturbing, are they a fair measure of how harshly particular defendants are actually sentenced and do they show a criminal justice system that is repressive and unjust? The answer is no. Because these figures do not take into account other societal factors such as the strength of the particular country's social services system, the availability of handguns, the rate of violent crime, the extent of the country's drug problem, etc., these dramatic figures do not tell us nearly as much about the criminal justice system in those countries as these figures in isolation would suggest. Ken Pease, an English criminologist who has tried to determine the level of comparative punitiveness among European countries, concluded that measuring a country's punitiveness according to the number of its citizens incarcerated compared to the country's total population "is liable to produce misleading results."

A recent article by Professor Richard Frase comparing sentencing practices in France with those in the United States illustrates just how difficult it is to compare different countries, even when the comparison is limited to only two countries. He describes France as a country that makes "very sparing use of custodial penalties" and as a country with a "less punitive attitude." He then explains how hard it is to document statistically the conclusion that France is less punitive than the United States because, among other problems, crimes are categorized differently and data are often not comparable between the two countries or are simply unavailable. Doing the best he can with the figures, he concludes that "it seems likely that, overall, fines and other noncustodial sentences are used less often in the United States than in France," and that "[i]t may also be the case that custodial terms are, on the average, longer in the United States." These are rather tentative conclusions considering that the incarceration rate of France is one-sixth that of the United States.

This is not to claim that the United States does not punish criminals more severely than many or even most other Western countries. But it is difficult to find data that would show exactly how much more criminals are punished in the United States and whether this is true for all crime categories and for all regions of the country. Like Professor Frase and other comparatists, I believe it to be the case that defendants in the United States are generally punished somewhat more severely than similar defendants on the continent. I am also worried that whatever disparity exists at present may be aggravated as legislatures continue to enact mandatory sentences (such as the "three strikes" legislation in California) and to increase sentencing ranges generally. Thus, in this article I will assume what I believe to be true — that defendants in the United States tend to receive sentences that are somewhat longer than those they would receive in other Western countries and that some defendants in the United States receive sentences that are much harsher than they would receive in Europe (including a death penalty, which does not exist in Europe). But while not denying that we have serious problems in our criminal justice system with the harshness of certain laws, I do not think it is fair to our system to use raw incarceration figures to suggest the system as a whole is barbaric or repressive, or to suggest that all defendants receive sentences in the United States that are terribly unfair and unjust. These comparative incarceration figures mean far less than they appear to mean. At a time when our criminal justice system has many serious problems, I do not think it is helpful to exaggerate the problems that do exist.

INCARCERATION RATES AND DEFENDANTS' RIGHTS

Professor Seidman presents the picture of a system in which constitutional protections have not done the job of protecting suspects, and as evidence of this, he points to our startling incarceration rate. He thinks prosecutors have an easy time of it in the United States, with most of our protections watered down and full of exceptions. This logic would certainly suggest that if we look to European countries with low rates of incarceration we would see criminal justice systems that make the prosecutor's job much more difficult and protections for defendants that dwarf those that exist in the United States.

But when you look at those systems, the relationship that Professor Seidman assumes exists between incarceration rates and protections for defendants doesn't hold at all. Consider, for example, the Netherlands, a country with an incarceration rate that is the lowest in Europe and with a reputation for tolerance and a tradition that has favored lenient sentencing policies. It is also a country that is well-known for its bold attempts to explore alternatives to incarceration for drug offenders, such as de facto legalization of soft drugs and novel measures to make sure addicts stay in treatment, for example, the "methadone bus" which brings methadone to the addict.

But when one looks at the Dutch system of criminal procedure, one sees a system with many features that would be violative of all sorts of constitutional rights in the United States. For example, the level of lay participation in the decision-making process is easily stated: it is zero. There is no right to a jury or even to lay judges as you find elsewhere in Europe. Moreover, the trial places considerable emphasis on the materials gathered during the closed pre-trial stage by the police and the investigating judge. Trials tend to center on a discussion of the materials contained in the dossier and place less emphasis on oral testimony and the examination of witnesses in open court. Because Dutch trials do not bar hearsay, there are cases in which the conviction is supported by statements from anonymous witnesses.

The Netherlands is unusual among European countries because it remains so heavily inquisitorial at a time when most other European countries have moved away from such a heavy emphasis on the investigatory phase of the procedure. But even compared to other continental countries, the notion that the American criminal justice system makes it too easy to convict defendants, leading to a high incarceration rate, seems ridiculous. Consider two other examples, Norway and Germany, both with incarceration rates much lower than that of the United States. In Norway, as is traditional in civil law systems, the judges always ask the defendant, after the state's attorney has read the charges, if he wishes to respond to the charges. The defendant need not respond—he has the right to remain silent—but in such an event the Norwegian code provides: "If the person charged refuses to answer, or states that he reserves his answer, the president of the court may inform him that this may be considered to tell against him." Adding additional pressure to respond to the charges is another feature of civil law trials: trials on the continent have the dual function of determining sentence as well as guilt. Both issues are resolved at the conclusion of the trial and announced in the court's judgment. The dual nature of the inquiry means that the defendant will not have the chance to speak prior to sentencing in the event of a conviction as would be the case in the United States. Thus, the fact that the trial has a dual function as well as that the factfinders are seeking the defendant's response means that defendants almost always choose to respond to the charges and answer the judges' questions. This means that the defendant is usually an important source of evidence at civil law trials. The fact that sentence is a possible trial issue has another advantage for the state's attorney: the defendant's criminal record is directly relevant to the issue of the appropriate sentence and so will always be brought out, whether the defendant chooses to respond to the charges or not.

Germany, like other civil law countries, accords victims of serious crimes (or the family of the victim in the case of homicide) far greater rights at trial than is the case in the United States. In Germany, victims of very serious crimes, such as homicide or rape, have the right to participate in the trial as a "secondary accuser" which gives the victim a status nearly equal to that of the defense during pretrial proceedings and at trial. There is even the possibility of appointed counsel if the victim is indigent. Because the defendant responds first to the charges, this means that in a rape case, for example, the defendant will give his account of the events before the victim has been called as a witness, the reverse of what it would be in the United States. As for removing the victim as part of a sequestration order when the defendant gives his account of the events, that would not be possible in Germany if the victim has chosen to participate at the trial because such a victim is treated like the defendant as far as presence in the courtroom is concerned and is entitled to remain in the front of the courtroom throughout the trial just like the defendant. Like the state's attorney or the defense attorney, the victim's attorney can ask questions of witnesses, suggest additional witnesses and even make a closing statement on behalf of the victim at the end of the trial. . . .

Professor Seidman complains that our Fourth Amendment is "riddled with exceptions and limitations." But I doubt that there is any common law country that would suppress the evidence in cases such as *Gates* or *Leon*, two of the cases complained about by Professor Seidman, where the officers were acting in good faith and had judicial approval based on a warrant for searches that resulted in the seizure of substantial amounts of drugs. In England, the courts have traditionally not seen it as their function to discipline police officers, believing that to be a function of the executive branch, not the judiciary. This has been changed under the Police and Criminal Evidence Act of 1984. But that act permits courts to exclude prosecution evidence only if the admission of such evidence "would have such an adverse effect on the fairness of the proceedings that the court ought not to admit it." Canada appears to take a somewhat similar stance, requiring suppression of evidence under Section 24 of the Charter of Rights and Freedoms "if it is established that, having regard to all the circumstances, the admission of it in the proceedings would bring the administration of justice into disrepute." Under either standard, it is doubtful in the extreme that suppression of important evidence would be likely in any situation where an officer was acting in a reasonable, good faith belief in the lawfulness of his action.

Professor Seidman also complains that while "the Supreme Court continues to insist on the ritualistic reading of *Miranda* warnings, judges have virtually gone out of the business of actually policing the voluntariness of confessions and regularly sanction the sort of coercive tactics that would have led to the suppression of evidence a half century ago." I don't know if this accusation is true—Professor Seidman cites no studies—but certainly the rights a suspect has in the United States under *Miranda* and its progeny to halt all questioning are far stronger than they would be for such a suspect in England. Suspects in England have the right to refuse to answer, but at the same time, it is understood that the police have the right to question. Thus, when a suspect refuses to answer a question, the police will often proceed to the next question. And while there is the right to representation during interrogation, it is not seen as the function of the defense solicitor to bar all interrogation, but rather to make sure that the questioning is fair and that the suspect is treated properly. Should a suspect refuse to answer questions, it will be reported at trial by the interrogating officer that the defendant was "cautioned" following his arrest and said nothing.

Given the acceptance of a system in which the police have a right to ask questions of a suspect as well as a system in which the refusal to answer questions is often introduced at trial, it is not surprising that a substantially greater percentage of suspects in England make damaging statements to the police compared to the United States. The percentage of suspects who refuse to answer questions in the interrogation room is likely to shrink in the future because the right to silence has been drastically narrowed under the Criminal Justice and Public Order Act of 1994. To mention just one change, section 34 of the act permits a negative inference to be drawn at trial from the failure of a suspect to mention any fact to the police at the time of questioning that the suspect could have mentioned at that time and which the suspect now relies on at trial.

The privilege against self-incrimination also provides protections for defendants in American courtrooms that have no equivalent in courtrooms in England (or most other common law countries). In *Brooks v. Tennessee,* the Supreme Court struck down a Tennessee statute that required the defendant to testify as the first witness on the defense case if the defendant chose to testify. The Court ruled that this statute violated the privilege against self-incrimination as well as due process, because the defendant must have complete freedom to testify whenever he chooses during the defense case. In England, the defendant has no right to decide when he will testify at trial. It remains the practice in England that the defendant must be the first witness for the defense if the defendant chooses to testify.

AN ALTERNATIVE PICTURE OF THE AMERICAN CRIMINAL JUSTICE SYSTEM

Professor Seidman sees the American criminal justice system as a harsh system, and he places the blame largely on the failure of our system of constitutional protections, which in his view do not make the prosecutor's job sufficiently difficult. I have accepted his premise to the extent of agreeing that the American criminal justice system punishes defendants more severely than other Western countries, but the evidence on this issue is not as clear as Professor Seidman suggests. I have strongly disagreed with his view that our constitutional protections make it too easy for prosecutors to convict the.guilty, and I think the case is fairly overwhelming that defendants have more rights and far stronger rights than defendants in other Western countries.

Professor Seidman seems frustrated and angry that our country would develop an elaborate system of constitutional rights that has no equivalent in other countries and, at the same time, punish defendants more severely than other countries, sometimes much more severely. But I think that it is not surprising to find extremes in procedure and punishment linked in this way because there is a synergy between procedure and punishment such that extremes in one encourage extremes in the other and vice versa. It is thus not an accident that a country with a system of criminal procedure that is the most complicated and the most expensive in the Western world and, if the truth be known, a trial system that is not very reliable, would also turn out to have a system that threatens, and sometimes inflicts, punishments that are harsh compared to those in other countries. Such a system needs to put pressure on defendants by threatening them with harsh punishments if they insist on trial, so that high mandatory minimums, habitual offender statutes, tough sentencing guidelines, and the like are encouraged by such a procedural system. Essentially, the system needs to work around its own procedures, and in the United States this is done by accepting types of charge bargains and sentence bargains—even bargains from defendants who insist that they are innocent—that would not be accepted in other systems.

Harsh punishments in turn encourage even more emphasis on procedure. Certainly, there is no better example than the death penalty, where even a single mistake in jury selection by a trial judge invalidates the death sentence no matter how heinous the crimes committed by the offender or how many such crimes he may have committed in the past. The system's reluctance to use the death penalty translates into a requirement of technical perfection in capital cases that can rarely be met. This in turn feeds anger at the system and the main outlet for that sort of anger is to pressure legislatures for ever harsher punishments for criminals. . . .

CONCLUSION

In this article I have taken strong issue with the claim that our system of constitutional protections are not nearly strong enough and that evidence of this is our high incarceration rate compared to other countries. I have tried to show that those who think our constitutional protections are riddled with exceptions or have been watered down by this or that decision of the Court have no perspective on our system. Compared to criminal justice systems in other countries, defendants in the United States have many procedural advantages that make the prosecutor's job more difficult. Among comparatists who have compared the American criminal justice system to other systems, it is not uncommon to conclude that if one is really guilty, one would prefer to be tried in the United States.

But there is a downside to going to trial in the United States: the risks at sentencing if found guilty. Not many offenders choose to go to trial in the United States because few can afford to run the risk of being sentenced if they are found guilty. I have suggested that this is part of the synergy between procedure and punishment and it ought not to surprise us that a country might tend to the extremes in both its procedures and its punishments.

Like many readers, I am sure, I would like to see our sentencing laws substantially reduced and prisons improved for those who must be incarcerated. Perhaps this is an impossible goal and other Western countries will tend to become more punitive like the United States as their crime rates rise and public apprehension about crime grows. But however unlikely reform of our sentencing laws may be, it becomes much more unlikely if we move in the direction Professor Seidman would like to see us go and substantially increase the rights that defendants have in our system.

Questions for Discussion

1. What are the rights that the Constitution gives a suspect in the criminal justice system?
2. To what extent have Supreme Court decisions on rights of suspects and defendants helped or hurt the prosecution?
3. What criteria would you use in evaluating the impact of constitutional rights on the conduct of the criminal justice system?
4. How do you account for the fact that while crime rates have remained static and even declined slightly in recent years, the rate of incarceration has skyrocketed?
5. How do you compare the fairness of the criminal justice system in the United States with the fairness of the system in other democracies? What are the reasons for your answer?

Suggested Readings

Butler, Paul. "Racially Based Jury Nullification: Black Power in the Criminal Justice System." *Yale Law Journal* 105, no. 3 (December 1995): 677–725.

Friedman, Lawrence M. *Crime and Punishment in the United States.* New York: Basic Books, 1993.

Hancock, Barry W., and Paul M. Sharp. *Public Policy, Crime, and Criminal Justice.* Upper Saddle River, N.J.: Prentice Hall, 1996.

Hopkins, Evans D. "Time and Punishment: From the Other Side of the Iron Bars, the Case for Parole." *Washington Post,* December 19, 1993, pp. C1, C2.

Huff, C. Ronald, Arye Rattner, and Edward Sagarin. *Convicted But Innocent: Wrongful Conviction and Public Policy.* Thousand Oaks, Calif.: Sage, 1996.

Kennedy, Randall. "Is Everything Race?" *New Republic* 214, no. 1 (January 1, 1996): 18, 20–21.

Leo, Richard A. "*Miranda's* Revenge: Police Interrogation as a Confidence Game." *Law and Society Review* 30, no. 2 (1996): 259–288.

Luban, David. "Are Criminal Defenders Different?" *Michigan Law Review* 91, no. 7 (1993): 1729–1766.

Miller, Jerome G. *Search and Destroy: African-American Males in the Criminal Justice System.* New York: Cambridge Univ. Press, 1996.

Puccio, Thomas P., with Dan Collins. *In the Name of the Law: Confessions of a Trial Lawyer.* New York: W. W. Norton, 1995.

Reiman, Jeffrey H. *The Rich Get Richer and the Poor Get Prison: Ideology, Class, and Criminal Justice,* 4th ed. Boston: Allyn & Bacon, 1995.

Rothwax, Harold J. *Guilty: The Collapse of Criminal Justice.* New York: Random House, 1996.

Tonry, Michael H. *Malign Neglect: Race, Crime, and Punishment in the United States.* New York: Oxford Univ. Press, 1995.

Uviller, H. Richard. *Virtual Justice: The Flawed Prosecution of Crime in America.* New Haven, Conn.: Yale Univ. Press, 1996.

Van den Haag, Ernest. *Punishing Criminals: Concerning a Very Old and Painful Question.* Lanham, Md.: Univ. Press of America, 1991.

Chapter 7

Is Affirmative Action a Desirable Policy to Remedy Discrimination?

In the decades following World War II, the civil rights movement in the United States achieved notable successes. The Supreme Court ruled that racially discriminatory practices were unconstitutional, and laws were adopted at the national, state, and local level ending practices of segregation and other forms of discrimination.

The civil rights movement focused initially on political gains — voting rights, school integration, and access to public accommodations. Although resistance was strong, the movement achieved legal guarantees of equal treatment. Achieving equal economic opportunity proved to be a more intractable problem. As many African Americans pointed out, it is all well and good to have the legal right to go to any fine restaurant or hotel, as civil rights laws required, but the legal right does not make much practical difference to the people who cannot afford to pay.

Civil rights legislation did not secure economic equality. Many companies hired only a few African Americans, and often the jobs they held were low level. Few African Americans rose to top positions in business. Many departments in colleges and universities had few African American teachers or administrators. And even professional sports — baseball, basketball, and football — which welcomed African Americans to their teams as athletes, hired few African Americans as coaches or executives. Many people in the civil rights movement saw this economic and social disparity between African Americans and whites as just another form of discrimination. They called upon government to guarantee equal employment opportunities.

Government responded in two ways: by enforcing antidiscrimination laws, and by adopting affirmative action programs, which required employers to take special measures to recruit, hire, train, and upgrade members of groups that have suffered harm from past discrimination. Both policies were not limited to African Americans but were applied to other racial minorities and to women.

Support for the enforcement of antidiscrimination laws was broad. Government agencies sought to ensure that employers made job information available to all groups, did not use tests or create standards that were unrelated to performance of jobs as an unfair screening device against minority groups, and placed no discriminatory barriers to advancement within an organization.

Affirmative action was — and remains — controversial. It is based on the idea that special measures are needed to benefit groups of people who suffered from a long history of discrimination. In this view, affirmative action is needed to make previously excluded groups of people more competitive in economic and professional life.

When a government agency or court determines that a private or public organization is engaged in discriminatory hiring practices, it may require the organization to end those practices. But detecting discrimination in hiring practices is difficult. At times, the government relies on a statistical analysis based on the composition of either the work force in an organization or the number of applicants to particular jobs there. Government agencies sometimes require employment "guidelines" or "targets," which the organizations are expected to follow to comply with civil rights regulations. But critics of affirmative action complain that these guidelines are actually "quotas" in which specific percentages are allotted to targeted groups.

Quotas are illegal in the United States. According to a landmark case, *Regents of the University of California* v. *Bakke,* the Supreme Court decided that an affirmative action program using quotas for medical school admissions violates the Civil Rights Act of 1964. The Court, however, declared that admissions committees can consider race as one of a complex of factors involved in admissions decisions.[1] Critics of affirmative action say that guidelines inevitably become quotas, while supporters of the policy say that they do not.

Since *Bakke,* affirmative action has increasingly come under attack in judicial and political arenas. In 1995, the Supreme Court decided in *Adarand Constructors v. Pena* that the federal government must adhere to the same strict constitutional standards that states had to obey when implementing affirmative action programs designed to benefit minorities and other groups that had suffered discrimination.[2] The Court applied a "strict scrutiny" test for federal programs, as already existed with states. This decision reversed earlier Supreme Court decisions that gave the federal government broader discretion than states had to implement affirmative action programs. *Adarand* was the first case in which the Supreme Court refused to uphold a federal affirmative action program.

In response, President Bill Clinton ordered a review of affirmative action policies in the federal government. In October 1995, the Department of Defense ended a program designed to help minority-owned firms win defense contracts. It was the first significant action by the Clinton administration following a review of affirmative action. President Clinton, however, remained committed to affirmative action. In a speech on July 19, 1995, he said: "We should reaffirm the principle of affirmative action and fix the practices. We should have a simple slogan: mend it, but don't end it."[3]

Many developments in affirmative action in 1995 and 1996 dealt blows to the program. In March 1996, in *Hopwood v. Texas,* a federal appeals court invalidated a race-based admissions policy at the University of Texas School of Law. The court held that race or ethnicity could not be used as a factor in admissions even to correct a perceived racial imbalance in the student body. The court also determined that the university had failed to identify past discrimination at the law school as a justification for a remedy that gives preferences to racial minorities.[4] And in April 1996, Georgia Attorney General Michael Bowers asked the state's thirty-four government-sponsored colleges and universities to change admission policies that give preference to racial minorities. He did so, he said, to comply with decisions of federal judges in recent cases.

One of the strongest attacks on affirmative action came from California. In July 1995, the California Board of Regents decided that considerations of "race, religion, sex, color, ethnicity, or national origin" in university admissions, hiring, and contracting would be prohibited. The universities could, however, consider a candidate's social and economic status. In February 1996, the California Board of Regents set a timetable of the spring 1998 term for repealing racial and sexual preferences in the admission of students. Under the old program, 40–60 percent of students had to be admitted on the basis of merit alone. For the remainder, the admissions officer could take into account factors such as race, ethnicity, and gender. The goal was to have a student body similar to that of the state as a whole. In the new plan, 50–75 percent would be admitted on the basis of merit alone. The rest could be admitted subject to considerations of socioeconomic and family background but not sex, religion, ethnicity, and national origin. In 1994, whites made up 49 percent of the student body, African Americans 4 percent, Hispanics 13 percent, and Asians 29 percent. It was widely believed that the new rule would decrease the percentage of Hispanics and African Americans and increase the percentage of Asians. And in November 1996, California voters approved Proposition 209, banning racial and sexual preferences in public hiring, contracting, and education in the state. The voters did so by a 54 percent majority. Opponents of the proposition immediately set forth legal challenges that the courts will eventually have to consider.

Affirmative action has been bitterly contested by people who believe the policy discriminates against them. They argue that they have not been hired or advanced because their employer has been forced to give preference to minorities or women. They say affirmative action is unfair, counterproductive, and unjust. Defenders argue that the policy is fair, just, and necessary to end discrimination. Some of the flavor of the controversy is seen in the debate below.

In testimony before the House Subcommittee on Employer-Employee Relations of the Committee on Economic and Educational Opportunities, Theodore M. Shaw, associate director-counsel of the National Association for the Advancement of Colored People (NAACP) Legal and Educational Defense Fund, Inc., makes the case for affirmative action.[5] He contends:

1. Affirmative action is a moderate, effective remedy for exclusion, to achieve equality that is real and not illusory.
2. Affirmative action has worked well. Millions of men and women have been provided an equal opportunity in employment, education, and housing because of affirmative action.
3. Discrimination against women and persons of color is still a tragic fact of life in America.
4. Both affirmative action programs to remedy discrimination and programs to address poverty and economic disadvantage continue to be necessary to overcome this country's history of gender-based and race-based exclusion and to achieve meaningful opportunity for all.

Brian W. Jones, president of the Center for New Black Leadership, a Washington, D.C., think tank, makes the case against affirmative action. He contends:

1. Affirmative action was justified when it was initiated thirty years ago but today it does more harm than good.
2. The modern beneficiaries of racial preferences tend to be individuals likely possessing the requisite advantages to compete effectively without the taint of preference.
3. The cost of preference policies can be measured in terms of: (a) the social discord created between preferred and nonpreferred groups, and among the preferred groups; (b) the opportunity cost of mismatched minority talent and capital; and (c) the economic cost to employers of complying with affirmative action mandates.
4. The inexorable trend of preference policies in America, as everywhere else in the world where they have been tried, is to ceaselessly elevate new groups to preferred status.
5. Instead of affirmative action, Congress should have an agenda that promotes equality of opportunity rather than equality of results.

NOTES

1. *Regents of the University of California v. Bakke,* 438 U.S. 265, 57 (1978).
2. *Adarand Constructors v. Pena,* 115 S. Ct. 2097 (1995).
3. Quoted in "Excerpts from Clinton Talk on Affirmative Action," *New York Times,* July 20, 1995, p. B10.
4. *Hopwood v. Texas,* 116 S. Ct. 2581 (1996).
5. The Legal and Educational Defense Fund was founded in 1940. It is no longer affiliated with the NAACP. It is a separate and independent organization in all respects, with separate board, staff, and budget.

Is Affirmative Action a Desirable Policy to Remedy Discrimination?

THEODORE M. SHAW

The Case for Affirmative Action

Several myths have been created about affirmative action:

1. affirmative action equals quotas;
2. affirmative action elevates unqualified blacks over more qualified whites;
3. affirmative action is no longer needed because discrimination has been eradicated;
4. affirmative action has not helped economically disadvantaged black people;
5. affirmative action is unfair and unAmerican.

I will address each of these myths, as well as the purpose, benefits, and continuing need for affirmative action.

THE PURPOSE OF AFFIRMATIVE ACTION

The goal of affirmative action is to break the cycle of discrimination and to enlarge opportunity for everyone. It is a moderate, effective remedy for exclusion, to achieve equality which is real and not illusory. As Justice Blackmun has eloquently stated, "In order to get beyond racism, we must first take racism [and sexism] into account."[1] (I add, as I am sure Justice Blackmun would agree, that this same principle applies to sex discrimination.)

I ask you and the entire nation to put aside polarizing rhetoric and devisive politics and to take a hard look at the facts — the history of and continuing need for equal opportunity and affirmative action measures. The facts reveal that well-designed and well-implemented affirmative action efforts still are necessary to overcome this country's history of gender-based and race-based exclusion and to achieve meaningful opportunity for all.

Affirmative action is not a single, rigid concept, but rather a mosaic of actions designed . . . to eliminate artificial barriers and to allow merit to shine through. The particular affirmative measures utilized will vary in different circumstances, flexibly addressing the problem at hand. Examples of affirmative action include student assignments to promote public school desegregation; site selections for public housing to promote residential desegregation; efforts to promote and support women and minority-owned businesses; and recruitment and hiring efforts to attract women and minorities into job categories from which they have been traditionally excluded. In every instance, affirmative action is the mechanism by which integration is encouraged and opportunities are opened to persons who have been traditionally excluded from them.

Affirmative action does not mean admitting or hiring unqualified or less meritorious candidates. However, it may mean refining our definitions of merit. Affirmative action recognizes that we have not achieved the ideal of either merit selection or a colorblind and genderblind society. In addition to invidious discrimination based on race, ethnicity and gender, our employment and contracting systems have always relied upon such non-merit-related criteria as nepotism, cronyism and the "old boy network." "Institutions of higher learning . . . have given conceded preferences . . . to the children of alumni, to the affluent who may bestow their largess on the institutions and to those having connections with celebrities, the famous and the powerful."[2] Alumni preferences alone, which inarguably favor whites, account for a greater number of persons admitted to colleges and universities than affirmative action programs. Affirmative action moves us closer to a true merit system, by shifting the focus to job-related qualifications and the potential of individuals, whatever their race.

Affirmative action has been endorsed by the federal government since the Kennedy administration. In contrast, quotas have never been endorsed by the federal government or the Supreme Court. They are now illegal.

Affirmative action does not put people into positions for which they are unqualified. As the federal courts have emphasized, its purpose is to create "an environment where merit can prevail."[3] "If a party is not qualified for a position in the first instance, affirmative action considerations do not come into play."[4] Affirmative action merely encourages institutions to develop realistic plans enabling them to go beyond business as usual and reach out to qualified persons not normally in the "old boy network."

In contrast to illegal quotas, one form of affirmative action which has been highly successful is goals or benchmarks used to aid in the evaluation of an employer's success in providing equal employment. This approach to measuring equal opportunity was recommended in the late 1960s to the Nixon Administration by a group of several hundred large corporations. These recommendations, accepted by President Nixon and implemented by Secretary of Labor George Shultz, included the "management-by-objectives" concepts of employment goals and timetables. In this form of affirmative action, the goal must be reasonably related to the number of women or minorities who are qualified and would likely be hired or promoted under a non-discriminatory system.

The Nixon Administration clearly differentiated between quotas, which were expressly rejected, and goals and timetables, which it explicitly endorsed. According to the Nixon Administration's 1973 Interagency Agreement, which still represents the position of the federal government:

> A quota imposes a fixed number of percentage which must be attained or which cannot be exceeded. If an entity fails to make the quota, it is subject to sanction.

A goal is a numerical objective. If an entity demonstrates that it has made every good faith effort to include persons from the targeted group, but has been unable to do so, it is not subject to sanction.[5]

Justice Sandra Day O'Connor referred to the 1973 Agreement with approval in her concurring opinion, "[t]his understanding of the difference between goals and quotas seems to me workable and . . . consistent with (Title VII)."[6]

A recent study of 3,000 employment discrimination cases shows that there is "no widespread abuse of affirmative action programs in employment." There are only a small number of so-called "reverse discrimination" cases (between 1 and 3 percent) and many of those were filed by "'disappointed' job applicants who were found by the court to be less qualified for the job than the chosen female or minority applicant." Bernard Anderson, Assistant Secretary of Labor, stated that he expects information being compiled by the Labor Department to show that the Nixon affirmative action program, which remains in effect, "has made a 'major difference' in expanding employment opportunities for women and minorities and should be continued."[7]

I would also point out that "quota-baiting" is not a new tactic. The Civil Rights Act of 1964 was enacted as the first modern statutory protection against invidious discrimination in employment and public accommodations. Opponents of equal opportunity protested this law as requiring "quotas," at a time when many jobs and unions were 100 percent white male. When Congress enacted the Civil Rights Act of 1991 to restore the law after several 1989 Supreme Court decisions restricting the ability of workers to recover for job discrimination, opponents applied the quota label. . . .

AFFIRMATIVE ACTION HAS WORKED WELL

Congress on numerous occasions, the courts, and many public and private studies all have concluded that affirmative action has been successful and is good for America. Literally millions of men and women have been provided an equal opportunity in employment, education and housing because of affirmative action. Affirmative action is good for families. Wives, daughters and mothers have been given access to education and the opportunity to compete in the workplace.

Affirmative action produces benefits for the entire community and nation. For example, as women have entered the medical profession and the United States Congress, more attention has been focused on crucial health needs of all women, such as breast cancer research. An LDF case involving the Detroit police department demonstrates the immense benefits of affirmative action in law enforcement. A federal court found that prior to the adoption of an affirmative action plan, the black citizens of Detroit were "a population . . . subjected to constitutional indignities as a *direct* result of the discriminatory practices which . . . created and maintained a white-dominated police force."[8]

After recruiting efforts failed to change the all-white nature of the force, the city adopted an affirmative action plan that included goals for the hiring and promotion of black police officers. The improvements resulting from this plan were dramatic. "There is clear evidence . . . that after the institution of the affirmative action program, police-community relations improved substantially, crime went down, complaints against the [police] [d]epartment went down, and no police officers were killed in the line of duty."[9]

Businesses have found that affirmative action is good for the bottom line. Productivity is improved in many instances and a work force that reflects the diversity of the markets they serve allows businesses to compete more effectively. The Business Roundtable and the National Association of Manufacturers have repeatedly endorsed affirmative action.

In May 1985, the directors of the National Association of Manufacturers endorsed a policy statement that supported affirmative action, with goals and timetables, as "good business policy." A 1984 poll by the National Association of Manufacturers registered overwhelming support for affirmative action policies. In the mid-1980s William McEwen, Director of Economic Opportunity at Monsanto Corporation and Chair of the National Association of Manufacturers Human Resources Committee, said "setting goals and timetables for minority and female participation is simply a way of measuring progress."[10]

In a March 1989 survey by *Fortune,* 68 percent of corporate chief executive officers said affirmative action programs were "good, very good or outstanding," while only 2 percent called them "poor."[11] An August 1994 *Fortune* article was titled "How to Make Diversity Pay" and described productivity gains attributable to increased workplace diversity. A February 1995, article in the *Wall Street Journal* reported that, with respect to all the legislative activity aimed at weakening or dismantling affirmative action, "business is wary." "This is not one of our key issues at the moment," says the U.S. Chamber of Commerce's Stephen Bokat.[12] A recent *Washington Post* article quoted Hugh L. McColl, Jr., chairman of NationsBank Corp., as saying "I am bothered, and I hope you are, . . . by the recent ideological siege against the purpose of affirmative action." McColl, who borrowed from Abraham Lincoln in describing affirmative action programs as "ensur[ing] for all 'a fair chance in the race for life,'" pledged that he would not let "go unchallenged . . . the dangerous and mean-spirited undertone of the public debate and the impact that [it] is having on our nation."[13]

DISCRIMINATION AGAINST WOMEN AND PERSONS OF COLOR IS STILL A TRAGIC FACT OF LIFE IN AMERICA

Much progress has been made on civil rights and women's rights, in large part because of the strong, bi-partisan commitment of Congress to the enactment and enforcement of laws prohibiting and remedying discrimination. Yet, persistent, widespread discrimination still prevents too many women, African

Americans, Latinos and other hardworking Americans from going as far as their abilities can take them.

The stubborn survival of discrimination on the basis of race, ethnicity and gender has been documented repeatedly by Congress over the past few years. Just since 1982, Congress has strengthened and extended both the Voting Rights Act (1982) and the Fair Housing Act (1988), restored the laws governing equal employment opportunities (Civil Rights Act of 1991) and discrimination by federally-assisted institutions (Civil Rights Restoration Act, 1988) and enacted new protections for persons with disabilities (Americans with Disabilities Act, 1990). On each of the occasions when Congress has acted to strengthen our laws providing for equal opportunity, this body concluded, after holding hearings and conducting extensive investigations, that invidious discrimination remains a real and tenacious force in American society.

Numerous public and private studies and experiences confirm the persistence of discrimination against women and minorities. In a 1990 study, the Urban Institute, a respected, nonprofit, nonpartisan research organization, conducted almost 500 hiring audits in Washington, D.C. and Chicago. Ten pairs of young men, one black and one white, were carefully matched on all characteristics that could affect a hiring decision, including age, education, employment experience, conventional dress and command of standard English. They applied for jobs advertised in the newspaper and the Institute compared their treatment at every stage of the hiring process. The Institute Report concludes that "unequal treatment of black job seekers is entrenched and widespread." When equally qualified black and white candidates competed for jobs, differential treatment was almost three times more likely to favor the white applicant.[14]

The *PrimeTime Live* television program used undercover cameras to show similar unequal treatment of a carefully matched pair, one African American and one white tester. The episode, which aired on September 26, 1991, documents blatant racial discrimination. For example, a white official at an employment agency offered courteous service to the white tester, while lecturing the black tester on laziness. The black tester was quoted a down payment on a car that was $1,000 higher than that quoted to the white tester for the purchase of the identical automobile from the same salesperson. The black tester was repeatedly told by a dry cleaning establishment that there were no jobs available, while the white tester was told there were positions available. The black tester was told that no apartment was available, after the white tester had been given a tour of a vacant apartment five minutes earlier. . . .

Discrimination on the basis of ethnicity and gender also persists on a wide scale. The Subcommittee is familiar, I am sure, with last week's Report of the Glass Ceiling Commission, a bipartisan panel appointed by President Bush to implement legislation sponsored by Senator Dole. The *Los Angeles Times* headline pretty much tells the story: "Glass Ceiling? It's More Like a Steel Cage." The *Los Angeles Times* found "there are simply no facts to support" the contention made by "some who want to abolish" affirmative action "that white males are being unfairly shunted aside in favor of lots of African Americans, Latinos, Asians and white women." This newspaper concluded: "The Glass Ceiling Commission based its findings on hard information, not unsubstantiated fears. Facts, and nothing but, should inform the intense debate over affirmative action."[15]

Women and minorities know that all is not right in the American workplace. "Seventy percent of . . . female managers polled believed that the male-dominated corporate culture was an obstacle to their success (up from 60 percent two years ago)."[16] "[I]n the prestigious [business school] programs paid for by corporations that round out a manager's credentials at a key career point, usually at age 40 or 45, companies are making only a token investment in developing female and minority executives. Only about 3 percent of 180 executives in Stanford's recent advanced-management program were women."[17]

The Department of Labor Glass Ceiling Commission found in 1991:

- "There was a point beyond which minorities and women had not advanced in some companies."
- "Minorities and women were concentrated in staff positions, and lacking in line positions where there is more of a career track to the executive suite and greater bonus and reward eligibility."
- "Recruitment practices prevented qualified women and minorities from being considered for management positions. . . . [P]ractices such as word-of-mouth recruiting and employee referrals were found to have an absence of minorities and women."
- "Minorities and women did not have access to development practices and career building experiences, including advanced education, as well as career enhancing assignments, such as corporate committees and task forces and special projects."[18]

The statistics confirm what the studies and our life experiences tell us: minorities and women still have not achieved anything close to equal opportunity. Women make up 80 percent of health service professionals, but "white males dominate the senior management positions."[19] Women are 37 percent of associates in large law firms but only 11 percent of partners.[20] Women are about 50 percent of entry level accountants, but less than 20 percent of accounting firm partners.[21] Women hold 40 percent of jobs in middle management but only 3 to 4 percent of top corporate jobs.[22]

African Americans, who constitute 11 percent of the total workforce made up less than 4 percent of the following occupations as of 1993: lawyers and judges (2.8 percent), dentists (1.9 percent), doctors (3.7 percent), engineers (3.7 percent), architects (3.1 percent), and managers in marketing, advertising and public relations (3.1 percent).[23] Average earnings of black workers, as a percentage of white workers' earnings, fell from 75.1 percent to 73.1 percent between 1980 and 1990.[24] A 1993 study by the *Wall Street Journal* showed that in the 1990–1991 recession, black males were the only group who suffered a net employment loss.[25] They suffered job losses in 36 states and in six of nine major industries: They held 59,479 fewer jobs at the end of the recession than they had held at the beginning.[26]

LDF SUPPORTS BOTH AFFIRMATIVE ACTION TO REMEDY DISCRIMINATION AND PROGRAMS TO ADDRESS POVERTY AND ECONOMIC DISADVANTAGE

Recent proposals suggest that affirmative action might be reconstituted as programs to help the disadvantaged. LDF had hoped that, with the basic structures to provide equal opportunity safely in place, the 1990s would be the decade in which the country could focus more attention on the problems of poverty and economic starvation of communities. We are distressed that, instead of moving forward to address these real and pressing concerns, we are forced to devote time and resources to preserving the remedies we have won and to fighting efforts to turn back the clock.

We believe that there ought to be more opportunity for *all* poor and working class people, who have been hurt by structural changes in our economy even while governmental and social policies much of the last fifteen years have been tilted in favor of the rich with the result that the wealthiest of Americans have become richer while the middle class has shrunk and millions of people joined the ranks of the impoverished. Some of those advocating the elimination of gender and race based affirmative action, however, are the same individuals who are advocating a war on the poor through social policies that include eliminating support for educational opportunities, school lunches, decent housing, job training, health care and basic safety net features.

Affirmative action programs for the economically disadvantaged are not a substitute for gender and race affirmative action. Racial and gender discrimination were enshrined in law; it took a constitutional amendment to guarantee women the right to vote, and we fought a civil war in the nineteenth century and a social revolution in the twentieth century over the issue of race. Women and people of color were not denied equality and opportunity on the basis of economic status. As the Supreme Court has repeatedly ruled, "the nature of the violation determines the scope of the remedy."[27]

Affirmative action has cast light on an entire generation of women, African Americans, Latinos and other people of color whose qualifications and potential would never have been identified for opportunity under the old "meritocracy" in which only white males need apply. The representation that it did not help economically disadvantaged African Americans is one of today's Big Lies — if you say it enough people will believe it. I grew up in a public housing project in the Southeast Bronx; but for affirmative action, I would not have had the opportunities I have had. We could fill the halls of Congress with tens of thousands and more women and people of color who are excelling in all walks of life, who have moved from economic disadvantage to middle class status, and who are beneficiaries of affirmative action. There is no stigma in that. Those who climb the ladder and who, once on top, look down and declare that their ascent was tainted because they received a hand on the way up, may have the luxury of advocating that no one else making the climb should receive a helping hand because it casts doubt on how those at the top got there. For African Americans, stigmatization did not begin thirty years ago with the advent of affirmative action; opportunity did. Affirmative action has been one of America's success stories, in spite of the fact that some have attempted to turn it into a pejorative.

To those who are attacking affirmative action with so much vehemence and conviction and who say that it is unfair and unAmerican, I put the following questions: What kind of country do you want? A nation in which African Americans, women, Latinos, Native Americans, and others who historically were excluded from access to mainstream opportunities as a matter of law and social practice will once again be relegated to marginality and exclusion in the name of theoretical color blindness and notions of a false meritocracy? Do you really believe that we can have prosperity and peace in a monochromatic male dominated society such as the one that existed before the profound changes of the last thirty years? Those entrusted with the noble responsibility of public office have an obligation to move beyond crass partisan interests on issues of such grave importance as race and gender. The clock runs in one direction — forward. There is no going back.

NOTES

1. *Regents of the University of California v. Bakke,* 438 U.S. 265, 407 (1978).

2. *Bakke,* 438 U.S. at 404 (opinion of Blackmun, J.).

3. *NAACP v. Allen,* 493 F.2d. 614, 621 (5th Cir. 1974).

4. *Bratton v. City of Detroit,* 704 F.2d 878, 892 (6th Cir. 1983).

5. "Permissible Goals and Timetables in State and Local Government Employment Practices," memorandum, March 23, 1973.

6. *Local 28, Sheet Metal Workers v. EEOC,* 478 U.S. 385, 496 (1986).

7. *BNA Daily Labor Report,* March 23, 1995, pp. AA-1.

8. *Bratton,* 704 F.2d at 897 n. 44.

9. *Baker v. City of Detroit,* 483 F. Supp. 930, 1000 (E.D. Mich. 1979), *aff'd Bratton.*

10. Quoted in Anne B. Fisher, "Businessmen Like to Hire by the Numbers," *Fortune,* September 16, 1985, p. 28.

11. Alan Farnham, "Holding Firm on Affirmative Action," *Fortune,* March 13, 1989, p. 87.

12. "Washington Wire," *Wall Street Journal,* February 10, 1995, p. A1.

13. Rudolph A. Pyatt Jr., "Hugh McColl's Affirmative Action Views Are Advice Well-Taken," *Washington Post,* February 16, 1995, p. B12.

14. *Opportunities Denied, Opportunities Diminished: Racial Discrimination in Hiring* (Urban Institute, 1991), p. 2.

15. "Glass Ceiling? It's More Like a Steel Cage," *Los Angeles Times,* March 20, 1995, p. B4.

16. U.S. Department of Labor, *Pipelines of Progress, A Status Report on the Glass Ceiling,* p. 5.

17. *Business Week* survey 1991, reported in ibid., p. 8.

18. Office of Federal Contract Compliance Programs, Director's Report, Fiscal Year 1991, pp. 9–10.

19. Foundation of the American College of Healthcare Executives, Hospital and Health Administration, December 22, 1994.

20. Claudia MacLachlan and Rita Henly Jensen, "Progress Glacial for Women, Minorities," *National Law Journal,* August 9, 1993, p. 1.

21. *Newsday,* June 14, 1994, p. A42.

22. Bryanna Latoof, "Still Fighting for Women's Rights," *St. Petersburg Times,* January 4, 1995, p. 1D.

23. *Statistical Abstract of the United States,* 1994, table 622, p. 393; table 637, pp. 407–410.

24. Andrew Hacker, *Two Nations* (New York: Ballantine Books; 1992), p. 101.

25. Rochelle Sharpe, "Losing Ground: In Latest Recession, Only Blacks Suffered Net Employment Loss," *Wall Street Journal,* September 14, 1993, p. A1.

26. Mark Lowery, "The War on Equal Opportunity." *Black Enterprise,* February 1995, p. 148.

27. *Swann v. Board of Education* 402 U.S. 1, 16.

☑ *NO*

Is Affirmative Action a Desirable Policy to Remedy Discrimination?

BRIAN W. JONES

The Case against Affirmative Action

I maintain that government-imposed preferential policies based upon race and gender, whether in the employment or education context, presently do a great deal more social harm than good. While thirty years ago such policies may have been an important tool for breaking down the systemic barriers to black entry into the economic mainstream, they have today, I think, reached the point of diminishing returns.

President Lyndon Johnson, speaking at Howard University in 1965, justified his Executive Order 11246, which we have heard discussed here this afternoon, by analogizing African-Americans to a "hobbled" runner in a race. In order to compete effectively in the race for economic and civic reward, he said, blacks needed to be given something of a head start.

At the time of President Johnson's pronouncement, the use of black skin as a proxy for social disadvantage was perhaps justifiable. Blacks were just emerging from the Jim Crow era in much of America and were not represented in any appreciable numbers in the economic or social mainstream. There was, so to speak, a relatively insignificant pool of prepared black talent from which the mainstream economy could draw. In 1965, approximately 15 percent of black families in America were considered middle class. Today, however, nearly half of all black families are middle class. Race today is no longer a sufficient proxy for social disadvantage.

Indeed, as the size of the black middle class expands, the pool of those best positioned to benefit from racial preferences becomes further removed from any manifest disadvantage. Hence, the lion's share of preference accrues to middle and upper class women and minorities. In short, the modern beneficiaries of racial preferences tend to be individuals likely possessing the requisite advantages to effectively compete without the taint of preference.

Conversely, the cost of preference policies can be measured in terms of: (1) the social discord created between preferred and nonpreferred groups, and among the preferred groups; (2) the opportunity cost of mismatched minority talent and capital; and (3) the economic cost to employers of complying with affirmative action mandates.

Furthermore, the costs associated with these divisive policies will likely only escalate over time, while the programs themselves will become ever more resistant to cradication. The inexorable trend of preference policies in America, as everywhere else in the world where they have been tried, is to ceaselessly elevate new groups to preferred status.[1] Indeed, while modern racial preference policies in America were originally intended to provide remediation to blacks disadvantaged by the legacy of slavery and Jim Crow laws, we are quickly approaching the day when nearly 70 percent of Americans will be members of "protected groups" eligible for government preferment.

Of course, the effect, if not the purpose, of this expanding pool of preference is to maintain the political viability of the program. Sadly, however, that trend is creating what one of my Center's directors, Shelby Steele, refers to as a "culture of preference." A culture in which rights accrue not to individuals, but rather to groups — groups which, incidentally, are not always easily defined. The inevitable consequence of this culture of preference is that groups must inevitably emphasize their differences and exalt their victimization to compete for preferred status. Thus, over the long-run, members of preferred groups are not substantially benefited and the larger society suffers the consequences of the social division created by competing groups. To stanch that inexorable tide, Congress, in my view, needs ultimately to eliminate government-sanctioned preference programs root and branch.

This, of course, is not to say that Congress should not have a positive civil rights agenda. Without question, it must. But that agenda must truly emphasize equality of opportunity, rather than equality of results. Over the past thirty years, the Congress, to its moral credit, has taken a valiant stand against invidious discrimination in America. It has erected an array of remedies for its victims.

In that vein, a positive civil rights agenda for the Congress should focus on four spheres of public activity: (1) stiffer enforcement of existing laws proscribing discrimination against individuals; (2) broader advertising and outreach efforts to ensure minority access to government employment and contracting opportunities; (3) encouraging efforts to improve the early education and disadvantaged individuals to ensure their preparedness to meet uniformly high standards for higher education, employment and contracting; and (4) encouraging industry and entrepreneurship within minority communities by reducing tax and regulatory burdens that retard economic development and hinder efforts at self-sufficiency.

With that agenda, Congress can rightly acknowledge that discrimination remains an obstacle to advancement in our society. However, it can also begin to forge a consensus in this country that the problems of our society are complex and are often more fundamental than preference policies admit. Only by encouraging individuals to empower themselves to improve their lives will we begin to see the kind of economic and civic progress we all agree is necessary to a strong and moral American future.

GENESIS OF PREFERENCES

The Federal Government's experiment with race and gender preferences began some thirty years ago with President Johnson's execution of Executive Order 11246, which requires private firms working on Federal projects to "take affirmative action to ensure that applicants are employed . . . without regard to their race, creed, color or national origin." In his Howard University address, Johnson stated clearly that the order was intended to achieve, "not just legal equity but human ability, not just equality as a right and a theory but equality as a fact and *equality as a result.*" (Emphasis added.) Therein lies the essential flaw of preference policies. They are designed in pursuit of the illusory goal of achieving equal results in the marketplace. But human talent and inclination have never been distributed in proportion to group representation in society. As Justice Thomas said in his important concurring opinion in this week's *Adarand Constructors v. Pena* decision, "[g]overnment cannot make us equal; it can only recognize, respect, and protect us as equal before the law."

Contrary to that notion, the Nixon Administration, with its implementation of the Philadelphia [contract set-aside] Plan, sought to impose equality of result in the procurement of Federal contracts. Under that Plan, the element of intent was essentially removed from the notion of illegal discrimination in contracting, just as the U.S. Supreme Court in *Griggs v. Duke Power Co.,* 401 U.S. 424 (1971), had removed it in the employment context. *Griggs* had held invalid employment practices, however neutral in intent, that caused a disparate impact upon a group protected under the Civil Rights Act of 1964.

From then on, discrimination would be discerned by racial imbalances in the workplace. The Office of Federal Contract Compliance Programs (OFCCP) then began requiring contractors to take "affirmative action" to achieve proportional representation of underrepresented groups in their subcontracts and workforces; and the Equal Employment Opportunity Commission began using demographic disparities in the workplace to discern discrimination in employment.

However, presuming "underrepresentation" to be the consequence of discrimination is wrong in two respects. First, the presumption ignores the fact that the talents and inclinations of individuals are not proportionately distributed. That 60 percent of dry cleaning establishments in New York City are owned by Korean-Americans does not suggest discrimination in the market-place. It rather underscores the talents, industry and inclinations of a great many Korean immigrants.

Second, the presumption of discrimination where representation is dispro-portionate leads policymakers and judges to impose group remedies like set-asides and "goals" that are often tantamount to quotas. The objective is to achieve proportional representation, even if that necessitates modifying the standard of competition for preferred groups in order to include "enough" members of a given group in the overall pool. That determination to define down deficiencies in performance by establishing separate standards in order to demonstrate "good faith" in pursuit of affirmative action "goals" ignores the hard work of confronting real deficiencies of academic and economic pre-paredness in some segments of minority communities — particularly the African-American community.

Indeed, Alfred Blumrosen, the first enforcement chief of the Equal Employ-ment Opportunity Commission, was unusually candid in conceding the expe-dient motive of presuming discrimination from "underrepresentation." In his book, *Black Employment and the Law,* Blumrosen wrote:

> If discrimination is narrowly defined, for example, by requiring an evil intent to injure minorities, then it will be difficult to find that it exists. If it does not exist, then the plight of racial and ethnic minorities must be at-tributable to some more generalized failures in society, in the fields of basic education, housing, family relations, and the like. *The search for efforts to improve the condition of minorities must then focus in these general and difficult areas, and the answers can come only gradually as basic institutions, attitudes, customs, and practices are changed.* We thus would have before us generations of time before the effects of sub-jugation of minorities are dissipated. (Emphasis added.)

In other words, holding blacks to the same objective standards as others would, in the short run, yield a disproportionately low representation in the marketplace. However, dealing with the "more generalized failures in society" that contribute to the underrepresentation would require too much time and social energy. Therefore, the government should endeavor to circumvent "the more generalized failures" by in effect requiring rough proportionality of rep-resentation in employment by whatever means practicable. Needless to say, rough proportionality could only be achieved through artificial, preferential means. Means that tragically abdicate any responsibility to confront the "more generalized failures" contributing to low performance.

Moreover, enforced proportionality necessarily discriminates against groups whose success exceeds their proportion of the population. For example, earlier in this century, Ivy League universities sought to impose quotas on the number of Jews permitted to enroll in order to maintain rough proportionality of repre-sentation. I trust we all agree on the immorality of that policy. Under the present affirmative action regime, however, the University of California was confronted some years ago by the Department of Education for discriminating against Asian-American students in admissions. And this year a group of Chinese-American parents is suing the San Francisco public school district, claiming that an affirmative action program at the premier magnet high school in town requires Chinese students to score much higher on an admissions test than students of any other ethnic group. In fact, each ethnic group applying to the school effectively has a separate score that its members must achieve to be admitted to the high school. This to maintain ethnic proportionality and to prevent Asian-American students from achieving too much success in the admissions process.

Enforced proportionality also has the frequent affect of mismatching talent and capital with the wrong opportunities. Much is often said about the cosmetic victory of achieving "diversity" at the front end of the hiring and admissions process. However, a glimpse at the back end often belies any claim of "victory." The University of California boasts about the diversity of its entering classes with nary a word about the fact that over 40 percent of its black students fail to graduate, as opposed to about 10 to 15 percent of whites and Asians. Indeed, statistics suggest that up to 70 percent of black college students at some universities fail to graduate.[2] While the statistics are tragic, the unwillingness to confront the reasons for them is shameful. By admitting black students with lower objective indicators than other students, universities concerned about their diversity numbers are placing some students in an environment where success is unlikely. Most individuals would be better off in settings more commensurate with their objective indicators.

The same is true of capital in the commercial context. By encouraging, through the use of set-asides and other preferences, poorly capitalized firms to enter markets in which they could not otherwise effectively compete, the government is imposing an inefficiency on the market. The same businessperson who is poorly capitalized for government contracting, may in fact be adequately capitalized in another segment of the economy. By directing that capital away from its most efficient use in the marketplace to a market where minorities are "underrepresented," we often in the long-run deprive that businessperson of the most efficient utilization of his or her economic potential.

THEORIES OF PREFERENCE

Despite their significant social and economic cost, race and gender preferences in America are today justified essentially on two grounds: (1) the remediation of disadvantage caused by past discrimination; and (2) the desire to promote diversity.

Remediation of Disadvantage

Remediation of disadvantage was in fact the original moral claim of the proponents of affirmative action. President Johnson's "hobbled runner" metaphor was an expression of that claim. However, that justification today contains insuperable laws. First, preferential policies today tend to benefit the least disadvantaged among and within preferred groups. Middle class white women are now the primary beneficiaries of preferences, largely due to their relatively high level of education and cultural advantage. And even within ethnic minority groups it is the middle class that is best positioned to profit from preference. Despite their well-intended genesis, preferential policies have evolved into a classic middle-class entitlement, almost wholly divorced from any manifest disadvantage of their beneficiaries.

Many defenders of preference maintain that an individualized showing of disadvantage is irrelevant; that the mainstream economy, "the system," is rigged hopelessly in favor of white men. However, the economic and educational success of many non-white immigrants today, as well as the black community's once proud history of overcoming the worst obstacles, militates against the argument that members of preferred groups can only succeed with the tug of government preferment. For example, the ethnic group with the highest rate of entrepreneurship in America today is Korean-Americans (28 percent of Korean-American men own their own business; 20 percent of Korean-American women do).[3] Forty percent of students at the University of California are Asian-American, a number representing the largest single ethnic group at the university, and one far exceeding the Asian-American population of California.[4]

Of course, this is not to suggest that discrimination no longer presents an obstacle to advancement for many minority individuals. It does. Rather, I mean only to rebut the notion that the playing field is hopelessly dominated by white men.[5] To be sure, white men continue to represent a disproportionate share of decision and policy makers in society; however, Asian-Americans, for example, are poised to begin a rapid assent up the ladder of economic and social status. That success is attributable not to preferential policies, but to a cultural emphasis on strong families, education, diligence and thrift.[6]

Diversity

The second justification for preferential policies is the notion of diversity. By diversifying the ranks of our employees, the theory goes, we will breed transracial familiarity and, consequently, harmoniously dynamic workplaces. Moreover, by bringing diverse faces into the shop, we can mitigate against the ostensibly natural tendency to hire and promote people who look like ourselves.

The anecdotal evidence suggests that both of these theories have been woefully inaccurate. Race relations in contexts where preference is writ large — college campuses and municipal employment, for example — have often become toxic as a result of increasing racial antagonism. Litigation over racial preferments in the workplace is escalating, suggesting that personal resentment caused by the policies is growing as well. Colleges, too, are experiencing growing self-segregation among students, rather than an increasing unity.

In the workplace, what Shelby Steele has called the "stab of racial doubt" has infected both preferred and non-preferred groups in such a manner as to impact minority advancement on the job.[7] Having hired members of protected groups based often on a separate, perhaps lower, standard than non-protected employees, it stands to reason that an employer may be marginally more hesitant to advance protected employees. This stigma attaching to minorities — one which presumes their lesser qualification — is often unfair. But it is not wholly unreasonable in a system that demands that minorities compete under a different — often lower — standard than nonminorities. The clear implication of these policies is that minorities simply cannot compete without "special" help from the government. Thus, the proverbial "glass ceiling" that is said to preclude protected minorities from reaching the professional pinnacle, may in part be a product of the multiple objective standards inherent in preferential policies. Preferential policies thus appear to exacerbate racial resentment and discrimination more effectively than they ameliorate them.

TOWARD A CONSTRUCTIVE CIVIL RIGHTS POLICY

The institutionalization of separate standards of performance for minorities who would otherwise fail to meet the prevailing standard in adequate numbers is what Shelby Steele has described as American society's attempt to buy racial absolution on the cheap. In contrast, the real work of helping disadvantaged people meet the highest standard of competition is not cheap in terms of either money or a community's sweat equity.

A truly constructive civil rights policy in America should focus on constructive efforts to confront the real underlying problems of performance in some of America's most distressed communities. Perhaps it is true that if preference policies are abandoned in education, hiring, and contracting, nonAsian minority representation in those spheres would be diminished. But the appropriate response to the diminution should not be to blindly fault discrimination and then to erect group remedies in the form of enforced proportionality and set-asides, in an illusory effort to confront an extraneous enemy. Rather, the diminished representation of some minorities absent preferential policies suggests a much deeper problem of individual performance. A truly affirmative civil rights policy must concern itself with the hard work of improving the performance of disadvantaged individuals.

A 1981 study prepared for this committee suggested that the costs to the Fortune 500 of complying with OFCCP regulations was about $1 billion. A *Forbes* magazine study estimated that cost in 1993 to be nearly $3 billion.[8] That figure suggests a tragic opportunity cost. The energy and resources expended on implementing preference policies would be much better spent on an earnest effort to improve the early education of truly disadvantaged individuals by supporting families and community institutions like churches and schools; by injecting an element of competition into our failing urban school systems; and, most importantly, by setting the same high standards for kids of all races and genders.

Of course, Congress must still acknowledge the regrettable fact that discrimination persists in America. To that end, reform existing civil rights laws to restore the element of intent to illegal discrimination. That done, Congress can then proceed to significantly strengthen the penalties for discrimination. The deterrent impact of making proven discrimination costly cannot be underestimated. Congress should also ensure that Federal contract and employment opportunities are advertised widely, through outreach programs directed at "underrepresented" communities.

Regulatory barriers to minority entrepreneurship should also be confronted by Congress. Regulations like the Davis-Bacon Act, OSHA [Occupational Safety and Health Administration], minimum wage laws and certain trade-licensing requirements often present insurmountable barriers to minority entrepreneurs, who are more likely than others to be undercapitalized. I urge this committee to hold hearings, similar to those held by a House Small Business subcommittee last week, which would examine the impact on minority entrepreneurship of a number of Federal and State regulations.

Such a constructive civil rights policy would do much to encourage us all to confront the very real problems that exist in many minority communities today. Preferential policies, on the other hand, despite all their good intentions, only divert precious energy and private resources from the fundamental problems facing us as Americans.

As the world marketplace moves into a new, competitive information age, we can ill-afford to say to some individuals that their skin color or chromosomes entitle them to opt-out of the highest standards of competition. We owe our children more than that. We owe America's future more than that.

CONCLUSION

The social cost of racial and gender preferences in America is today prohibitive. The ceaseless emphasis on group difference and victimhood which is demanded by the existing structure is corrosive of social relations in the workplace and the larger society. Moreover, the significant economic costs associated with maintaining the present system represent a tragic opportunity cost: by requiring an adaptation of standards to fit performance, rather than the converse, we simply allow problems of performance to fester and deteriorate. The Congress should remove itself from the burgeoning business of racial and gender preferences. Absent a truly constructive civil rights approach, one that encourages individual achievement of uniformly high standards, we allow the middle class in America to play the fiddle of preference while truly disadvantaged communities burn.

NOTES

1. See Thomas Sowell, *Compassion versus Guilt and Other Essays* (New York: William Morrow, 1987), p. 197.

2. See e.g., Thomas Sowell, *Preferential Policies: An International Perspective* (New York: William Morrow, 1991), pp. 107–112.

3. Heather MacDonald "Why Korean Americans Succeed," *City Journal*, Spring 1995, p. 14.

4. Peter Applebome, "Gains in Diversity Face Attack in California," *New York Times*, June 4, 1995, p. 1, col. 2.

5. Indeed, see John Sibley Butler, *Entrepreneurship and Self-Help Among Black Americans* (New York: SUNY Press, 1991), for a discussion of the significant economic development of black communities during the apex of the Jim Crow era, an era without preferential policies or government cooperation of virtually any kind. For example, between 1929 and 1932—despite Jim Crow and the Great Depression— black Americans owned some 26,000 retail establishments in America with total net sales in excess of $100 million (p. 148).

6. See generally MacDonald, "Why Korean Americans Succeed."

7. Shelby Steele, *The Content of Our Character* (New York: St. Martin's Press, 1990), p. 120.

8. Peter Brimelow and Leslie Spencer, "When Quotas Replace Merit, Everybody Suffers," *Forbes*, February 15, 1993, p. 80.

Questions for Discussion

---

1. What criteria should be used in deciding which groups should be included in a category warranting affirmative action?
2. Do guidelines inevitably lead to quotas? What are the reasons for your answer?
3. What criteria should be used by a university admissions committee of a prestigious college or university in selecting students for admission? What is the relevance of your answer to the issue of affirmative action?
4. What effect does affirmative action have on the beneficiaries of affirmative action programs?
5. How would you recognize when affirmative action programs should be ended?

Suggested Readings

"Affirmative Action: Pro & Con." *Congressional Digest* 75, nos. 6–7 (June/July 1996): entire issue.

Bergmann, Barbara R. *In Defense of Affirmative Action.* New York: New Republic/Basic Books, 1996.

Cole, David. "Hopwood v. State of Texas: The End of Affirmative Action?" *Legal Times* 18, no. 46 (April 1, 1996): 18, 20.

Eastland, Terry, *Ending Affirmative Action: The Case for Colorblind Justice.* New York: Basic Books, 1996.

Jost, Kenneth. "Rethinking Affirmative Action." *CQ Researcher* 5, no. 16 (April 28, 1995): 369–392.

Kahlenberg, Richard D. *The Remedy: Class, Race and Affirmative Action.* New York: New Republic/Basic Books, 1996.

Lemann, Nicholas. "Taking Affirmative Action Apart." *New York Times Magazine,* June 11, 1995, pp. 36–43, 52, 54, 66.

Loury, Glenn C. "Not-So Black and White: The Two Americas Are Actually Converging." *Washington Post,* October 15, 1995, p. C3.

Shipler, David K. "My Equal Opportunity, Your Free Lunch." *New York Times,* March 5, 1995, sec. IV, pp. 1, 16.

Sowell, Thomas. *Preferential Policies: An International Perspective.* New York: William Morrow, 1990.

Steele, Shelby. *The Content of Our Character: A New Vision of Race in America.* New York: St. Martin's Press, 1990.

Sullivan, Andrew. "Let Affirmative Action Die." *New York Times,* July 23, 1995, sec. IV, p. 15.

U.S. Cong., House of Representatives. *Hearings on Affirmative Action in Employment.* Hearings before the Subcommittee on Employer-Employee Relations of the Committee on Economic and Educational Opportunities, 104th Cong., 1st Sess., 1995.

———, Senate. *Affirmative Action and the Office of Federal Compliance.* Hearing before the Committee on Labor and Human Resources, 104th Cong., 1st Sess., 1995.

Wilson, James Q. "Sins of Admission." *New Republic* 215, no. 2 (July 8, 1996): 12, 14, 16.

Popular Participation

D| emocracies pride themselves on the freedom of people to participate in the political process. Such participation takes many forms, including forming private associations known as interest groups, getting involved in political campaigns, voting, working for political parties, and expressing ideas through speech or the mass media.

The traditional definition of an interest group is a collection of people with common interests who work together to achieve those interests. When a group becomes involved in the activities of government, it is known as a political interest group.

More than a century ago, Alexis de Tocqueville observed that the people of the United States have a propensity to form associations. This observation has become as valid a description of the 1990s as it was of the 1830s. The United States has a large number of political interest groups — business, labor, professional, religious, and social reform. At the same time, many citizens do not belong to organizations other than religious and social groups, which in some cases have no significant political role.

Interest groups engage in a variety of activities, including making financial contributions to candidates for public office and to political parties, getting their viewpoints known to the general public and to other groups, organizing demonstrations, and influencing government officials. Legitimate political behavior in a democracy allows for great freedom to participate in these ways. The First Amendment of the Constitution is often cited as the basis for such political behavior. That amendment states:

> Congress shall make no law respecting an establishment of religion, or prohibiting the free exercise thereof; or abridging the freedom of speech, or of the press; or the right of the people peaceably to assemble, and to petition the government for a redress of grievances.

One form of political activity is involvement in political campaigns and elections. In a democracy people are free to support candidates of their choice. Such support may consist of merely voting in an election, but it may also include organizing meetings, soliciting support for candidates, raising and spending money for candidates, and publicizing issues.

An effective democracy requires that information be widely disseminated. The same First Amendment that protects the rights of individuals and groups to engage in political activities also safeguards the press and other media such as television, radio, and magazines. Television, particularly, has become the chief source of news for many people.

What people do and what they think are of vital importance to government officials. In democracies (and even in many dictatorships) government makes every effort to know what public opinion is on many issues. Sometimes government leads and sometimes it follows public opinion.

Although modern dictatorships rely on political participation, that participation is generally controlled by the ruling elite. Interest groups are not spontaneous organizations designed to be independent from government but are linked to government primarily through government-controlled leadership. And so, for example, trade unions are not free to strike or engage in protest activities — at least not legitimately. People are not free to form competitive political parties, and often there is only one political party that dominates elections. That party is regarded as having a special role in mobilizing the masses.

In many modern dictatorships elections do take place, but they are generally rigged. Where opposing candidates are permitted to compete, there is generally no significant difference between the candidates on issues. Protest movements and mass demonstrations are broken up, sometimes ruthlessly, unless those movements are controlled by the government. To be sure, protest movements and demonstrations do exist in some modern dictatorships, but government tries to control or suppress them.

In modern dictatorships, moreover, the media are not free to report the news in an objective manner. Instead, the media reflect the wishes of the ruling dictators. News is suppressed; opposition newspapers are closed down. There is only one truth — that of the government — disseminated through television, radio, magazines, and newspapers.

Although democracies are fundamentally different from dictatorships, even democracies do not always live up to the standards of freedom they cherish. In this regard, the political behavior of nongovernmental organizations in the United States poses problems for those interested in protecting democratic processes. Although it is relatively easy to discuss democracy in the abstract, actual practices raise thorny questions. Part III considers five issues pertaining to popular participation in the democratic process in the United States: the use of the English language to strengthen national unity, the meaning of voting and elections, the fairness of campaign finance laws, the character of the electoral college system, and the bias of the media.

Chapter 8

Would the Adoption of English As the Official Language of the United States Strengthen National Unity?

The United States is a multiethnic society. Even before independence, immigrants who settled here spoke different languages, a matter of concern to some English-speaking Americans. In 1753, for example, Benjamin Franklin feared that so many people in the colony of Pennsylvania spoke German that the legislature would need interpreters. Later he complained that many Philadelphia street signs were written in German.

In the past as in the present, many non-English-speaking immigrants learned English. But many did not and were able to communicate in their native languages by living in ethnic communities. In the late nineteenth and early twentieth centuries, when immigration from Eastern and Southern Europe soared, many native-born Americans worried that these newcomers could not be assimilated into an American culture. In response, in 1906, Congress passed a law requiring an understanding of English for a person to become a naturalized American citizen. This requirement continues to this day.

Following adjustments in immigration law in 1965, a new wave of immigrants arrived, mostly from Latin America, the Caribbean, and Asia. Many could not speak English, and schools had difficulty teaching children who did not understand English. In 1968, Congress passed the Elementary and Secondary Education Act. Its Bilingual Education Amendments allocated $7.5 million for local demonstration bilingual projects to help Hispanic children gradually shift to classes in English. By the early 1990s, federal funds for bilingual programs reached $750 million annually. The program serves not only Hispanics but other immigrant groups as well.

In the 1970s, the Office of Civil Rights in the U.S. Department of Health, Education and Welfare issued guidelines requiring help for non-English-speaking children through participation in bilingual programs. And in 1974 the Supreme Court decided in *Lau v. Nichols* that school districts had to make certain that non-English-speaking children could participate in the U.S. educational system. The Court gave school districts flexibility in meeting the regulations of the Department of Health, Education and Welfare.[1]

Concerned about the status of English in America, S. I. Hayakawa, a U.S. senator from California, introduced a constitutional amendment that would make English the official language of the United States. An immigrant and a linguistics professor, in 1983 Hayakawa became a founder of U.S. English, an organization committed to making English the official language of the United States and encouraging the teaching of English in schools. By 1996, twenty-three states had made English their official language. The scope of the state laws varied from state to state. Arizona, for example, requires state employees to conduct business in English but does provide for exceptions in matters of criminal justice.

Supporters of making English the official language of the United States differ in some points, but most want English to be used by government agencies for conducting their work and to appear as the only language on electoral ballots. Some would end or greatly weaken the bilingual program in schools, which they see as promoting languages other than English. Unless immigrants understand English, according to proponents of English-language laws, they will miss economic opportunities that are available to English-speaking people in the United States.

A central idea of the movement to make English the official language is that the English language is a unifying element to American society. If people who live in the United States are not able to speak English, they may not be able to assimilate into American culture, and the United States could experience secessionist movements like those in Canada and Yugoslavia.

The English language movement has produced a reaction. In 1987, the English Plus Information Clearing House (EPIC) was formed to promote English *plus* mastery of a second or more languages. EPIC is a coalition of fifty-six groups established under the auspices of the National Immigration, Refugee and Citizenship Forum and Joint Committee for Languages. In general, opponents of English language laws feel that the purpose of the laws is to deny immigrants their rights and even their democratic representation. They argue that most immigrants want to and will learn English, in are enthusiastic about the United States, and seek to become assimilated over time.

What the adoption of English as the official language would mean would depend on the wording of the legislation and court interpretations. Two proposals are for "Official English" or "English Only." Official English would require that English be used for official government functions as determined by law. For example, legislative meetings would be conducted in English, but the legislature could decide to translate deliberations into other languages. Some advocates of English Only favor more restrictive policies, such as requiring people in the United States to speak English in public places.

In the selection below, S. I. Hayakawa makes a case for English as the official U.S. language. He argues:

1. English unites us as Americans — immigrants and native-born alike — encouraging trust while reducing racial hostility and bigotry, allowing us to discuss our views and maintain a well-informed electorate, the cornerstone of democratic government.

2. For the United States to move in the direction of multilingualism would fracture national unity, as the experience of countries with multilingualism shows.
3. Bilingualism is also a costly and confusing bureaucratic nightmare.
4. While employing a child's native language to teach him or her English is entirely appropriate, many bilingual programs fail to teach English efficiently and perpetrate dependency on the native language.
5. Students in bilingual programs should move into mainstream, English-language classes as quickly as possible.
6. The use of English ballots does not deprive citizens of their right to vote, while a policy of providing bilingual voting ballots erodes government support for a common language and is racially biased by including some languages while excluding others.
7. Making English the official language by law sends a signal to newcomers about the importance of learning English.

James C. Stalker makes several points in opposition to English language laws:

1. It is legitimate for all Americans to maintain some part of their native heritage. Cultural diversity is one of the factors that separates the United States from other countries. It enables the nation to maintain an open society in the face of political, economic, and social strains that prevent other countries from realizing their full potential.
2. Passing a law declaring English as the official language is unlikely to have a bearing on the effectiveness of bilingual programs. Outlawing bilingual programs is even less likely to improve the English of the children and adults now in those programs.
3. We can deal with communication problems stemming from multilingualism more objectively than we can deal with problems of cultural and political difference.
4. The historical experience of immigrant groups, especially the Germans, suggests that English probably is not threatened by immigrants speaking languages other than English. Today most Spanish-speaking immigrants learn and speak English.
5. Immigrants learn English because it has utility to them. But if a group of people wish to speak a language other than English, there is little that we can do about it legally or otherwise and still maintain that we are a free country.
6. For the United States to continue to be an important economic and political power in the world, Americans of whatever variety will need two languages — their first language and English, or

English and a second language. Knowing a second language increases our abilities to use our first language.
7. Multilingualism is potentially dangerous only if it promotes cultural divisiveness; otherwise it is a benefit of great economic and political value.

NOTE

1. *Lau V. Nichols*, 94 S. Ct. 786 (1974).

☑ *YES*

Would the Adoption of English As the Official Language of the United States Strengthen National Unity?

S. I. HAYAKAWA

Bilingualism in America: English Should Be the Only *Language*

During the dark days of World War II, Chinese immigrants in California wore badges proclaiming their original nationality so they would not be mistaken for Japanese. In fact, these two immigrant groups long had been at odds with each other. However, as new English-speaking generations came along, the Chinese and Japanese began to communicate with one another. They found they had much in common and began to socialize. Today, they get together and form Asian-American societies.

Such are the amicable results of sharing the English language. English unites us as Americans — immigrants and native-born alike. Communicating with each other in a single, common tongue encourages trust, while reducing racial hostility and bigotry.

My appreciation of English has led me to devote my retirement years to championing it. Several years ago, I helped to establish U.S. English, a Washington, D.C.-based public interest group that seeks an amendment to the U.S. Constitution declaring English our official language, regardless of what other languages we may use unofficially.

As an immigrant to this nation, I am keenly aware of the things that bind us as Americans and unite us as a single people. Foremost among these unifying forces is the common language we share. While it is certainly true that our love of freedom and devotion to democratic principles help to unite and give us a mutual purpose, it is English, our common language, that enables us to discuss our views and allows us to maintain a well-informed electorate, the cornerstone of democratic government.

Because we are a nation of immigrants, we do not share the characteristics of race, religion, ethnicity, or native language which form the common bonds of society in other countries. However, by agreeing to learn and use a single, universally spoken language, we have been able to forge a unified people from an incredibly diverse population.

Although our 200-year history should be enough to convince any skeptic of the powerful unifying effects of a common language, some still advocate the official recognition of other languages. They argue that a knowledge of English is not part of the formula for responsible citizenship in this country.

Some contemporary political leaders, like the former mayor of Miami, Maurice Ferre, maintain that "Language is not necessary to the system. Nowhere does our Constitution say that English is our language." He also told the *Tampa Tribune* that, "Within ten years there will not be a single word of English spoken [in Miami] — English is not Miami's official language — [and] one day residents will have to learn Spanish or leave."

The U.S. Department of Education also reported that countless speakers at a conference on bilingual education "expounded at length on the need for and eventuality of, a multilingual, multicultural United States of America with a national language policy citing English and Spanish as the two 'legal languages.'"

As a former resident of California, I am completely familiar with a system that uses two official languages, and I would not advise any nation to move in such a direction unless forced to do so. While it is true that India functions with 10 official languages, I haven't heard anyone suggest that it functions particularly well because of its multilingualism. In fact, most Indians will concede that the situation is a chaotic mess which has led to countless problems in the government's efforts to manage the nation's business. Out of necessity, English still is used extensively in India as a common language.

Belgium is another clear example of the diverse effects of two officially recognized languages in the same nation. Linguistic differences between Dutch- and French-speaking citizens have resulted in chronic political instability. Consequently, in the aftermath of the most recent government collapse, legislators are working on a plan to turn over most of its powers and responsibilities to the various regions, a clear recognition of the diverse effects of linguistic separateness.

There are other problems. Bilingualism is a costly and confusing bureaucratic nightmare. The Canadian government has estimated its bilingual costs to be nearly $400,000,000 per year. It is almost certain that these expenses will increase as a result of a massive expansion of bilingual services approved by the Canadian Parliament in 1988. In the U.S., which has 10 times the population of Canada, the cost of similar bilingual services easily would be in the billions.

We first should consider how politically infeasible it is that our nation ever could recognize Spanish as a second official language without opening the floodgates for official recognition of the more than 100 languages spoken in this country. How long would it take under such an arrangement, before the U.S. started to make India look like a model of efficiency?

Even if we can agree that multilingualism would be a mistake, some would suggest that official recognition of English is not needed. After all, our nation has existed for over 200 years without this, and English as our common language has continued to flourish.

I could agree with this sentiment had government continued to adhere to its time-honored practice of operating in English and encouraging newcomers to learn the language. However, this is not the case. Over the last few decades, government has been edging slowly towards policies that place other languages on a par with English.

In reaction to the cultural consciousness movement of the 1960s and 1970s, government has been increasingly reluctant to press immigrants to learn the English language, lest it be accused of "cultural imperialism." Rather than insisting that it is the immigrant's duty to learn the language of this country, the government has acted instead as if it has a duty to accommodate an immigrant in his native language.

A prime example of this can be found in the continuing debate over Federal and state policies relating to bilingual education. At times, these have come dangerously close to making the main goal of this program the maintenance of the immigrant child's native language, rather than the early acquisition of English.

As a former U.S. senator from California, where we spend more on bilingual education programs than any other state, I am very familiar with both the rhetoric and reality that lie behind the current debate on bilingual education. My experience has convinced me that many of these programs are short-changing immigrant children in their quest to learn English.

To set the record straight from the start, I do not oppose bilingual education *if it is truly bilingual.* Employing a child's native language to teach him (or her) English is entirely appropriate. What is not appropriate is continuing to use the children of Hispanic and other immigrant groups as guinea pigs in an unproven program that fails to teach English efficiently and perpetuates their dependency on their native language.

Under the dominant method of bilingual education used throughout this country, non-English-speaking students are taught all academic subjects such as math, science, and history exclusively in their native language. English is taught as a separate subject. The problem with this method is that there is no objective way to measure whether a child has learned enough English to be placed in classes where academic instruction is entirely in English. As a result, some children have been kept in native language classes for six years.

Some bilingual education advocates, who are more concerned with maintaining the child's use of their native language, may not see any problem with such a situation. However, those who feel that the most important goal of this program is to get children functioning quickly in English appropriately are alarmed.

In the Newhall School District in California, some Hispanic parents are rais-ing their voices in criticism of its bilingual education program, which relies on native language instruction. Their children complain of systematically being segregated from their English-speaking peers. Now in high school, these stu-dents cite the failure of the program to teach them English first as the reason for being years behind their classmates.

Even more alarming is the Berkeley (Calif.) Unified School District, where educators have recognized that all-native-language instruction would be an inadequate response to the needs of their non-English-speaking pupils. Chal-lenged by a student body that spoke more than four different languages and by budgetary constraints, teachers and administrators responded with innova-tive language programs that utilized many methods of teaching English. That school district is now in court answering charges that the education it pro-vided was inadequate because it did not provide transitional bilingual educa-tion for every non-English speaker. What was introduced 20 years ago as an experimental project has become — despite inconclusive research evidence — the only acceptable method of teaching for bilingual education advocates.

When one considers the nearly 50 percent dropout rate among Hispanic students (the largest group receiving this type of instruction), one wonders about their ability to function in the English-speaking mainstream of this coun-try. The school system may have succeeded wonderfully in maintaining their native language, but if it failed to help them to master the English language fully, what is the benefit?

ALTERNATIVES

If this method of bilingual education is not the answer, are we forced to return to the old, discredited, sink-or-swim approach? No, we are not; since, as shown in Berkeley and other school districts, there are a number of alternative methods that have been proven effective, while avoiding the problems of all-native-language instruction.

Sheltered English and English as a Second Language (ESL) are just two pro-grams that have helped to get children quickly proficient in English. Yet, polit-ical recognition of the viability of alternate methods has been slow in coming. In 1988, we witnessed the first crack in the monolithic hold that native-language instruction has had on bilingual education funds at the Federal level. In its reauthorization of Federal bilingual education, Congress voted to in-crease the percentage of funds available for alternate methods from 4 to 25 percent of the total. This is a great break-through, but we should not be satis-fied until 100 percent of the funds are available for any program that effec-tively and quickly can get children functioning in English, regardless of the amount of native-language instruction it uses.

My goal as a student of language and a former educator is to see all students succeed academically, no matter what language is spoken in their homes. I want to see immigrant students finish their high school education and be able to compete for college scholarships. To help achieve this goal, instruction in English should start as early as possible. Students should be moved into English mainstream classes in one or, at the very most, two years. They should not continue to be segregated year after year from their English-speaking peers.

Another highly visible shift in Federal policy that I feel demonstrates quite clearly the eroding support of government for our common language is the requirement for bilingual voting ballots. Little evidence ever has been presented to show the need for ballots in other languages. Even prominent Hispanic organizations acknowledge that more than 90 percent of native-born Hispanics currently are fluent in English and more than half of that population is English monolingual.

Furthermore, if the proponents of bilingual ballots are correct when they claim that the absence of native-language ballots prevents non-English-speaking citizens from exercising their right to vote, then current requirements are clearly unfair because they provide assistance to certain groups of voters while ignoring others. Under current Federal law, native language ballots are required only for certain groups: those speaking Spanish, Asian, or Native American languages. European or African immigrants are not provided ballots in their native language, even in jurisdictions covered by the Voting Rights Act.

As sensitive as Americans have been to racism, especially since the days of the Civil Rights Movement, no one seems to have noticed the profound racism expressed in the amendment that created the "bilingual ballot." Brown people, like Mexicans and Puerto Ricans; red people, like American Indians; and yellow people, like the Japanese and Chinese are assumed not to be smart enough to learn English. No provision is made, however, for non-English-speaking French-Canadians in Maine or Vermont, or Yiddish-speaking Hasidic Jews in Brooklyn, who are white and thus presumed to be able to learn English without difficulty.

Voters in San Francisco encountered ballots in Spanish and Chinese for the first time in the elections of 1980, much to their surprise, since authorizing legislation had been passed by Congress with almost no debate, roll-call vote, or public discussion. Naturalized Americans, who had taken the trouble to learn English to become citizens, were especially angry and remain so. While native-language ballots may be a convenience to some voters, the use of English ballots does not deprive citizens of their right to vote. Under current voting law, non-English-speaking voters are permitted to bring a friend or family member to the polls to assist them in casting their ballots. Absentee ballots could provide another method that would allow a voter to receive this help at home.

Congress should be looking for other methods to create greater access to the ballot box for the currently small number of citizens who cannot understand an English ballot, without resorting to the expense of requiring ballots in foreign languages. We cannot continue to overlook the message we are sending to immigrants about the connection between English language ability and citizenship when we print ballots in other languages. The ballot is the primary symbol of civic duty. When we tell immigrants that they should learn English — yet offer them full voting participation in their native language — I fear our actions will speak louder than our words.

If we are to prevent the expansion of policies such as these, moving us further along the multilingual path, we need to make a strong statement that our political leaders will understand. We must let them know that we do not choose to reside in a "Tower of Babel." Making English our nation's official language *by law* will send the proper signal to newcomers about the importance of learning English and provide the necessary guidance to legislators to preserve our traditional policy of a common language.

Would the Adoption of English As the Official Language of the United States Strengthen National Unity?

JAMES C. STALKER
Official English or English Only

Whether English should be the official language of the United States is a debater's dream — there are no absolutely right or wrong answers. We can prove pretty conclusively that a nuclear bomb will kill people; it is somewhat harder to prove that making English our legally official language will harm anyone or to prove the opposite, that pursuing a policy of multilingualism will aid anyone. However, we can get a clearer view of the topic by avoiding the flaming rhetoric and the smoke generated from the flames and exploring the question to see what issues are involved.

"Official English" and "English Only" are apparently synonymous terms. However, the two phrases are not the same. To call for an "official" English is to call for a law specifying that English is the language which is to be used for official government functions, functions which would, of course, need to be specified in the law. Presumably, if English were declared the legally official language of the federal government, it would then be required that all federal documents would be printed in English, that federal legislative sessions would be conducted in English, perhaps even that government officials would be required to be fluent speakers and writers of English. But legislation that specifies that English be the official language of the United States need not require that English be the only language in which the government conducts its business or communicates with the public it serves. It is quite conceivable that legislation requiring that English be the official language should also require that important legislation or legislative debates be translated into the major languages in use in the United States.

Legislation requiring that English should be the *only* language used in the United States is clearly much more restrictive, and although it could have those consequences touched on in the previous paragraph, other possible consequences might arise as well, consequences not so clearly obvious. It is possible that English-only legislation could be used to prohibit children from speaking a language other than English in public places, such as public school playgrounds. It could mean that languages other than English could not be spoken in any public places — the street, public offices. It could mean that we must designate certain areas in which languages other than English could be used, much as we now do for cigarette smokers in some states. Such consequences may seem facetious, but they are not. Laws require or prohibit certain specified actions. A law declaring English as the only legal language must inevitably be tested in court to determine the contexts and situations in which the law operates. In California, the recently approved official-English constitutional amendment prohibits printing ballots in any language other than English; that is a specified part of the law as passed. The group that supported the amendment most vigorously, U.S. English, has also sought the prohibition of advertisements in any language other than English, including those in the Yellow Pages, a quite legal attempt to test how far the law can be extended.[1] In how many and what kinds of situations can the use of a language other than English be prohibited? English as an official language does not necessarily prohibit the use of any other language, although it opens the door for such a prohibition. English as the only legal language opens the prohibitive doors immediately and obviously, and in many cases the call for an official status for English is a thinly disguised call for English as the only legal language.

CLARIFICATION OF THE ISSUES

Before we consider further the practical consequences of our two possibilities — official English and English only, we need to consider the underlying concerns which have brought this question to the level of importance that it now has, and we need to separate the nonlinguistic, political issues from the linguistic ones. One of the primary expressed reasons for the call for an official English centers on bilingual programs and on Hispanic and Asian immigrants. The most common statement is that the Hispanic and Asian populations prefer not to assimilate into mainstream American culture, that they do not want to learn English or adopt traditional, mainstream cultural norms, and that bilingual programs support their desire for separateness by enabling them to maintain their native language under the guise of learning English. The emotional reactions to such a position by many people who regard themselves as "traditional, mainstream" Americans is all too predictable. Those immigrants who are different and wish to remain different should go back where they came from, go back to the culture which they hold as more valuable and dear to them than "our" culture. They should go back where they are comfortable and everyone speaks their language.

There are really three issues here: (1) the legitimacy of cultural maintenance, (2) the intention and effectiveness of bilingual programs, and (3) simple communication. For the first of these issues, we can say the obvious: that we are all culturally different in some way or another; that each of us very probably values and wishes to maintain or obtain some part of our native heritage, whatever it is; that we are all immigrants, except for Amerindians; and that we expect others to be tolerant and accepting of our Scots, Polish, Russian, or African heritage. (During periods of high immigration, claims that assimilation is not happening seem to be more prevalent.[2] We must also remember that as a nation, we at least give lip service to the notion that our cultural diversity is one of the factors which separates the United States from many other countries in the world, one of the factors that has enabled the U.S. to maintain an open society in the face of political, economic, and social strains which prevent other countries from realizing their full potential. We have been coping with political and cultural diversity since before the Revolution and engaging in cultural maintenance for at least that long.

The second issue, that of the intention and effectiveness of bilingual programs, should be handled as a separate problem. If bilingual programs are ineffective in teaching children English, then something should be done about the programs themselves. Passing a law directed at the official status of English is relatively unlikely to make the bilingual programs better. Outlawing the programs through an English-only law is even less likely to improve the English of the children and adults now in those programs.

The focus on bilingual programs is in part prompted by an often unarticulated fear that we will become a nation which will need interpreters in the legislature. It is a concern over communication, a concern that we might be able to deal with somewhat more objectively than the problem of cultural and political difference.

HISTORICAL BACKGROUND

Language diversity was already an issue before the Revolution. As early as 1753, in a letter to a friend, Benjamin Franklin expressed the fear that German would be so prevalent in Pennsylvania that the legislature would need interpreters. He noted that a good many of the street signs in Philadelphia were in German, without an English translation.[3] By 1745 there were approximately 45,000 German speakers in the colonies, and by 1790 there were some 200,000, nine percent of the population.[4] Enough of them settled in Pennsylvania to cause Franklin to envisage the possibility of that colony's becoming a

German-speaking region. In 1795, the Germans of Virginia (not Pennsylvania) petitioned Congress to print laws in German for those immigrants in Virginia who had not yet learned English. The subcommittee turned in a favorable report on the petition, but it was tabled. A later request that same year also received a favorable review in committee but was defeated on the floor of Congress by a vote of 42 to 41.[5]

Even with such a rebuff, the German speakers did not go away or learn English. Rather, their numbers increased: 1.5 million arrived between 1830 and 1860, and another 1.5 million arrived during the decade of the 1880s. In 1990, the German immigrants and their children numbered approximately 8 million compared to the 2.5 million English immigrants and their children.[6] These latter arrivals were no more eager to abandon their native language than were their cultural ancestors. As a consequence, there were German bilingual schools in Pennsylvania during the latter half of the nineteenth century; German newspapers were common in New York and Pennsylvania, down the Ohio River valley, into Missouri and Texas.

We can get some retrospective idea of how substantial the influence of the German immigrants would have been throughout nineteenth- and early twentieth-century America, linguistically and culturally, by consulting the 1980 census, in which the number of people who reported themselves as being of German heritage was only slightly less than the number reporting themselves as being of English heritage — 49.6 million English to 49.2 million German. Scottish and Irish heritage people add another 50.2 million, but many of those immigrants did not think of themselves as English, nor did they speak the same dialect.[7]

Other language groups desired to maintain their native languages when they came to the United States, and a look into our history turns up some interesting results of that desire. The Louisiana constitution allowed the publication of laws in French, and they were so published until about seventy years ago. California (1849) and Texas allowed the publication of laws in Spanish, and New Mexico still maintained Spanish and English as official languages of the state until 1941. In 1842 Texas required the publication of its laws in German as well as Spanish and English and added Norwegian in 1858.[8] After the Civil War, several states required the use of English as the language of instruction in the public schools, but several allowed the use of other languages in one way or another. In Louisiana, French could be used in those parishes where the French language was spoken. Hawaii allowed the use of other languages by petition. Minnesota required books in English, but explanations could be in other languages.[9] What all of this tells us is that we have never been absolutely certain that we need to or should require that everyone speak and read and write English. On the other hand, there has been a rather constant pressure to maintain a common language, and that language has been English. German had the strongest chance to displace English; in fact, it had nearly two hundred years to do so, but it did not succeed. The conclusion that we can draw is that English is probably not seriously threatened. It has maintained its position as the common language and likely will continue to do so.

THE STATUS OF SPANISH: PRESENT AND FUTURE

The assumption that Spanish will succeed in displacing English where German did not is probably unfounded, but we must recognize that the possibility exists. However, certain conditions must prevail for that eventuality to take place. The Spanish speakers must not only want to maintain Spanish, but they must also refuse to learn any English at all. Even in those sections of the country in which there are large Spanish-speaking populations, it does not seem to be economically possible for all Spanish immigrants to remain monolingual. In fact, the evidence points to the opposite conclusion. Results from a 1976 study indicate that of 2.5 million people who spoke Spanish as their native language, 1.6 million adopted English as their principal language.[10] Fifty percent of the population switched from Spanish to English as their principal language. In order to offset this large loss of native speakers, Veltman calculates that Spanish-speaking women would need to produce 4.5 children each, but the average Chicano woman has only 2.9 children. A 1985 Rand Corporation study found that "more than 95 percent of first-generation Mexican-Americans born in the United States are proficient in English and that more than half the second generation speaks no Spanish at all."[11] Another study found that 98 percent of Hispanic parents in Miami felt it essential that their children read and write English perfectly.[12] In other words, Spanish speakers in the United States show a strong tendency to become English speakers, and as a result we are unlikely to become a Spanish-speaking country.

The loss of native speakers might be offset by the immigration of new Spanish speakers, but the evidence is that 50 percent of Spanish speakers who immigrate to the U.S. already speak some English.[13] They obviously are not Spanish-only speakers and can be reasonably expected to learn more English. It is simply maladaptive and dysfunctional not to do so. If the only way to prevent the maintenance of Spanish among a particular part of the population is to control immigration, then we must take the bull by his horns rather than his tail. We must control immigration through restrictive immigration laws rather than by trying to control immigration through a constitutional amendment mandating English as the official language. Would such an amendment then enable us to control immigration by preventing anyone who does not speak English from migrating to the U.S.? That would be a very interesting law indeed.

To be complete, we need to consider the possibility that the statistics I have given are inaccurate — that Spanish speakers are not learning English at any great rate, that Spanish speakers will pour into the country in such large numbers that their number will equal or exceed the number of speakers of English, and that as a consequence, we will become a country with two major languages. If that should happen, the U.S. could also become a country socially, politically, and linguistically divided, like Canada or Sri Lanka or any of several African countries. Countries which are composed of two largely monolingual groups do seem to have more tensions that tend to pull the nation apart rather than aid it in retaining unity. It is not generally politically wise for a nation to possess two major, equally important languages, especially when each group attaches great emotional value to its own language and culture and becomes xenophobic about the other language and culture. Will passing a law declaring English as the official language prevent the rise of a second major language? Only if we also pass a set of restrictive laws, among them a law which limits immigration to those people who already speak English, and a law which prohibits the use of any language other than English.

LEGISLATION: EFFECTS AND ALTERNATIVES

We have to question the effectiveness of these two additional laws. Limiting immigration might indeed work, if we are willing to build an eight-foot concrete wall along the Mexican-American border and convert a significant portion of our defense budget (or perhaps that portion of our education budgets now devoted to bilingual education) to patrolling our Southern borders. We have not been very effective in enforcing the immigration restrictions that we already have, and a new, more restrictive law is unlikely to accomplish any more than the current laws do.

The money for massive enforcement of current or new immigration restrictions is unlikely to materialize, so let's consider the ramifications of the other major possibility, prohibition of the use of any language other than English. If any language group, Spanish or other, chooses to maintain its language, there is precious little that we can do about it, legally or otherwise, and still maintain that we are a free country. We cannot legislate the language of the home, the street, the bar, the club, unless we are willing to violate the privacy of our people, unless we are willing to set up a cadre of language police who will ticket and arrest us if we speak something other than English. What we can do is disenfranchise all of those who have not yet learned or cannot learn English. We can exclude them from the possibility of taking part in our political system and from our schools, and because they will be uneducated, we can prevent them from benefiting from the economic system. We can insure a new oppressed minority. If that minority becomes a majority, through immigration (legal or illegal) and through birth, we will live with the consequences of our actions.

I dwelt on the German immigration into our country in the eighteenth and nineteenth centuries because that group very deliberately maintained its language and culture. Thus, those parts of the Spanish and Asian populations which are reluctant to abandon their culture and language because they had to abandon their countries for political and economic reasons are not unique to the United States. This is not a new problem. The Germans, for the most part, have eventually become users of English, not because of repressive linguistic policies or legislation, but for that most effective reason of all — utility. People learn a new language or dialect if they see that that language or dialect has high potential value for them, not because they are legally required to. The very fact that our current evidence says that more Spanish speakers are learning English than are retaining their own language is a pretty good indication that a good many of them believe English to be more useful and therefore more valuable than Spanish. English enables them to gain more than they have, to partake in the political and economic life of the United States more fully than Spanish (or Vietnamese or Chinese) does.

Our need is not to insure that everyone in the United States be a monolingual speaker of English but rather to insure that our country continues to hold its own politically and economically in the world at large. To accomplish this task, all Americans must be less provincial and less linguistically ethnocentric. English is now the predominant world language, especially in business, technology, and education, the mainstays of traditional, mainstream American culture. Because of the worldwide importance of English as an international language, it is unlikely that the United States will lose English as its common language at a time when other countries are seeking more speakers of English and teaching their own populations English. However, we will need people who can speak the languages of other countries. For the United States to continue to be an important economic and political power in the world, Americans of whatever variety will need two languages — their first language and English, or English and a second language. English is indeed a world language, but as every international tourist or business traveler learns, not everyone in the world speaks English. Rather than eliminate the second language of our immigrants, we need to help them learn English and maintain that valuable resource they already have, the use of a second language, and we need to teach our native English speakers a second language.

The United States has always been a polyglot country. It is part of our strength. It is unlikely that nonnative speakers of English, be they immigrants or born here, will remain monolingual, because they need English to talk with other Americans whose native language is not English and with other people in the world who do not speak Vietnamese or Spanish or French or Arabic or whatever. Multilingualism in a country is potentially dangerous only if it becomes the rallying point for cultural divisiveness. Otherwise, it is a benefit of great economic and political value.

Aside from the purely utilitarian economic value of knowing more than one language, there is evidence that knowing a second language increases our abilities to use our first language. People who know two languages generally perform better on tests of verbal ability administered in their native language than do monolingual speakers. That is to say, if your native language is English, and you learn Japanese, you will perform better on tests which measure your knowledge of and abilities in English.[14] Parents who know and accept the research that shows that "bilingual youngsters are more imaginative, better with abstract notions and more flexible in their thinking" are enrolling their children in private language programs to give them the advantage that bilingual programs give other groups of children.[15]

CONCLUSION

Neither our Congress nor any other national legislature has ever had much success in legislating morals or beliefs. Making English the official or only language of the United States will not alter my personal beliefs about the value of my language or my beliefs about yours. Rather than taking the path of linguistic legislation, we are much more likely to be successful in maintaining a common language in the United States by pursuing the American tradition of persuasion and demonstration. The very fact that English speakers (whether English is their first or second language) are economically and politically more powerful than non-English speakers is a better argument for learning English than an argument based on the fact that English is the official or only language of the United States. (See Carlin for a similar argument from the viewpoint of politics.)

I have tried to point out some distinctions here, perhaps the most important of which is that *official, only,* and *common* are not synonymous when coupled with *English.* A great many of us wish to maintain English as the *common* language of the United States, but that goal need not, and probably should not, entail legislating English as the *only* language or the official language. The problems that we have as a multilingual society have been with us since at least 1753 when Benjamin Franklin noted them, and we have managed to overcome them or turn them to our advantage without depriving anyone of the freedom of speech that we value so highly. There are distinct advantages for our culture, for our children, and for each of us individually to be multilingual, especially if we all share a language in common. If we are concerned about the quality and intent of bilingual programs or about the effects of our immigration policies, let's be direct and honest and focus on those and not pretend that legislating language choice will improve or change bilingual programs or slow immigration.

NOTES

1. Geoffrey Nunberg, "An 'Official Language' for California," *New York Times,* October 2, 1986, late ed., sec. 3, p. 23; and John D. Trasvina, "'Official' English Means Discrimination," *U.S.A. Today,* July 25, 1986, p. 10A.

2. See e.g., Packhurst Whitney, "They Want to Know What Their Children Are Saying," *Collier's Magazine,* July 14, 1923, pp. 13, 21; "Immigrants Who Don't," *Literary Digest* 88, no. 11 (1926): 50; and Edward M. Chen and Wade Henderson, "New 'English-only' Movement Reflects Old Fear of Immigrants," *Civil Liberties,* no. 358 (1986): 8.

3. H. L. Mencken, *The American Language: Supplement I* (New York: Knopf, 1945), p. 140.

4. Charles Anderson, *White Protestant Americans* (Englewood Cliffs, N.J. Prentice Hall, 1970), p. 80.

5. Mencken, p. 139.

6. Anderson, p. 80.

7. "Charting the Great Melting Pot," *U.S. News & World Report,* July 7, 1986, p. 30.

8. Mencken, p. 141.

9. J. C. Ruppenthal, "The Legal Status of the English Language in the American School System," *School and Society* 10 (1919): 658–66.

10. Calvin Veltman, *Language Shift in the United States* (The Hague: Mouton, 1983), p. 14.

11. Nunberg, sec. 3, p. 23.

12. Trasvina, p. 10A.

13. Chen and Henderson, p. 8.

14. Kenji Hakuta, *The Mirror of Language: The Debate on Bilingualism* (New York: Basic, 1986).

15. Stacy Wells, "Bilingualism: The Accent Is on Youth," *U.S. News & World Report,* July 28, 1986, p. 60.

Questions for Discussion

1. What effect does bilingualism have on learning English?
2. Are English language laws discriminatory? What are the reasons for your answer?
3. Should the federal and state governments communicate only in English? What are the reasons for your answer?
4. What would be the consequences to the United States if large numbers of American people spoke only languages other than English?
5. What motivates the groups that want to adopt English as the official U.S. language?

Suggested Readings

Baron, Dennis. "English in a Multicultural America." *Social Policy* 21, no. 4 (Spring 1991): 5–14.

Califa, Antonio. "Declaring English the Official Language: Prejudice Spoken Here." *Harvard Civil Rights–Civil Liberties Law Review* 24, no. 2 (Spring 1989): 293–348.

Chavez, Linda. *Out of the Barrio: Toward a New Politics of Hispanic Assimilation.* New York: Basic Books, 1991.

Citrin, Jack. "Language Politics and American Identity. *Public Interest,* no. 99 (Spring 1990): 96–109.

Crawford, James. *Hold Your Tongue: Bilingualism and the Politics of "English Only."* Reading, Mass.: Addison-Wesley, 1992.

Donegan, Craig. "Debate over Bilingualism." *CQ Researcher* 6, no. 3 (January 19, 1996): 49–72.

Gallegos, Bee, ed. *English: Our Official Language?* New York: H. W. Wilson, 1994.

Imhoff, Gary, and Gerda Bikales. "The Battle over Preserving the English Language." *USA Today Magazine* 115, no. 2500 (January 1987): 63–65.

Kirschten, Dick. "Speaking English." *National Journal* 21, no. 24 (June 17, 1989): 1556–1561.

Levine, Herbert M. *Immigration.* Austin, Tex.: Raintree Steck-Vaughn, 1998.

Porter, Rosalie Pedalino. *Forked Tongue: The Politics of Bilingual Education.* New York: Basic Books, 1990.

Schlesinger, Arthur M., Jr. *The Disuniting of America.* New York: W. W. Norton, 1992.

Sowell, Thomas. *Ethnic America: A History.* New York: Basic Books, 1981.

Wattenberg, Ben J. *The First Universal Nation.* New York: Free Press, 1991.

Worsnop, Richard L. "Bilingual Education." *CQ Researcher* 3, no. 30 (August 13, 1993): 697–720.

Chapter 9

Do Voting and Elections Mean Very Much?

A central feature of political democracy is universal suffrage. With the exception of people under the age of eighteen, felons, or the insane, every U.S. citizen has the right to vote. Restrictions based on registration and residence impose the only limits on this right.

While today U.S. citizens enjoy universal suffrage, even forty years ago there were significant restrictions on the right to vote. Under Article I, Section 4 of the Constitution, the states can determine the "times, places, and manner" of elections, but Congress is permitted to alter such regulations except as to the places in choosing senators. (Until 1913, senators were chosen by state legislatures.) In the early years of the Republic only white male property owners were allowed to vote in most states. The trend has been to expand the franchise to include groups previously excluded. At first, property ownership as a voting requirement was eliminated. The Fifteenth Amendment to the Constitution, adopted in 1870, forbade any state to deny or abridge the right to vote "on account of race, color, or previous condition of servitude."

States, however, found ways to prevent African Americans from voting. In effect, African Americans were excluded from exercising their votes in the South through such devices as literacy tests, the white primary, and the poll tax, which required the payment of a fee to vote. Intimidation by some whites made it unlikely that African Americans would organize for the purpose of exercising the right to vote. Primaries were considered to be conducted by "private organizations" and, consequently, not subject to the Fifteenth Amendment. Some restrictions also effectively disfranchised some whites. The poll tax kept poor whites from voting, and literacy tests were used to keep immigrants from voting.

The twentieth century brought major changes. The Nineteenth Amendment, adopted in 1920, allowed women to vote. The Twenty-Fourth Amendment, adopted in 1964, made the payment of a poll tax or any tax illegal in federal elections, including primaries. The Voting Rights Act of 1965 protected the right of African Americans to vote in every state. The Twenty-Sixth Amendment, adopted in 1971, established that all persons eighteen or older could not be denied the right to vote on account of age. Supreme Court decisions and state legislation eliminated literacy tests. And in 1993, President Bill Clinton signed the National Voter Registration Act, more popularly known as the "Motor-Voter Law," which requires states to allow people to register to vote by mail, or when applying for driver's licenses and government benefits, or when enlisting in the armed services. The law succeeded in registering millions of people in this manner.

Yet many U.S. citizens do not exercise the right to vote. In the 1996 presidential election, for example, the turnout rate of the voting-age population was 48.8 percent, compared to 55.2 percent in 1992, 50.2 percent in 1988, 54.4 percent in 1976, and the post–World War II high of 63.1 percent in 1960. The 1996 turnout rate was the lowest since 1924 and the second lowest since 1824. In state and local elections the turnout is generally lower than in national elections.

The failure of many U.S. citizens to vote has raised the issue of whether voting and elections mean very much. Political scientists Gerald M. Pomper and Susan S. Lederman argue that they do and summarize their findings in a selection from their study. Specifically, they contend:

1. On the basis of empirical evidence, there appears to be a linkage between the appeals of parties and the demands of the electorate. Politicians do redeem most of their promises.
2. The effect of elections is indirect.

Elections constitute endorsements or rejections of a politician's policies. Voting serves to influence rather than to control the actions of politicians.

Political scientist Howard L. Reiter argues that voting is not effective in translating the beliefs of the people of the United States into public policy. He contends:

1. It is difficult to determine the meaning of a candidate's victory or defeat because different people vote for the same candidate for different reasons.
2. Most of the major issues of U.S. history have been resolved not by elections but by other historical forces, such as mass movements.

Reiter emphasizes that he is not saying elections are unnecessary, or that people shouldn't vote, only that elections are not all that they are claimed to be. Because voting is individualistic and private, it should not be considered the highest public endeavor of the citizen. Democracy requires more than taking a few minutes to vote once in a rare while. As African Americans who achieved the vote since learned, elections play a limited role for citizens and the system as a whole.

Do Voting and Elections Mean Very Much?

GERALD M. POMPER AND SUSAN S. LEDERMAN
Elections and Democratic Politics

Political theorists have emphasized the dangers of direct voter control, while finding benefits in indirect influence. Our examination has revealed little evidence of the former process, but we have uncovered many indications of the latter. American institutions serve to limit the electorate's command over government actions, but they do provide many opportunities for the expression of voters' demands. The character of the electorate is consistent with these expectations. The voters are not prepared to exercise a sovereign control over policy, but they are ready and able to press their personal interests.

Empirical studies confirm these generalizations. In presidential elections, the voters' principal role has been to maintain or displace the party in power. Programs have followed from the actions of the governing coalition, retrospectively judged by the electorate, not from explicit popular directives. In gubernatorial contests as well, the voters have not consistently demanded either low state taxes or high spending, but have responded differently to the varying initiatives of politicians.

These initiatives, as expressed in national party platforms, have been relatively specific and related to the apparent interests of the citizenry. Despite the apparent lack of direct control, therefore, there seems to be a linkage between the appeals of parties and the demands of the electorate. The existence of such a linkage is confirmed by actions on platform promises. Politicians do redeem most of their promises, and the parties reveal considerable internal unity and interparty difference in their actions. Another indication of linkage between official policies and voter interest is provided by the history of southern blacks. Despite their generally depressed state, blacks have found better protection of their natural rights when they have had the vote as a means of defense.

The policy effects of elections are not their only functions. Many other results may follow from popular selection. For example, the choice of rulers by ballot promotes the recruitment of officials with characteristics distinct from those designated through inheritance, lot, or force.[1] Suffrage may also affect the personal characteristics of the citizens. Mill believed that individuals developed more competence, awareness, and ambition when they participated in government.[2] In the struggle for civil rights as well, demands for voting rights have been the stimulus to broad mobilization of the black community.[3]

A major function attributed to elections is the promotion of political stability.[4] Through its votes, the populace is seen as expressing its allegiance to the existing constitution. Whether elections are only ritualistic as in the Soviet Union, or involve some real choice, their common effect is to bolster the legitimacy of the holders of power. "Elections commit the people to a sense of responsibility for their own betterment. . . . It seems clear that they are essential to us as props of the sentiment of legitimacy and the sentiment of participation."[5]

Our stress has not been on these important intangible effects of elections, but on their policy consequences. It remains now to draw our varied findings together in a general conception of the effects of popular intervention on the action of government. We first examine the theory of elections as mandates. Subsequently, we analyze the process of indirect electoral influence and its implications for American politics.

ELECTIONS AS MANDATES

A mandate would be the most general form of direct voter control. In this theory, political contests are seen as debates over future governmental policies, and the ballot as the means of resolving the debates. Consequently, voting is presumed to result in a relatively specific set of instructions by the electors to officials. Voters are principally concerned with issues, and candidates elected on the party ticket and platform are bound to implement the policies prescribed by the electorate. This theory has been particularly associated with the Labour party of Great Britain, although it is supported in other nations as well.

Under the mandate principle, issue conflicts or broad policy innovations are decided by "going to the country" for a final decision. According to this rule, even a party's legislative majority "does not necessarily entitle it to introduce a major change of policy, of a kind likely to arouse intense public controversy, if the electors have not had the chance to express their view on the subject."[6]

For example, the British Liberal party in 1906 successfully campaigned on behalf of a low-tariff policy. Finding the results a mandate, the Commons subsequently resolved: "That this House, recognizing that in the recent general election the people of the United Kingdom have demonstrated their unqualified fidelity to the principle and practice of the Free Trade, deems it right to record its determination to resist any proposal . . . to create in this country a system of Protection."[7] Similarly, in the United States, many persons interpreted the successive presidential elections of 1964, 1968, and 1972 as mandates to limit American involvement in Vietnam.

For elections to serve as mandates, three conditions would need to be fulfilled: (1) governmental institutions would facilitate the implementation of popular verdicts in official policy; (2) voters would be concerned primarily with future policy questions; (3) majority preferences on these questions as expressed in elections could be ascertained. However, in the United States at least, none of these three conditions is substantially satisfied.

It would be difficult to implement a mandate in America. A popular program must overcome the multiple cracks of federalism; the decentralized party system; the independent powers of bureaucracies, courts, and public authorities; and manifold checks and balances. Critical areas of policy affecting the public are outside the normal work of government, and are determined by "private" corporations. If public support for a given proposal is strong and definitive, these barriers are not insurmountable. In most instances, the electorate's wishes are not that clear.

Moreover, voters are not necessarily activated by policy considerations, at least not in the coherent and prospective fashion suggested by the mandate theory. Traditional partisanship and candidate evaluations account for much of the balloting. While many voters are concerned with their particular interests, only a minority are aware of or interested in the entire range of policies or general ideological postures. The relevant "issues" of a campaign therefore differ from one individual or group to another, and a common interpretation of the mandate of an election would be difficult to secure. Furthermore, voters are more conscious of past than future policies. They make retrospective judgments on the record of the incumbent party more often than prospective choices between alternative programs.

Even if voters were primarily motivated by future policy questions, the popular mandate would be difficult to define. Victory for a given party does not necessarily mean that a majority supports each of its programs. Voters are not always consistent in their policy or partisan preferences. In the postwar period the electorate has generally favored the Democrats on domestic welfare issues, but has been more favorable to the Republicans on questions of foreign policy.[8] In state politics, as seen in the controversy over California's Proposition 13, voters may support both lower taxes and high levels of government spending.[9]

To the extent that voters are concerned with policy questions, their involvement normally extends only to a limited number of issues. On any given matter of public policy, the party's voters will include not only advocates of its position but also many who are indifferent to or ignorant of this stand, and some who oppose the party but still vote for it because of other considerations. In fact, by combining "passionate minorities" it is theoretically possible for a party to win a majority vote, even though each of its individual policies is supported only by a fraction of the electorate.[10]

A total popular majority is composed of many policy minorities. Rarely, if ever, is this minority united on all particular issues. The victory of a party thus cannot be interpreted as endorsement of its total platform. Presidents often attempt to claim popular mandates for their preferred policies, but their efforts should be regarded as tactical assertions in their legislative struggles, not as demonstrable arguments.[11] Jimmy Carter's victory in the 1976 presidential race cannot be taken as popular support for his energy policy or any other "moral equivalent of war." Even less can a 1976 decision of the electorate be seen as endorsing his actions in the unforeseen Iranian crisis of 1979 and 1980.

Furthermore, even a majority of voters would not include a majority of the total adult population. Nearly half of American adults now do not participate in presidential balloting. It is possible that the nonvoters, concentrated among persons of low social and economic status, may have sharply different policy views from those of the active citizenry. While current research does not indicate such a discrepancy of views, we cannot fully predict the future behavior of any newly mobilized voters.[12]

For a mandate to be valid, it should be based on an informed choice of the electorate. If a party's voters support its policies without thought and simply because of their partisanship, this loyalty clearly does not impose any restraints on the government. Nor is a mandate discernible if no alternatives to the winning party's program are available. In order for the voters to make a decision on public policy, they must have a defined choice. On most issues, American parties do not offer different policies. This similarity is often due to the fact that both parties support a program of proven popularity. In other cases, however, the absence of a choice makes it dubious that the voters clearly supported the policy in question.

Mandates are difficult to achieve, determine, and implement. The difficulties were made evident in the presidential election of 1920, which Woodrow Wilson had hoped would be a "great and solemn referendum" on American participation in the League of Nations. His hopes were disappointed. National institutions did not provide for a referendum or any other direct test. In the presidential campaign the issue was clouded by other questions, by vagueness, and by the personalities of the candidates. Interpretation of the results was difficult. "The Republicans and Harding, however, victors by a seven million vote majority and hence free to interpret the election results as they saw fit, declared that the American people had, once and for all, rejected the notion of the League of Nations."[13] If a mandate could not be clearly obtained on this issue, policy decisions in elections must be unlikely in general.

The Vietnam war issue, significant in three different presidential elections, provides further illustration of the complexities of popular mandates. In each of the three races from 1964 to 1972, many observers, and particularly critics of American involvement, read the returns as a popular call for restraint on U.S. military action. Examination of voter opinion, detailed in Table 1, does not support this view. In the earliest stages of the American intervention, President Johnson received support from advocates of both quick withdrawal and an escalated use of force, with fullest endorsement from those taking the moderate position, to "keep our soldiers in Vietnam, but try to end the fighting."

By 1968, with American involvement and casualties at their height, overall opinion had begun to turn against the war, but the election results did not show a sharp polarization. Hubert Humphrey did receive more support from "doves" than "hawks," but the differences were not extreme. Not until the third election, that of 1972, was there a distinct alignment of policy preference and voting choice. Democrat George McGovern drew exceptional support from those favoring immediate withdrawal. His defeat, then, could be ac-

Table 1 Opinion on Vietnam and Democratic Presidential Vote, 1964–1972

		Policy Position	
Democratic Vote	Withdrawal	Moderate	Use All Force
1964	63[a]	82	52
1968	50	44	33
1972	57	26	14

[a]Entries are the percentage voting Democratic of those holding the stated opinion in each year.

curately interpreted as a rejection of that policy and an apparent endorsement of the Nixon administration's alternative position of gradual disengagement.[14]

Even this agonizing case shows the limitations of particular mandates. It was not until after a decade of substantial American involvement in Vietnam — and fifty thousand casualties — that the electorate was presented with distinct alternatives and was prepared to choose. Furthermore, it still was not provided with full and honest information, as the Nixon administration engaged in deception, subversion, and secret bombings while claiming to be negotiating for a rapid truce. In the end, American policy did change, but the actions of war protestors and the growing doubts of experts may be credited with the result as much as the electorate at large.[15]

The general absence of mandates is consistent with our specific findings on direct voter control. We have found new programmatic directives by the citizenry in presidential elections, gubernatorial contests, or southern history. In these instances, as in the debate on Vietnam, "the vocabulary of the voice of the people consists mainly of the words 'yes' and 'no'; and at times one cannot be certain which word is being uttered."[16]

POWER AND INFLUENCE

The effect of elections must be indirect. Initiatives in a democratic system lie not with the voters but with politicians. A realistic theory of elections would define mandates, when they exist, not as programmatic but as personal. As British Conservatives and Liberals have argued, "the party which wins an election has 'a mandate to govern, it being understood that unless the election happens to have been dominated by a single issue (which is exceptional), the government should be free to pursue whatever policies it finds appropriate."[17]

An electoral victory does not commit the politician to the voters' program, but rather serves as popular endorsement of his policies; the politician offers a proposal, and the electorate approves, condemns, or fails to respond. A proper analogy might be an auction, with the candidates and parties offering their wares, and waiting hopefully for a response from the audience. It is this sort of endorsement that Lyndon Johnson requested and received in 1964, when he declared, "I ask the American people for a mandate, not to preside over a finished program, not just to keep things going. I ask the American people for a mandate to begin."[18] The voters granted the mandate, but the President and his party largely determined its content.

Politicians in a democracy enjoy wide discretion. "The leading statesmen in a free country have great momentary power. They settle the conversation of mankind. . . . It is they who, by a great speech or two, determine what shall be said and what shall be written for long after. . . . In excited states of the public mind they have scarcely any discretion at all. The tendency of the public perturbation determines what shall and what shall not be dealt with. But, upon the other hand, in quiet times statesmen have great power; where there is no fire lighted they can settle what fire shall be lit."[19]

Elections are important as limits on these initiatives. In a theoretical sense, elections are significant not as *power* in government, but as an *influence* on government. Power "manifests itself by the behavior of a person or group when it conforms to the preferences, whether expressed or implied, of another person or group." If mandates controlled official behavior, then voters would be exercising power, but the absence of mandates also implies the absence of power. What the voters do exercise is influence, an effect rather than a control, on the conduct of officials. Influence "rests upon the capacity of human beings to imagine and thus to anticipate the reactions of those who are affected by their actions. Influence flows into the human relation whenever the influencer's reaction might spell disadvantage and even disaster for the actor, who foresees the effect the action might have and alters it more or less in accordance with this foresight."[20] Because politicians might be affected by the voters in the next election, they regulate their conduct appropriately.

To exert their influence, voters have the most obvious and vital sanction: they control the politician's job. They can quickly and bloodlessly dismiss an offensive official and thereby end his power, prestige, and profit. No explanations need be given by the electorate, and no appeal can be taken from its decisions, however arbitrary and capricious. The voters are not informed or interested enough to decide specific policy, but their final control over the politician means that he must make great efforts to satisfy popular needs and notions, wants and whims.

The existence of the vote does not make politicians better as individuals; it simply forces them to give greater consideration to demands of enfranchised and sizable groups, who hold a weapon of potentially great force. As Tocqueville wrote: "The men who are entrusted with the direction of public affairs in the United States are frequently inferior, in both capacity and morality . . . but they will never systematically adopt a line of conduct hostile to the majority; and they cannot give a dangerous or exclusive tendency to the government."[21]

There are other means of influence than the pressures of elections. Money, status, and skill can be used by groups devoid of any significant number of votes, as demonstrated by the political strength of such diverse interests as physicians and criminals. The influence of elections is still unique because votes provide a vital sanction. The ability to punish politicians is probably the most important weapon available to citizens. It is direct, authoritative, and free from official control. Other pressures on politicians gain in potency when supported by votes, whereas the lack of votes diminishes the impact of alternative methods. "It is because there are elections from time to time that the precise demands made on the people's behalf are always listened to. Elections are important not only for what happens at them but for what happens because of them."[22]

An extensive study of American local communities illustrates the point. Agreement between leaders and followers on the relative importance of issues was found to be higher in communities of high voting participation. Leaders gave more attention to mass concerns where voting rates were high. Moreover, voting increased the impact of other forms of political participation. Where turnout was high, citizens engaged in such activities as campaigning, community organizations, or personal contacting were also more likely to have their preferences reflected by public officials. "Elections themselves may not be capable of dealing with the vast array of specific problems faced by citizens and groups, but the general pressure of the vote appears to enforce the effectiveness of the other, more specific modes of participation."[23]

The voters usually employ their powerful sanction retrospectively. They judge the politician after he has acted, finding personal satisfactions or discontents with the results of these actions. Such judgment is within the competence of the electors. They need not be experts, able to judge the technicalities of law or the merits of contrasting proposals for the future. They need only be able to perceive improvement or deterioration in their personal situation. An uneducated South Carolina Negro in 1877 perfectly expressed the workings of retrospective control. Explaining his rejection of the Redeemers' promises, he explained, "Den say dem *will* do dis and dat. I ain't ax no man what him *will* do — I ax him what him *hab* done."[24]

The fact of retrospective judgment affects the politician's initiatives as well. Knowing that a day of reckoning is fixed by the calendar, he must strive to make that day pleasant for the voters. Knowing the voters' past attitudes, the parties must plan their future behavior accordingly. Having made promises for which they will be called to account, they must seek to fulfill these pledges. Politicians are free from popular dictation, but not from popular responsibility. "By virtue of the combination of the electorate's retrospective judgment and the custom of party accountability the electorate can exert a prospective influence if not control. Governments must worry, not about the meaning of past elections, but about their fate at future elections."[25]

The issue of Vietnam is again illustrative. The war in Southeast Asia became politically important in 1968, when the effect of the Johnson administration's actions had been brought home to the voters, not in the pre-escalation year of 1964. The electorate responded to the reality of that policy, not because it violated a presumed mandate.

By 1968 public disillusionment with the American intervention was widespread, and the Democratic incumbents were subject to criticism within and outside their own party. The decline in public support of the war brought all major candidates to promise its end. The Republicans, and particularly Richard Nixon, joined the pledge, but provided no specific program, instead seeking the support of all critical voters. Within the Democratic party, discontent with the administration found expression in the nominating campaigns of Senators Eugene McCarthy and Robert Kennedy. Ultimately the party convention, and its nominee, Hubert Humphrey, joined in pledging a peace effort.

No specific mandate came from the voters. Nevertheless, their expression of dissatisfaction led all parties to repudiate past policy and brought a new administration to power. Even though reluctant and slow, the new Nixon government had no political option open but eventually to remove American troops from Vietnam. It then used its record of gradual withdrawal from the war to win resounding approval of its actions in the 1972 race.

The ambiguous mandate of 1964 became a major issue for the citizenry in 1968, and a record for judgment in 1972. Incumbent and prospective Presidents heard, solicited, and responded to the retrospective judgment of the electorate. The political process provided an outlet for criticism, an opportunity for choice, and a means of change. Moreover, the voters' judgment also had a prospective effect. The war was clearly an electoral liability, and this political fact conditioned presidential actions throughout the 1970s. Whether for good or ill, American military power was restricted in Angola, Cambodia, Sinai, and other areas, most notably Iran. The political consequences of Vietnam made new American initiatives unlikely. The governors were shown ultimately dependent on the consent of the governed.

LINKING GOVERNED AND GOVERNORS

Decisions at the ballot box are intermittent and generalized. An election for any particular office occurs only once every two or four years, and the judgment made is of a total record, not individual actions. The significance of elections extends beyond these limited occasions. Their influence is considerably magnified by politicians' anticipations of the reactions of the voters. These anticipated reactions are the vital link between the interests of the voters and the actions of government. They affect politicians continuously and on all issues. In most cases, the politician "is free to act as he thinks best because the ordinary citizen is not pounding on his door with demands for action." Nevertheless, the politician remains responsive, for "his freedom to act is limited by the fact that he believes there *will* be pounding on his door if he does not act in ways that are responsive."[26]

In looking ahead to the next election, politicians cannot take comfort in the ignorance or apathy of the majority of voters on any particular problem. We have seen . . . that voters are aware of their particular interests, even though they are not typically concerned with the broad range of issues. Winning politicians therefore believe that their policy positions are important and act accordingly.[27] Victory may depend on marginal votes, and the politician must therefore be sensitive to any group which can provide that crucial margin. "Public spokesmen, be they congressmen or others, have a sharp ear attuned to complaints that foreshadow discontent. They react, not to actual opinion, but to their image of what opinion could become if not forestalled by action on their part. And often they are right. The very lack of concern for small grievances might well crystallize a genuinely hostile community sentiment."[28] The electoral threat feared by politicians may not actually materialize, but "because of its *possible* occurrence, the person or persons under the influence of another will anticipate the reaction of him who exercises the influence."[29]

Anticipation of voter reactions is manifested in the policies that politicians reject, adopt, and propose. One important, though elusive, manifestation is the exclusion of certain issues from political debate. "Leaders respond to many elements of public opinion that *could* affect an electoral decision, even though these opinions may not have influenced the public's choice in any actual election. In gauging popular attitudes, political leaders develop a strong sense of what the permissible bounds of policy are."[30]

Illustratively, while the level of governmental support for schools is still debated, the more fundamental question of the desirability of free public education is so fully accepted that it never becomes an election issue. The consensus of the society is maintained by the parties' foresight of the electoral consequences of denying that consensus. By contrast, the massive Goldwater defeat in 1964 followed the apparent Republican denial of the settled principle of governmental responsibility for social welfare.[31] . . . We also found protection for blacks associated with suffrage. Oppressive actions were less likely to be taken when the oppressed might retaliate at the polls.[32]

Anticipated reactions help to account for the actions politicians take as well as those they forego. Parties and officials follow policies they believe the voters want, even though there is no demonstrable mandate. . . . The advent of a national majority party usually results in new public policies to meet the presumed interests of the party's voting coalition. Judging past performance, the voters continue the existing majority party in office, in a Maintaining or Converting election, or install its opposition in a Deviating or Realigning contest. In state politics, governors raise and lower taxes and expenditures in anticipation of popular demands. These actions follow more from the governors' commitments than from decisions at the polls. The case of the New Jersey income tax . . . is illustrative. Intervention by the voters does not dictate, but legitimizes, party control and programs.

Similar behavior is evident in Congress. The representative must rely on his own perceptions of the voters' present and future demands, rather than awaiting an electoral mandate. "A Congressman has a very wide range of choices on any given issue, as far as his constituency is concerned. There is no district viewpoint as such to be represented on the overwhelming majority of issues. A few will care one way, and a few the other, but the issue will be insignificant or unknown to the great majority."[33] In his actions, the representative must guess the uncertain reactions of the electorate. Congressmen are apt to vote as they believe their constituents desire. In fact, these perceptions are more strongly related to the congressman's roll-call votes than either his personal attitudes or even the district's surveyed opinion.[34]

Anticipated reactions explain both common and unusual behavior of these legislators. On most votes, representatives see no conflict between the demands of their constituency, their party, and their own views. When such differences are perceived, their vote is for the constituency interest, leading oil-state Democrats to oppose taxes on energy producers and New England Republicans to seek to control the prices "free enterprise" can charge consumers. Much to the legislators' efforts are directed toward the voters at home — advertising their efforts, claiming credit for the benefits received, taking positions for recognition among the voters, and explaining their actions in speeches or in personal appearances.[35]

In seeking to satisfy the voters, politicians also deal with emerging questions. Many of their initiatives are attempts to arouse a favorable response from the electorate, so as to maintain and increase their own popular support. Candidates are advanced who may catch the public fancy. Promises are made in the hope that the voters will be attracted to a new program. Governmental benefits are provided for the citizenry and then stressed in the incumbents' campaign for reelection. These actions are not necessarily demanded by the voters. They are trade goods offered by politicians in the speculative hope that constituents will purchase them with the currency of their votes.

We have seen . . . how the parties anticipate the desires of the voters, making specific pledges of future action in their platforms, particularly on issues involving tangible and divisible benefits. Having made a large number of such pledges, the winning party honors most of its commitments, thereby mitigating opposition attacks, and then seeks reelection on its achievements. Relative party cohesion on disputatious pledges and the concentration of platforms on the incumbents' performance allow the voters to render a retrospective judgment on these initiatives.

Similar behavior has been evident in the South. . . . Afro-Americans have rarely had control over state governments, but the existence of a black electorate has been associated with the protection of vital rights. To appeal to blacks, white officials have protected life, limited segregation, and promoted education. Anticipated reactions have brought politicians to favor a degree of racial equality in their initiatives.

Elected governments are not unique. Anticipated reactions may influence all regimes, and a sensitivity to public opinion is expedient even in primitive or authoritarian societies. When faced with electoral sanctions, however, the government not only may, but must, anticipate these reactions. Recent history indicates the efficacy of the ballot. No freely elected leader has made the disastrous decisions of a Hitler to conduct a suicidal war or of a Stalin virtually to destroy his nation's defense or of an Idi Amin to engage in the genocide of his own people. Leaders in democracies have not necessarily been personally wise or moral, but they apparently have been restrained by the need to win public favor in an election. Elections can provide the protection envisioned by theorists favorable to democracy.

Without elections, some protections are still available, but they are extraordinary and uncertain. A tribal chief who is especially unfit may be killed or abandoned.[36] Assassinations, revolutions, and foreign intervention are available to remove officials who are particularly onerous. Government may have the good sense to restrain itself. Nevertheless, without the ballot, as Mill recognized, rulers "can with impunity disregard" the citizens' desires, but they "are under a necessity of considering the interests of those who have the suffrage."[37]

The ballot does not guarantee full responsiveness on the part of rulers. They may misperceive or disregard citizen needs. As the history of blacks in both South and North has demonstrated, other resources are useful, and even necessary, for the full protection of individuals. The limitations of elections can be particularly serious for such socially deprived groups. They are unlikely to have other resources, and their reliance on the ballot must be correspondingly greater. Failure to achieve their goals may cause bitter despair and even rejection of the electoral process, as exemplified by the extreme advocates of "black power."

Elections still remain the primary way of achieving popular goals. Deprived groups with few resources other than their numbers must be aware particularly of the uses of politics. Their vital resource must be employed where it is most effective — at the polls. The ballot does not guarantee improvement, but it does create opportunities for the amelioration of social conditions by bringing officials to consider the interests of any significant group. Elections in democracies allow a change of rule in ordinary ways and without awaiting extraordinary occasions. In such systems, therefore, officials avoid not only the extremely unpopular action but even the uncomfortable. A greater sensitivity by politicians to the anticipated reactions of the public is necessitated. No better means of protection has been devised. Security has not been provided by depending on the good will of rulers, on the presumed identity of interests between governed or governors, or on institutional controls, such as a federal structure, or supervision by a monopolistic political party. To the ancient question "Who will guard the guardians?" there is only one answer: those who choose the guardians.

CONCLUSION: THE MEANINGFUL BALLOT

To provide guardianship, elections must be well designed. There is no protection from the ballot unless each of the links in the chain between governed and governors is tempered and strong. To forge these links, however, is difficult. The initiatives of politicians may be irrelevant or appropriate. Their anticipation of voter reactions may be erroneous or accurate. The voters may be ready or unprepared to express their interests and to exercise a retrospective judgment. Meaningful elections require more than the casting of ballots. Other important conditions must be met.

Implicit in this study has been the assumption of an appropriate election structure. Without attempting an elaborate analysis in this conclusion, we can suggest some of the elements of this structure.[38] The first necessity for meaningful elections is an organized party system. . . . We have noted the vital role of political parties. They provide the means through which voter needs and discontents are heard and resolved. Without a choice between at least two competing parties, the electorate is powerless to exert its influence.

A related vital requirement is for free competition between the parties. The voters must be able to hear diverse opinions and be able to make an uncoerced choice. To provide this opportunity, the parties must be allowed significant opportunities to make their appeals. Nomination and campaigning must be available to the full range of candidates, and the means provided for transmitting their appeals to the electorate. A legitimate democratic election also requires that all of the adult population be enfranchised, that the ballot be intelligible to the voters, and that the winning party have some claim to explicit or tacit support by an electoral majority. It is also obviously necessary that the votes be honestly cast and counted.

Elections in the United States do largely meet the standards of meaningful popular decisions; true voter influence exists. The two parties compete freely with one another, and the extent of their competition is spreading to virtually all states. Access to the voters is open to diverse candidates, and no party or administration can control the means of communication. Suffrage is virtually universal, and voters have fairly simple choices to make for regular offices. In the overwhelming number of cases, voting is conducted honestly.

To fully effectuate popular influence, however, improvements are required in the American electoral system. Most critically needed are measures to strengthen the political parties, the vehicles for effective voter choice. Throughout the past two decades, the parties have deteriorated. They have lost campaigning functions to the mass media and political consultants. Waves of "reform" have limited their ability to nominate candidates and organize effectively. Electoral financing has been taken over by interest groups, government, and individual contributors. Legislative leaders have lost their few powers of party discipline within national and state legislatures. With the decline of parties have also come decreasing participation in elections but increasing levels of public cynicism and political alienation.[39] Party revival is necessary if these trends are to be reversed.

Party — and democratic — renewal in the United States will require a detailed and sustained program. It will necessarily involve providing funding for political parties as well as candidates, limiting the open and exhausting primaries in presidential nominations, and rebuilding a local base for popular participation in the parties. Without such changes, and even without parties, elections in America will certainly remain. Yet, to be meaningful, they must also be organized by the parties, our long-standing agencies with a collective responsibility to the public. Without parties, elections will be only plebiscites or rituals.

Whatever the future may hold, present conditions in the United States do enable the voters to influence, but not control, the government. The evidence of this study does not confirm the most extravagant expectations of popular sovereignty. Neither are elections demonstrably dangerous or meaningless. Most basically, we have found the ballot to be an effective means for the protection of citizen interests. Elections in America ultimately provide only one, but the most vital, mandate. Echoing the words but not the despair of Linda Loman, of *Death of a Salesman,* the voters authoritatively command: "Attention must be paid."

NOTES

1. Change in the character of public officials on the advent of universal suffrage is illustrated in Robert A. Dahl, *Who Governs?* (New Haven: Yale University Press, 1961), chaps. 2–5.

2. John Stuart Mill, *Considerations on Representative Government* (New York: Liberal Arts Press, 1958), chap. 3.

3. William R. Keech, *The Impact of Negro Voting* (Chicago: Rand McNally, 1968), chap. 1.

4. The "allegiance-maintaining" function of voting and the choice of leadership through elections is stressed in the thorough survey of Richard Rose and Harve Mossawir, "Voting and Elections: A Functional Analysis," *Political Studies* 15 (June 1967): 173–201.

5. W. J. M. MacKenzie, "The Export of Electoral Systems," *Political Studies* 5 (October 1957): 256. Cf. R. S. Milne, "Elections in Developing Countries," *Parliamentary Affairs* 18 (Winter 1964–65): 53–60.

6. A. H. Birch, *Representative and Responsible Government* (London: Allen & Unwin, 1964), p. 117.

7. Cecil S. Emden, *The People and the Constitution* (2nd ed.; London: Oxford University Press, 1956), p. 225. The discussion of mandates, in both normative and empirical terms, is related to the debate over "responsible party government." This issue is ably discussed by Allan P. Sindler, *Political Parties in the United States* (New York: St. Martin's, 1966), chap. 5.

8. Donald E. Stokes, "Some Dynamic Elements of Contests for the Presidency," *American Political Science Review* 60 (March 1966): 20–21; and Gerald M. Pomper, *Voters' Choice* (New York: Harper & Row, 1975), pp. 151–58.

9. Everett Carl Ladd et al., "The Polls: Taxing and Spending," *Public Opinion Quarterly* 43 (Spring 1979): 126–35. See also Robert Axelrod, "The Structure of Public Opinion on Policy Issues," *Public Opinion Quarterly* 31 (Spring 1967): 51–60.

10. See Anthony Downs, *An Economic Theory of Democracy* (New York: Harper & Row, 1957), pp. 55–60. . . .

11. Richard Pious, *The American Presidency* (New York: Basic, 1979), pp. 107–11.

12. Steven J. Rosenstone and Raymond E. Wolfinger, "The Effect of Registration Laws on Voter Turnout," *American Political Science Review* 72 (March 1978): 39–41. See also E. E. Schattschneider, *The Semi-Sovereign People* (New York: Holt, Rinehart & Winston, 1960), chap. 6.

13. Richard L. Merritt, "Woodrow Wilson and the Great and Solemn Referendum, 1920," *Review of Politics* 27 (January 1965): 78–104. The quotation is from p. 103. The Republican platform was ambiguous, the party pledging no more than "such agreements with other nations as shall meet the full duty of America to civilization and humanity" (Donald B. Johnson, *National Party Platforms* [Urbana: University of Illinois Press, 1978], 1:231).

14. See Sidney Verba et al., "Public Opinion and the War in Vietnam," *American Political Science Review* 61 (June 1967): 319–25, for the early period; and Warren E. Miller and Teresa E. Levitan, *Leadership and Change* (Cambridge, Mass.: Winthrop, 1976), pp. 133–36, for the later elections.

15. Among the more useful books in a burgeoning literature on this period, see Townsend Hoopes, *The Limits of Intervention* (New York: Longman, 1973); and William Shawcross, *Sideshow* (New York: Pocket Books, 1979).

16. V. O. Key, Jr., *Politics, Parties and Pressure Groups* (5th ed., New York: Crowell, 1964), p. 544.

17. Birch, *Representative and Responsible Government*, pp. 116–17.

18. In accepting the Democratic nomination; *The New York Times,* August 28, 1964, p. 12.

19. Walter Bagehot, *The English Constitution* (Garden City, N.Y.: Doubleday Dolphin Books, n.d.), pp. 18–19.

20. Carl J. Friedrich, *Man and His Government* (New York: McGraw-Hill, 1963), pp. 199, 201.

21. Alexis de Tocqueville, *Democracy in America,* ed. Phillips Bradley (New York: Vintage, 1954), 1:248.

22. John Plamenatz, "Electoral Studies and Democratic Theory: A British View," *Political Studies* 6 (February 1958): 9.

23. Sidney Verba and Norman Nie, *Participation in America* (New York: Harper & Row, 1972), pp. 322–27.

24. George B. Tindall, *South Carolina Negroes, 1877–1900* (Columbia: University of South Carolina Press, 1952), p. 13.

25. V. O. Key, Jr., with the assistance of Milton C. Cummings, Jr., *The Responsible Electorate* (Cambridge, Mass.: Harvard University Press, 1966), pp. 76–77.

26. Gabriel A. Almond and Sidney Verba, *The Civic Culture* (Boston: Little, Brown, 1965), p. 352.

27. John W. Kingdon, "Politicians' Beliefs about Voters," *American Political Science Review* 61 (March 1967): 137–45.

28. Raymond A. Bauer, Ithiel deSola Pool, and Louis A. Dexter, *American Business and Public Policy* (New York: Atherton, 1963), p. 315.

29. Friedrich, *Man and Government,* p. 204.

30. Angus Campbell et al., *The American Voter* (New York: Wiley, 1960), p. 547.

31. See Philip Converse et al., "Electoral Myth and Reality: The 1964 Election," *American Political Science Review* 59 (June 1965): 321–36.

32. Another example is provided by the former leader of Tammany Hall. He finds that electoral tickets "balanced" among ethnic groups are required to avoid potential protest, rather than to satisfy any explicit demand. See Edward N. Costikyan, *Behind Closed Doors* (New York: Harcourt Brace Jovanovich, 1966), pp. 181–82.

33. Lewis A. Dexter, "The Representative and His District," *Human Organization* 16 (Spring 1957–58): 4.

34. Warren E. Miller and Donald E. Stokes, "Constituency Influence in Congress," in Angus Campbell et al., *Elections and the Political Order* (New York: Wiley, 1966), pp. 362–66. See also Charles F. Cnudde and Donald J. McCrone, "The Linkage between Constituency Attitudes and Congressional Voting Behavior: A Causal Model," *American Political Science Review* 60 (March 1966): 66–72.

35. The constant concern for voter reaction is a unifying theme in three recent and excellent works on Congress: John Kingdom, *Congressmen's Voting Decisions* (New York: Harper & Row, 1973); David Mayhew, *Congress: The Electoral Connection* (New Haven: Yale University Press, 1974); and Richard Fenno, *Home Style* (Boston: Little, Brown, 1978).

36. See I. Schapera, *Government and Politics in Tribal Societies* (London: Watts, 1956).

37. Mill, *Considerations,* p. 131.

38. For a fuller discussion, see Henry B. Mayo, *An Introduction to Democratic Theory* (New York: Oxford University Press, 1960), chaps. 5–8.

39. For analysis of the problems, see Austin Ranney, *Curing the Mischiefs of Faction* (Berkeley: University of California Press, 1975); David Broder, *The Party's Over* (New York: Harper & Row, 1972); and Everett Carll Ladd, *Where Have All the Voters Gone?* (New York: Norton, 1978).

Do Voting and Elections Mean Very Much?

HOWARD L. REITER
The Limits of Voting

On Tuesday, November 8, 1988, more than ninety-one million Americans trooped to the polls, and a majority of them elected George Bush president. It was a remarkable exercise — ninety-one million people, each convinced that the act of voting was worthwhile. Some observers commented warmly upon this latest example of the vigor of American democracy; others noted that a million *fewer* people voted in 1988 than had voted four years earlier, and that only *half* the eligible voters had cast a ballot — one of the lowest turnout rates in American history.

Exactly one year later, on Wednesday, November 8, 1989, Eastern Europe was in turmoil. In most of the nations that for more than forty years had been considered satellites of the Soviet Union, crowds were gathering regularly to call for the overthrow of their regimes. On November 8, for example, most of the ruling body of East Germany resigned, and on the following day the Berlin Wall was opened to allow free access between east and west. The day after that, the man who had headed Bulgaria's Communist party for thirty-five years abruptly resigned.

Where was democracy more effectively exercised: in the United States, with all the democratic trappings but a citizenry so uninvolved that only 50 percent of eligible voters showed up at the polls in 1988, or in Eastern Europe, where meaningfully competitive political parties and elections did not exist, but where mass popular movements overthrew long-entrenched regimes? If the answer seems unclear, is it possible that competitive political parties and elections are not necessary for the effective exercise of democracy? And if competitive political parties and elections are not necessary for a meaningful democracy, what does this say about the political system of the United States?

THE PROBLEM WITH VOTING

When the subject of democracy arises, most Americans turn naturally to thoughts of voting. Indeed, when we evaluate other countries in terms of how democratic they are, the first thing we look at is whether they have free elections. In our own country, the least controversial of the demands of the civil rights movement was to guarantee to African-Americans in the South the right to vote; even defenders of the old system of segregation seldom claimed that denying people the vote was a good thing in principle.

Why has voting been so venerated by Americans? The usual answer is that voting is the way in which the political beliefs of the American people are translated into government policy. Since we are given a choice of leaders, we supposedly can select the one whose views are closest to our own and, therefore, get those views carried out; of course, the stipulation is that a majority of the voters agree with us. In this way, the majority rules in our political system. This view of how American democracy works is pleasant, but it has a number of problems.

Most advocates of democracy agree that some form of election and that some sort of representative government is essential, especially in a large community where not everyone will fit in the same arena. In addition to voting, however, there are many other ways for the people to participate in democratic decision making. Some of these ways include telephoning and writing letters to officials, working for organizations that promote a specific cause, organizing and joining demonstrations, and even participating in civil disobedience.

Is Voting the Best Means of Democratic Participation?

In some respects, of course, voting has its advantages. It is easy to do, easy to understand, and does not require a high level of articulation. A person who votes for Bush or Dukakis does not have to give any reason for his or her vote. In the privacy of the booth, an individual does not have to explain anything to anybody. Unlike some other methods of political participation, voting takes little time, it can be done inconspicuously, and a person will not get arrested for doing it. For these reasons, voting remains the most widespread form of political participation.

On the other hand, there are clear drawbacks to voting as well. The vote is a blunt instrument; all it "says" is that you prefer Bush to Dukakis. It doesn't say, "On every issue, Bush is better than Dukakis." It doesn't say, "Bush is a better *person* for the job, but on many *issues* I like Dukakis better." It doesn't say, "I like Bush, but I wish he'd change his position on abortion." And it doesn't say, "I'm only voting for Bush as the lesser evil." All the other forms of political participation are superior to voting because they are more articulate.

Of course, victorious politicians love to read more into the vote than they legitimately can. They talk of a "mandate" for their policies — instructions on how they should behave in office — as though everyone who voted for them must have agreed with them completely on all issues. In fact, despite Bush's victory, many Americans polled in 1988 disagreed with him on many issues. A majority favored *more* government spending on liberal programs in such areas as social security, health, education, the environment, children, the elderly, the homeless, and fighting AIDS, and *less* spending on the Nicaraguan contras; moreover, a plurality wanted less spent on the Star Wars program.[1] This is often the case with elections, and people should treat with more than their usual degree of skepticism any elected official's claim to have a mandate.

In other words, any victorious candidate is likely to have received many votes from people who disagreed with him or her on many issues. Even those voters who agreed with the victor on most or all of the highly visible issues probably dissented without realizing it from their candidate's less-publicized positions. Indeed, it is possible for a candidate to win a majority of the vote while the voters reject most of his or her stands on issues. Imagine that Bush and Dukakis are running against each other in a three-person electorate; we'll call those voters John, Cathy, and Lee. There are five issues that are important to the voters: the Equal Rights Amendment (ERA), budget cuts, arms control, abortion, and busing. In the following table, we can see which candidate each voter agrees with on each issue:

	John	Cathy	Lee
ERA	Bush	Bush	Dukakis
Budget cuts	Bush	Dukakis	Dukakis
Arms control	Dukakis	Bush	Dukakis
Abortion	Bush	Dukakis	Dukakis
Busing	Dukakis	Bush	Dukakis

If you read *across* each issue in the table, you will see that two out of three voters agreed with Dukakis on every issue except the Equal Rights Amendment. If you read *down* each voter's column, you will see that John and Cathy voted for Bush — assuming that each voter chose the candidate with whom he or she agreed the most — and Lee voted for Dukakis. Therefore Bush won two-thirds of the voters, who agreed with him on only one out of five issues! I do not suggest that this kind of outcome ordinarily happens, but it is a good illustration of why an election does not always serve as an expression of public opinion.

Another variation of this problem is the possibility that a candidate may win by amassing a coalition of small groups of voters, each of which favors a policy that is highly unpopular with all other voters. By making selective appeals, a candidate can win the votes of people who want to bring back slavery, people who want to outlaw the eating of meat, people who want to expel New England from the union, and so forth, until that candidate has a majority — but on a platform that nobody supports.

As though these problems with voting were not serious enough, they are magnified when we consider how many people do not vote. Even if Bush could claim a mandate for his views, he was supported by only 53 percent of the 50 percent of the eligible voters who showed up at the polls. Therefore slightly more than one out of four eligible voters supported him, in an election that has been referred to as a solid victory or even a landslide!

Another problem with voting as the prime means of democratic participation is that it is less effective than other means. First, despite all the denials by civic groups, one vote has only an infinitesimally small chance of affecting the outcome. In the average state in 1988, nearly two million people voted, and the chances of any one voter's changing the outcome in a statewide election was just about zero. In the case of a presidential election, the odds are much less that your one vote will affect the outcome. First, your vote would have to be the swing vote in your state, and second, your state's electoral votes would have to swing the election. Compare this situation to the potential influence of one persuasive participant in a town meeting, an organization, or a demonstration.

Another problem with voting follows from the two previous arguments that one vote is (a) a poor way to express an opinion on an issue, and (b) likely to be lost in the shuffle. If these two arguments are true, then voting for someone who shares your view on an issue is not a very effective way to put that view into effect. First, your vote is highly unlikely to affect the outcome of the election, and second, even if your candidate wins, he or she may not conclude that it was *your* issue that helped him or her to win.

In fact, in American history, the great causes were typically won *outside* the ballot box. Slavery ended not because Abraham Lincoln won the election of 1860; he did not run on an abolitionist platform. Only when he thought that emancipation would help to win the Civil War did Lincoln decide to abolish slavery. In 1932, Franklin D. Roosevelt won the White House on vague promises to balance the budget and end the prohibition of alcoholic beverages. His New Deal program of economic recovery was a slogan that took definite shape only after he was in office. Elections played a strange role in the Vietnam War. American involvement in Vietnam escalated in 1965, right after Lyndon Johnson overwhelmingly defeated Barry Goldwater, who had called for a military victory. The treaty that signaled the withdrawal of American forces was signed in 1973, soon after Richard Nixon crushingly defeated George McGovern, who had called for an end to the war. In both cases, the *defeated* candidate's policies seem to have won out.

If elections have not been nearly as effective at getting the people's views into public policy as defenders of the American system would have us believe, then what *is* effective? The abolition of slavery, the New Deal, and the ending of the war in Vietnam were all promoted by mass movements that pressured government and other elites to change certain policies. We can add to this inventory the civil rights movement and such recent examples as the mass movements around women's issues (including both sides of the abortion controversy), environmentalism, consumerism, and antitax protests. In all these cases, people took to the streets and lobbied officials in ways that were more pointed, and had much greater impact, than elections ever have.

THE LESSONS OF VOTING

In the final analysis, voting is an odd way to foster the participation of the masses, for it is like a spectator sport. If the authorities promote voting as the prime way to get involved in politics, then they are sending certain messages:

Politics is Individualistic

At various times and places in history, people have conducted politics by bringing the community together in one place to determine collectively the outcome of major issues. The best-known examples include the ancient Greek city-states, Israeli *kibbutzim,* New England town meetings, and communes of various kinds. This concept is based on the argument that if politics is society's way of deciding its collective future, then what better way than to have people resolve the issues through face-to-face argumentation and brainstorming? In contrast, voting is an isolated, individualized act. People do not share their ideas or persuade each other. Each person is like an unconnected atom; Americans tend to see social life in general in this manner.[2]

Politics is Private

Which question is a greater invasion of privacy, whom did you vote for in the last election, or what deodorant do you use? There is no obvious answer. People whose only political activity is voting are left to infer that politics is intensely personal and private, almost shameful. We vote not only individually, but often in booths with curtains, like Roman Catholics confiding their sins in the confessional. Again, instead of treating politics as the most *public* of activities because it is concerned with the future of us all, we treat it as something to be hidden. I do not suggest that there is no reason for a secret ballot, only that a nation whose most important political act is conducted in private is one that does not take politics seriously as the highest *public* endeavor of the community.

Politics is Episodic

Politics, we are encouraged to believe, occurs once a year on election day, and for most of us it occurs only every four years, if that. We discharge our highest civic responsibility by taking a few minutes to go into a booth and make a few choices, once in a rare while. Although we are all free to engage in other political activities, such as collective action, writing to officials, working on campaigns, or organizing protests, most adults are content to limit their political activity to that occasional act of choice. And if we think of voting as the core of what democracy means, we will not think that democracy requires anything else.

This emphasis on a passive citizenry, bestirring itself from its lethargy — getting up from the couch, if you will — once every four years in order to go to the polling place and flip a few levers, is consistent with a broader view of politics that has long been dominant in the United States. This view is the doctrine of classical liberalism, the philosophy of long-ago theorists such as Thomas Hobbes, John Locke, and David Hume, as well as the framers of the U.S. Constitution. Among the most important tenets of classical liberalism are *individualism,* the notion that people's identities and fates are essentially derived from their individual talents rather than from some group to which they belong, such as a social class or a race (as though children born into wealthy families have no greater chance of material success than those born into poor families); *individual rights,* the concept that we all have certain claims with which nobody else, including government, should interfere (as though we have no responsibilities to others, only claims against them); and *limited government,* the idea that some of the most important activities in which we engage must be protected from such broader interference (as though the state cannot expand freedoms by guaranteeing them to all people). Among the other products of classical liberal thought, although not shared by all its major proponents, has been *capitalism,* the economic doctrine that vests ownership of the means of production in private hands.

From this brief inventory we can see that the emphasis of classical liberalism and capitalism alike is on private affairs rather than public activities. The people are to be left alone; government, in this view, as Ronald Reagan often said, is the problem and not the solution. If government is at best a necessary evil — in James Madison's words, "If men were angels, no government would be necessary"[3] — then involvement in public life is not very attractive. Pursue private activities, and stay out of trouble. Leave politics to the sleazy politicians, and community affairs to the do-gooders. Good citizens should vote, but nobody will object if they spend their leisure time at sports, watching television, or washing the car. Better yet, if they spend their spare time at the mall, they will be supporting the economy by consuming goods. Politics can seem simply another form of consumption, rather than the way in which a community decides its future.

Contrast this picture with a view of citizenship that assumes that people will be active participants in the decisions that affect their lives. Assume that most people take a strong interest in the issues and candidates of their day, and discuss them frequently with friends, neighbors, and relatives. This situation is not difficult to imagine, for historians of nineteenth-century American politics tell us that people back then were far more engaged in politics than they have been in our century. When Charles Dickens traveled to the United States in

1842, not long after a presidential election in which 80 percent of the eligible voters participated, he noticed that on trains,

> Quiet people avoid the question of the Presidency, for there will be a new election in three years and a half, and party feeling runs very high: the great constitutional feature of this institution being, that (as soon as) the acrimony of the last election is over, the acrimony of the next one begins; which is an unspeakable comfort to all strong politicians and true lovers of their country: that is to say, to ninety-nine men and boys out of every ninety-nine and a quarter.[4]

Note the reference to "men and boys," because women (and, for that matter, most nonwhites) were not in the pool of eligible voters in the nineteenth century. That issue aside, compare Dickens's picture with the often dispirited lack of interest shown in elections today. At the climax of the 1988 campaign, for example, a national survey found that only 28 percent of Americans were "very much interested" in the campaign, and that nearly half had discussed politics no more than one day during the preceding week.[5] Compare your experience with Dickens's: have you ever been on a train or public bus where everyone was arguing about politics? Why has politics, arguably the subject of the most far-reaching and universal concerns that we have, become so remote from ordinary citizens? And what meaning remains to citizenship when people are drawn to their private interests and to such matters as sports and celebrity gossip, to the virtual exclusion of public life?

A COUNTERARGUMENT

I should emphasize here that I have not been saying that elections are unnecessary, or that people shouldn't vote. I *am* saying that voting isn't all it's claimed to be. Some readers are undoubtedly uncomfortable reading this disparagement of the significance of elections for democracy, and have some hard questions to ask. Let us examine one such rebuttal: Hasn't the acquisition of the vote made a huge difference for African-Americans in the South? Until the 1960s, few African-Americans were permitted to vote, and the politics of the region was dominated by white politicians who often made racist appeals as they sought votes. Today, as a result of the mass enfranchisement of blacks in the South, the region has been transformed. From local officials to Governor L. Douglas Wilder of Virginia, African-Americans have won public office, and even where they have not, their presence has had a major influence on white politicians: some, such as Governor George Wallace of Alabama, dropped their racist appeals and began to court black voters, and others, such as Senator James Eastland of Mississippi, retired from politics when they saw that African-American votes were going to keep them from getting re-elected. Some scholars have argued that having the vote has also gotten southern blacks returns in the form of more favorable government policies.[6]

There is no question that being able to vote has been a major development for African-Americans in the South, but this fact does not negate the arguments of this chapter. The fact that many African-Americans were forcibly denied the vote until the 1960s and 1970s makes this truly a special case. For any group emerging into a position of legal equality, rights and practices that other citizens regard as trivial or take for granted assume a special role. At the same time that black southerners were winning their voting rights, for example, they were ending such practices as segregated drinking fountains and rest rooms. For the remainder of society, drinking fountains and rest rooms were not an important political concern; for this oppressed group, every gain in status was a major breakthrough. So it was with voting.

How much did African-Americans achieve with the vote? Have the underlying conditions that plague so many been overturned? Certainly, the overt forms of official discrimination died, partly as a result of black votes. But the election of numerous African-Americans to office has not ended unofficial segregation and substandard conditions in housing, schools, and jobs, or the tacit discrimination that continues in those realms. Indeed, most examinations of the changing status of blacks since the 1960s conclude that, while a substantial number have "made it" into the middle class, the rest have fallen farther behind than they used to be.[7] The vote, helpful to some, has not overcome many underlying conditions.

Indeed, we might cynically (and with only some exaggeration) suggest that most African-American candidates are elected to high office under two conditions: first, that they can only take charge of such troubled areas as the "rust belts" cities of the North and poverty-stricken rural towns of the South, leaving whites in control of the most comfortable places; and second, that they must not rock the boat. Successful black politicians such as Governor Wilder and Mayors Tom Bradley of Los Angeles and David Dinkins of New York are often bland and moderate figures who were elected by showing that they could be as accommodating to the local business community and to the needs of "responsible" leadership as any white conservative.

Finally, there is an underlying irony to gaining the vote, and that is that the vote was *not* achieved through the ballot box. From organizing voter-registration campaigns under threats of violence in the South to massive rallies in the North, the civil rights movement resorted to almost every form of political participation *besides* voting in order to overthrow the old system in the South. To be sure, the federal government played an important role, notably through the Voting Rights Act of 1965, which was made possible by the election of President Lyndon Johnson and an overwhelmingly Democratic Congress the year before. Yet there were probably few political contests in 1964 outside the South that focused mainly on civil rights, and it is unlikely that a purely electoral strategy would have been enough to get the Voting Rights Act passed.

So we conclude that for an oppressed group, the vote certainly has a greater significance than it has for most citizens. Even there, however, we should realize that it has been of only limited help to African-Americans — or to anybody else.

POLITICS WITHOUT ELECTIONS?

Whether my arguments here are valid, some political scientists believe that elections are beginning to play a smaller role in American politics. Fewer people are voting; many elective offices are becoming less and less competitive as one party or the other seems to have a firm lock on one office or another. "Rather than engage voters directly," argue Benjamin Ginsberg and Martin Shefter, "contending political forces have come to rely upon such weapons of institutional combat as congressional investigations, media revelations, judicial proceedings, and alliances with foreign governments."[8] Another reason elections are becoming less important than they used to be is due to the widespread use of public opinion polls. These polls lead many high-ranking politicians to believe that they don't need elections to know what people are thinking; the official can simply commission a poll to take the public's pulse. Also, interest-group activity has increased to the extent that it overshadows the popular forces that elect legislators. Finally, the growth of political movements with their extensive fund-raising apparatus creates another way to involve people in politics competitive with the electoral process.

If the foregoing claims are correct, we have a strange situation. Elections are considered to be the heart of democracy, but currently they are playing a less important role for citizens and for the system as a whole. This fact should lead us to examine how democratic the American political system is and what *really* is the role of elections in our society today.

NOTES

1. These are the results of two nationwide surveys conducted by reputable academic teams, the American National Election Study from the Institute for Social Research at the University of Michigan, and the General Social Survey from the National Opinion Research Center at the University of Chicago.

2. For an extended argument for face-to-face democracy, see Benjamin Barber, *Strong Democracy* (Berkeley and Los Angeles: Univ. of California Press, 1984).

3. This famous quotation is from *Federalist* 51.

4. Charles Dickens, *American Notes* (London: Chapman and Hall, 1842), 149.

5. The source of these figures is the American National Election Study from the Institute for Social Research at the University of Michigan.

6. See, for example, Gerald M. Pomper, with Susan S. Lederman, *Elections in America* (2d ed.: New York and London: Longman, 1980), 179–209; and Richard Bensel and Elizabeth Sanders, "The Impact of the Voting Rights Act on Southern Welfare Systems," in Benjamin Ginsberg and Alan Stone, eds., *Do Elections Matter?* (Armonk, N.Y., and London: M. E. Sharpe, 1986), 52–70.

7. For a summary of research in this area, see Gerald David Jaynes and Robin M. Williams, Jr., eds., *A Common Destiny: Blacks and American Society* (Washington: National Academy Press, 1989).

8. Benjamin Ginsberg and Martin Shefter, *Politics by Other Means* (New York: Basic Books, 1990), 1.

Questions for Discussion

1. Do elections matter? What are the reasons for your answer?
2. What should elections determine?
3. What would be the political consequences of a major expansion in voting turnout?
4. What effect has the enfranchisement of African Americans had on their political power?
5. What effect does voting have on an individual's participation in other forms of political activity?

Suggested Readings

Bibby, John F. *Politics, Parties, and Elections in America,* 3d ed. Chicago: Nelson-Hall, 1996.

Chen, Kevin. *Political Alienation and Voting Turnout in the United States, 1960–1988.* San Francisco: Mellon Research Univ. Press, 1992.

DeSipio, Louis. *Counting on the Latino Vote: Latinos as a New Electorate.* Charlottesville: Univ. Press of Virginia, 1996.

Flanigan, William H., and Nancy H. Zingale. *Political Behavior of the American Electorate,* 8th ed. Washington, D.C.: Congressional Quarterly Press, 1994.

Ginsberg, Benjamin, and Alan Stone, eds. *Do Elections Matter?* 2d ed. Armonk, N.Y.: M. E. Sharpe, 1996.

Luttbeg, Norman R., and Michael M. Gant. *American Electoral Behavior, 1952–1992,* 2d ed. Itasca, Ill.: Peacock Publishers, 1995.

Maisel, Louis Sandy. *Parties and Elections in America.* New York: McGraw Hill, 1993.

Miller, Warren E. *The New American Voter.* Cambridge, Mass.: Harvard Univ. Press, 1992.

Rosenstone, Steven J., and John M. Hansen. *Mobilization, Participation, and Democracy in America.* New York: Macmillan, 1993.

Teixera, Ruy A. *The Disappearing Voter.* Washington, D.C.: Brookings Institution, 1992.

Chapter 10

Is Campaign Finance Reform Necessary?

For most of U.S. history the funding of political campaigns was left entirely to private sources. Unlike the practice in countries where the government underwrites the expense of campaigning, in the United States political parties and candidates have had to attract donations from individuals and groups.

In the twentieth century, campaign contributions have come under greater government regulation. In 1907 Congress passed a law prohibiting corporations from using their own funds in federal election campaigns. A similar prohibition was enacted for labor unions in 1943. Between 1947 and 1962 the law governing campaign expenditures forbade both corporate and union contributions and expenditures in federal primaries, general elections, and nominating conventions.

A number of laws were passed in the 1970s to deal with campaign finance. Many resulted from the revelations of illegal corporate contributions to the Committee to Reelect the President, the campaign organization for the reelection of President Richard Nixon in 1972. Challenges to provisions in these laws resulted in Supreme Court decisions invalidating some restrictions on campaign finance in federal elections.

Today, campaign laws require that all federal candidates must disclose their campaign contributions. For presidential contests, a system of matching grants and public financing was established, and expenditure limits were set. But a presidential candidate who uses only his or her own personal funds in a campaign is not subject to any spending limits. Independent Ross Perot used his own funds in his unsuccessful attempt to win the presidency in 1992. But when he ran again on the Reform party ticket in 1996, he relied on government financing and, consequently, was subject to the kinds of restrictions faced by his Democratic and Republican party presidential opponents. No limits are placed on how much a congressional candidate's campaign committee can spend on the candidate's campaign.

One of the consequences of the campaign reform legislation of the 1970s was the growth of political action committees (PACs). A PAC is a private organization concerned with promoting economic, social, or ideological goals in public policy through electoral and other forms of political activity. PACs contribute money to candidates for public office. In addition, some of them help with voter registration and turnout.

PACs originated with trade unions in the 1930s. Their rapid growth occurred in the 1970s and thereafter as a result of campaign finance reform. According to the FEC, there were 608 PACs at the end of 1974. By July 1996, the number of PACs had increased to 4,033.[1] Not only has the number of PACs increased, but so, too, have PAC expenditures. FEC figures show the increase. For the election cycle of 1977–1978, PACs contributed $35.2 million to all federal candidates. In the 1993–1994 election cycle, the PAC contribution figure rose to $189.6 million.[2]

Critics of campaign finance practices complain about the influence of private money. Specifically, they criticize PACs as well as "soft money" — donations for administrative costs and activities that help state, local, and federal candidates with party advertising and voter mobilization campaigns. Corporations and unions are legally prevented from contributing money directly to federal candidates, and individuals can give no more than $20,000 a year to national party committees to directly aid federal candidates. But corporations and unions can contribute soft money, which both major parties accept. Soft money is exempt from federal contribution and spending limits.

Campaign finance reform is an issue that has political support in principle. But because the stakes are so high for legislators considering reform as well as interest groups affected by the existing system, Congress has been unable to adopt reform legislation since 1974. In 1995, President Bill Clinton and Speaker of the House Newt Gingrich shook hands in support of legislation favoring campaign finance reform. But in 1996, a bipartisan reform bill sponsored in the Senate by Wisconsin Democrat Russell Feingold, Arizona Republican John McCain, and Tennessee Republican Fred Thompson did not survive a filibuster. Provisions of the bill (S. 1219, the Campaign Finance Reform Bill) would have given reduced-rate television time and postal discounts to candidates who agreed to meet voluntary campaign spending limits.

The issue of campaign finance became the subject of much media attention after the 1996 election. Republicans criticized practices of President Clinton in giving perquisites, such as overnight stays in the White House's Lincoln bedroom and golf games with the president, to donors of the Democratic party. They also attacked possible illegal contributions to the Democratic party from foreign sources and Vice President Al Gore's use of his White House office to solicit contributions. The Clinton administration and the Democratic party denied that they had engaged in any illegal behavior. Congressional practices, too, came under suspicion. For example, a lobbyist said that Indiana Republican congressman Dan Burton, chairman of the House Government and Reform Oversight Committee, threatened to move clients away from the lobbyist if the lobbyist did not raise $5,000 for Burton's campaign fund. Burton denied the story. In the spring of 1997, committees in both the House and Senate prepared for investigations of campaign finance practices.

In testimony before a Senate committee considering S. 1219, Ann McBride, president of the public-interest organization Common Cause, argues that campaign finance reform is necessary to correct the wrongs of the finance system. In her view, the current system shuts out citizens and lets the rich and powerful harm democratic processes. She asserts that large contributions buy access and influence in all aspects of legislative decision making. The 1974 campaign finance law opened the door to tremendous growth in the number of PACs. The beneficiaries of the current system are the special interests, such as the tobacco, insurance, and telecommunications industries, which are able to evade regulation through soft-money contributions to political parties. McBride argued in support of S. 1219, which sought to impose voluntary spending limits, provide benefits to participating candidates, restrict special-interest PACs, and ban soft money. She objects to the amount of money that is raised for elections, which she regards as unnecessarily high.

Law professor Bradley A. Smith argues that efforts to regulate campaign finance have distorted the political process, hindered grass-roots political involvement, infringed on the First Amendment, helped to entrench incumbents in office, and done nothing to deal with the corrupting influence of money in politics. Contending that the assumptions behind campaign finance reform are flawed, Smith concludes that campaign finance reform will harm the political system. Smith calls for deregulation of the electoral funding process.

NOTES

1. Federal Election Commission news release, "PAC Count–1974 to Present," July 11, 1996.

2. Federal Election Commission news release, "PAC Activity Shows Little Growth over 1992 Level, Final FEC Report Finds," November 1995.

 YES

Is Campaign Finance Reform Necessary?

ANN McBRIDE
The Need for Campaign Finance Reform

This bill [S. 1219] is the first bipartisan comprehensive campaign finance reform bill introduced in Congress in a decade, and the first ever bicameral bipartisan comprehensive campaign finance reform bill. I also want to note the steadfast support on the campaign finance issue provided by several Rules Committee members, including Senator Wendell H. Ford [D.-Ky.] and Senator

Robert C. Byrd [D.-W.Va.], and acknowledge their longstanding efforts on behalf of real campaign finance reform.

We are at a critical juncture in the fight for reform. First, both Houses of Congress have passed strong gift bans and passed the first reform of the lobby disclosure law in 50 years. Both of these important victories were made possible by strong bipartisan support in both bodies. Second, last year a bipartisan group of Senators joined together to successfully save the presidential campaign finance system — the most important government integrity reform of this century. Third, last year, by a bipartisan vote of 57 to 41, the Senate went on record for consideration of campaign finance legislation before the end of the 104th Congress.

We challenge the leadership of this body to make good on the Senate's commitment to act in this Congress — and soon. Too often in the past, delay of consideration of campaign finance reform has meant that the legislation died in the final days of the Congress. We call on Majority Leader Robert Dole (R.-Kans.) to schedule floor consideration of this bill in March to ensure enough time for the bill to make it through the legislative process before the 104th Congress adjourns.

THE PROBLEM

The new dynamic at work on this issue does not arise here in Washington, but swells out from the anger and outrage of Americans who are sick and tired of [a] system that shuts them out and lets the rich and powerful in and who want leaders who are going to do something about it. The people want change in the campaign finance system, and they want it now.

Over the last year as the new President of Common Cause, I have traveled extensively and met with hundreds and hundreds of Americans across this nation. Our fellow citizens are deeply troubled by the cynicism and mistrust running rampant in our country. They are deeply disturbed by an unresponsive government and by a political process that has grown increasingly mean-spirited. They sense with alarm the growing divisions among us as a nation and the loud voices of negativism and hate. But perhaps most of all, they decry elected officials who listen more to big money and Washington lobbyists than to their own constituents.

The influence-money culture that pervades Washington D.C. has become the symbol and the reality of what's wrong in our nation's capital and in our democracy. The American people have come to understand that our political system is rigged to benefit campaign contributors and incumbent officeholders at the great expense of citizens. And their anger has reached the boiling point.

This disgust with the current system is echoed by prominent national figures of all political stripes who have called for campaign finance reform. This past November, a diverse group of national figures sent a letter to the leaders of the

House and Senate, criticizing the obscene spending in congressional campaigns and demanding immediate action on reform. They wrote,

> It is our collective judgment that private interest money is having a corrosive effect on our representative democracy. Congressional campaigns are in too many cases spending obscene sums in the quest for victory. Special interests are all too happy to supply the funds via PAC [political action committee] contributions and so-called "soft money," increasing the access and influence of those who make them to the point that the Congress' agenda and actions no longer are determined solely on the basis of what is good for the majority. We all see the frightening erosion in the trust and confidence of the American people in their government.

Signers included Republican presidential candidate Pat Buchanan, Senators John Kerry (D.-Mass.) and Alan Simpson (R.-Wyo.), a number of former Senators including Warren Rudman, David Boren and Paul Tsongas, and Ross Perot of United We Stand America. And retired General Colin Powell said simply of the current campaign finance system, "Fix it."

In addition a group of 19 religious leaders representing Catholic, Protestant and Jewish faiths have proclaimed, "From churches and synagogues across the nation, we hear their sense that this is not an esoteric issue of technical election regulations, but one that goes to the essence of the ethical and moral life of our nation."

Here in Congress, retiring Senators and Representatives are adding their voices to [a] chorus for change. While each of the record number of Senate retirees has individual reasons for leaving, a near-universal lament is their distress over a campaign finance system that dominates congressional elections and undermines congressional decision-making. Senator Bill Bradley (D.-N.J.) called campaign finance reform the number one priority, "the most important issue out there. You can't change anything until you deal with the money in politics." Senator Sam Nunn (D.-Ga.) noted, "Too much of the time and efforts of Members of Congress are consumed by fundraising efforts. The ability to raise big money and buy saturation television ads have become the dominant theme of our political races." Senator Alan Simpson (R.-Wyo.) said the current campaign financing system is "poisoning the system, it is prostituting ideas and ideals. It is demeaning democracy and debasing debate."

But the loudest voices demanding change are those of the American people. They have come to understand that campaign finance reform is not an abstract issue, but one that directly affects their lives, their pocketbooks and their democratic form of government. A survey conducted jointly earlier this year by a Democratic and a Republican pollster found that in response to the statement, "Those who make large campaign contributions get special favors from politicians," 68 percent of the people were deeply and seriously troubled; 34 percent said it was one of the things that worries them the most; and another 34 percent said it worries them a great deal. The fact is Americans recognize exactly what is going on in Washington these days — large contributions buying access and influence in all aspects of legislative decision-making.

Just how this insidious system works can be seen by looking at what has happened to the House Republican freshmen who were elected to change the way business is done in Washington and who dubbed their class the "reform class." In fact, it hasn't taken many of these freshmen long to learn their way around the influence-money culture of Capitol Hill. During the first half of 1995 — their first six months in Washington — these freshmen received $5 million from special-interest PACs. The average freshman raised 45 percent of his or her campaign money from PACs in the first half of 1995. Compare that to their 1994 election campaigns when as open seat and challenger candidates PACs provided just 22 percent of their funds.

Many of these freshmen have become "instant insiders" — as dependent on PACs as their well-seasoned colleagues. *Business Week* recently editorialized, "[T]he greediest gorgers on PAC money these days are the freshmen Republicans elected in 1994 on a platform of changing Washington. How sad it is to see them in Congress, shoulder-to-shoulder with lobbyists, thanking them for helping write legislation that will only benefit their clients."

Special-Interest Political Contributions

There is an inherent problem with a system in which individuals and groups with an interest in government decisions can give substantial sums of money to elected officials who have the power to make those decisions. In the current system, special-interest PAC contributions have become a dominant force in the financing of congressional campaigns. This dependence of Members of Congress, particularly in the House, on PAC contributions has seriously compromised the integrity and public credibility of the congressional decision-making process.

Contrary to myth, and contrary to the assertions of those who oppose campaign finance reform, PACs did not spring from the reforms initiated by the 1974 amendments to the Federal Election Campaign Act. PACs have existed since the 1950s, and were recognized as problematic in the early 1970s. Instead of solving this problem, however Congress bowed to business and labor pressure and, in 1974 — over the opposition of Common Cause — changed the law specifically to authorize for the first time the establishment and operations of PACs by those with government contracts. This provision opened the door to tremendous growth in the number of PACs, since many businesses and labor unions had contracts with the government. In other words, there is nothing unintended about the resulting explosion in PACs.

The explosion of PACs has resulted in a growing dependence on PAC contributions. PACs contributed a record $189 million to federal candidates during the 1994 election cycle. In House races during the last election, winning candidates received 40 percent of their campaign money from PACs. The average successful Senate candidate took in slightly over $1 million in PAC money in 1994. PAC money constituted nearly a quarter of the money raised by Senate candidates in 1994.

PAC money is special-interest money that is strongly linked to a special interest group's legislative agenda. It is often used as part of sophisticated lobbying campaigns by these special-interest groups to affect the public policy decisions made by Congress. PACs multiply their influence because of the cumulative effect of giving by all of the PACs in a particular industry — such as banking, insurance, telecommunications or tobacco. And because PACs give money year after year, they build up enormous aggregate contributions to Members of Congress over time — investments that they can then "cash in" when a critical piece of legislation of interest to that industry is under consideration.

And perhaps most troubling, PAC money goes overwhelmingly to incumbents. Used to buy access and influence to Members of Congress, PAC money helps to unbalance the political process because it makes it harder for challengers to mount credible campaigns. In 1994, challengers in House races on average received less than 15 percent of their campaign funds from PACs. Senate challengers in 1994, on average, received less than 5 percent of their campaign funds from PACs.

Washington Influence-Money Culture

To see the Washington influence-money culture at work, you only need to look at the insidious corporate welfare system that will cost American taxpayers $265 billion over the next five years. Under this system, the beneficiaries are huge corporations and other wealthy special interests who use millions in political contributions to carve out lucrative government perks, massive tax breaks and other special benefits. While virtually all government programs are under intense scrutiny, these programs almost always stay off the table.

Let me cite one example. Archer-Daniels-Midland (ADM) and its chair, Dwayne Andreas, enjoy an enormous government tax subsidy that benefits producers of ethanol, an alcohol-based fuel. ADM has about 80 percent of the ethanol market. The ethanol subsidy costs taxpayers about $3.6 billion over five years. Since the Watergate era, when his contributions to the Nixon re-election campaign made headlines, Mr. Andreas has been a major player in the political money world, with contributions from the Andreas family and ADM totalling some $4 million since the 1970s.

The impact of the influence-money culture is also evident in federal policy on tobacco. While the tobacco industry has been attempting to salvage its image with an enormous public relations campaign, tobacco giants are also carefully targeting millions of dollars in political contributions in their efforts to influence government decision-making. Since 1985, tobacco interests have contributed more than $17 million in PAC and soft money to congressional candidates and the national parties. In the first six months of 1995, the to-bacco industry poured more than $1.5 million into the coffers of the national parties — a record for soft money giving during the period.

Special-interest money has also poured in from the health insurance indus-try and doctors who could potentially reap billions of dollars and favorable regulations as Medicare undergoes an overhaul. Since 1985, health insurance interests and doctors' associations have given nearly $50 million to congres-sional campaigns and national party committees. Nine out of ten current members of Congress have accepted contributions from both health insurance and doctors' PACs during the past decade.

Similarly, the telecommunications industry gave almost $31 million in PAC contributions in the last decade to aid their fight for less regulation and greater profits, a goal they have almost realized in new telecommunications legisla-tion passed by both Houses last year. Other heavy political givers include the oil and gas industry, the gambling industry, and the alcohol industry.

A Spending Race Unfair to Challengers

But let's look at the problem from another side — from a candidate's perspec-tive. The present campaign finance system has played a central role in shap-ing an electoral landscape that is grossly unfair to challengers. Democracy de-pends on having real elections with real choices if people truly have the power to elect representatives who can be held accountable. Congressional incumbents now have such an extraordinary advantage over challengers that we are losing the ability to hold real elections for Congress.

Under the current system it is far easier for incumbents to raise money than challengers. In 1976, Senate winners spent an average of $610,000; in 1986, the average Senate winner spent $3 million. By 1994, that figure soared to $4.5 million. For the past decade, the general rule has been that, on average, Senate incumbents outspent challengers in the general election by at least a 2-to-1 margin. For example, in 1992, while the average Senate incumbent spent almost $4.2 million for [his or her] campaign, the average challenger could only counter with less than $1.8 million. In that election year, Senate incum-bents outspent their general election challengers in 27 out of 28 races, and only four incumbents lost. In 1994, in an exception to the general rule, two challengers — Michael Huffington and Oliver North — had huge war chests. However, when those two races are excluded, the spending of an average Senate incumbent is again twice that of the average challenger.

The picture in the House is bleaker. By 1994, winning a seat in the House of Representatives cost an average of $450,000, and House incumbents out-spent House challengers by a ratio of 2.6 to 1, or $549,801 on average spent by incumbents to $209,922 on average spent by challengers. In 1976, that ratio was 1.6 to 1.

PAC contributions point up the fundraising advantage incumbents enjoy: in 1994, labor PACs gave 68 percent of their contributions to incumbents; business PACs on average gave 77 percent to incumbents. It is also, in large part, for this reason that, even in the "revolutionary" 1994 election, the incumbent reelection rate in the House was still over 90 percent. Incumbents generally are able to vastly outraise challengers and typically swamp their challengers by outspending them. The need to raise this enormous amount of money makes elected officials dependent on those special-interest groups and wealthy individuals with money to contribute and which want to use those political contributions to buy access and influence.

Soft Money

The most destructive and dangerous money in the political system today is so-called "soft money." Soft money is a scandal. This loophole has given a re-birth to the kinds of huge contributions in the political process that have not been seen since Watergate.

Soft money is a loophole that has developed in recent years to provide candidates, contributors and political parties a means to evade federal contribution limits. Soft money is money that is *illegal* under federal law — it either violates federal source restrictions (such as money from corporations) or federal limits (such as large contributions from individuals in amounts often exceeding $100,000). Since 1907, federal law has prohibited corporations from contributing any money to federal campaigns. The prohibition on labor unions funds dates to the 1940s. Federal law also limits an individual to contributing no more than $1,000 to a federal candidate per election, and no more than $20,000 to a political party per year.

To evade these restrictions, soft money contributions are solicited by federal candidates and national party officials from individuals, corporations, unions or others and funneled through designated non-federal accounts of the national political parties. The national party committees then transfer the money from these accounts to the state parties. The state parties then spend the money on campaign activities that directly affect federal elections — activities such as generic advertising, voter registration drives or get-out-the-vote drives. Thus, the soft money contributions are laundered through the political parties in a way that allows federally illegal money to nonetheless be used to influence federal elections.

In the 1994 election cycle, Republicans raised more than $45 million in soft money, while the Democrats raised $40 million. During the first six months of 1995, the two parties raised a record $30.6 million in the soft money slush fund. The Republican party raised a record $20 million in soft money, of which $7.8 million came in contributions of more than $50,000. The Democrats raised $10.5 million, of which $5.3 million, more than half, came in contributions in excess of $50,000. The largest single soft money contributor on record is a $2.5-million donation from Amway to the Republican National Committee in October 1994.

Any campaign finance reform bill that does not end the soft money system is not reform. Instead, two systems will be created — one with limits and another one where money flows freely.

THE SOLUTION

While the amounts of influence money in Washington are enormous, the opportunity for reform has never been better. The bipartisan campaign finance reform legislation — S. 1219 — presents a real opportunity to enact campaign finance reform this year. S. 1219 is tough, fair and comprehensive, and should be passed by the Senate before the April recess.

Voluntary Spending Limits

A poll taken this past summer found that 87 percent of Americans favor limiting the amount of money candidates can spend on a political campaign. Eighty-eight percent believe it will be effective to reduce the amount of money special-interest groups can contribute to a candidate. A system of voluntary spending limits combined with clean campaign resources will control congressional campaign spending — spending which gives advantages to incumbents over challengers. S. 1219 establishes voluntary spending limits for Senate candidates based on a state's voting-age population. The spending limits range from $950,000 for candidates in smaller states like Wyoming to $5.5 million in large states like California. By putting a cap on spending, the bill will hold down the costs of a campaign, will give challengers a fairer chance, and will reduce the pressure on candidates to raise ever increasing amounts of money.

As the *Washington Post* has noted, "At the moment, it is the *absence* of [spending] limits that hurts challengers. In 1994 incumbents outspent challengers in House races by better than 3 to 1. Properly set spending limits *help* challengers by preventing incumbents from burying them under money." By inducing both incumbents and challengers to abide by a common spending cap, a spending limits system *with real benefits* will give challengers a real opportunity to compete with incumbents.

Providing Real Benefits to Participating Candidates

Under S. 1219, Senate candidates who abide by the spending limits would be eligible to receive an aggregate of thirty minutes of free television time and would be able to purchase additional TV time at a 50-percent reduction of the lower-unit-rate cost. Qualified candidates would also be eligible to receive a reduced-rate mailing benefit for up to two mailings to all state voters. Candidates would be required to demonstrate a threshold level of support by raising 10 percent of the spending limit with 60 percent coming from individuals who reside in the candidate's home state. Candidates would also be required to limit the use of their personal wealth.

Restrictions on Special-Interest PACs

S. 1219 bans special-interest PACs. However, if the PAC ban is ruled unconstitutional — as many believe it would be — the legislation provides a fallback provision that would limit PAC contributions to no more than 20 percent of the candidate's spending limit and would reduce the amount any one PAC can contribute to a candidate from $5,000 to $1,000 per election.

Soft Money Ban

S. 1219 bans soft money. The bill requires that *any* money solicited or received by the national political parties must comply with federal law. So too, *any* money spent by the state parties on any activities which might influence federal elections — including voter registration and get-out-the-vote drives — must comply with federal law. And *any* money raised by a federal candidate or federal officeholder for federal elections must comply with federal law. These three provisions, taken together, will close the corrupting soft money loophole.

S. 1219 also closes other loopholes in the current system including banning bundling which allows PACs, registered lobbyists, agents of corporations or labor unions to evade federal contribution limits, banning the use of the frank for mass mailings in election years, banning the use of campaign funds for personal uses, banning members' PACs and strengthening enforcement.

S. 1219 contains some provisions dealing with independent expenditures, particularly tightening the definition of independent expenditures to ensure that there is no coordination or consultation between the supposedly independent spender and the campaign of the candidate who benefits from the spending. . . . In addition we believe there are ways the bill could be strengthened to deal with independent expenditures. For example, if independent expenditures over a threshold amount are made against a complying candidate, or in favor of the opponent of a complying candidate, the complying candidate should be provided with free response time adjacent to the independent spenders' broadcast advertisement.

BIPARTISAN BREAKTHROUGH ON REAL BENEFITS: BROADCAST TIME

Under S. 1219, candidates who agree to spending limits are provided free- and reduced-cost television time. Free television time is a concept which has been supported by Majority Leader Dole, Senator Mitch McConnell (R.-Ky.) and others.

Broadcast advertising is not only one of the most successful ways a congressional candidate can reach voters, it is also one of the most expensive. For many challengers, TV ads are often prohibitively expensive. In 1992, broadcast advertising was the single largest expense for Senate candidates — accounting for more than 40 percent of their expenditures, according to Congressional Quarterly's *Handbook of Campaign Spending.*

Asking broadcasters to provide time to qualified candidates is in keeping with the broadcasters' responsibility to their viewers. The airwaves are owned by the public. The broadcasters receive a license to use and profit from the public's airwaves. Congress has the power to condition that license on the broadcaster's agreement to provide a reasonable amount of air time at free or reduced rates for the sake of improving the political process. Broadcasters have a responsibility to the public in return for the broadcasting licenses they receive. That public responsibility should include providing TV time to candidates who agree to spending limits.

In a recent speech, Reed Hundt, chairman of the Federal Communications Commission, stated his support for requiring broadcasters to provide air time to candidates, and laid out why such proposals are constitutional. Hundt noted that the average Senate candidate in a contested election in 1992 spent $2.4 million on media expenses; in California, the two candidates spent over $50 million. In the aggregate, in 1994, candidates spent $355 million on media advertising. In 1996, this figure is expected to be over $500 million.

Hundt noted that these media costs, in themselves, place a huge burden on candidates, "The cost of TV time-buys makes fundraising an enormous entry barrier for candidates for public office, an oppressive burden for incumbents who seek reelection, a continuous threat to the integrity of our political institutions, and a principal cause of the erosion of public respect for public service." He debunked the notion that free- or reduced-rate broadcast time provided to candidates would amount to an unconstitutional "taking." He said, "As everyone acknowledges, broadcasters are granted commercial use of the public's airwaves as long as they serve the 'public interest.' Since the beginning of modern broadcasting after World War II, the FCC has regarded that 'public interest' as including the use of TV to develop 'an informed public opinion through the dissemination of news and ideas concerning the vital public issues of the day.'"

Instead, as Hundt noted, "numerous commentators have concluded that TV has enslaved politicians and degraded the electoral process." The obligation to serve the 'public interest' provides the basis for requiring broadcasters to provide free- or reduced-rate broadcast time. Further, Hundt rejects the notion that such a requirement will unconstitutionally take the property of broadcasters. "Under the Communications Act of 1934, broadcast licensees have no property claim to the airwaves or to a particular frequency."

OPPONENTS OF REFORM

...Speaker Gingrich has publicly opposed the companion bipartisan bill in the House. He also recently testified that there is too little money spent on political campaigns. He argued that the total amount spent on House and Senate races in 1994, a record $724 million, was only twice as much as the advertising budgets for the three leading antacid manufacturers, and that this shows the money currently spent in politics is not excessive.

This view — not enough money is spent on politics — badly misses the point and is seriously wrong. The problem is not simply how much money is *spent*, but how much money must be *raised* and what candidates must *do* to raise it. The fundraising, the reliance on PACs and wealthy individuals, and the advantage of incumbents with access to money distort the political process.

For example, the pressure to raise the $4.5 million Senate average means that Senate candidates have to spend much of their time fundraising. Fundraising becomes an enormous distraction that interferes with Members doing the job they were elected to do. The $4.5 million the average Senate candidate must raise means a Senator must raise approximately $15,000 a week, every week for six years, starting the moment he or she is sworn into office.

As Senator Paul Simon noted, "A great many people visit the United States Senate, and they will see two or three of us on the floor debating some issue, and they get discouraged. . . . But they would be even more discouraged if they knew the reality. Probably at that point, there are more Senators on telephones trying to raise money, than there are on the floor of the United States Senate." The need to raise this enormous amount of money makes elected officials dependent on those special-interest groups and wealthy individuals which have money to contribute — and who want to use those political contributions to buy access and influence.

Recent press reports indicate that part of Speaker Gingrich's proposed solution is to increase the influence of wealthy individuals by increasing the individual contribution limits five-fold. This increase would mean that one couple could give $20,000 to a congressional candidate — close to the average annual pay of working Americans. There is not too little money in politics today, but too much — too much fundraising, too much spending, too much special-interest money. And Mr. Gingrich's solution — raising the individual contribution limit five-fold — would only increase the influence of the wealthiest Americans at the expense of the average taxpayer.

To say that the current individual contribution limit is $1,000 actually understates the reality. The *cycle* limit on what an individual can contribute to a candidate is $2,000 — $1,000 each for the primary and general election. And when, as is often the case, both spouses make the maximum contribution, a married couple thereby contributes $4,000 per candidate per election cycle. Thus, the existing contribution limit gives the very wealthy the ability to contribute a sum of money that is well beyond the capacity of average Americans. To increase the contribution limit — to $20,000 for a couple during an election cycle—is a change that would work to the benefit only of the very wealthy, and would further increase the disparity between the wealthy and average citizens in the relative ability to influence campaigns.

Speaker Gingrich also recently said that the number one problem in political campaigns is the wealthy candidate who spends his or her own money in a campaign. There is no doubt that, under the existing campaign finance system, a wealthy candidate who is willing to spend an unlimited amount of his or her own personal fortune on a political campaign has an advantage today. It is difficult under existing rules for an opponent to raise the money necessary to compete with a wealthy candidate because spending by a wealthy candidate cannot be directly restricted due to constitutional limitations. Certainly this is an issue of concern but it is also an issue which can and should be addressed within the confines of the Supreme Court decision. S. 1219 provides valuable alternative resources to complying candidates that can be used to compete effectively with a wealthy opponent who chooses not to comply with the spending limits.

The broadcast provisions in S. 1219 give complying candidates running against wealthy candidates several advantages in response. Complying candidates are eligible to receive the free- or reduced-rate broadcast time, and the wealthy candidate is not. The 50 percent discount on television means that $1 million of campaign funds spent on television is actually worth $2 million. Thus, complying candidates are able to buy an unlimited amount of broadcast time at half of the cost to the wealthy candidate purchasing the same amount of time. This is a significant advantage to complying candidates. Under S. 1219, wealthy candidates may continue to have an advantage, but opponents of wealthy candidates will be provided real resources with which to counter that wealth.

In truth, wealthy candidates who have spent their own money on their campaigns have not gotten much bang for their buck. While 14 Senate candidates each used $1 million or more of their own money in 1994 Senate races, only four of them were successful. Three of the four were incumbents — a group with a 90 percent reelection rate in any case. Overall, personal wealth accounted for only eight percent of 1994 Senate winners' campaign funds, while 20 percent of their funds came from PACs, according to the Congressional Research Service. In 1994 House races, 16 candidates each used $400,000 or more of their own personal wealth for their campaigns. Only two of the sixteen won a seat in Congress. Overall, winners in 1994 House races relied on personal wealth for only 1 percent of their campaign funds, while raising 38 percent of their funds from their PACs. And in the one federal system with limits that do exist — the presidential system — only two of the major party candidates have elected not to participate in the spending limits system, and only one — current candidate Steve Forbes — has chosen to use his own money.

Another approach of opponents is to say that you do not need contribution limits but only disclosure. Of course, you could say the same thing about a bribe — don't make bribery a crime, just disclose it and let the voters decide. The fact is, however, that Americans want a political process that is based on standards of integrity and fairness, a process where big money cannot dominate.

Disclosure *is* a critically important part of campaign finance regulation, but in itself will not make the campaign finance system fair, open and accountable. We have disclosure now, and that has not stopped wealthy individuals and special-interest groups from using campaign contributions to buy access and influence with elected officials. To remove contribution limits would say the sky is the limit. Mere disclosure of such corruption would not control it, but explode it. Disclosure of rampant corruption would serve only to increase public cynicism about politics and further the alienation of average voters from their government.

PRESERVING AND PROTECTING THE PRESIDENTIAL CAMPAIGN FINANCE SYSTEM

In the midst of the growing call for reform of congressional campaign finance, the most important political reform of the past 90 years — the presidential campaign financing system — is under attack. On May 24 of last year [1995] the Senate rejected an effort to gut the presidential system.

The presidential campaign finance system — enacted in the wake of the Watergate scandals — initially met its goal of dramatically improving the way the President is elected. The system provides optional public matching funds during the primary election, and full public funding for the major party candidates in the general elections. Candidates who choose to accept the public funds also agree to adhere to spending limits in both the primary and general elections.

All but two of the 66 major party candidates since 1976 have opted into this system. For the first decade of its existence, the presidential system reduced the role of special-interest influence money in presidential campaigns and made presidential elections more competitive by equalizing spending between candidates. It also has successfully restrained spending: in 1972, the Nixon campaign spent $60 million, the equivalent of over $200 million in inflation-adjusted dollars. By contrast, spending by each of the candidates in 1992 was about $90 million, well below the rate of spending prior to the reform. Further, a challenger has defeated an incumbent in three of the four campaigns conducted under the system (excluding the 1988 race, which had no incumbent), a competitiveness that contrasts sharply with congressional campaigns where incumbent reelection rates always exceed 90 percent.

In addition, far more citizens give to political campaigns through the voluntary checkoff system than through direct contributions. While approximately one in seven Americans now contribute to presidential campaigns through the checkoff, only one in 22 Americans contributed to political campaigns in 1994, according to a University of Michigan study. With that support, the presidential system has been able to fund elections since its inception in 1976.

Former Senator Paul Laxalt (R.-Nev.), who chaired numerous campaigns for President Reagan, has said that the presidential campaign system "worked, and it was like a breath of fresh air." A bipartisan study commission headed by Republican Melvin Laird and Democrat Robert Strauss concluded in 1985 that the system "has clearly proven its worth in opening up the process, reducing undue influence of individuals and groups, and virtually ending corruption in presidential election finance."

Since the mid-1980s, however, the emergence of the soft money loophole has greatly undermined the integrity of the presidential system by reintroducing Watergate-style contributions in presidential campaigns. Again we see huge corporate donations and $100,000 (or more) individual contributions being raised by national political leaders and by the political parties. This is a pernicious loophole that can and must be closed and would be closed by S. 1219.

While ending the soft money system is absolutely critical to ensuring the continued success of the presidential campaign finance system, there are several other reforms Common Cause believes would significantly improve the system:

End State-by-State Limits

Common Cause supports eliminating the state-by-state limits for publicly financed Presidential primary candidates. There has been a general consensus among both candidates and observers of the system that the state limits do not reflect the realities of the primaries — in which only a few states, especially those with the earliest primary dates, are the targets of substantial spending by candidates. The Federal Election Commission reported that "the limitations have had little impact on campaign spending in a given state, with the exception of Iowa and New Hampshire. In most other states, campaigns have been unable or have not wished to expend an amount equal to the limitation."

Although several other states are holding early primaries in 1996, the overall spending limit for the primary season will continue to act as a necessary constraint on spending by candidates. While candidates will have to exercise care in allocating their spending, elimination of the limits will give them greater discretion in the running of their campaigns.

Free- and Reduced-Cost Television Time

Common Cause supports extending the concept of free- and reduced-cost television time to presidential candidates in both the primary and general elections. Television is especially important to presidential candidates. Although the early primaries in Iowa and New Hampshire focus on face-to-face campaigning, television remains an important element in those states. In the larger states which now have earlier primaries — New York, California, Texas—television is the key element in the campaigns and it is where most campaign funds are spent.

We strongly believe that providing the resource of free- or reduced-cost television time is critical for congressional candidates and is equally so for presidential candidates. Providing candidates with this additional resource would offer additional clear resources for candidates who agree to spending limits and would help blunt the impact of wealthy candidates' spending their own money.

Fix the Underfunding of the Presidential Election Campaign Fund

As you know, 1996 presidential primary candidates did not receive the full allotment of matching funds to which they are entitled on January 2. While the shortfall was partially due to the large amounts of funds raised by candidates in 1995 and the fact that the $3 checkoff amount has only been in effect for two years, another factor is Treasury Department regulations which do not allow anticipation of funds which taxpayers will check off in early 1996 and which will be available to the fund later in the primary season. We believe the Federal Election Campaign Act should be amended to explicitly allow a reasonable estimation of anticipated revenue to make it possible for primary candidates to be fully funded.

In the long term, we believe it will be necessary for Congress to index the $3 checkoff amount to inflation, in order to bring the revenue to the fund in line with the already indexed payments to candidates.

Provide Candidates with Matching Funds at an Earlier Date

Common Cause believes the committee should consider moving the current date for providing the first payment of matching funds to presidential primary candidates from the beginning of the election year to an earlier time in order to accommodate the now "front-loaded" primary season. Public funding of primary candidates is intended to provide candidates with a source of funding free of special-interest influence and to free the candidates themselves from the burden of spending most of their time raising money rather than meeting with voters. Allowing the use of matching funds at an earlier date would recognize the reality that primary campaigns do not begin on January 1 of the election year.

CONCLUSION

Mr. Chairman, campaign finance reform is a test of the willingness of politicians to support truly revolutionary change in our government. If the Senators and Representatives who have spent much of the last year talking about changing business as usual in Washington are sincere, they will join as a sponsor of S. 1219. The alternative — one the American people will no longer tolerate — is to continue to support the current campaign finance system that is fundamentally corrupt.

We urge support for S. 1219 and will support only strengthening amendments that do not undermine the bipartisan support for the bill.

Is Campaign Finance Reform Necessary?

BRADLEY A. SMITH

*Campaign Finance Regulation: Faulty Assumptions
and Undemocratic Consequences*

INTRODUCTION

Efforts to control political campaign spending have met with little ideological resistance since the turn of the century, and efforts over the past 25 years to reform campaign finance, primarily by limiting contributions to and spending by campaigns, have been exceptionally popular. However, despite its popularity, there is no serious evidence that campaign finance regulation has actually accomplished any of the goals set out for it by its supporters. Rather, continued support for campaign finance reform by groups such as Common Cause seems to stem more from habit than from any serious argument that those reforms already enacted are working or that proposed reforms might meet their stated goals. In fact, efforts to regulate campaign finance have been little short of disastrous. They have distorted the political process, hindered grassroots political involvement, infringed on First Amendment rights, and helped to entrench incumbents in office while doing nothing to address the allegedly corrupting influence of money in politics.

This paper examines the fundamental assumptions behind campaign finance reform efforts and finds them largely flawed. Because these assumptions are flawed, campaign finance reform will not achieve the objectives set out for it and, in fact, has already had a detrimental effect on the electoral process. Rather than continue down the path of greater government regulation, the country would be best served by deregulating the electoral process, as intended by the drafters of the Constitution.

THE STRUCTURE OF CAMPAIGN FINANCE REGULATION

The first state laws regulating campaign finance were passed in the latter part of the nineteenth century. These laws were typically limited to minimal disclosure requirements of campaign donations and expenditures, although four states also banned all corporate contributions beginning in 1897. The first federal law, a narrow provision banning some corporate contributions, was passed in 1907. Over the next six decades, the federal government passed several laws requiring disclosure of contributions and the filing of reports, but these laws remained generally toothless and were largely ignored. Only with passage of the Federal Election Campaign Act [FECA] in 1971 and, more important, the 1974 amendments to FECA, did campaign finance regulation become a significant factor on the American political landscape.

The Federal Election Campaign Act

The 1974 amendments to FECA constituted the first effort to establish a comprehensive, national system of campaign finance regulation. Specifically, the amendments established the following framework of contribution and spending limits for federal campaign finance:

- Individual contributions were limited to $1,000 per candidate per election, with primary and general elections counting as separate elections.

- Individuals were limited to $25,000 per calendar year in total contributions to candidates, party committees, and political action committees (PACs).
- PACs and party committees were limited to contributing $5,000 per candidate per election.
- Candidates were limited to personal spending of $25,000 in House races and $35,000 in Senate races, a provision later struck down as unconstitutional by the Supreme Court.
- Absolute ceilings were placed on the amount that could be spent in any campaign: $70,000 for a House seat and $100,000, or eight cents per eligible voter, in the Senate. That provision was also struck down by the Supreme Court.
- Independent expenditures by nonparty committees — that is, expenditures on behalf of a candidate without the cooperation or knowledge of the candidate — were limited to $1,000 per candidate per election. That, too, was struck down by the Supreme Court.
- Political party committees, in addition to being limited in the amounts they could directly contribute to candidate campaigns, were limited in spending on behalf of their candidates to $10,000 in House campaigns and $20,000 in Senate campaigns. Both figures were indexed for inflation, and the Senate figure also allowed for adding spending based on population.

In addition, the 1974 amendments established the presidential financing system of matching funds to candidates for amounts raised in contributions of $250 or less, established overall spending limits for eligibility to receive matching funds, and provided for public funding of major party candidates in the general election for president.

In the years surrounding the passage of the 1974 amendments to FECA, many states passed similar laws regulating the financing of state campaigns. The amendments and their state counterparts were hailed at the time as marking an end to the corrupt system of elections that the United States had used since its founding.

Buckley v. Valeo

One of the more remarkable features of the decades-long effort to regulate campaign finance, which culminated in the 1974 amendments to FECA, was the almost total absence of ideological opposition to regulation. Yet scarcely had FECA been enacted when a formidable ideological and constitutional challenge against it was launched in the federal courts.

In *Buckley v. Valeo,* a coalition of liberals and conservatives attacked FECA as a violation of First Amendment guarantees of free speech. Restrictions on campaign contributions and spending, they pointed out, constitute restrictions on speech as surely as would a statute directly prohibiting an individual from speaking. "Presumably dollars are not stuffed in ballot boxes. . . . The mediating factor that turns money into votes is speech. More money leads to more communications supporting the candidate. More communications supporting the candidate leads to additional votes. . . . Advocacy cannot be proscribed simply because it may be effective."

In a lengthy opinion, the Supreme Court agreed that campaign finance restrictions burdened First Amendment rights but declined to strike down the entire statute. Citing the government interest in preventing the "appearance of corruption," the Court upheld restrictions on the size of campaign contributions but struck down limits on candidate spending and independent expenditures in support of a candidate. The Court held that the provision of taxpayer funds to support campaign activity could be conditioned on a candidate's agreement to limit total campaign expenditures. It also held that Congress could require the disclosure of campaign donors' names, addresses, and amounts contributed.

The net result of the *Buckley* decision is that Congress and state legislatures can limit the amount an individual or entity can give to a campaign and can require disclosure of campaign donors and expenditures. However, Congress cannot limit the amount a campaign spends, nor can it limit the amount individuals or organizations spend on their own to support a candidate's campaign so long as these expenditures are made independent of the campaign. It is within these limits that proposals to regulate campaign finance must operate.

In a partial dissent from the judgment in *Buckley,* Chief Justice Warren Burger warned that contribution limits would restrict the amount of political speech and have a "chilling" effect on grassroots political activity. The loss of "seed money" in the form of early, large contributions would, he argued, discriminate against many candidates. He further argued that the legislation, and in particular its provisions for public funding of presidential campaigns, would be used by incumbents to disadvantage challengers, third parties, and independent candidates.

In the 20 years since the Buckley decision, all of Burger's fears have been realized. However, supporters of campaign finance limitations continue to argue for still more regulation. This regulatory approach is doomed to fail, not only because the reformers have incorrectly assessed the probable results of legislation but also because they have based their legislation on faulty assumptions.

FAULTY ASSUMPTIONS OF CAMPAIGN FINANCE REFORM

John Gardner, founder of the interest group Common Cause once stated, "There is nothing in our political system today that creates more mischief, more corruption, and more alienation and distrust on the part of the public than does our system of financing elections." In a nutshell, Gardner's statement sums up the general assumptions underlying the arguments made in favor of campaign finance regulation: first, there is too much money being spent in political campaigns; second, this money has a corrupting influence, buying both votes and elections and thereby excluding ordinary citizens from the political process; and finally, the growth in campaign spending has made the electoral process in some way less "democratic." However, as Professor Frank Sorauf of the University of Minnesota, the nation's foremost commentator on campaign finance, points out, "Very few aspects of American politics better fit the metaphor of Plato's cave than the realities of American campaign finance." What most political scientists and other experts know as reality is vastly different from the "grotesque images projected onto the wall of the cave." The common public perception of the role of money is, in Sorauf's words, "difficult to square with the evidence." But any rational policy discussion of campaign finance must be based on the world as it is, not on the distorted images projected onto the wall of the cave and heralded as reality by the campaign finance reformers. Close scrutiny of the assumptions underlying most campaign finance reform efforts is long overdue.

Do We Spend Too Much on Campaigns?

One often hears that too much money is spent on political campaigns. Indeed, the language in which campaigns are described in the general press constantly reinforces that perception. Candidates "amass war chests" with the help of "special interests" that "pour" their "millions" into campaigns. "Obscene" expenditures "careen" out of control or "skyrocket" upwards. Rarely is there a dispassionate discussion of actual expenditures on politics. For the campaign finance regulators, this lack of calm discussion is a good thing. If truth be told, there is substantial reason to believe that Americans spend too little on political campaigns.

To say that too much money is spent on campaigning is to beg the question, compared to what? For example, Americans spend more than twice as much money each year on yogurt as on political campaigns. As the *Washington Post* reported recently, "Close to $100 million will be spent promoting the 'Seinfeld' launch into syndicated reruns this fall — more than it costs to run a presidential campaign." In the two-year election cycle culminating in November 1994, approximately $590 million was spent by all congressional general election candidates. Although this set a new record for spending in congressional races, the amount is hardly exorbitant, amounting to roughly $3 per eligible voter spent over the two-year period. Total direct campaign spending for all local, state, and federal elections, including Congress, over the same period can be reasonably estimated at between $1.5 billion and $2.0 billion, or somewhere between $7.50 and $10 per eligible voter. When one considers that that money was spread over several candidates, it is hard to suggest that office seekers are spending obscene sums attempting to get their messages through to voters. By comparison, Americans spent two to three times as much money in 1994 alone on the purchase of potato chips. Procter & Gamble and Philip Morris Company, the nation's two largest advertisers, spend roughly the same amount each year on advertising as is spent by all political candidates and parties.

If it is hard to suggest that too much money is spent on political campaigns in some absolute sense, it may be fairly suggested that the perception that too much is spent stems from a belief that what is spent is largely ineffective. In other words, the problem, on closer examination, may not be that too much is spent but that too little benefit seems to come out of it. Voters are tired of what they perceive as the relentless negativity of televised campaign advertisements, and they do not believe that political advertisements add significantly to their store of real political knowledge.

This perception may itself be influenced by press reporting and editorials critical of campaign advertising. But whether modern, televised campaign advertising is overly negative may simply be a matter of individual voter preference. Negative advertising is popular for a simple reason: it works. Indeed, as Bruce Felknor, former executive director of the Fair Campaign Practices Committee, states, "Without attention-grabbing, cogent, memorable, negative campaigning, almost no challenger can hope to win unless the incumbent has just been found guilty of a heinous crime." It is a mistake to assume, as many campaign finance reformers do, that the elimination of negative campaigning would necessarily serve the public. Negative advertising that is relevant to the issues can serve the public well. Felknor notes that without negative campaigning aimed at showing up an opponent's bad side, "any knave or mountebank in the land may lie and steal his or her way into the White House or any other elective office." To suggest that candidates should not point to each other's perceived shortcomings, writes Felknor, is "preposterous." Negative campaigning — that is, efforts to expose corruption, unpopular positions, or weak character in an opponent — has been prevalent in American elections since 1796.

Even if one concedes that the elimination of negative advertising would be a good thing, efforts to limit spending on campaigns — either directly, through spending limits, or indirectly, through contribution limits — bear no relationship to the negativity of the campaign. Less spending only reduces the amount of communication, not any negative tone of that communication.

Increased campaign spending does translate into a better informed electorate. Gary Jacobson's extensive studies have shown that "the extent and content of information [voters] do have has a decisive effect on how they vote." Voter understanding of issues clearly increases with the quantity of campaign information received. In short, spending less on campaigns will not elevate the level of debate, but it will result in less public awareness and understanding of issues. This reduction in the flow of information may even make well-produced negative advertising more valuable, as candidates will need to get the maximum political mileage from each expenditure and a poorly informed electorate may be more susceptible to misleading political advertisements.

There are no objective criteria by which to measure whether "too much" is spent on political campaigns. What is spent, we might fairly say, is the amount that individuals feel is worthwhile to contribute and candidates find is effective to spend. Considering the importance of elections to any democratic society, it is hard to believe that the expenditure of less than $10 per voter for all local, state, and national campaigns every two years constitutes a crisis requiring government regulation and limitations on spending.

Does Money Buy Elections?

The second assumption of campaign finance reform is that money buys elections in some manner incompatible with a functioning democracy. Of course, it is true that a candidate with little or no money to spend is unlikely to win most races. Furthermore, the candidate spending more money wins more often than not. But correlation is not the same as cause and effect, and one must be careful not to make too much of such simple numbers. The correlation may stem simply from the desire of donors to contribute to candidates who are likely to win, in which case the ability to win attracts money rather than the other way around. Similarly, higher levels of campaign contributions to and spending by a candidate may merely reflect a level of public support that is later manifested at the polls.

Moreover, higher spending does not necessarily translate into victory. Michael Huffington, Lewis Lehrman, Mark Dayton, John Connally, and Clayton Williams are just a few of the lavish spenders who wound up on the losing end of campaigns. As Michael Malbin, director of the Center for Legislative Studies at the Rockefeller Institute of Government, explains, "Having money means having the ability to be heard; it does not mean that voters will like what they hear." In the end, so long as voters have the final say among various candidates of differing views, the democratic process is well served.

While money does not ensure election, those few studies that have attempted to quantify the effect of campaign spending on votes have found that additional spending does affect a limited number of votes. However, the positive effect of added spending is significantly greater for challengers than for incumbents. In fact, studies show an inverse relationship between incumbent spending and incumbent success. Heavy spending by an incumbent usually indicates that the incumbent is in electoral trouble and facing a well-financed challenger. But the incumbent's added spending is likely to have less effect on vote totals than the challenger's added spending. Thus, limits on campaign spending would hurt challengers more than incumbents. Accordingly, efforts to limit spending, whether mandatory or through incentive-based "voluntary" caps, should not be viewed as benign. Incumbent lawmakers will always have an incentive to draw campaign regulations to their advantage; commentators have noted that campaign finance legislation routinely favors the party or candidate putting forth the proposal and always favors incumbent legislators.

Incumbency is already the single best predictor of electoral success. Limits on campaign financing can tend to add to political ossification. Although incumbent reelection rates have been consistently above 75 percent since the turn of the century, they have risen to record heights in this era of extensive campaign finance regulation. Even in the November 1994 elections, which resulted in significant political realignment, 91.4 percent of congressional incumbents seeking reelection were victorious. The Republican gains came primarily from the GOP's near sweep of "open" seats — that is, seats to which the incumbent did not seek reelection. While money can help buy votes, it buys far more votes for challengers than for incumbents. This being the case, money is an equalizer in the system, helping challengers to overcome the otherwise tremendous advantages of incumbency. Despite all the alarmist rhetoric, it is once again difficult to see what all the fuss is about.

Does Money Buy Votes in the Legislature?

Many Americans have come to view legislative politics as a money game. Indeed, states with few restrictions on campaign spending are frequently referred to as "pay to play" states. For many casual observers, legislative politics in the U.S. Congress can be summed up in the words of former representative Ozzie Myers (D.-Pa.), who was caught on videotape taking a bribe while declaring, "Money talks, bull . . . walks!" The fact that Representative Myers was expelled from the House is often overlooked.

In fact, those who have studied voting patterns on a systematic basis are almost unanimous in finding that campaign contributions affect very few votes in the legislature. The primary factors in determining a legislator's votes are party affiliation, ideology, and constituent views and needs. That has been reflected in study after study over the past 20 years. Where contributions and voting patterns intersect, it is primarily due to the fact that donors contribute to candidates believed to favor their positions, not the other way around.

In response to these repeated studies showing little or no "vote buying," campaign reformers generally offer a simple response: experience and human nature generally tell us that legislators, like other people, are influenced by money, even when it goes not directly to their pockets but to their campaigns. Yet the issue is not so simple, and to accept the findings of the repeated studies does not require us to check our common sense at the door.

First, people who are attracted to public office generally do have strong personal views on issues. Second, there are institutional and political incentives to support party positions. Third, money is not the only political commodity of value. For example, in 1993–94, the National Rifle Association contributed nearly $2 million to congressional campaigns through its PAC. However, the NRA also has 2.8 million members, "who focus intently, even solely, on NRA issues in their voting." Groups advocating gun control often complain that the

NRA outspends them but rarely mention that the NRA also outvotes them. Is the NRA's influence based on dollars or votes? When the NRA faced a liberal Congress and president in 1993–94, money did not gain the NRA victory over the Brady bill or the assault weapons ban. However, the election of a new congressional majority in 1994 may result in the repeal of both aforementioned pieces of legislation. Yet a fourth reason why campaign contributions have minimal effect on legislation is that large campaign contributors are usually offset in legislative debate by equally well financed interests who contribute to a different group of candidates. In fact, large PACs and their parent organizations frequently suffer enormous losses in the legislative process.

If campaign contributions have any meaningful effect on legislative voting behavior, it appears to be on a limited number of votes that are generally related to technical issues arousing little public interest. On such issues, prior contributions may provide the contributor with access to the legislator or legislative staff. The contributor may then be able to shape legislation to the extent that such efforts are not incompatible with the dominant legislative motives of ideology, party affiliation and agenda, and constituent views. Whether the influence of campaign contributions on these limited issues is good or bad depends on one's views of the legislation. The exclusion of knowledgeable contributors from the legislative process can just as easily lead to poor legislation with unintended consequences as their inclusion. But in any case, it must be stressed that such votes are few.

Campaign finance reformers seem to envision a world in which career officeholders, freed from the corrupting influence of money, lobbyists, and — dare it be said? — public opinion, would produce good, wise, and fair legislation. This notion of the philosopher-bureaucrat, popular during the Progressive Era at the turn of the century, has been discredited as an unattainable and, indeed, undesirable ideal. And although campaign finance reformers have long posed as disinterested citizens seeking only good government, Lillian BeVier of the University of Virginia Law School has surveyed reform efforts and found that campaign finance regulators have targeted certain types of campaign activities, "at least in part because [those activities] are closely tied to political agendas the reformers oppose." In other words, the motivation for efforts to limit campaign contributions and spending may not be that money sways votes in the legislature, but that those being elected to office reflect ideologies and voting tendencies with which many campaign finance reformers do not agree. The reformers therefore favor regulation that would tilt the electoral process in favor of preferred and, as it turns out, largely liberal candidates.

Given the popular perception otherwise, it simply cannot be stated strongly enough: no significant causal relationship has been found between campaign contributions and legislative voting patterns. In the end, just as money can buy speech but cannot ensure that voters will like what they hear, money can buy access to officials but cannot ensure that those officials will like what they hear. The safeguard is in an informed voting public.

Has the Growth in Campaign Spending Altered the Democratic Nature of the Process?

The final basic assumption motivating efforts to limit campaign contributions and spending is the notion that the growth in campaign expenditures over the past 30 years has created an unequal distribution of electoral power, in which monied interests dominate the system. Like the notion that money buys elections and legislative votes, this assumption contains a kernel of truth surrounded by a heavy coating of myth.

Contrary to the image created by campaign finance reformers, there has never been a "golden age" of American politics in which money was unimportant and the poor participated on the same level as the rich. Wealth has always been important in democratic politics, and never have more than a small minority of Americans contributed to politics with their dollars.

Indeed, in early U.S. elections, most campaign expenses were paid directly by the candidates. Such expenses were relatively minimal, such as publishing an occasional campaign pamphlet and, especially in the South, treating voters to food and drink at public gatherings and rallies. Candidates did not "run" for election but "stood" for office, relying on their reputations and personal recommendations to carry them to victory. However, far from being more "democratic" than current campaigns, elections in this early period were generally contested by candidates representing aristocratic factions before a relatively small, homogeneous electorate of propertied white men.

This genteel system of upper-class politics began to change in the 1830s, when Martin Van Buren organized the first popular mass campaigns around Andrew Jackson and the Democratic party. It was the very democratization of the process that created the need for significant campaign spending. Money became necessary not only for the traditional expenditures on food and liquor, but also for advertisements, widespread pamphleteering, organization of rallies, and logistical support. However, even the new, mass parties obtained financing from a small number of sources. Funding for the new style of mass campaigning initially fell on those who benefited most directly from gaining and/or retaining power: government employees. Absent a professional civil service, all government employees relied on their party retaining power if they were to retain their jobs. It became common practice to assess those employees a percentage of their salaries to support the party's campaigns.

Similarly, would-be officeholders allied with the opposition served as a major source of challenger funds. As late as 1878, roughly 90 percent of the money raised by the Republican congressional committee came from assessments on federal officeholders. However, after the passage of the Pendleton Act in 1883, which created a federal civil service, and of similar laws in the states, campaign money from assessments on officeholders began to dry up. Only then did politicians look for new sources of funds. Two dominant sources emerged: wealthy individuals and corporations.

The acceleration of northern industrialization that accompanied and followed the Civil War created the new phenomenon of large, national corporations. These corporations and government regulation grew in a symbiotic relationship. Wartime government contracts created the foundations of many a corporation, and government land and cash grants to railroad companies became common. Corporations also benefited as Republican Congresses sheltered many industries behind high tariff walls. To tame the corporate power it had helped to create, in 1887 Congress created the Interstate Commerce Commission. More business regulation followed, including the Sherman Antitrust Act in 1890. State regulation of railroad rates, business competition, and working conditions became common.

With both state and federal governments claiming previously unprecedented powers to both regulate and subsidize industry, corporate America recognized the need for political participation. The goal was not to buy votes but to elect candidates supportive of corporate interests. By 1888, roughly 40 percent of Republican national campaign funds came from manufacturing and business interests. State parties were probably even more reliant on corporate funding. In the last years of the nineteenth century, Republican National Chairman Mark Hanna systematized these contributions through a system of assessments on banks and corporations. By 1904, corporations contributed more than 73 percent of Theodore Roosevelt's presidential campaign funds. The Democratic party relied less on corporate contributions but was also heavily wedded to funding from the personal wealth of a handful of wealthy industrialists to finance their campaigns. Industrialist Thomas Fortune Ryan and banker August Belmont contributed roughly three-quarters of the Democrats' 1904 presidential campaign fund ($450,000 and $250,000, respectively); Henry Davis, a mine owner and the party's vice presidential candidate, contributed much of the rest.

In other words, contrary to the myths of campaign finance reformers, the role of the average citizen and the small contributor in financing campaigns has not been reduced over the years. For most voters, familiarizing themselves with the candidates and voting in elections have always been the extent of political involvement. Today, approximately 10 percent of Americans make any financial contribution to a political party, candidate, or PAC in an election cycle. That represents a far broader base of financial support than has historically existed. Yet few would argue that it has made the political system more democratic or responsive.

Just as it is a mistake to assume that reliance on small number of contributors is necessarily undemocratic, it is a mistake to believe that large expenditures are inherently undemocratic. If, for example, we assume that reliance on numerous small contributions makes a campaign in some way more democratic, then the U.S. Senate campaign of Oliver North was the most democratic of all 1994 campaigns. Yet it was also one of the most expensive, costing nearly $20 million. Despite his reliance on small donations from many people, North was roundly castigated by many campaign finance reformers for the high cost of his campaign. Yet North lost.

Unfortunately, campaign finance regulation actually limits voter choice by discouraging challengers and favoring political insiders. Neither increased campaign spending nor reliance on a small fundraising base is inherently undemocratic. Those who seek to broaden the fundraising base by limiting large contributions are searching for a holy grail that never was, and their efforts tend to make the system less democratic rather than more so. . . .

CONCLUSION

Efforts to regulate campaign finance, in particular, the Federal Election Campaign Act, have been based on mistaken assumptions about the role of money in politics and on the mistaken belief that eliminating or reducing money will in some way make the process more fair, the playing field more level. In fact, spending on political campaigns is hardly extravagant, amounting to only a few dollars per eligible voter every two years. Because there is no a priori correct allocation of political advantages, including money, efforts to control this one feature of the political landscape have tended to have serious detrimental side effects, including the entrenchment of incumbents and the stifling of new, alternative political choices. FECA and its state counterparts have served to limit grassroots political activity and to enhance the power of campaign professionals and insiders. Overall, campaign finance regulation has served to make the political process less open and less democratic.

Moreover, efforts to limit campaign contributions and expenditures run directly counter to the assumptions of the First Amendment. The First Amendment was based on the belief that political speech is too important to be regulated by the government. Campaign finance laws operate on the directly contrary assumption that campaigns are so important that speech must be regulated. The result has been a series of Supreme Court decisions making largely arcane, questionable distinctions between different types of entities, campaigns, and campaign activities. These decisions are hard to justify under the First Amendment and have clearly limited the opportunities for Americans to engage in what at least one sitting justice has recognized as "core political speech."

After nearly 25 years, FECA has done nothing to change the alleged evils that led to its adoption. This suggests either that the evils are inevitable if not beneficial, or that the solution to the alleged problems must lie elsewhere — in measures such as term limitations, abolition or modification of legislative seniority and pension systems, or other structural reforms from which Congress has shied away.

In short, the solution to the alleged problems of campaign finance is far simpler than the arcane web of regulations that leads to citizens being fined for distributing homemade leaflets, to trade groups being prohibited from communicating with their members, and to personal wealth serving as an indicator of a viable political candidate. The solution is to recognize the flawed assumptions of the campaign finance reformers, dismantle FECA and the FEC bureaucracy, and take seriously the system of campaign finance regulation that the Founders wrote into the Bill of Rights: "Congress shall make no law . . . abridging the freedom of speech."

Questions for Discussion

1. Although McBride and Smith disagree about the need for campaign finance reform, in what ways do their analyses of campaign finance agree?
2. Who are the supporters of campaign finance reform? Why do they favor reform?
3. Who are the opponents of campaign finance reform? Why do they oppose reform?
4. Who would be the principal beneficiaries of public financing for congressional campaigns? Why?
5. What effect would denial of private funding have on First Amendment rights?

Suggested Readings

"Campaign Finance Legislation: Pro & Con." *Congressional Digest* 73, no. 4 (April 1994): entire issue.

Carney, Eliza Newlin. "Defending PACs." *National Journal* 28, no. 28 (July 13, 1996): 1518–1523.

Center for Responsive Politics. *Ten Myths about Money in Politics.* Washington, D.C.: Center for Responsive Politics, 1995.

Dewer, Helen. "Complex Forces Halt Campaign Finance Reform." *Washington Post,* July 8, 1996, pp. A1, A6.

Dionne, E. J., Jr. " . . . And the Rest of the System Too." *Washington Post,* June 25, 1996, p. A17.

Jost, Kenneth. "Campaign Finance Reform." *CQ Researcher* 6, no. 6 (February 9, 1996): 121–144.

Ornstein, Norman. "Bad Contribution." *New Republic* 214, no. 24 (June 10, 1996): 14, 16.

Smith, Bradley A. "Faulty Assumptions and Undemocratic Consequences of Campaign Finance Reform." *Yale Law Journal* 105, no. 4 (January 1996): 1049–1091.

Smith, Linda. "Campaign Finance: Fix Washington." *Washington Post,* June 25, 1996, p. A17.

U.S. Cong., House of Representatives. *Campaign Finance Reform Legislation.* Hearings before the Committee on House Oversight, 104th Cong., 1st Sess., 1995.

Wertheimer, Fred, and Susan Weiss Manes. "Campaign Finance Reform: A Key to Restoring the Health of Our Democracy." *Columbia Law Review* 94, no. 4 (May 1994): 1126–1159.

Wright, John R. *Interest Groups and Congress: Lobbying, Contributions, and Influence.* Boston, Mass.: Allyn and Bacon, 1996.

Chapter 11

Should the Electoral College Be Abolished?

When citizens vote in presidential elections, they do not cast their ballot for presidential candidates but for electors who are pledged to support particular candidates. These electors constitute the Electoral College, which officially elects the president.

The Framers of the Constitution created an Electoral College because they feared popular election as the means for filling the nation's highest office. Instead, they hoped that wise electors would make independent judgments. Today electors are committed to supporting their party's candidate, but they are not uniformly required to do so. Still, citizens can generally be certain that electors will vote as pledged.

In the Electoral College the number of electors for each state is equal to the number of senators and representatives from that state. Heavily populated states have more electors than sparsely populated states because they have more representatives. In all but two states the slate of electors that gets the largest number of popular votes (a plurality or a majority) gets all the Electoral College votes of that state. In Maine and Nebraska, where electors represent congressional districts and two electors are selected at-large, it is possible to have a divided electoral vote. To become president, a candidate must win a majority of the votes in the Electoral College. If no candidate wins a majority, the House of Representatives makes the choice from the three candidates with the largest number of electoral votes. In this runoff election state delegations vote as units, each state having one vote.

Even if an election is not thrown into the House of Representatives, it is possible for a person to become president although he or she has fewer popular votes than the opponent. In 1876, for example, Samuel Tilden received more popular votes than Rutherford B. Hayes, yet Hayes became president. Grover Cleveland experienced the same kind of loss to Benjamin Harrison in 1888.

The effect of the Electoral College system on the distribution of power has been to give advantages to the heavily populated states, like New York, California, and Illinois, because these states have large electoral votes. Presidential candidates usually devote their attention to these more populous states because of the Electoral College's winner-take-all system.

From time to time, Congress has conducted hearings about changing the Electoral College system. Three new procedures for electing the president have been proposed:

1. Require electors to vote for the candidates to whom they are pledged.
2. Replace the winner-take-all system with a system in which candidates get the same proportion of a state's electoral vote as they receive in its popular vote.
3. Eliminate the Electoral College altogether and establish direct popular election of the president.

The debate below, drawn from a hearing before the Subcommittee on the Constitution of the Committee on the Judiciary in 1992, considers the value of the Electoral College. Political Scientist Lawrence D. Longley argues that the Electoral College is a highly imperfect method of electing the president and ought to be abolished. It performs poorly both at its best and at its worst. At its best, Longley makes the following criticisms:

1. The Electoral College is a distorted counting device.
2. Candidate strategy is shaped and determined by these distortions; candidates focus on large, swingable states in order to win their large blocs of electoral votes.
3. The importance of a large, swingable state's parochial interests, political leaders, and unique local factors are magnified by the Electoral College.
4. The Electoral College differs in impact on different types of candidates. Regional third-party candidates are advantaged by the winner-take-all feature, while third-party candidates with broad-based but nationally distributed support are disadvantaged.
5. Faithless electors may further distort the popular will.

At its worst, Longley notes:

1. In a very close electoral vote count, ambitious electors could determine the outcome.
2. An election can produce a divided verdict, with one candidate receiving the most popular votes and the other candidate winning the election in electoral votes.
3. An election may be undecided on election night, with deals and actions by the electors or the mid-December Electoral College meetings deciding the outcome.
4. If the Electoral College fails to produce a majority in December, the extraordinary procedure would be followed by election of the president by the House of Representatives in January.
5. A final and definitive decision by the House in January is by no means certain.

Political scientist Judith A. Best favors a continuation of the Electoral College. She finds the proposals to amend the electoral system would deform rather than reform the system. She attacks the contingency procedure as one that will make runoff elections the rule, proliferate parties and candidates, and turn the selection process into a national ordeal. The proposal to establish a direct election would convert a direct popular federal election into a plebiscite that would destroy the balance of power in the U.S. governing system.

In defending the Electoral College system, she makes the following points:

1. The general election should be and, for all practical purposes, is now the only election.
2. Like a contingency election, a runner-up presidency is extremely unlikely under the electoral vote system.
3. Faithless electors have never been a problem and can be handled short of a constitutional amendment by the states and the parties.
4. In no case in our history has the electoral vote system rebuffed a man who had an undisputed majority of the popular vote.
5. The electoral system is a major support for our moderate two-party system, and this would be the worst time to further weaken the two-party system.
6. To abandon the Electoral College system would be to radically change the fundamental structure of the Constitution by removing the federal constraints on the power of the presidency, and it would lead to attacks on the legitimacy of other federally districted intermediary institutions such as the state equality principle of the Senate and the amending process.

$\boxed{\checkmark}$ *YES*

Should the Electoral College Be Abolished?

LAWRENCE D. LONGLEY
The Case against the Electoral College

WHAT IS TO BE DONE?

Many years ago, political columnist and sage Arthur Krock wrote, "The road to reform in the method of choosing the Presidents and Vice-Presidents of the United States is littered with the wrecks of previous attempts." I commend this Subcommittee for being willing to travel once more down that difficult road to reform. The last substantial effort at electoral college reform occurred over a thirteen year period from 1966 through 1979. These efforts came very close to success, with a constitutional amendment providing for direct election of the President being overwhelmingly adopted by the House of Representatives in 1969 by a vote of 338–70 and enjoying enormous support from diverse groups. This measure was, however, to be defeated in 1970 in the Senate, not by a substantive vote on its merits, but rather by an undeclared yet effective filibuster. This defeat was extremely disheartening to electoral reform supporters. Despite this 1970 setback, the Senate returned to electoral college reform efforts in 1973, 1977, and again in 1979. S. J. Res. 28, a proposed constitutional amendment to abolish the electoral college, received 51 votes in the Senate in 1979, a clear majority, but unfortunately insufficient to constitute the necessary two-thirds vote. It is a measure of the determination and courage of electoral reform supporters, as well as a measure of a growing awareness of the electoral college's inadequacies, that this Subcommittee is meeting now to consider once more a constitutional amendment in this area. I compliment the Subcommittee and its Chairman for its initiative, and wish it success in finally doing away with the arcane institution of the electoral college.

I would be less than honest, however, if I did not also point out the great difficulties in this task. These difficulties lie not only in the constitutional amending process itself, but also in the necessity of convincing oneself, other Senators, and the public of the desirability and even necessity of abolishing the electoral college. These difficulties lie also in the divisions and occasional self interest calculations of reformers themselves. Perhaps my occasional co-author, Washington journalist Neal R. Peirce, put this best when he once wrote:

> The cause of electoral reform seem to be endangered by two age-old threats — the unwillingness of reformers to agree on a single system and the insistence of some that they could reform the system for their own partisan advantage.

It is my conviction that this Subcommittee must unite in support of one electoral college reform plan — and I hope this is S. J. Res. 297, as introduced by Senators David Pryor and David L. Boren. This Subcommittee must put the national interest ahead of any self-interest advantage perceived — accurately or not — as inherent in the present electoral college system, and ensure that the vote of the American people for the people's president is counted fairly and conclusively in determining the U.S. President.

THE INSTITUTION

The electoral college is a highly imperfect method of electing the President of the United States. At best, it distorts campaign strategy and poorly represents the popular will. At worst, it can create political and constitutional crises in determining who should be President. The 1992 election illustrates vividly these distortions and imperfections and further contains the potential for crisis in the electoral college.

THE ELECTORAL COLLEGE AT ITS BEST

The electoral college means of presidential election is of great significance, even when it produces a clear decision. The electoral college is not a neutral and fair counting device for tallying popular votes cast for President in the form of electoral votes. Instead, it counts some votes as more important than others, according to the state in which they are cast. As a result, these distortions of popular preferences greatly influence candidate strategy: certain key states, their voters, parochial interests, political leaders, and unique local factors, are favored. The electoral college election of the President also discriminates among types of candidates. Independent or third party contenders with a regional following have great opportunities for electoral college significance, while independent or third party candidates with broad-based but nationally distributed support may find themselves excluded. Such candidates can prove decisive in terms of swinging large blocs of electoral votes from one major party candidate to the other. Finally, the electoral college can reflect inaccurately the popular will because of the action of faithless electors — individual electors who vote differently in the electoral college from the expectations of those who elected them.

In short, the electoral college is neither neutral nor fair in its counting of the popular votes cast for the President of the United States.

The Electoral College Is a Distorted Counting Device

There are many reasons why the division of electoral votes will always differ from the division of popular votes. Among these are the apportionment of electoral votes among the states on the basis of census population figures that do not reflect population shifts except every ten years, the assignment of electoral votes to states on a population basis rather than a voter turnout basis, the "constant two" constitutional allocation of two electoral votes equally to each state regardless of size, and the winner-take-all system for determining each state's entire bloc of electoral votes on the basis of a plurality (not even a majority) of popular votes.

As a result of the census determination of electoral votes, states that are growing quickly during the 1990s will not have their new population growth reflected in their electoral vote total until the census in the year 2000, which will establish the electoral college apportionment for each state for the presidential elections of 2004 and 2008. In other words, population changes in any state which will have occurred since 1990 will not be reflected in the 1992 electoral college and will not be taken into account in the electoral college for up to fourteen years, in the year 2004.

The electoral college also does not reflect differing levels of voter turnout, either over time, or among states. The electoral votes each state commands is constant for either two or three presidential elections (1984 to 1988, or 1992 to 2000) despite increases in voter turnout in a state or, alternatively, continued low levels of voter participation. In a classic example, Mississippi and Kansas both had an identical 8 electoral votes in the presidential election of 1960, but Mississippi had an astonishing low voter turnout of 25.5 percent, while Kansas had a far greater voter turnout of 70.3 percent. As a result, in that election, Mississippi enjoyed one electoral vote per 37,271 actual voters, while Kansas had but one electoral vote per 116,003 voters. It is indeed a curious feature of the electoral college that low levels of voter participation are rewarded.

It is in the "constant two" and "winner-take-all" characteristics of the electoral college that one finds the most significant distortions of the electoral college. The extra two electoral votes, regardless of population, provides an advantage to the very smallest states by giving them at least three electoral votes while their population might otherwise entitle them to barely one. However, the importance of the winner-take-all feature overshadows all the other distortions: by carrying New York or California — even by just the smallest margin of popular votes — a candidate will win *all* of that state's 33 or 54 electoral votes. As a consequence, the electoral college greatly magnifies the political significance of the large electoral vote states — even out of proportion to the millions of voters living there.

Candidate Strategy Is Shaped and Determined by These Distortions

Strategists for presidential candidates know full well the importance of these distortions of the electoral college. In the 1992 election, candidates Bush, Clinton, and Perot will spend inordinate time in the largest states of the country. A candidate's day, an extra expenditure of money, a special appeal — any of these might be pivotal in terms of winning an entire large bloc of electoral votes — in the case of California, 54, or 20 percent of the 270 electoral votes needed to win. Candidates and their strategists do not look at the election just in terms of popular votes, but rather in terms of popular votes which can tilt a state's entire bloc of electoral votes.

In the case of a three candidate race — as in 1992 — the plurality win and winner-take-all features take on a special significance. A candidate — be it Bush, Clinton, or Perot — does not need 50 percent of California's vote to win its entire bloc of 54 electoral votes. Forty percent or even 35 percent might well do it. A close three-way division of popular votes in a large state even further magnifies the pivotal value of that state.

The Importance of a Particular State's Parochial Interests, Political Leaders, and Unique Local Factors Are Magnified by the Electoral College

As has been previously argued, the distortions of the electoral college lead candidates to focus on large, swingable states in order to win their large blocs of electoral votes. The best way of appealing to these states is, of course, to concern oneself with the issues and interests special to that state. As a consequence, candidates Bush, Clinton, and Perot are likely, in 1992, to be exceedingly articulate about the problems of Pennsylvania's coal fields or California's defense industry or New York City's crime rates. A special premium is also placed on the role of key large state political leaders who might be significant in that state's outcome. Mayors Dinkins of New York, Bradley of Los Angeles, and Goode of Philadelphia, as well as Governors Cuomo of New York, Edgar of Illinois, and Wilson of California will be consulted — and courted — by the candidates, as will be leaders of the California Hispanic and New York Jewish communities. Local factional feuds and diverse issues in the large pivotal states will play an unusually major role in presidential campaign politics.

In contrast, other states will be neglected. Smaller states, where a narrow plurality win could at most tilt only 3 or 4 electoral votes, will be relatively ignored. Additionally evident will be the lack of candidate time given to states of any size that are viewed as "already decided." No candidate has incentive, under the electoral college, to waste his campaign time or resources on a state or region already likely to go for him — or against him. In short, Delaware, a very small state, is unlikely to be contested vigorously by any candidate: likewise, the Rocky Mountain states may well be conceded to Perot (or alternatively to Bush) and, as a consequence, be "written off" by all the candidates.

In short, the electoral college focuses candidates' attention and resources on those large states seen as pivotal, and away from voters in other states that are too small or that are seen as predictable in outcome. The political interests of the large, swingable states are more than amply looked after; those of the other states are relatively neglected.

The Electoral College Differs in Impact on Different Types of Candidates

Besides the distorting effect of the electoral college in terms of voters, the electoral college also discriminates among candidates. The two major party nominees start off on a relatively equal footing as far as the electoral college goes, assuming each enjoys comparable potential in the large swingable states. Independent or third party candidates, however, differ greatly in their potential in the electoral college.

Regionally based independent or third party candidates — such as George Wallace in 1968 or Strom Thurmond in 1948 — may enjoy potential benefits from the electoral college. Because of their regional strength, they can hope to carry some states and, with them, those states' entire blocs of electoral votes. Their popular vote need not even be an absolute majority in a state: a simple plurality of votes will suffice. In 1968, for example, major party candidates Richard Nixon and Hubert Humphrey together split slightly over 61 percent of the popular vote in Arkansas, while George Wallace, a regional candidate who nevertheless won only 38 percent of that state's vote, received 100 percent of Arkansas' electoral votes. Dixiecrat candidate Strom Thurmond in 1948 benefited significantly from such splits. While winning 1.1 million votes over-all, only 2.4 percent of the national popular vote, he carried four southern states. He received, consequently, 39 electoral votes — 7.3 percent of the national electoral vote total or an inflation of almost three times over his national popular vote strength. Regional candidates can be advantaged by the electoral college's winner-take-all feature; this advantage is in addition to and separate from whatever benefits might conceivably result from such a candidate being able to deadlock the electoral college. (This latter possibility will be discussed subsequently.)

Independent or third party candidates with broad-based but nationally distributed support are, on the other hand, sharply *disadvantaged* by the electoral college. Without plurality support somewhere, such a candidate will be shut out of any electoral votes. Such was the problem which plagued independent candidate John B. Anderson in 1980. Unless his support had been sufficiently unevenly distributed among the states to allow him to win in some states, his voter support — even had it run as high as 20 to 30 percent — was destined to result in total eradication in the electoral college. A significant factor leading to the sharp decline of Anderson's popular support in 1980 resulted precisely from this feature of the electoral college: since his popular vote support was unlikely to carry any state and its electoral votes, a vote for Anderson was widely seen as a wasted vote. As a result of this and other factors, his support dwindled sharply over the six months of his independent presidential candidacy from a high of some 24 percent to a final vote tally of 6.6 percent. A similar decimation of a third party candidate's strength occurred in the 1948 election. Former Vice President Henry A. Wallace ran in that year's presidential contest as the candidate of the Progressive party. He received virtually the same popular vote as Dixiecrat candidate Thurmond in the same election — 1.1 million votes or 2.4 percent. While regional candidate Thurmond saw his strength swell into 7.3 percent of the electoral votes, however, Wallace's vote was completely wiped out by the electoral college. In 1966, less successful independent candidate Eugene McCarthy suffered a similar fate. Although he received around 750,000 popular votes, his votes totally disappeared in terms of electoral votes.

The problem here is more than just unfairness to nationally-based independent or third party candidates when their popular votes result in no electoral
votes. A major factor limiting the support of these very same contenders is the
view that a popular vote for them is a "wasted vote": "He can't win — at least in
this state. I want to cast a vote that counts — a vote for one of the major candidates." This problem could constitute an enormously difficult one for Ross Perot
— or alternatively Bill Clinton or George Bush — in 1992. As the election campaign comes to its conclusion, millions of voters who are possibly inclined to
vote for one of these candidates may decide not to do so because of the electoral
college. Voters may reason: "My preferred candidate — Perot (or Clinton or
Bush) — isn't likely to carry this particular state. One of the other candidates
will. I had best vote for one of them (or against one of them by voting for the
other). I want to have my vote mean something in deciding the election."

There is, however, another way that a "third place" contender with widely
distributed national appeal like Perot (or Clinton or Bush) could be truly significant in the 1992 election, even should he not be in a position to win a large
number of electoral votes. This is by his candidacy and his votes being decisive in tilting some of the large, closely competitive states, and with them tilting the outcome of the national election between the other two candidates.
Such was the role minor independent candidate Eugene McCarthy nearly
played in 1976. Although he received less than 1 percent nationally of the
popular vote, he received more votes in four states (Iowa, Maine, Oklahoma,
and Oregon, totalling 26 electoral votes) than the margins in these states by
which Ford defeated Carter. In these four states, McCarthy's candidacy may
have swung those winner-take-all blocs of electoral votes to Ford. Even more
significantly, had McCarthy been on the New York ballot, it is likely that his
votes would have been sufficiently drawn from Carter's strength in that one
state to have tilted New York's bloc of 41 electoral votes to Ford instead of
Carter. If New York had gone to Ford, he would have then won the election
by thus securing an electoral college majority — this despite Carter's indisputable national popular vote majority.

The prospects of Ross Perot being decisive in the outcome of — or even
winning — the 1992 election are, of course, presently unknown. Polls as of
mid-year are unclear and somewhat contradictory as to his enduring support
and as to whether his support comes principally from Bush or Clinton: further
they do not speak meaningfully as to the final outcome in specific states in a
three-way race. Such initial polls early in the campaign season are very fragile
and momentary indicators indeed, and certainly cannot predict the dynamics
of popular vote shifts in the crucial final months of the campaign. Most importantly, they also do not indicate conclusively how Perot's support, at whatever
level, will translate into possible electoral votes for him, or into shifts of electoral votes in individual states between the major party candidates Bush and
Clinton. Nevertheless, it is absolutely clear that, because of the presence of
three electorally viable candidates, the electoral college, as a vote tabulating

mechanism, will be an important and profoundly inequitable institution that will play a significant role in the presidential election of 1992.

In short, the electoral college at best treats candidates unequally, and creates enormous potential difficulties for many independent or third party candidates, difficulties which Ross Perot may or may not be able to overcome in 1992. Whatever their level of success, however, independent or third party candidates may have great significance in electoral outcomes because of the powerful impact of relatively few popular votes on tightly contested large marginal states where the determination of a substantial bloc of electoral votes may ride on small and shifting pluralities.

Faithless Electors May Further Distort the Popular Will

A final problem of the electoral college "at its best" — in other words while still producing a clear decision — lies in the potential occurrence of faithless electors. In seven of the eleven most recent elections we have seen an individual deciding, after the November election, to vote for someone other than expected. In each of these instances, however, such elector defections have been both singular in occurrence and insignificant in outcome. They do constitute, however, a distortion of the popular will. When one of the state of Washington's nine Republican electors decides, as in 1976, not to vote for the state's popular vote winner, Jerry Ford, the voters of Washington have lost a portion of their franchise.

Individual elector defections for whatever reason — strongly held issues or personal whim — have been of minor significance in the past. Such faithless electors, however, would likely proliferate in the instance of an election producing a very close electoral vote count. In any case, the occurrence of faithless electors, even on an individual basis, is one more way by which the electoral college fails — even when definitive in its choice — to reflect faithfully and accurately the popular vote. The electoral college is not a neutral and fair means of electing the President. Neither, as we shall now see, is it a *sure* way of determining who shall be President.

THE ELECTORAL COLLEGE AT ITS WORST

The electoral college does not inevitably result in a clear determination of the election outcome. Rather, the result of the popular vote, when transformed into the electoral votes which actually determine the President, may be uncertain and unresolved through December and even into January.

In a Very Close Electoral Vote Count, Ambitious Electors Could Determine the Outcome

Individual electors have defected from voter expectations in the past for highly individual reasons. In the case of an electoral college majority resting on a margin of but a few votes, electors seeking personal publicity or attention to a pet cause could withhold — or just threaten to withhold — their electoral votes from the narrow electoral vote winner.

The 1992 popular vote may well produce a relatively close election, especially if candidate Perot — as it now appears likely — should win a significant number of electoral votes. A clear majority of electoral votes for Bush or Clinton — or even Perot — might still result, but if that electoral vote majority of 270 rested on a thin margin of but a few votes, such an electoral vote majority could be hostage to elector threats and reconsiderations. Uncertainty and suspense over whether there actually would be an electoral vote majority when the electors voted in December would make the five week period following the November election a period of political disquiet.

An Election Can Produce a Divided Verdict, with One Candidate Receiving the Most Popular Votes and the Other Candidate Winning the Election in Electoral Votes

An electoral outcome with a divided verdict might well be conclusive in the sense that the candidate with the majority of electoral votes would become President with little question of outright popular upheaval. The electoral college would be seen at its worst, however, in the effect of such a "divided verdict" election on the legitimacy of a President. Should a person be elected — or re-elected — as President despite having run clearly second in popular preference and votes, his would be a presidency weakened in its ability to govern and to lead the American people.

Such divided verdict elections have occurred two or three times in our nation's history, the most recent indisputable case being the election of 1888 when the 100,000 popular vote of Grover Cleveland was turned into a losing 42 percent of the electoral vote. It might be noted that the electoral vote winner in 1888, Benjamin Harrison, lost the subsequent election of 1892 to Grover Cleveland, this time in both popular votes *and* electoral votes.

A divided verdict election is, of course, entirely possible in 1992, especially if at least two of the candidates run close to each other in popular votes. Our most recent close Presidential election, that of 1976, contained a real possibility of an electoral vote reversal of the popular preference. If a total of 9,244 votes had been cast for Ford instead of Carter solely in the two states of Ohio and Hawaii, Ford would have won those two states, with them a national total of 270 electoral votes, and thus the presidential election — despite Carter's clear lead in popular votes. One hesitates to contemplate the consequences had a non-elected President such as Jerry Ford been inaugurated for four more years as president after having been rejected by a majority of the American voters in 1976, his only presidential election.

An Election May Be Undecided on Election Night with Deals and Actions by the Electors at the Mid-December Electoral College Meetings Deciding the Outcome

The most frequently expressed fear about the electoral college concerns the possibility of an electoral college deadlock — no candidate winning an electoral vote majority on the basis of the election night results. Most analysts assume that, in this case, an undecided election would go directly to the House of Representatives in January. In fact, it is entirely possible that an apparent electoral college deadlock, based on the November returns, would set off a sequence of possible deals and actions including the electors themselves.

The 41 days between the 1992 election day, November 3, and the day on which the electors will meet in their respective capitals in 1992, December 14, would be a period of speculation, conjecture, and crisis. Most electors will follow party lines, but some might deviate in order to vote for the popular vote winner, or to help a candidate who had almost achieved an electoral vote majority. Certainly, this period would be a period of intense uncertainty and unease, as unknown and obscure presidential electors decided the outcome of the 1992 presidential election.

Such an occurrence is entirely possible in any close election, especially should a third party or independent candidate such as Ross Perot be able to win a number of electoral votes. In the last presidential election marked by a third party candidate winning electoral votes, that of 1968, third party candidate George Wallace carried 45 electoral votes. In that election, had a total of 53,000 popular votes been cast differently in the three states of New Jersey, Missouri, and New Hampshire, Nixon would have lost his electoral vote majority and instead had only 269 electoral votes — one short of the necessary majority. In the 1976 election, even without the presence of an independent or third party candidate able to win electoral votes, the possibility also existed of an electoral college deadlock. If 11,950 popular votes in the two states of Delaware and Ohio had shifted from Carter to Ford, Ford would have carried those two states and won their 28 electoral votes. The results of the 1976 election, then, would have been *an exact tie in electoral votes:* 269 to 269! The presidency would have been decided *not* on election night, but through deals or switches at the electoral college meetings in December, or the later uncertainties of the House of Representatives.

If the Electoral College Fails to Produce a Majority in December, the Extraordinary Procedure Would Be Followed of Election of the President by the House of Representatives in January

Election of the President by the House of Representatives would be an exceedingly awkward undertaking. According to the Constitution, voting in the House would be by equally weighed states, with an absolute majority of 26 states needed for a decision. The House would choose from among the top *three* candidates in electoral votes — no other "compromise" candidate could be considered.

Congressmen could be in a great quandary as the House started to vote on January 6, 1993. Many Representatives would vote strictly along party lines, totally ignoring any strength shown by an independent or third party candidate such as Ross Perot. Other House members might feel it appropriate or even politically necessary to vote for the candidate (the opposing major party contender or even an independent candidate) who had carried their district. Some House members might even feel influenced by the national popular vote result or by who had received the most popular votes in their state. . . . In other words, should an election be thrown into the House, congressmen would vote in different ways for a number of different reasons. A final outcome would be difficult to predict, despite whatever partisan divisions existed.

As of 1992, the House is controlled by the Democratic party, not only in terms of the total number of seats, but also in terms of state delegations. Thirty-one state delegations have a Democratic majority, 10 are Republican, 8 are evenly divided between the two parties, and one state delegation (Vermont) consists solely of Socialist Representative Bernard Sanders. This Democratic favorable position as of mid-1992, however, is likely to be eroded by the results of the November 1992 House elections: fifteen of the Democratic state delegations presently have Democratic majorities by only one seat: a loss of one Democratic Representative in these fifteen states would make it either a tied or a Republican majority state. If the Republican party should gain two dozen or more House seats in the 1992 election — a widely anticipated possibility — the newly elected House which takes office on January 4, 1993, will almost certainly have significantly fewer state delegations with clear Democratic majorities.

Beyond such calculations, however, lurks the fact that such partisan projections do not take into account the previously mentioned factors of congressional voting in accord with district results, voting in correspondence with state vote outcome, voting influenced by the national popular vote results, or voting even in terms of personal preferences. Vermont, for example, is one of the seven states (Alaska, Delaware, Montana, North Dakota, South Dakota, and Wyoming are the others) which have only one congressman. Each of these seven Representatives individually would be able to cast one of the 26 House state votes which could elect the President and these seven Congress-

men would outvote the 156 total House members from the six largest states —
California, New York, Florida, Ohio, Michigan, and Texas. Vermont's lone
congressman, as previously noted, is Socialist Bernard Sanders — who at one
point hinted that he might cast his state's vote in a House election of the President for independent Ross Perot. In order to forestall such a possibility, Representative Sanders recently has been courted by both House Republican and
Democratic leaders: the *Washington Post* described him at mid-year 1992 as
"The Lonely Guy No More." Under any scenario, House voting for President
would at best be confused as members sort out pressures of party, constituency, political self-interest, and personal preference.

A Final and Definitive Decision by the House in January Is by No Means Certain

The House would commence its deliberations and voting on January 6, 1993,
only 14 days prior to the constitutionally mandated Inauguration Day of January 20. Such a House vote would be divided in 1993 between Bush, Clinton,
and Perot. No matter how this vote splits, no matter how many state delegations are divided and consequently not able to vote, the constitutional requirement of 26 state votes will remain. . . .

If no President has been elected by the House of Representatives by noon
on January 20, the Twentieth Amendment provides that the Vice-President-
elect shall "act as President." (The Vice-President probably would have been
elected by the U.S. Senate since the voting there is one vote per Senator, and,
most importantly, is limited to the top *two* contenders. A difficulty might arise
if the Democratic presidential–vice-presidential ticket had run *third* in electoral votes, thus requiring the presumably Democratically-controlled Senate to
choose only between Republican Vice-President Dan Quayle and Ross Perot's
running mate for election as Vice President-elect and potentially as acting
President.) The result of such a presidential election, then, would not be the
decisive determination of a President, but rather the designation of a Vice
President who would act as President. He would fill that office for an uncertain tenure, subject to possible removal at any time by renewed House voting
later in his term — especially following the midterm congressional elections
when, undoubtedly, the partisan balance in the House would shift to the disadvantage of the acting President. His would be a most unhappy and weakened presidency, subordinate to Congress because of his administration's congressional creation and possible termination, limited by a non-existent
electoral mandate, and crippled by uncertainty as to how long his temporary
presidency could continue.

The electoral college in the 1992 election may, unhappily, exhibit some or
even many of these shortcomings. On the other hand, the American people
may be lucky once more in this election year and not be faced by crisis in the

electoral college. In any case, the electoral college will be a crucial determining factor in the 1992 election — and possibly even in subsequent elections — shaping and distorting the popular will.

At its best, the electoral college operates in an inherently distorted manner in transforming popular votes into electoral votes. In addition, it has enormous potential as a dangerous institution threatening the certainty of our elections and the legitimacy of our Presidents. These defects of the contemporary electoral college cannot be dealt with by patchwork reforms such as abolishing the office of presidential elector. This distorted and unwieldy counting device must be abolished, and the votes of the American people — wherever cast — must be counted directly and equally in determining who shall be President of the United States. It is all too likely that the 1992 presidential election will finally provide the American public with indisputable evidence of the failings of the electoral college as a means of electing the people's president.

Should the Electoral College Be Abolished?

JUDITH A. BEST
In Defense of the Electoral College

When it is not necessary to change, it is necessary not to change
— John Kennedy

To paraphrase an old truism: hard election years can lead to bad constitutional law. The current movement to change the method of selecting the president arises from a fear that in the 1992 race, with three strong contenders, no candidate will achieve an electoral vote majority, thereby triggering a contingency election in the House or the prospect of faithless electors in the college itself. It has also renewed old fears of a runner-up president.

The proposed amendments would deform rather than reform the system. The proposals to make the contingency procedure a runoff election will make runoffs the rule, proliferate parties and candidates and turn the selection process into a national ordeal. The proposals for what is called a direct election would convert what is, in practice, a direct popular *federal* election into a plebiscite that will destroy the balance of power in our governing solar system. Both kinds of proposals would be a death blow to our already weakened moderate two party system. These proposals arise from a misconception of American democracy or a misunderstanding of the workings of the present system or both.

There are several points to be made. First, the general election should be and, for all practical purposes, is now the only election. Second, like a contingency election, a runner-up presidency is extremely unlikely under the electoral vote system, and for the same reason. Third, faithless electors have never been a problem and can be handled short of a constitutional amendment by the states and the parties. Fourth, the electoral system is a major support for our moderate two party system, and this would be the worst time to further weaken the two party system. Finally the electoral vote system is a paradigm, the very model, of the American democracy. To abandon it would be to radically change the fundamental structure of the Constitution by removing the federal constraints on the power of the presidency, thereby increasing its power, and would lead to attacks on the legitimacy of other federally districted intermediary institutions such as the state equality principle of the Senate and the amending process.

The federal electoral vote system, in practice, is a popular plurality system which not only magnifies the plurality winner's electoral vote margin of victory over the runner-up, it also gives the runner-up a monopoly of opposition and thus effectively provides us with a single election. For more than 160 years, since the most universal adoption of the state unit rule, the electoral vote system has provided us with a single election. It will do so again.

Fears that it will not are produced by polls that report a dead heat, but that is because they ignore the election laws and especially the federally districted unit rule. For example the *Wall Street Journal*/NBC poll conducted July 5th through 7th drew its sample of 1,105 registered voters from 263 randomly selected geographic points in the continental U.S. without regard for state boundaries. Such polls imply that we already have amended the Constitution, that we currently have a plebiscitary, all-national election, that it is not necessary for a candidate to win states. Such implications are a proposition contrary to present fact — a proposition contrary to the campaign strategies of the 1992 candidates who do know that they must win statewide pluralities if they are to win any electoral votes. The only polls that are relevant to the issue at hand are statewide polls, and they do not report anything like a dead heat.

In early July, according to *Hotline,* which looked at statewide polls, Perot was leading in twenty-two states with enough electoral votes to win. Bush was leading in twelve states, and Clinton in four. Depending on one's personal choice for president, one may lament or rejoice over these figures, which, of course, will change as the campaign progresses, but the Constitution should not be amended because we don't like the prospective outcome of a particular election.

Some people fear that deadlock in the electoral vote is likely when there is a strong third party movement or today's strong Perot candidacy. The historical evidence is to the contrary. The electoral vote system magnifier effect has given the victory to the winner of the popular plurality in the five elections when there were three or more strong contenders.

Strong Third Party Election in Years
(candidate popular vote percentages; winners' electoral vote percentage underlined)

1856	Buchanan		Frémont	Fillmore	
	45.6%	58.7%	33%	21%	
1860	Lincoln		Douglas	Breckinridge	Bell
	39.79%	59.4%	29.4%	18%	13%
1912	Wilson		T. Roosevelt	Taft	
	41.85%	81.9%	27.4%	23%	
1924	Coolidge		Davis	La Follette	
	54%	71.7%	28.9%	16.6%	
1968	Nixon		Humphrey	Wallace	
	43.4%	55.9%	42.7%	13.5%	

In 1856, the year predicting party realignment, when Fillmore, the Whig, won 21 percent of the popular vote, and Frémont of the new Republican party won 33 percent, Buchanan's popular plurality of 45.6 percent became 58.7 percent of the electoral vote. In 1860, contending against not only Douglas but Breckinridge and Bell (the latter two together achieving 31 percent of the popular vote), Lincoln won because his 39.79 percent of the popular vote was magnified to 59.4 percent of the electoral vote. In 1912, running against both Taft and Teddy Roosevelt, Wilson's 41.85 percent of the popular vote was converted to 81.9 percent of the electoral vote. In 1924, when third party candidate Robert La Follette won 16.6 percent of the popular vote, Coolidge's 54 percent popular majority became 71.7 percent of the electoral vote. In 1968, when George Wallace won 13.5 percent of the popular vote, Nixon's popular vote plurality of 43.4 percent was converted to 55.9 percent of the electoral vote.

In a real three-way race under the electoral vote system, the likelihood is not electoral vote deadlock but an electoral vote landslide for one of the three candidates. There is no imminent danger of this election triggering a contingency election in the House or a spate of faithless electors or a runner-up presidency.

While *highly* unlikely, a contingency election is possible. Some members of Congress are genuinely concerned that a contingency election would be a political disaster for the presidency, the Congress and the nation. There are some real problems with the existing contingency process including the possibility of a President and Vice President of different parties, the injustice of depriving a state of its vote if its delegation is tied, the possibility that the winner of the popular plurality would lose if he belonged to the minority party in the House, the specter of corrupt deals among candidates and members of the House, or even the appearance of such deals.

The contingency election reforms proposed, however, will produce equal or greater evils. They will certainly weaken the two party system, promote multi-factionalism and multiple candidacies, delay coalition building, promote deals and bargains between and among candidates after the general election, make runoffs the rule and not the rare exception and increase the premium on fraud.

A popular runoff provision changes candidate psychology. Factional candidates, single issue candidates, and extremist ideological candidates will have a greater incentive to continue in the race. The more candidates there are the greater the likelihood of a runoff election, and in a runoff they could win something — a Supreme Court nomination, a cabinet post, agreement to promote some position on say abortion or gay rights or gun regulation — in return for their support. And such bargains need not be and often would not be struck in the open.

When you change the rules, you change the game, and you change the skills and strategies needed to win. A runoff provision is an invitation to contingency-election strategies that would utterly destroy the parties' already weakened control over nominations, and reduce the influence of state party leaders in the campaigns.

A campaign is normally a very fluid period. This one may be more so. In this election the voters are angry, and the polls reflect it. But support for all three candidates is soft. As the election draws near, the wasted vote psychology will begin to take effect, particularly as voters realize they won't have a second chance to vote. If the contest appears to be close, many voters, especially those whose support for a candidate is soft, whose support is a protest against the other two candidates, will act to ensure the defeat of the candidate they most oppose. This voter psychology has served the two party system well. It is *the very existence of a runoff* — a second chance to vote — that could turn the general election into a national primary.

The proposals for a popular runoff if a candidate doesn't achieve a 50 percent or a 40 percent popular plurality fail to take this second chance candidate and voter psychology into account. The runner-up spot in the general election would become a worthwhile prize, the hope of many more candidates. The voters could indulge the temptation to send a message and cast a protest vote thereby delaying coalition building until the runoff.

If the 50 percent popular vote requirement had been in effect in our history, we would have had at least 15 runoff elections and probably many more. If the 40 percent runoff rule had been in effect there is at least one election that we know of that would have required a runoff — the election of 1860. It would have meant a loss for Lincoln for the supporters of Breckinridge and Bell would have preferred Douglas. What a loss for the nation! But, no doubt, there would have been many more runoffs. There is nothing magical about the 40 percent figure. It is the fact of a runoff process not a numerical percentage that changes attitudes about the general election. Even the proposal to require a popular runoff if no candidate achieves a majority of the electoral vote undermines this candidate and voter psychology.

The simplest solution to the problems of the present contingency provision is to have no contingency election, to change the requirement for election from a majority of the electoral vote to a plurality of the electoral vote. This would solve all of the aforementioned problems with the existing contingency process and would make the general election the only election. Since the major party candidates do not adopt a contingency election strategy, this would not change their behavior in that regard. It would highlight the need for party unity. Some third party candidates would attempt to run as spoilers or to promote special causes, but to little avail as it would not change but only reinforce the voter psychology about casting a wasted vote.

Some may fear this would produce a president with an insufficient mandate, though this seems ironic coming from the supporters of a 40 percent runoff rule. To those who would require a 50 percent popular percentage, I would point out that the majority principle is a very stringent one in a heterogeneous, continental nation — one not required for the election of Senators, or congressmen, most governors and mayors because it institutionalizes runoffs.

Under the electoral vote system, we have had 15 presidential terms with presidents who polled less than 50 percent of the popular vote. Seven of these presidential terms are considered to be among the best in our history including Polk, Lincoln, Cleveland twice, Wilson twice and Truman. Lincoln with 39.79 percent of the popular vote is considered to be the greatest of all our presidents. We have even had one president, Gerald Ford, who reached the office without participating in a presidential election. The American people consider all of these presidencies to be legitimate.

To those who would require a 50 percent electoral vote percentage, I say, you can rely on the magnifier effect of the electoral vote system. For more than 160 years, it has always provided an electoral vote majority for one of the candidates, whether in closely contested two-way or three-way contests. A popular runoff election provision is an incentive, an open invitation, to multiple parties, candidates and elections. There comes a point in time where a decision must be made, and a decision that is swift, sure clean, clear, proven in practice and legitimated through time is desirable. The existing system, even with its faults, possesses these characteristics.

I would abolish the office of elector but not the electoral votes. I see no pressing necessity to do this, but if we are talking about perfecting the system this might as well be included. There have been only eight faithless electors out of more than 16,000, and in no case did these faithless votes come remotely near to affecting the outcome, nor were they intended to do so. The problem can be addressed by the states through statutory law and by responsible party choice of and pledging of electors. I recommend North Carolina's law which not only fines a faithless elector but declares that failure to vote as pledged is a resignation from the office and allows for the appointment of another elector in his place.

As for the runner-up president, in no case in our history has the electoral vote system rebuffed a man who had an undisputed majority of the popular vote. In every case but one the electoral vote system gave the victory to the winner of a popular plurality. In 1888, Cleveland lost because he failed to seek a broad mandate and ran a sectional campaign. But a sectional campaign (promising everything to one section of the country, say the populous Eastern megalopolis, to the detriment of the rest of the country) is a formula for alienation, inability to govern and even for civil war. The American people are better served by a system that does not allow sectional majorities to dominate the presidential contest.

The 1888 election was the fifth closest in our history. In terms of popular votes, the margin between Cleveland and Harrison was only 0.8 percent. Two other candidates won popular votes in this election, each with more than the 0.8 percent margin Cleveland had over Harrison. This was an election that any reasonable person would call a draw. As a popular vote contest reaches toward a draw, the majority principle becomes arbitrary, and the electoral vote requirement that candidates win states is both desirable in a continental nation and a satisfactory way of resolving the draw.

Moreover, close popular vote contests, those verging on a draw, do not themselves produce runner-up presidents unless a candidate runs a sectional campaign. In the closest popular election in our history, 1880, when the margin of popular votes was only 9,457, a margin of 0.1 percent, the electoral vote system gave the victory to the winner of the popular plurality. Garfield won with 57.9 percent of the electoral vote. In 1844, 1884, 1960 and 1968, the other close, near draw elections, we see the same phenomenon — the electoral vote magnifier effect that gives the victory to the winner of a popular plurality.

It is absurd to cling rigidly to the principle of "the most popular votes" in a situation that is a near draw because the popular votes do not reflect the intensity of preferences, nor do all the people vote. And the vote is merely a kind of one time temperature taking. It would be different a few days, weeks or months later. Presidential support polls go up and down, and many a voter has quickly rued his November ballot. As Alexander Bickel said, to resolve deadlocks "all that is needed is settlement in advance upon one sensible and well-understood method." The people may not understand the complexities of the electoral vote system, but they do understand the need to win states. In a media age, the networks, on election night, present maps of the United States usually coloring the states red or blue, as their voters decide how the state's electoral votes will be cast.

John Kennedy said, "If it is not necessary to change, it is necessary not to change." And why in this case? The answer is that, as Martin Diamond said, the electoral vote system is "a paradigm of the American democracy" because it is both democratic and federal, because it mandates more than arithmetical majorities; it mandates the formation of political majorities that can govern because of their broad cross-sectional, federal base. It is one of "the intermediary institutions" that, as James Burnham pointed out, were created by the founders to make democracy both safe and stable — in a phrase, to make it serve the end of human liberty. We are not, never have been and were not intended to be a simple democracy, a plebiscitary democracy or a Perot electronic town meeting democracy, the kind of democracy whose end is Caesar, whose end is tyranny.

We are a democratic federal republic. We have a representative, constitutionally limited government of carefully balanced, separated powers. The president as selected by the electoral vote process with its federally districted, federally aggregated vote requirement, is an integral part of this balanced system. To change this process and establish a plebiscitary presidency will destroy this balance and increase the power of the President in relation to Congress.

And, to create a plebiscitary presidency will lead to attacks on the Senate because if we abandon the federal principle in presidential elections, why shouldn't we abandon it for the Senate? If numbers of voters are the only test for legitimacy then the Senate of the United States is unfair. A state with half a million people has the same representation as a state with fifteen or twenty million people, and this in the Senate which passes on Supreme Court nominations and treaties.

Nor will we be likely to stop there for the so called direct election movement is part of a centralizing, simplifying constitutional heresy which would abandon the fundamental principles of the founders. If the majority principle is the only legitimate one, why should each state have an equal vote on constitutional amendments? Surely it is unfair that a state with half a million people should have the same vote as one with twenty million. Why don't we forget the states altogether and have a plebiscite, a direct national vote, on constitutional amendments? If the argument is that the people should vote directly for the president because he represents them all, why shouldn't we vote directly on constitutional amendments which rule and limit us all? And, why shouldn't we vote directly on Supreme Court Justices who interpret our Constitution, and have the power to directly remove them as well?

The founders knew the answers to these questions — it is majority faction — majority tyranny. The federal principle in presidential elections is but one of the important devices the founders used to prevent and control majority faction. There is no principled or logical way to abandon the federal principle in presidential elections without undermining it for the Senate and the amendment process. The last thing the founders wanted was a plebiscitary democracy for they knew it is the form of government in which majority factions oppress minorities of all kinds.

Let us remember we are a nation of states — the United *States* of America. The federal principle and the separation of powers are the two fundamental structural principles of our Constitution. The federal principle requires that all our elected national officials represent this continental nation in its diversity because they are chosen in districted constituencies. The federal principle places a geographic rider on the formation of majorities, recognizing that people who live together, sharing the same roads, parks and schools, sharing the same climate and natural resources, sharing the same local economy, sharing a particularly composed ethnic, religious and racial local community, have common interests and needs that must be recognized by and represented in a national government. We are not an amorphus mass, randomly scattered across the nation. We live in distinct local and state communities. Like the members of Congress, the president, who has the veto power, must be made sensitive to state and local needs. Because the electoral vote system requires that to win the presidency a candidate must win states, the presidency is incorporated into the federal system.

The founders were right. The people can be trusted to govern themselves *if* they are provided the proper process, a process that creates political not simply arithmetical majorities, a process that requires the creation of broad cross-sectional, federal majorities. We have the process, proven through time and practice. The people must be and can be trusted to use this process even in atypical, strange election years.

If anything this election year provides more reason than ever to preserve the electoral vote system for it is a major support of another essential intermediary institution — our moderate two party system, which has served both the unity and the stability of the nation. The electoral vote system works to reduce multifactionalism. It has a bias against sectional, single issue, extremist and self-nominated candidates and against a multiparty system. This atypical election year will either prove the rule that the electoral vote system supports the two party system, or be a party realigning election like that of 1856. In any case, this is hardly the time to destroy a major support of the two party system. Rather, it is a time for the two parties to do some soul searching about how and why they have failed to perform their proper functions of majority formation, rejecting and recruiting candidates for the office of president, and structuring voter choice. Especially, it is the time for the presidential Out party to consider the causes of its failure to serve as a focal point for all those seriously dissatisfied with the In party.

In sum, the case for abandoning the federal principle in presidential elections has not been made. It is clear that this election year has created panic, but it has not proven the need for change; nor have any of the proponents of reform made the case that their reforms will eradicate the evils they fear, and not bring greater evils in their wake.

Questions for Discussion

1. How would direct election of the president affect the two-party system?
2. How would direct election affect the power of racial minorities in the United States?
3. If a president were elected with a minority of the popular vote but a majority of the Electoral College vote, how would popular support of the presidency be affected?
4. How would a system of direct election of the president affect the political campaigning strategy of presidential candidates?
5. Which groups benefit and which are hurt by the Electoral College system?

Suggested Readings

Best, Judith A. *The Choice of the People?* Lanham, Md.: Rowman & Littlefield, 1996.

Bickel, Alexander M. *Reform and Continuity: The Electoral College, the Convention and the Party System.* New York: Harper & Row, 1971.

Committee on Federal Legislation of the Association of the Bar of the City of New York. "Proposed Constitutional Amendment Providing for Direct Election of the President and Vice-President of the United States." *Record of the Association of the Bar of the City of New York* 48, no. 7 (November 1993): 821–833.

Diamond, Martin. *The Electoral College and the American Idea of Democracy.* Washington, D.C.: American Enterprise Institute for Public Policy Research, 1977.

Durbin, Thomas M. "The Anachronistic Electoral College: The Time for Reform." *Federal Bar News and Journal* 39, No. 9 (October 1992): 510–518.

Glennon, Michael J. *When No Majority Rules.* Washington, D.C.: Congressional Quarterly Press, 1992.

Hardaway, Robert M. *The Electoral College and the Constitution.* Westport, Conn.: Praeger, 1994.

Josephson, William, and Beverly J. Ross. "Repairing the Electoral College." *Journal of Legislation* 22, no. 2 (1996): 145–193.

Longley, Lawrence D., and Neal R. Peirce. *The Electoral College Primer.* New Haven, Conn.: Yale Univ. Press, 1996.

Peirce, Neal R., and Lawrence D. Longley. *The People's President: The Electoral College in American History and the Direct Vote Alternative,* rev. ed. New Haven, Conn.: Yale Univ. Press, 1981.

U.S. Cong., Senate. *The Electoral College and Direct Election of the President.* Hearing before the Subcommittee on the Constitution of the Committee on the Judiciary, 102d Cong., 2d Sess., 1992.

Chapter 12

Do the Mass Media Have a Liberal Bias?

By most accounts the mass media — television, newspapers, magazines, and the radio — play a central role in the U.S. political system. Some observers believe that the media's influence is so powerful that they function as the fourth branch of government. The media's perception of political leaders and events affects what people believe, so that political leaders neglect the media at their peril. In May 1987, for example, reporters for the *Miami Herald* staked out the Washington townhouse of then Democratic presidential front-runner Gary Hart, after the newspaper received information that a woman was staying with Hart while his wife was in Colorado. Media attention forced Hart to withdraw from the campaign, and although he subsequently returned, his organization suffered setbacks in support and funding.

Whether allegations made against Hart on the subject of sexual morality in this and other instances were accurate or not, the reporting of such a matter had a profound impact on his candidacy and the entire presidential campaign as well. In previous years newspapers had adhered to a professional code that forbade reporting on certain aspects of the private lives of public figures.

The media's influence is derived not only from the stories presented but from the prominence given them. An analysis of the media's reporting on a single day will show a diversity of emphases. News, or the importance of particular items of news, is not so self-evident that everyone in the profession of journalism agrees on what is, and what is not, significant. Some critics of the media have noted the importance of emphasis in coverage of the Vietnam War, coverage they claim was detrimental to U.S. foreign policy interests. Television news reporting that highlighted the killing by U.S. soldiers of Vietnamese civilians or the use of drugs by GIs was biased, these critics argue, because the enemy's actions and problems were not also exposed. Not only was the coverage unbalanced, but it was much less sensitive to U.S. government needs than news reporting during World War II. Supporters of the media counter that these critics simply do not like the news and so are "killing the messenger." Reporters are simply doing their job, media supporters contend, and political leaders who try to dominate the news are always going to be annoyed when news stories cast them in unfavorable light.

Media critics often claim that the media have a bias, but they differ about what the bias is. Syndicated columnist Robert Novak argues that the mass media have a liberal bias. He contends that many journalists have crossed the line from reporting to advocacy. He claims that the Washington press corps is elitist. In Novak's view, members of the national media owe their liberal ideology to left-of-center experiences in their university education, tightly knit peer groups, and the milieu of the popular culture since the 1960s. Few reporters and editors are conservatives, and few editorial pages in the United States are conservative. On issues involving wealth disparities, taxes, the role of government, a balanced budget amendment, health care, the "religious right," abortion, school choice, the command of U.S. forces, and the nature of conservatism, the media have adopted a liberal philosophy. Although conservatives like William F. Buckley Jr. and Rush Limbaugh appear in the media, they are opinion journalists and make no pretense about being objective reporters.

William H. Rentschler, publisher of *The Rentschler Report*, argues that the mass media are not biased. In his opinion, most newspapers are run by editors who believe their prime duty is to give a fair airing to countervailing points of view. But Limbaugh's programs and a broad array of magazines, such as *National Review* and *American Spectator*, the National Empowerment Television Network, and Hillsdale College's newsletter, *Imprimis*, are openly one-sided, espousing a conservative viewpoint. The assault on the mass media from the right, conducted with unbending rancor and arrogance, has undermined public trust in traditional sources of news and opinion. The right-wing attack on public broadcasting as liberal has been responsible for cutting funding for public radio and television. Yet mainstream media are instinctively fair. As evidence, Rentschler observes that a majority of the nation's daily newspapers endorsed Ronald Reagan and George Bush in three successive presidential elections.

 YES

Do the Mass Media Have a Liberal Bias?

ROBERT NOVAK

Political Correctness Has No Place in the Newsroom

A free press is one of the foundations of a free society. Yet, Americans increasingly distrust and resent the media. A major reason is that many journalists have crossed the line from reporting to advocacy. In effect, they have adopted a new liberal creed — "all the news that's 'politically correct' to print."

How does one define political correctness in the newsroom? One need look no further than the stylebook of the *Los Angeles Times,* one of the largest, most influential newspapers in the nation. It forbids reporters to write about a "Dutch treat" because this phrase allegedly is insulting to the Dutch. Nor can one report that a person "welshed on a bet" because that would be insulting to the Welsh. Moreover, one certainly can not write about a segment of the population once known simply as Indians — they always must be referred to as Native Americans. Jokingly, I asked one of the *Los Angeles Times* editors, "How do you refer to Indian summer? Is it now Native American summer?" He replied that he would substitute "unseasonably warm weather late in the year."

This is what political correctness can do to language — it destroys meaning. It also demeans the ethnic groups it supposedly protects. Do we really think that these groups are so unintelligent as to be unable to distinguish between conventional idioms and genuine prejudice? Is their identity so fragile that it must depend on censorship? People who believe in the real dignity of the individual, no matter of what race, sex, ethnicity, or other condition, shouldn't embrace political correctness because it is bad philosophy; and reporters shouldn't do so either because it is bad journalism.

In 1972, I wrote a paper in which I alienated many of my colleagues (and won the approval of a few) for publicly stating that the national media — the 500 or so reporters and editors based mainly in Washington, D.C., who work for newspapers, wire services, and television networks — had become elitist. I noted that reporters no longer were the typical working-class populists of earlier years who lived on small salaries and had constant contact with ordinary people, problems, and views.

Today, the members of the Washington press corps are even more elitist. I am not referring just to media stars like Diane Sawyer, who is earning $7,000,000 annually. Most run-of-the-mill reporters and editors in the national media are in the top 1–2 percent of income earners in the nation. A Washington bureau chief makes more than $100,000 a year; a senior reporter, over $70,000. Is it surprising that many of them have trouble understanding and appreciating the difficulties other Americans face or that they think differently about such issues as taxes, government regulation, crime, family values, and religion?

I also declared in 1972 that members of the national media tend to share a uniformly liberal ideology. This does not mean they are meeting secretly every other week in someone's basement to get their marching orders. Rather, their ideology originates from a number of left-of-center experiences in their university education, tightly knit peer groups, and the milieu of popular culture since the 1960s.

Am I exaggerating the impact of this liberal ideology? Of the approximately 500 reporters and editors I mentioned earlier, I am aware of just two who are well-known, admitted conservatives. Nationwide, there are about 10 editorial pages in America that properly could be called "conservative," and that stance does not extend beyond the editorial page at more than a handful. At the very least, this striking imbalance speaks volumes about the potential for liberal ideology to dominate the news.

Of course, many journalists hotly deny that they are liberals. Others claim that they do not allow their liberalism to influence their reporting. Yet, here are some unquestionably liberal "axioms" that I believe (based on polls and other sources as well as my own experience) are held almost universally by the members of the national media:

- The rich are getting richer and the poor are getting poorer. The income of the rich should be redistributed to the poor.
- Americans are undertaxed. U.S. taxes are well below those imposed in Europe, and the Federal government therefore should raise them, especially for those who earn, save, and invest more.
- Government, on the whole, is a positive force in America that has done vastly more good than harm.
- The proposed balanced budget amendment is a dangerous idea.
- Term limit amendments are even more dangerous, as well as undemocratic.
- There is a nationwide health care crisis, and only the government can solve it by establishing universal coverage for health insurance.
- The "religious right" — a term that lumps millions of ordinary believers together with a few extremists — is a serious menace to the future of American society.
- Being pro-choice is not enough; there should be absolutely no interference with the reproductive rights of women.
- To support school choice, whether through vouchers or tax credits, is to support the destruction of all public education.
- It is far better for U.S. forces to be under multinational command than for them to be controlled by American military commanders.
- Conservatism is a narrow philosophy: liberalism, by contrast, is more broad, unprejudiced, and compassionate.

The strongest trend in the media industry is toward advocacy journalism. The news sections of most newspapers are even more ideological than when I first criticized them in 1972. Once, the editorial page was the place for journalists to express their opinions, but now they do so on every page, including the front one, under the misleading banner of objective reporting.

Increasing selectivity is leading to increasing bias. Members of the media not only are more subjective in determining whether a story will make it into the news, but in deciding what sort of "slant" it will be given and how much coverage it will receive. Even the wire services have succumbed, running (or not running) stories that, in the past, would have gotten the reporters and editors responsible fired. The worst examples of bias and selectivity are seen on network television programs, which have come to value entertainment more than the news.

Liberals often argue that conservative bias — as evidenced by a growing number of conservative journalists ranging from William F. Buckley, Jr., to Rush Limbaugh — makes up for any liberal bias in the media and leads to "balance." They are being disingenuous, and not just because liberals greatly outnumber conservatives in the journalistic profession. Buckley, Limbaugh, and others like them are opinion journalists. They never have tried to represent themselves otherwise. Moreover, bias of one kind cannot possibly make up for other kinds. By all means, liberal and conservative views are welcome in certain areas of journalism, but when they intrude on the objective reporting of the news, they are equally harmful.

How do we return to the old standards of objectivity and a fair press? While it is important for Americans to make their views known and to convince the media that reform not only is desirable, but necessary, this is not enough. In 1972, I predicted that the pressure of public opinion would force the media into more responsible behavior, but that has not happened.

Special care must be taken to educate properly the young men and women who want to pursue a career in journalism. This is not an automatic recommendation for journalism school. Most of these institutions are in the business of spreading bias and political correctness, not curbing them. There are none (with the exception of the National Journalism Center in Washington, D.C.) that challenges the dominant liberal ideology in the media. Nevertheless, one does not have to attend journalism school to learn the fundamental principles of good writing, reporting, and editing, or to understand bias and how to avoid it. A good liberal arts education can provide ethical as well as academic training.

Finally, action must be taken at the top. People who are dedicated to the principles of good journalism as well as the principles of good business must take leadership positions at or even buy newspapers, magazines, and television stations. They cannot merely wait for the current establishment to change — they must lead the way.

The stakes are high. When the media is out of touch with citizens, the nation is vulnerable; when facts bow to bias, truth is in jeopardy.

Do the Mass Media Have a Liberal Bias?

WILLIAM H. RENTSCHLER
Resisting Pressures on a Free Press

Who, in his own words, is "the poster boy of free speech"? To hear him tell it, in melodious, self-satisfied tones, it is Rush Limbaugh, one of the reigning superstars of talk radio, who also describes himself as "undaunted, undistracted, serving humanity." Through the 600-plus stations that carry his one-sided, egocentric, wildly popular talk show, he proclaims grandly, "This is Rush Limbaugh, with my brain tied behind my back, just to make it fair."

Limbaugh was credited by former Rep. Vin Weber (R.-Minn.), leading the House Republican Orientation Conference for newly elected GOP Congressmen, with being "as responsible as any person" for the November, 1994, landslide.

"No, I'm not running for President," maintains this self-styled paragon of family values. "But I should be." All this might seem ludicrous if it weren't for his enormous influence with rank-and-file, rightward-tilting voters, who otherwise feel themselves voiceless. Meanwhile, there is a sinister element in Limbaugh's message that gravely threatens the credibility of the mainstream media, which generally adhere to the journalistic obligation of presenting both sides of controversial issues, encouraging dissent, and allowing debate to flourish on their pages and TV screens.

This is not the Limbaugh way. He is unapologetically biased, unbalanced, and partisan. Among his weapons are a supercilious sneer and cackle of dismissive laughter, the nasty putdown, and ridicule of the "traditional liberal media" and those "liberal" political figures he fixes in the crosshairs of his lethal verbal assault weapon, especially Pres. Bill Clinton and First Lady Hillary Clinton.

"The Left is never gonna go away. They're arrogant and they hide from people what they really are," he tells his listeners in his confidential, I'm-letting-you-in-on-a-dirty-little-secret tone of voice. "You try to like these people, but it's not easy." He suggests a tactic: "Don't ever mention the names of liberal columnists."

"And I," Limbaugh gloats, "am the liberals' worst nightmare." This is probably so. As the Greek dramatist Sophocles said in 409 B.C., "Everywhere among the race of men, it is the tongue that wins and not the deed."

Journalism is more than a job; it is a calling, a quasi-public service occupation. The duties of the devoted, committed journalist are wide-ranging, exacting, intimidating, and severe. Today, many in the print field veer away from those stringent obligations and seek the greater glory of TV panel spots, celebrity status, and a giant leap forward in compensation.

It wasn't so long ago that a reporter was simply a reporter, who covered his or her assignments factually, fairly, fully, "without fear or favor," as *The New York Times* demanded of its staff. Some of that ethic persists across the entire field of print journalism, and some pursue it rigorously, but it has been diluted by the ever-quickening pace of the rapidly changing world of communications. Despite that accelerating and unsettling trend, most newspapers are run by editors who believe it continues to be their prime duty to give a fair airing to countervailing points of view.

The *Times,* deplored by Limbaugh and his conservative coterie, exemplifies this balance day in, day out. On its February 1, 1995, editorial page, for instance, in the premier position adjacent to the masthead, were two letters that effectively stated diametrically opposing points of view on the critical matter of defense spending. The first letter, from the national vice president of the Air Force Association, made a strong, predictable case for beefed-up military outlays and greater preparedness in the post–Cold War era. The second, written by a Fellow at Harvard's Russian Research Center, stated that the U.S. military budget of $273 billion in 1993, plus that of its allies, "outstrips sevenfold [the combined] spending of $66 billion by our potential enemies." He noted that U.S. defense outlays exceed by $39 billion those of the next nine nations, including France, Great Britain, and Germany. He argued persuasively for shifting some of our defense budget to meet civilian needs and reduce the Federal budget deficit.

The Times' balanced approach follows closely a sound and thoughtful admonition by its publisher, Arthur Hays Sulzberger, in 1948:

> Obviously, a man's judgment cannot be better than the information on which he has based it. Give him the truth and he may still go wrong when he has the chance to be right, but give him no news or present him only with distorted and incomplete data . . . and you destroy his whole reasoning processes, and make him something less than a man.

No such balance exists on Limbaugh's "Excellence in Broadcasting" Network. He preaches the gospel according to St. Rush, and most callers seem to agree with his bombastic right-wing propaganda. Limbaugh's tone of certainty destroys the entire reasoning processes of most of his callers. The articulate dissenters are few.

"Discussion in America means dissent," author and cartoonist James Thurber noted in 1961. John F. Kennedy warned in 1959, before his election as president, "Let us not be afraid of debate or dissent — let us encourage it. For if we should ever abandon these basic American traditions . . . what would it profit us to win the whole world when we have lost our soul?"

Limbaugh, free speech's "poster boy," would argue that he is the very manifestation of dissent. However, he is so good at what he does mainly because Limbaugh has no one across the table to challenge on equal terms some of his outrageous ideological assertions. His program is largely a lovefest of like-minded listeners/callers massaging the giant ego of their hero.

What is dangerous to the free flow of conflicting ideas and balanced reporting — so critical to the effective functioning of a free society — is the increasing domination of the print media and air waves by a lavishly financed propaganda campaign that reached its present zenith in the 1994 political races.

Because the Far Right sees the Public Broadcasting System — TV and radio — as a balancing force, and thus threatening to its agenda, Republicans in Congress have set out to disembowel the beast by eliminating or severely restricting its Federal funding. In an ominous opening salvo, Sen. Larry Pressler (R.-S.D.), new chairman of the Commerce Committee, which controls PBS funding, demanded sensitive information on the sex, ethnic and professional backgrounds, and political leanings of the system's employees. He quickly backed off after a firestorm of protest based on invasion of privacy, according to the Associated Press. Total Federal support for all public broadcasting nationwide, AP reported, is $285,000,000, about equal to the cost of one military jet.

The media assault from the right is by no means limited to Limbaugh or the spate of conservative talk shows, including that of Watergate conspirator G. Gordon Liddy, and dozens of local offerings. It is far broader. Consider several examples:

- William F. Buckley's *National Review* and R. Emmett Tyrrell's *American Spectator* trumpet a right-wing agenda without much pretense of fairness and balance. As far as they are concerned, they are right; they know it; and that is all that matters. There is little dissent or debate in their pages.
- The comparatively new National Empowerment Television Network, with a claimed "reach" of 11,000,000 homes, is a venture of longtime professional conservative Paul Weyrich. It provides a forum for House Speaker Newt Gingrich (R.-Ga.) and is being supported by, among others, Michael Huffington, who spent $28,000,000 of his own fortune in barely losing the 1994 senatorial race to Dianne Feinstein (D.-Calif.). The network sponsored an intimate $50,000-a-couple soiree in early February, 1995, at Washington's Hay Adams Hotel honoring Gingrich, who is their featured superstar host and contributor of his views to the network.
- Hillsdale College in Michigan aggressively promotes the conservative agenda in its newsletter, *Imprimis,* with a circulation of 565,000.

Not all so-called conservatives relish the strident message of the movement's present-day leadership. In a July, 1994, interview, Barry Goldwater, the patron saint of modern-day conservatism, former five-term U.S. senator, and 1964 Republican presidential candidate, was asked, "Are you still a conservative?"

"Oh, yeah, of course I am, always will be," he responded.

A lot of so-called conservatives today don't know what the word means. They think I've turned liberal because I believe a woman has a right to an abortion. That's a decision that's up to the pregnant woman, not up to the Pope or some do-gooders or the religious right. . . . One problem today is with these neo-conservatives, the radical right, the religious extremists whose interpretation is very narrow and who want to destroy everybody who doesn't agree with 'em. I see them as betrayers of the fundamental principles of conservatism.

Goldwater was reminded that GOP chairman Haley Barbour, an architect of the 1994 Republican sweep, charges critics of this group with "religious bigotry" and "Christian bashing."

Snorted Goldwater, "That's a crock. He's way the hell off base, dead wrong. That religious bunch is crazy. They're dangerous. They'll destroy the Republican Party. Maybe eventually the Democratic Party, too."

The increasingly powerful organs of the right — print and electronic — contrive to blunt the impact and counter the influence of what conservatives deride as the "liberal media" — especially the nation's largest daily newspapers and a handful of TV superstars — which they believe pose a danger to "their" America. This assault is patently phony, strictly strategic in its intent to undermine public trust in traditional sources of news and opinion. What the conservatives deride as "liberal" are, for the most part, those mainstream daily newspapers that, whatever their editorial positions, attempt to provide some semblance of balance in their coverage. This above all else infuriates the "Johnny-One-Notes" like Limbaugh, who accept only their own brand of orthodoxy.

In reality, considerably less than a majority of the body politic, they are so sure they, and only they, are right that they feel it is their God-given right, even duty, to suppress, derogate, and ridicule any and all contradictory viewpoints. Their dogmatism and certainty are scary and dangerous to the foundations of a free society. They cluster under the protective banner of the First Amendment, ignoring the fact that it at least implies a sense of responsibility.

Supreme Court Justice Oliver Wendell Holmes, Jr., opined that the First Amendment, at its most basic level, does not give a person the right to "shout fire in a crowded theater." Later, Chief Justice Warren Burger noted dryly that the same principle applies even if the theater is largely empty. With Limbaugh's audience of approximately 25 million comes an unprecedented level of arrogance and mean-minded, destructive rhetoric meant not only to wound, but to destroy perceived foes of the conservative movement.

As a former editor and publisher of community newspapers, I would not suggest the press giants are above reproach — far from it. They can be infuriating and grossly irresponsible at times, as well as shoddy in their attention to high principle. Nor by any means are the TV networks exemplary, as they jostle for ratings and profits by exploiting violence, sex, and all things sensational. Largely gone are the days when the likes of Edward R. Murrow, Chet Huntley, and Walter Cronkite were dominant, rational, evenhanded, and widely respected.

Still, there remains among the mainstream media a certain compelling instinct for some measure of fairness. If you or I are slandered on TV, we usually can get our face and view before a camera within hours. If we are attacked in the press, the offending paper probably will carry a rebuttal, apology, or letter to the editor. That won't necessarily undo the damage, but it may assuage the hurt to some degree. That is not generally so with most staunchly conservative media outlets.

In 1994, for example, former Delaware governor and onetime presidential aspirant Pete duPont wrote a "Conservative Manifesto" for *National Review,* where he serves as chairman of the National Review Institute. Included was a section on crime and punishment that was a draconian rehash of failed, counterproductive programs incredibly expensive to taxpayers, a pitch for "tough on crime," but counter to the conservative mission of reduced Federal spending. As a longtime member of the Board of Directors of the National Council on Crime & Delinquency, I responded with a point-by-point rebuttal letter to the editor. I received a gracious response from duPont, but *National Review* adamantly refused to publish my letter.

My experience with *The Wall Street Journal's* editorial page is similar. The paper often buries input that takes issue with some of editor Robert Bartley's favorite conservative nostrums.

Such, of course, is the prerogative of Buckley and Bartley. However, they express outrage when perceived "liberal" bias creeps into a news story in a major daily, such as *The New York Times, Washington Post, Los Angeles Times, San Francisco Chronicle, Philadelphia Inquirer, St. Louis Post-Dispatch, Atlanta Journal and Constitution, Milwaukee Journal, Minneapolis Star Tribune,* or *Boston Globe.*

They seem to ignore the fact that a sizeable majority of the nation's daily newspapers endorsed Ronald Reagan and George Bush in three consecutive presidential elections. Thus, the blanket "liberal media" charge has a hollow ring when such conservative ideologues as press lords Rupert Murdoch and Conrad Black, Jack Welch of General Electric (owner of NBC), and other deep-pocket owners control so much of the nation's press capacity and airtime. Certainly, the *Chicago Tribune* can't be categorized as "liberal." There are many others that simply don't fit the pejorative term of "liberal press," used relentlessly by the Limbaughs and Buckleys, but they drum it home anyway.

What is most worrisome is the carefully orchestrated frontal attack on the mainstream media by a band of zealots whose unabashed aim is to destroy their credibility and influence. The ultimate effect is to sow seeds of doubt in the public mind; to narrow — not broaden — rational national debate, and thus widen the chasm that separates Americans from one another.

"Freedom to differ is not limited to things that do not matter much," Supreme Court Justice Robert H. Jackson said in 1943. "That would be a mere shadow of freedom. The test of its substance is the right to differ as to things that touch the heart of the existing order."

If it is necessary to differ, it is a time to do so in a spirit of civility, reason, and goodwill, rather than unbending rancor and arrogant certainty as the urgent issues of these troubled times are debated. Americans must bridge what writer Studs Terkel has called "the great divide" if they are to approach full potential for decency and greatness.

For all its faults, foibles, prejudices, excesses, and its sometimes resort to baser instincts, Americans should thank God for the free press that is denied most of the world's peoples. Neither the press nor other avenues of communications are truly free when they promote — under government fiat or their own free will — rigid conformity, an "official" doctrine, or a "party line." It only occurs when they provide accurate, complete, balanced news and information, which give a citizen, as the *Times'* Sulzberger put it so aptly, "the chance to be right."

We should be thankful, too, that our early leaders had the wisdom and foresight to give us the First Amendment, thus protecting even those who abuse and misuse its protective cloak. It is our duty to be vigilant against every assault on that right so vital to preserving our liberty.

Journalist Max Lerner wrote in 1949: "The problem of freedom in America is that of maintaining a competition of ideas, and you do not achieve that by silencing one brand of idea." What is more important in a free society than safeguarding, continually advancing, and guaranteeing "a competition of ideas"?

Questions for Discussion

1. What criteria should be used in determining whether a newspaper or television program is biased in presenting the news?
2. How does the approach used in presenting the news affect the receiver of the information?
3. If there is a media bias, what is it? What is your evidence?
4. How do political leaders attempt to shape the news? Are they successful?
5. How does corporate ownership affect the presentation of the news?
6. How do the attitudes of the journalists, producers, and executives affect the shape of the news?

Suggested Readings

Barone, Michael. "The Return of Partisan Journalism." *American Enterprise* 7, no. 2 (March/April 1996): 29–31.

Dowd, Maureen. "Raffish and Rowdy." *New York Times*, March 31, 1996, sec. IV, p. 15.

Fallows, James. *Breaking the News: How the Media Undermine American Democracy*. New York: Pantheon Books, 1996.

Feder, Don. "Why Liberals Find Talk Radio So Threatening." *American Enterprise* 7, no. 2 (March/April 1996): 24–28.

Glaberson, William. "The New Press Criticism: News as the Enemy of Hope." *New York Times,* October 9, 1994, sec. IV, pp. 1, 4.

Glassman, James K. "The Press: Obvious Bias. . . ." *Washington Post,* May 7, 1996, p. A19.

Herman, Edward S., and Noam Chomsky. *Manufacturing Consent: The Political Economy of the Mass Media.* New York: Pantheon Books, 1988.

Maureckas, Jim, and Janine Jackson, eds. *The FAIR Reader: An Extra Review of Press and Politics in the '90s.* Boulder, Colo.: Westview Press, 1996.

Parenti, Michael. *Inventing Reality: The Politics of News Media.* New York: St. Martin's Press, 1993.

Sabato, Larry J. *Feeding Frenzy: How Attack Journalism Has Transformed American Politics.* New York: Free Press, 1991.

Policy-Making Institutions

A s indicated in Part I, the Framers of the Constitution established a system of separation of powers and checks and balances constituted in three branches of government — legislative, executive, and judicial. The Framers feared that the concentration of powers in the hands of one branch would be a danger to liberty.

The Constitution, as has so often been said, is a living document, and it has changed over time through formal constitutional amendment, statutes, political practices, and customs. In part because of the ambiguities in some provisions of the Constitution and in part because of historical developments, power has shifted in different eras from one branch to another.

Constitutional amendments have modified the major branches of government. For example, the Seventeenth Amendment, adopted in 1913, changed the method of choosing U.S. senators from election by the state legislatures, as provided in Article I of the Constitution, to direct popular election in each state. Statutes have also changed the Constitution. Congress passed numerous laws in the nineteenth and twentieth centuries establishing new departments and government agencies. When the Constitution was adopted, the role of government in society was minimal, but through statutes passed, particularly in this century, Congress has given executive agencies — the bureaucracy—vast powers in both domestic and foreign policy.

The formal constitutional actors in the U.S. political system have had their own impact on constitutional development. The Constitution says nothing about the power of judicial review, but the Supreme Court, under John Marshall, asserted that power in *Marbury v. Madison* in 1803. Today the power of judicial review is an accepted principle of the U.S. political system. The Constitution, moreover, says nothing about the organization of Congress into committees, but congressional committees today play important roles in the enactment of legislation.

Custom, too, influences the Constitution. George Washington left office at the end of his second term, and a two-term tradition was widely accepted over time until Franklin D. Roosevelt was elected to a third term in 1940 and a fourth term in 1944. Adopted in 1951, however, the Twenty-Second Amendment limited presidential terms to two, thus giving formal constitutional sanction to what had been a custom until Roosevelt's third term.

The power of the principal institutions of government depends, then, on a variety of factors. The Constitution and laws provide the basic structure and define the formal powers of the major actors in the political system. The relationship of policy makers over time, however, depends on the personalities of the policy makers, the ties between the president and influential members of Congress, the character of judicial decisions, the astuteness of top bureaucrats, and historical developments.

Part IV deals with some of the important issues about the power, role, and behavior of policy makers in the national government today. The debates consider the limitation of terms for members of Congress, the authority of the president to commit armed forces, the scope and power of the federal bureaucracy, the confirmation process, the philosophy of the Supreme Court, and the standard by which a federal judge should be removed from office.

Chapter 13

Should the Number of Congressional Terms Be Limited?

The Constitution specifies the duration of the terms of office for members of Congress: two years for representatives and six years for senators. Although the Framers considered limiting the number of terms a member of Congress may serve, they abandoned the idea. They did not limit the number of presidential terms either.

George Washington established a precedent for the presidency when he voluntarily stepped down at the end of his second term. Franklin D. Roosevelt upset the tradition of a two-term presidency when he won re-election to third and fourth terms. Roosevelt's experience may never be duplicated because in 1951 the Twenty-Second Amendment, limiting the number of presidential terms to two, was adopted. Though spear-headed by Republicans, it may have adversely affected two Republican presidents, Dwight D. Eisenhower and Ronald Reagan, who would have been strong contenders for third terms had they chosen to run again.

From time to time, proposals for limiting congressional terms have been put forward. The idea has won the support of Presidents Abraham Lincoln, Harry S. Truman, Dwight D. Eisenhower, and John F. Kennedy. In 1990, new proposals were made, most notably by a group composed largely of Republicans — Americans to Limit Congressional Terms.

It is not difficult to understand why Republican support for limiting congressional terms was strong. Between 1955 and 1994, the Democratic party was in continuous control of the House of Representatives, and it was the majority party in the Senate for most of that time. Democrats benefited mostly from incumbency during those years since incumbents tended to get reelected. In the campaign of 1994, many Republican candidates for Congress supported congressional term limits.

The movement for term limits also developed a momentum because of popular dissatisfaction with legislators. Particularly in the late 1980s and early 1990s, the prestige of Congress was hurt by stories about "perks" of legislators, such as no-interest loans for members of the House of Representatives at the House Bank and special parking spaces at National Airport for senators and representatives. Scandals involving sexual harassment and the taking of bribes and questionable contributions from private and corporate sources contributed to the further tarnishing of Congress's image. In the minds of many people, Congress was becoming a privileged class with benefits and behavior patterns that were unreasonable and costly to the American people. To many, it seemed that one reason Congress had lost touch with ordinary people was because so many members were in Congress too long.

The dissatisfaction with Congress had grown to such a point that in 1992 term limitation measures were placed on the ballots in fourteen states. All of them were passed. In 1995, the Supreme Court decided in *U.S. Term Limits v. Thornton* that the states may not add to, amend, or otherwise restrict the qualifications clause of the Constitution, which set the requirements for serving in the House and Senate.[1] At the time of the Court's decision, twenty-three states had passed term limits for their congressional representatives. A proposed term limits amendment was defeated in the House in 1995, and the Senate filibustered the proposed amendment in 1996. Interest in term limits continues, however.

The debate below is taken from congressional hearings on term limits. David M. Mason, director of the U.S. Congress Assessment Project of the Heritage Foundation, argues for congressional term limits. He contends:

1. Limiting terms is a legitimate democratic method of limiting the power of elected officials and of assuring representation. In this regard, term limits seek to prevent an acquired familiarity with government and its functions from creating among officials a set of interests and views different from those of the public generally. Term limits also prevent elected officials from bending their legally acquired powers to expand their influence or perpetuate their incumbency.

2. Changes in Congress and the nation indicate the need for term limits. These include the increased rate of reelection and return to Congress; the broadening of Congress's management and administration of federal programs, which has decreased political accountability and isolated members of Congress from their constituents; and post–cold war expansions in government.

3. With term limits, legislators would be more willing to question established programs and policies and would have greater independence from existing administrative and political arrangements.

4. A term-limited Congress would be less willing to delegate broad powers to the executive branch so that a better defined separation of powers would emerge as a result.

5. Term limits would almost certainly result in greater diversity in the Congress.

6. Arguments against term limits denigrate the very concept of democratic rule.

7. Term limits would no more limit popular choice than do other means that are built into the current electoral system.

8. Term limits have broad and consistent support.

Thomas E. Mann, director of government studies at the Brookings Institution, argues against term limits. He contends:

1. The crux of the case for term limits is a rejection of professionalism in politics. But professionalism is an essential feature of a complex and specialized world. The perceived ills of contemporary American government — from policy deadlock to pork-barrel spending — have little connection to careerism in Congress.
2. There is no permanent Congress. The membership of the House and Senate is largely remade every decade, and term limits are unlikely to increase the competitiveness of congressional elections.
3. There is no reason to believe that a term-limited Congress would be more accountable to the American people or that it would be more inclined to advance the public interest. If anything, term limits are likely to shift the focus of members of Congress even more in the direction of local and immediate concerns.
4. It requires a leap of faith to believe that term limits will achieve what its proponents claim: transform the institution of Congress, making it more productive, more deliberative, less dependent on staff and special interests, less disposed to micromanage programs and agencies, and better structured to reward members on the basis of ability rather than seniority.
5. Term limits are antidemocratic, restricting people's electoral choices.
6. Although opportunities should exist for new people to hold congressional positions, many people who have seniority in Congress have legislative talent. That talent encompasses among other traits a respect for the public, a capacity to listen to people who disagree with you, bargaining skills, a willingness to compromise, an appreciation for parliamentary procedure, and a capacity to move easily between technical knowledge and ordinary experience.

NOTE

1. *U.S. Term Limits v. Thornton*, 115 S. Ct. 1842 (1995).

Should the Number of Congressional Terms Be Limited?

DAVID M. MASON
Term Limits and Political Conscience

TERM LIMITS AS A DEMOCRATIC PRINCIPLE

A principal purpose of representative democracy is the limitation of power. Our constitution represents an effort to divide, define and limit power in such a way as to provide for the governing of a large and powerful nation while limiting the size and power of the government. Term limitation is simply another method of limiting the power of elected officials and of assuring genuine representation. Periodic elections themselves are the most fundamental expression of these limitations, but . . . limits on service in public office have been integral to democracy since its origins. In America, limits on executive officials in particular have existed since the founding, and are now so ingrained as to pass almost without comment. In my own state of Virginia, for instance, the governor can serve only one four-year term, a situation which most voters and politicians seem satisfied with. With increasing frequency in recent years, term limits have also been imposed on mayors: in Philadelphia in 1951, in Wilmington, Jacksonville and Nashville in the 1960s and in Atlanta in 1973, among others. Somewhat more recently, cities began to impose term limits on members of city councils, including Bangor, Maine in 1976, Dallas in 1981, Tacoma and Tampa in 1983 and El Paso in 1984. Thus, while to many term limits seem to have sprung inexplicably into public view in about 1990, in fact, the concept has been applied continuously in America and increasingly since the 1960s, with the new twist being its application to legislative offices. As a matter of fundamental principle, however, it is difficult to distinguish between limitations on executives and legislators, particularly, as I will discuss further, as legislative offices become full-time positions.

There are at least two general objectives in limiting the terms of elective officials: the first [is] to prevent an acquired familiarity with government and its functions from creating among officials a different set of interests and views than among the public generally. This was a great concern among the founders, who held out regular and frequent elections at which times officials would presumably be returned to private status, and the principle that Congress could make no law that did not apply to itself, as protections against a tyranny of democratically elected officials. A second and related objective of term limits is to prevent the ability of elected officials to bend their legally acquired powers in order to expand their influence or perpetuate their incumbency. The House of Representatives recognizes both of these functions of term limitations in its own rules in regard to service limitations on the Intelligence and Budget Committees. An explicit purpose of the six-year limit on Intelligence Committee service is to prevent Members from becoming overly familiar with and presumably captive to the intelligence bureaucracy. The limits on the Budget Committee arose in response to fears on the part of Members of other standing committees that the Budget Committee might acquire too much power over the other organs of the House. In addition, Republicans have recently imposed limitations on service by their Ranking Members, and Democrats on certain members of their party leadership, apparently for similar reasons.

Term limits, then, are not so much a solution in search of a problem, as has been suggested by one commentator, as a valid principle in need of application. It is appropriate and necessary to engage in a discussion of term limits on the level of fundamental principle, but blanket assertions that term limits are undemocratic or that the idea is unthoughtful can be dismissed out of hand. Instead, we need to ask, in this context, whether conditions in Congress or in the country at large merit the application of this legitimate principle to election to the House and Senate.

CHANGES IN CONGRESS AND THE NATION SUPPORTING TERM LIMITS

The founders incorporated the rotational principle in the Constitution through varying terms of office and staggered service in the Senate, and seemed to assume that there would be frequent turnover in federal office. Though they obviously knew about explicit term limits, they did not impose them on Congress, and a respect for their judgments and for the usage of over 200 years compels us to ask whether conditions have changed in such a way as to make term limits appropriate for Congress today.

Among the most frequently discussed factors in regard to term limits is the rate of reelection and return to Congress. Counting retirements and election defeats, return rates to the House had generally increased from about 75 percent just after World War Two to around 90 percent until last year, when the rate dipped back down to about 75 percent. Senate trends have been less obvious, with the return rate of the relevant class dipping below 50 percent for three successive elections from 1976 to 1980. These rates are significantly higher, however, than those that prevailed in the founding era, when House turnover was frequently in the 50 percent range. In addition to return rates, there is a substantial body of work on what have been referred to as the vanishing marginal districts: the increasing trend, again broken in the last election [1992] for House incumbents to win reelection by margins greater than 60 percent.

A number of factors have been advanced as contributing to increased reelection rates, including a decline in intraparty competition, the increase in the population of districts, a more vigorous exploitation of the advantages of office, such as constituent service operations and the frank, and the increasing regulation of political campaigns, which has led, among other results, to a large and growing financial advantage for incumbents over challengers. Left unaltered, these factors will continue to keep reelection rates higher than they would be otherwise, meaning that the House has become more resistant to political change, though not immune to it. I believe this development is unhealthy, even undemocratic, and that the general reduction in turnover, and the factors contributing to it, constitute a valid reason to support term limits.

There is demonstrable evidence that Members change their views in predictable ways over time. Economist James Payne has documented in *The Culture of Spending* (ICS Press, San Francisco, 1991) that Members of Congress tend to support more government spending as their tenure increases, and that this tendency operates across the ideological spectrum. The National Taxpayers' Union Budget Tracking System shows similar results. Public choice economists as well have contributed important new insights into the actions of public officials, arguing that there is unavoidably, and perhaps even unconsciously, a heavy dose of self-interest in the actions of public officials. Representative Tim Penny, among others, has criticized the Congressional pension system as a heavy contributor to an inappropriate careerist attitude.

A more important argument for term limits is the significant change in the role and operation of the professionalized legislature, particularly since the 1960s. In general terms, Congress has taken an increasingly active role in the management and administration of federal programs, which has resulted in a blurring of the separation of powers, with a consequent loss of political accountability, and has permitted an expansion of the scope and scale of federal activities far beyond what would have been permitted by earlier Congresses. The emergence of essentially continuous sessions of Congress is both a result of and reinforcement to this managerial impulse, as is the rapid growth in Congressional staff, most of which occurred during the 1960s and 1970s.

As Congress has become a continuously meeting body, and as opportunities for outside income, and consequently for non-political outside activities, were reduced and then eliminated, as Congress exempted itself from the application or objective enforcement of various social policy laws, Members of Congress unavoidably became more detached from, or in the words of *The Federalist,* less sympathetic to, the plight and concerns of ordinary citizens. For most Members, election to Congress means that you no longer work, shop, commute or send your children to school among your constituents. The attitudes and outlook inside the beltway among what has become a professional political class is indeed different from that in the rest of the nation, and Members of Congress spend far more time here than they did twenty or thirty years ago, and vastly more time than was the case in the founding period. Also importantly, time spent back in the district is as campaigner and officeholder, rather than as businessowner, commuter or parent. The reply that Congress is, to the contrary, hypersensitive to changes in public opinion, only strengthens the case that Congress is indeed out of touch. Members who have a firm grasp of their constituents' opinions and views are unlikely to be swayed by transient changes in polls or by superficial public relations efforts. It is those who put their own job security first in order of priority who are more likely to react inappropriately to such factors.

The professional, managerial Congress clearly acts differently than its predecessors. This new Congress is, for instance, far more willing to delegate broad powers to executive agencies, on the assumption that Members and committees will have a major say in the implementation and execution of their mandates. Indeed, there has arisen an unfortunate tendency to pass particularly contentious issues into the bureaucracy, but under procedural mandates that allow Congress to attempt to manage or prejudice the outcome. Such practices leave voters who are frustrated with government performance in general or with particular policy outcomes with no one to hold accountable: Congress points to the bureaucracy and the president points back at Congress, yet both sides have incentives to postpone and temporize rather than to resolve issues clearly.

The development and increasing use of non-legislative means of exercising power has aided the career Congress in avoiding accountability while managing the executive branch policy process. Among these practices are: insistence on adherence to report language as equivalent to law; attempts to construct detailed and definitive legislative histories; detailed requirements on executive branch decisionmaking procedures, including, incredibly, prohibitions on contact among executive officials; reporting requirements to Congress; and, the Independent Counsel law, particularly the Congressional triggering mechanism. All of these practices and many others less formal permit (if they are not themselves per se) violations of the separation of powers. The result, again, is a lack of accountability to voters as to who is responsible for the results. This entanglement also robs legislators of the objectivity which is essential to proper legislative oversight of executive activity: to the extent that Congress is involved in executive branch decisions it simply cannot be a fair judge or referee.

To the degree that the president, governors and mayors had their tenure limited because of the full-time nature of their offices, the extent of their powers and the resources under their control, the same imperative applies to Congress, state legislatures and even city councils as they lengthen sessions, increase staffs and budgets, and take a larger role in government management.

In addition to changes in the legislature, changed conditions in government generally seem to have contributed to support for term limits. The entire developed world is experiencing a post–cold war revolution in government, as we have seen in Italy, Japan and Canada even more dramatically than in the United States. Much as in situations of active wars, governments have grown in scope and power while policies in a broad range of areas have ossified, becoming increasingly at variance with changing public opinion. As with tectonic forces that build up over time, the sudden reduction in military and foreign policy tension is likely to result in large and sudden changes in other areas of policy and society, changes that have by no means yet been spent.

BENEFITS OF TERM LIMITS

In assessing the likely effects of term limits, honest observers on both sides of the issue are likely to admit that predictions are uncertain. Because most term limits laws have included grandfather clauses, we have no significant experience with term limited legislatures, and the judgments would take years to form in any case. Unintended and unpredicted consequences are certainly likely. While I disagree . . . in predicting that term limited legislatures would tend to produce more limited government, though not necessarily lower spending, I agree that the results would by no means be consistently conservative, and that predicting specific policy outcomes is impossible. This simply drives home the point that support for term limits is on the level of principle, and is not driven by any narrow ideological view.

The most important changes under term limits would be in the political process and system itself. Most importantly, term limits would change the role, outlook and attitude of elected officials. Legislators would be more willing to question established programs and policies and would have greater independence from existing administrative and political arrangements. Legislators would be more inclined to fix problems than to manage them. One case in point is the genuine scandal of existing Congressional constituent service operations. Political Scientist Morris Fiorina has detailed the demonstrable political benefits of casework to Members of Congress, and internal congressional documents emphasize the media and political aspects of securing proper credit for casework. Yet lawmakers across the political spectrum defend constituent service as essential to the representative function, among conservatives, notably, as an essential means for individual citizens to deal with the federal behemoth. What is lost in the discussion is that fact that Congress collectively is responsible for the bureaucratic messes that make casework so voluminous while individual Members profit from solving the problems one at a time. The incentive, intended or not, is to manage problems rather than to solve them, a system which, overall, serves the public poorly. A term limited Congress would likely demonstrate a different attitude.

As discussed above, I also believe a term limited Congress would be less willing to delegate broad powers to the executive branch, and that a better defined separation of powers would emerge as a result. Internally to Congress, except under the most lengthy of term limits, the seniority system, and the system of standing committees which depends on it, would be destroyed, and there needs to be greater discussion than there has been to this point about how the committee system might be replaced or changed under term limits. Term limits might well revive the possibility of a return to a part time legislature, or at least to some reduction in the length of sessions. There is at least one survey comparing states with and without gubernatorial term limits which indicates that term limited states have more competitive elections, even in the terms in which the seat is not open, contrary to the claim that term limits would result in a free ride after the first election since competitors would wait for an open seat. Finally, term limits would almost certainly result in greater diversity in the Congress, as we saw in the results of the large turnover last year. Even more than the 1992 elections, term limits would open service in Congress to people from a wider range of backgrounds, and to citizens at different stages in their lives and careers.

OBJECTIONS TO TERM LIMITS

The first, but least credible, objection to term limits heard in Washington is that they are a plot designed by frustrated Republicans who could otherwise never gain a majority in Congress. The positions of Republican officeholders, and the Republican record in open seats over the past decade or more indicate that this theory is both implausible and unlikely to succeed. Further, the emergence, growth and progression of the term limits movement indicates that Congress, and even Democrats generally are not the intended targets. The first statewide term limit initiative, in Oklahoma, applied to the state legislature only, as did California's 1990 initiative. While the Colorado initiative, also that year, applied term limits to a Congressional delegation for the first time, it also applied to the Republican-controlled state legislature. The initiative in Washington state the next year was led by a liberal peace activist. In municipalities around the country citizens have applied term limits to various local officials, including some areas such as New Orleans and Kansas City, and now New York, where no one expects a change in the partisan or racial composition of officeholders as a result of term limits. There is nothing personal about the term limits movement, and the prevailing Congressional reaction to the contrary simply confirms the suspicions of most term limits advocates.

Opponents also argue that term limits will deprive the nation of talented legislators. Certainly there are many long-time Members of Congress who I admire greatly. But this argument ignores the genius, and indeed the basic supposition of democracy: that people are capable of ruling themselves. To argue that only one among over a half million people is well qualified to serve in Congress is simply insupportable. This argument also ignores the design of most term limit measures. Not only are politicians permitted to sit out a term or more [and] run again, but most state limits allow incumbents to run as write-in candidates, a route which has been successful in some cases.

Opponents also argue that staff, bureaucrats and special interests would run a non-professional Congress. As a former staffer, I would assert that junior Members rely far less on staff than their senior colleagues. Further, Congressional Management Foundation surveys indicate that the average tenure of Congressional staff in their current position is between six and eighteen months, probably depending on the age of the Congress itself. While there are certainly a number of long term staffers, their tenure is largely a result of the seniority system and the tenure of their patrons. Term limited legislators will have no compunctions about making their own staffing arrangements.

As for bureaucrats and special interests, the infamous iron triangles that serve them were born of the Congressional committee and seniority system. Term limited legislators would be more suspicious of bureaucrats, and special interests would have less leverage and less incentive to pressure or cultivate them. A cursory look at the major contributors to anti-term limit efforts will show that the most infamous of the special interests find it in their interest to oppose term limits.

The charge that inexperienced legislators would, whatever their intentions, be manipulated by these interests again denigrates the very concept of democratic rule, and misunderstands the role of the legislature, which is to apply well-informed common sense rather than narrow expertise.

Finally, opponents charge that term limits are undemocratic because they limit choice. We have discussed how term limits are analogous to other institutional arrangements that distinguish our republican system from pure democracy. Beyond that, it is difficult to argue that term limits have a more limiting effect on voter choice than other prejudices and barriers built into the current electoral system which would be relieved by term limits. The first of these are the electoral advantages of officeholding for the incumbent, many deriving directly from the use of public funds. Even if constituent service staffs, pork barrel spending and newsletters were eliminated from the Congressional arsenal, continuing biases toward incumbents would exist in the political and media structures, and increasingly in the federal regulation of political campaigns. The argument for unlimited tenure also runs counter to the basic premise of representational democracy, the focus of which is not on the officeholder but on his selection from among the people.

CONSTITUTIONAL ISSUE AFFECTING TERM LIMITS

The principal activity on Congressional term limits thus far has been through state initiative. A number of constitutional questions arise as a result, along with declarations, particularly from opponents, that state limits on Congressional tenure are clearly unconstitutional. Honest commentators would have to admit, however, from their view of the arguments, that no one really knows what the Supreme Court might say, that the issue would be genuinely one of first impressions. . . .

Advocates of state authority rely heavily upon the time, place and manner clause, under which the Supreme Court has given states wide latitude to regulate ballot access, including prohibitions on write-in candidates and prohibitions on losing major party primary candidates running in the general election. Clearly the courts have determined that there is no fundamental right to ballot access, making claims by officeholders of a Fourteenth Amendment equal protection right to run unlikely to prevail. Advocates also claim a Tenth

Amendment reserved powers right for states or citizens to limit the tenure of their representatives. While I believe that the arguments in favor of state power to limit Congressional terms ought to prevail, and probably will, we simply will not know until the Supreme Court acts. It would be unfortunate, however, if this matter were simply relegated to the courts, and a decision were sprung on a hapless electorate or on Congress without a more general debate and discussion of the constitutional issues, or of alternative approaches. This committee in particular should consider holding additional hearings focusing specifically on the constitutional and other legal issues involved in term limits.

Of course, these arguments would be moot if, as most term limit advocates prefer, Congress approved a constitutional amendment. Nearly everyone would agree that a national system would be more fair and rational. Skeptics are justly concerned about cavalier changes in the Constitution, and I would like to suggest one intriguing possibility should the courts determine that term limits are permissible under the time, place and manner clause. As this committee well knows, Congress has the right to supersede state laws under that clause, as has been done under the Voting Rights Act, the Motor Voter bill and other legislation. I see no reason why Congress should not act by statute to limit Members' terms. For advocates, once implemented, such a change is unlikely to be reversed, and for skeptics, a statutory approach would allow for adjustments or emergency changes with relative ease. Unfortunately, it is the continuing and vociferous resistance to term limits on the part of elected officials that lead advocates to seek the surest fix, a constitutional one. If advanced in a timely fashion, compromise is entirely possible. Bitter end resistance is likely to result in less favorable outcomes.

TERM LIMITS AND POLITICAL CONSCIENCE

Finally, I would address the question of why officeholders continue to oppose term limits in large majorities while the public supports them, by margins as high as 80 percent in some opinion polls. This is not a matter of a shallow or transient blip in public opinion. Support for term limits is broad, remaining remarkably consistent across every demographic and political grouping. It is persistent, having been successful, with only one notable exception which was later reversed, in elections in diverse areas over three successive years. Notably, for referendum measures, support seems to hold up relatively well when applied to a specific proposal, and even when supporters are outspent by large margins. A recent issue of *The American Enterprise* contained some interesting polling data from the Gallup Organization indicating that support for term limits has grown from 49 percent in 1964 to 64 percent in 1990, and to 67 percent in 1992 on the specific question of twelve year limits for the House and Senate. *The American Enterprise* also notes that support for term limits was lowest in 1964 among college graduates, but is now highest among the best educated portions of the electorate.

Term limits have been enthusiastically supported for a variety of offices, municipal, state and federal. Voters in many California jurisdictions have supported the concept three different times for these different levels of government. Voters in San Jose went so far as to impose retroactive term limits on city officials, as have Houston voters. Seventeen states and scores of cities and counties have voted for term limits. With the probable addition of Illinois and Massachusetts among others next year, well over 50 percent of the population will have had the opportunity to vote on term limits at least once. No issue in recent memory has commanded such broad and consistent support.

It may be time for elected officials to ask themselves honestly, whether they are thinking about term limits as their constituents are, or whether they are reacting on the basis of their own employment and career situations. For exactly to the extent that judgments are formed on that basis, public officials have lost sight of the public interest. When the public supports term limits broadly and overwhelmingly, over time and in specific referenda for a variety of offices, it is time for elected officials to reflect honestly on why their own judgment is at variance with that of their constituents, whether this is a matter of conscience or of self interest. And if opposition is a matter of conscience, ask why in a democracy the judgments of representatives and citizens are so much at variance, for such is surely an unhealthy situation if it long persists.

Should the Number of Congressional Terms Be Limited?

THOMAS E. MANN
The Case against Term Limits

I take as my point of departure that a constitutional amendment is required to accomplish this objective. The efforts to limit congressional terms by state initiative are, I believe, unconstitutional and will be so ruled by the courts. In any case, your responsibility as members of the Subcommittee on Civil and Constitutional Rights is to consider whether the U.S. Constitution should be amended to add an additional qualification for service in the Congress — namely that one not have served more than a specified number of total or consecutive terms in the House of Representatives or Senate.

I applaud you for initiating a process of public deliberation on a question that has heretofore generated considerably more heat than light. In the last several years term limits have become the preferred vehicle for expressing public frustration and anger with the political system. Citizen initiatives to limit congressional terms have succeeded in all 15 states where they were on the ballot, most by overwhelming margins. Numerous state and local jurisdictions have voted to limit the terms of their legislators. Public opinion polls reveal overwhelming popular support for term limit proposals. If our Constitution could be amended by national initiative, I have no doubt that term limits would soon be enshrined in the fundamental charter of our democracy.

Fortunately, however, we enjoy a representative system of government that requires a level of deliberation before our basic democratic rules can be altered. We are forced to stop and think before acting. Precious little reasoned discussion has accompanied the debates over term limits in the states. Advocates have skillfully tapped the reservoir of public distrust of politicians and stimulated visceral reactions in favor of term limits. Opponents of term limits have largely abdicated their responsibility for joining the debate. Many politicians, fearful of arguing against a proposal that appears to enjoy such broad popular support and of embracing a position that is transparently self-serving, have removed themselves from the fray, trusting that one way or another the term limit movement will be stopped before its objective is achieved. This myopia has produced a one-sided debate and increased the probability that term limits will someday soon be applied to members of Congress.

These hearings mark the beginning of what I hope will be a thoughtful public discussion of congressional term limits — what they are designed to achieve, what their consequences might be, and whether more effective remedies might be available for dealing with the problems identified by term limit advocates. During these hearings it is important to remember that the burden of proof — diagnosing the problem and demonstrating that the cure is likely to work without debilitating side effects — properly falls on those who would alter the constitutional order. My view is that a persuasive case for term limits has not been made. What I intend to do here is review and assess that case, based on my reading of an extensive scholarly and popular literature, as well as on my own research on congressional elections and collaborative work with Norman Ornstein on congressional reform.

CAREERISM

The crux of the case for term limits is a rejection of professionalism in politics — or legislative careerism. Careerism is seen as fostering in members of Congress an exclusive focus on reelection and power and a devaluation of the public interest. Advocates see rotation as a way to cure these ills, by preventing a concentration of political power and enhancing government by amateurs — selfless citizens who temporarily answer their country's call to legislate in the public interest. In support of this, they point to the extensive American experience with rotation in office as well as the philosophical underpinnings for rotation expressed in the founding period, particularly by the Antifederalists.

Most advocates of term limits embrace a conception of democracy that is plebiscitary in character. This concept makes a series of related assertions: Representation is a necessary evil that works only if elected officials closely mirror the instincts and wishes of their constituents. Careerism breeds an arrogance among officeholders that insulates them from the concerns of the people. A permanent political elite turns a deaf ear on the citizens it is elected to serve and pursues its own self-interested agenda.

However, one prominent proponent of term limits, George F. Will, argues that legislative careerism produces just the opposite effect: risk-averse members hypersensitive to public sentiment and unwilling to exercise independent judgment. Will champions term limits as a means of restoring deliberative democracy; his compatriots in the movement prefer to empower the people and revitalize direct democracy. What unites them is a belief that citizens legislators, by virtue either of their more accurate reflection of public sentiment or their wisdom, independently expressed and untainted by career considerations, will more faithfully pursue policies that term limit proponents favor, which in most cases means a government that spends, taxes and regulates less.

Since careerism or professionalism is the central malady term limits are designed to cure, it is important that the several components of the professionalism critique be evaluated. Were the founders truly sympathetic to mandatory rotation? Is professionalism damaging to our politics and policymaking? Is professionalism in government avoidable? Will term limits replace professionals with amateurs in the Congress? Let me address each of these questions in turn.

Whatever the objections raised by the Antifederalists, the Constitution speaks clearly on the issue of mandatory limits. The founders directly and unanimously rejected the idea of term limits. After much debate, they concluded that frequent elections would be a sufficient safeguard against abuse by incumbents. Indeed, their strategy was not to deny or negate personal ambition but to channel that ambition to serve the public interest. That required giving members a longer-term stake in the institution so that they might look beyond the public's immediate concerns and in Madison's words "refine and enlarge" the public view. Will argues rather lamely that a vastly changed political and social situation necessitates trying to restore core values of the founders' generation by embracing measures that they deemed unnecessary. But Hamilton's words in 1788 ring true today: "Men will pursue their interests. It is as easy to divert human nature as to oppose the strong currents of selfish passions. A wise legislator will gently divert the channel, and direct it, if possible, to the public good."

What can we say of the costs of professionalism to our politics? Critics of Congress routinely attribute everything they dislike about the institution to careerism. Careerists in Congress are said to be more corrupt, more beholden to special interests, more consumed with pork barrel projects, more supportive of increased spending and less responsive to the public interest than amateurs would be.

If these claims were true, we would expect that to be revealed by differences in the behavior of more and less professional legislators. We can search for these differences by comparing junior and senior members in the contemporary Congress. We can compare the behavior of the more professionalized twentieth-century Congress to the more amateur nineteenth-century Congress. We can compare amateur and professional legislatures across countries, states and localities. None of these comparisons show that professional legislators are more corrupt, parochial, or influenced by interest groups than their amateur counterparts.

Instead, careful study of Congress and every other sector of society suggests that greater professionalism is a necessary offshoot of the growth and specialization of the modern world. If the political rules are rewritten to make it impossible to build a career in Congress, then the institution will have to rely on the professionalism of others to do its job, whether they are staff members, bureaucrats or lobbyists. The revolt against professionalism is part of a broader populist resentment of elites in all spheres of society and a nostalgia for a bygone "Golden Era." But advocates of term limits are hard pressed to offer any examples of amateurism operating successfully in contemporary society, in the United States or abroad. George Will got it right the first time when he wrote: "The day of the 'citizen legislator' — the day when a legislator's primary job was something other than government — is gone. A great state cannot be run by 'citizen legislators' and amateur administrators."

Finally, there is the critical issue of whether term limits would succeed in replacing career politicians with citizen legislators and whether the latter would fit the image sketched by term limit proponents. The precise form of the term limit would have a bearing on this question: simple limits on continuous service in one house would have a very different effect on candidate recruitment than a lifetime limit on service in Congress. The former is likely to foster a class of itinerant professionals who move up and within a hierarchy of term-limited legislatures, no less engaged in the profession of politics but probably less committed to the larger purposes of the institution of which they are a part. The latter, depending upon the severity of the limit, would alter recruitment patterns but would the average member fit the image of the disinterested citizen legislator? I think not.

Absent other changes in the legal and political context of congressional elections, the enormous costs — personal and financial — of running for Congress would not diminish under term limits. Candidate-centered, media-dominated, weak-party campaigns require entrepreneurial skills and resources that are not evenly distributed across American society. Removing the possibility of developing a legislative career would skew the membership of Congress even further in the direction of a social and economic elite. As political scientist Morris Fiorina has observed, "amateur political settings advantage the independently wealthy, professionals with private practices, independent business people, and others with similar financial and career flexibility." Moreover, Syracuse University professor Linda Fowler is almost certainly correct in arguing that patterns of recruitment and forced retirement under term limits will increase the influence of special interests in the legislature.

In sum, the linchpin of the case for term limits — the desirability and feasibility of ending legislative careerism and returning to the citizen legislature originally conceived by the founders — fails on every key dimension. Mandatory rotation destroys the primary incentive used by the Federalists in writing the Constitution to nurture a deliberative democracy. The perceived ills of contemporary American government — from policy deadlock to pork barrel spending — have little connection to careerism in Congress. Professionalism is an essential feature of a complex and specialized world. Finally, any effort to use term limits to replace careerists with citizens legislators is likely to produce some combination of musical chairs by professional politicians with weak institutional loyalties and of participation by elite amateurs with sufficient resources and connections to make a brief stint in Congress possible and profitable.

COMPETITION AND TURNOVER

Another crucial argument advanced on behalf of congressional term limits is the need to restore electoral competition and turnover to a body in which incumbents exploit the advantages of their office to ensure automatic reelection and perpetuate a permanent Congress. Term limits, it is argued, will reinvigorate democracy by leveling the playing field between incumbents and challengers, preventing dynasties from forming in Congress, and guaranteeing that fresh blood and new ideas reach Washington on a regular basis.

There is much to be said for this critique of congressional elections. My colleague at Brookings, Bill Frenzel, a former Republican member of the House from Minnesota, has developed the argument in "Term Limits and the Immortal Congress: How to Make Congressional Elections Competitive Again," which appeared in the Spring 1992 issue of *The Brookings Review.* I have responded to Frenzel's argument in an accompanying article entitled "The Wrong Medicine: Term Limits Won't Cure What Ails Congressional Elections." Rather than review in detail our respective assertions and evidence, I will provide the Committee with a copy of the two articles. Here I will simply summarize what I see as the major problems with this argument for term limits.

One concern of critics can easily be put to rest. There is no permanent Congress. Indeed, it is ludicrous that the term continues to be used following the 1992 elections, which produced the most turnover in the House since 1948. Many analysts overgeneralized from the quiescent House elections between 1984 and 1988. The fact is that the membership of the House and Senate is largely remade every decade. The years between 1974 and 1982 produced a high level of turnover from retirements and incumbent defeats. By the early 1980s three-fourths of senators and representatives had served fewer than 12 years. Membership stabilized during the rest of the decade as new members settled in and the public showed little interest in throwing the rascals out. That pattern began to change in 1990, although a weak field of challengers kept House incumbent losses to 15 in spite of the widespread signs of public discontent. But 1992 confirmed that we are once again in a period of rapid membership turnover. Every indication is that high levels of voluntary retirement and incumbent defeat will continue in 1994.

While achieving a healthy flow of new blood is not a serious problem for the House or Senate, ensuring a reasonable level of competition is. Incredibly high reelection rates and large margins of victory (more so in the House than in the Senate) are a legitimate concern. But term limits are unlikely to increase the competitiveness of congressional elections. Increased competition requires more high-quality, well-financed challengers, but term limits would not materially reduce the disincentives to running for Congress or increase the effectiveness of party recruiting mechanisms. Potential candidates would continue to weigh the disruptions to family life and career, loss of privacy, demands of fundraising, and the other unpleasantries of modern campaigns. Moreover, there is no reason to believe that term-limited incumbents would be any less determined to retain their seats for the full period permitted by the amended Constitution. The odds of a challenger defeating an incumbent would not increase under term limits. Indeed, a term limit would very likely turn into a floor, with would-be candidates deferring their challenge and awaiting the involuntary retirement of the incumbent. If a norm of deference to term-limited incumbents took root, elections would be contested only in open seats, and then only those not safe for one political party or the other. This would mean a net reduction in the competitiveness of congressional elections.

One important (though usually unstated) target of term limit proponents is the permanent majority status of the House Democratic party. Presumably Republicans would have a better chance of climbing out of the minority if the cohort of veteran Democratic legislators were forced to give up their seats without a fight. I am sympathetic with the goal — an occasional change in the House majority party in line with national political tides would be good for politics and governance — but dubious of the means. Yet during the 1980s, while Republicans fared better in open seats than in those contested by an incumbent, even here their performance fell short of the Democrats. Term limits just won't get the job done, whether the job is increasing competition generally or elevating the Republicans to majority status. The right responses are more targeted interventions to build a stronger Republican "farm team" of candidates; to put more resources into the hands of challengers and limit the material advantages of incumbency; and to raise the national stakes in congressional elections.

ACCOUNTABILITY

Another argument advanced by term limit supporters, one that is related to the critique of careerism, is that members of Congress are not genuinely accountable to the people that send them to Washington. The overriding goal of reelection leads members to pursue a manipulative relationship with their constituents — they buy safe districts by shoveling pork and catering to special interests with access to campaign resources. Ordinary citizens are anesthetized and potential challengers discouraged, thereby allowing members to pursue their own agendas in Washington without any realistic fear that they will be held to account for their actions.

There are grounds for concern here. Uncontested elections and halfhearted challenges are unlikely to have a bracing effect on incumbents and over time may breed an unhealthy feeling of invulnerability and arrogance. Moreover, heavy investments in constituent service tend to depoliticize the relationship between representatives and constituents and minimize the possibility of policy accountability. Yet most members of Congress remain unbelievably insecure about their political futures and highly responsive to the interests of their constituencies. One major reason incumbents are so successful is that electoral accountability is alive and well: representatives conform to the wishes of their constituents and are in turn rewarded with reelection.

The problem is not individual accountability. Voters show no signs of suffering from inattentive or unresponsive representatives. If anything, members of Congress are too solicitous of their constituencies and insufficiently attentive to broader national interests, too consumed with their personal standing in their district or state and too little dependent on their political party.

What many of us sense is in short supply in the contemporary Congress is a collective accountability that provides an appropriate balance between local and national interests, between narrow and general interests, between short-term preferences and long-term needs. The present system appears to favor local, special and immediate interests over national, general and future concerns. Will believes the way to right that balance and to restore congressional deliberation in service of the public interest is to remove members of Congress from the unseemly and demeaning business of elections, to proscribe ambition in public life rather than channel it, to take the politics out of government.

I believe this effort is self-defeating. It would deny the democratic connection rather than revitalize it. There is simply no reason to believe that a term-limited Congress would be more accountable to the American people or that it would be more inclined to advance the public interest. If anything, term limits are likely to shift the focus of members of Congress even more in the direction of local and immediate concerns.

CONGRESSIONAL ORGANIZATION AND POWER

The final argument offered by proponents is that term limits would transform the institution of Congress, making it more productive, more deliberative, less dependent on staff and special interests, less disposed to micromanage programs and agencies, and better structured to reward members on the basis of ability rather than seniority. As I understand the logic of this argument, term limits would change the motivations of legislators and subsequently their behavior by removing the incentive to put reelection and personal power within the chamber above other considerations, such as making public policy in the national interest.

It requires an extraordinary leap of faith to believe that term limits will produce these desirable institutional changes, especially in light of my earlier discussion of the electoral effects of term limits. We have no direct evidence on which to rely — term limits have been in effect in the states for too short a time to provide an empirical basis for any reliable generalizations. Indeed, there is much to be said for taking advantage of our federal system by assessing the state experiments with term limits before enshrining them in the U.S. Constitution. A number of very interesting scholarly studies are now being launched and pertinent findings will begin to emerge as state term limits take effect over the next several years. But I suspect my call for experimentation and deliberation will not mollify leaders of the term limit movement.

Absent any reliable evidence, I simply note that the institutional changes mentioned above do not logically follow from the imposition of term limits. Take legislative productivity. As Michael Malbin and Gerald Benjamin have observed, a legislature of well-meaning amateurs, determined to decide on the merits of an issue unsullied by career considerations, have no guarantee of success. While critics often attribute stalemate to cowardly politicians unwilling to make tough decisions, it more often occurs among legislators who want to do the right thing but disagree over what the right thing is.

Or take deliberation, which George Will sees as occurring in a legislature where "members reason together about the problems confronting the community and strive to promote policies in the general interest of the community." Ironically, the term limits movement is the very antithesis of deliberation. It is riding the crest of a plebiscitary wave in our politics which favors initiatives, referendums and other forms of direct democracy over the reasoned discussion insulated from public passions preferred by Will. I find it hard to imagine how term limits would foster deliberation in Congress. Members would continue to have a reelection incentive until they came up against the limit. A greater impatience to build a record of achievement would not necessarily augur well for the national interest; short-sighted solutions to immediate problems could just as easily be the result.

More importantly, the intense individualism of the contemporary Congress would be strengthened, not weakened, under term limits. There would be little incentive for members to follow the lead of others, be they party leaders or committee chairmen. The elimination of seniority as a basis for leadership selection, a likely consequence of term limits, would intensify competition and conflict among members but devalue the authority of those positions. Few rewards and resources would exist for institutional maintenance and policy leadership — protecting the independence and integrity of the Congress, setting legislative agendas, mobilizing majorities. With little change in the media and interest group environment of Congress, the centrifugal forces in Congress would remain strong while the centralizing instruments are weakened.

Much the same can be said for the other improvements in the institutional performance of Congress that allegedly would flow from term limits. Term-limited members could prove to be more dependent on special interests for campaign funds, information and a job after service in Congress than present members. Less experienced members would perforce rely more heavily on congressional staff and executive branch officials.

Indeed, the more one examines the claims of term limit advocates, the more one is struck by the utter failure of advocates to make a convincing case connecting remedies with problems. If Congress were to legislate in a complex policy area on the basis of theories and evidence no better than I have summarized here, it would be roundly (and properly) criticized by many of those who now embrace term limits. There is, I believe, no substantive case for amending the U.S. Constitution to limit the terms of members of the House and Senate.

While I believe the failure of proponents to present a convincing argument for term limits is sufficient reason for rejecting a constitutional amendment, there are two additional reasons for resisting popular sentiment on this issue.

DEMOCRACY

Term limits would diminish our democracy by restricting it unnecessarily. Voters now have the power to end the career of their representatives and senators by the simple exercise of the franchise. At present they also enjoy the power to retain in office those officials whom they believe merit reelection. The Constitution properly precludes the citizens of one district or state from limiting the electoral choice of those residing somewhere else.

I fully support efforts to increase the supply of able, well-financed challengers and to enhance the quality and quantity of relevant information about incumbents available to citizens. Such steps would increase the competitiveness of congressional elections and expand the choices available to voters. But an arbitrary limit on terms of congressional service is an anti-democratic device masquerading as the champion of democratic revival. Alexander Hamilton said it best: It is a "fundamental principle of our representative democracy that 'the people should choose whom they please to govern them,' [and that] this principle is undermined as much by limiting whom the people can select as by limiting the franchise itself."

EXPERIENCE

Longevity and experience do not correspond perfectly with wisdom and effectiveness. Some incumbents overstay their productive periods in Congress and are treated too generously by their constituents at reelection time. Every legislative body needs regular infusions of new members to reflect changing public sentiments and put new ideas into the legislative process. Opportunities should exist for junior members to participate meaningfully in the legislative process.

That being said, I believe it would be a terrible mistake to end all careers in Congress after 6 or 12 years. Legislative talent — which encompasses among other traits a respect for the public, a capacity to listen to people who disagree with you, bargaining skills, a willingness to compromise, an appreciation for parliamentary procedure and a capacity to move easily between technical knowledge and ordinary experience — is not in overabundant supply. Able people must be encouraged to make substantial investments in developing these skills and applying them on behalf of the public interest. Anyone familiar with the current Congress can name dozens of senior members in both parties whose careers defy the stereotype of term limit supporters. They have serious policy interests, they are legislative workhorses, they have the confidence to resist temporary passions and interest group pressures and they demonstrate a respect for their institution and the pivotal role it plays in the American constitutional system. History is filled with examples of legislative careerists who made substantial contributions to their country, including such notables as Robert LaFollette, Jr., Arthur Vandenberg, Edmund Muskie and Sam Ervin. Term limits would have ended their careers in Congress before they made their mark. Rather than demonstrate our contempt for such careers, we should think about how we might encourage others to make comparable investments.

CONCLUSION

Term limits are a false panacea, a slam-dunk approach to political reform that offers little beyond emotional release of pent-up frustrations with the performance of the economic and political system. Shortcoming in the electoral process and in the organization of Congress should be dealt with directly, in ways that strengthen representative democracy and the institution closest to the people.

Questions for Discussion

1. Are term limits for members of Congress democratic? Why or why not?
2. Why do incumbents have an advantage in getting reelected?
3. What effect would public financing of congressional campaigns have on incumbent reelection prospects?
4. What effect would term limits have on the character, integrity, and professional competence of candidates for congressional office?
5. What effect would term limits have on the power of special interests?
6. What effect would term limits have on voting turnout?

Suggested Readings

Bandow, Doug. "Push for Term Limits." *New York Times,* May 25, 1995, p. A29.

Carey, John M. *Term Limits and Legislative Representation.* New York: Cambridge Univ. Press, 1996.

"Congressional Term Limits: Pros & Cons." *Congressional Digest* 74, no. 4 (April 1995): entire issue.

Crane, Edward H., and Roger Pilon, eds. *The Politics and Law of Term Limits.* Washington, D.C.: Cato Institute, 1994.

Frenzel, Bill. "Term Limits and the Immortal Congress: How to Make Congressional Elections Competitive Again." *Brookings Review* 10, no. 2 (Spring 1992): 18–22.

Harris, Fred R. *In Defense of Congress.* New York: St. Martin's Press, 1995.

Hibbing, John R., and Elizabeth Theiss-Morse. *Congress As Public Enemy: Public Attitudes toward American Political Institutions.* New York: Cambridge Univ. Press, 1995.

Jost, Kenneth. "Judgment Time for Term Limits." *ABA Journal* 80 (November 1994): 80–83.

Mann, Thomas E. "The Wrong Medicine: Term Limits Won't Cure What Ails Congressional Elections." *Brookings Review* 10, no. 2 (Spring 1992): 23–25.

Penny, Timothy, and Major Garrett. *Common Cents: A Retiring Six-Term Congressman Reveals How Congress Really Works — and What We Must Do to Fix It.* Boston: Little, Brown, 1995.

Polsby, Nelson. "Some Arguments against Congressional Term Limitations." *Harvard Journal of Law and Public Policy* 16, no. 1 (Winter 1993): 101–107.

Robinson, Peter, ed. *Can Congress Be Fixed? (And Is It Broken?).* Stanford, Calif.: Stanford Univ. Press, 1995.

Schrag, Peter. "The Populist Road to Hell: Term Limits in California." *American Prospect,* no. 24 (Winter 1996): 24–30.

U.S. Cong., House of Representatives. *Term Limits for Members of the U.S. Senate and House of Representatives.* Hearings before the Subcommittee on Civil and Constitutional Rights of the Committee on the Judiciary, 103d Cong., 1st and 2d Sess., 1993–1994.

———, Senate. *Constitutional Amendment to Limit Congressional Terms.* Hearing before the Subcommittee on the Constitution, Federalism, and Property Rights of the Committee on the Judiciary, 104th Cong., 1st Sess., 1995.

Chapter 14

Should the War Powers Act Be Repealed?

The Constitution gives roles in military policy to *both* Congress and the president. Article I of the Constitution grants Congress the power to declare war; raise and support armies; provide and maintain a navy; make rules for the government and regulation of the land and naval forces; provide for calling forth the militia to execute the laws of the Union; and provide for organizing, arming, and disciplining the militia. Other provisions add to Congress's constitutional role. Such provisions include the Necessary and Proper Clause of Article I, Section 8, allowing Congress broad scope to carry out the powers specifically enumerated in the Constitution and its general constitutional powers of taxation and appropriation. The president's constitutional powers over military policy are set forth in Article II. That article gives the president executive power and designates that office as commander in chief.

Inherent in the Constitution itself are conflicts between the legislative and executive branches of government. One principal issue that has developed over time has involved the president's right to send military forces into actual or potential combat situations without the consent of Congress.

One of the most important reasons for the growth of executive power anywhere is the existence, or the imminent prospect, of war among nations or war within a nation. Executive power tends to increase during wartime, sometimes because the legislature grants the president emergency powers and sometimes because the executive takes action without asking for the approval of Congress.

At the outbreak of the Civil War, President Abraham Lincoln took steps that, according to the Constitution, were illegal. These included spending money that had not been appropriated by Congress and blockading southern ports. Lincoln expanded the powers of the president as commander in chief beyond the intent of the Framers of the Constitution. In 1940, President Franklin Roosevelt transferred fifty ships to Great Britain in return for the leasing of some British bases in the Atlantic — without congressional authorization to take such actions. He also ordered U.S. ships to "shoot on sight" any foreign submarine in waters that he regarded as essential for the nation's defense. In giving such an order, he was making war between the United States and Germany more likely.

Presidential power in foreign policy has also increased because of the changing character of the technology of warfare. In an age of jet aircraft, nuclear weapons, and intercontinental ballistic missiles, the president may be required to make quick decisions that cannot wait for congressional deliberation.

Since the end of World War II, the United States has become a principal actor in world politics — a status in the international community that will be discussed in Part V. Here it is only essential to state that as a major world power, the United States has had to concern itself with global security issues in a manner unprecedented in its history.

The permanent emphasis of foreign and national security considerations has plagued executive-legislative relations since 1945. President Harry Truman sent U.S. troops to Korea without a formal declaration of war. President Dwight Eisenhower approved actions by the Central Intelligence Agency (CIA) to help bring down one government in Guatemala and put the shah in power in Iran. John Kennedy authorized the CIA to assist a military operation planned by Cuban exiles against a communist regime in Cuba — an operation that turned out to be a foreign policy disaster for the young president. He also increased the number of military advisers to Vietnam from several hundred to about seventeen thousand.

The actions of Presidents Lyndon Johnson and Richard Nixon in the war in Indochina sparked an increasing involvement by Congress in the conduct of foreign policy. Johnson raised the number of U.S. troops to five hundred thousand. Nixon engaged in a "secret" air war in Cambodia in 1969 and sent U.S. troops into that country in 1970.

The 1970s were marked by massive congressional involvement in the conduct of foreign policy. In 1971 Congress adopted legislation forbidding the expenditures of funds to carry on the war in Cambodia. Overriding a veto by President Nixon, it passed a War Powers Act (1973) sharply limiting the president's ability to send troops. Under the act the president has the power on his own authority to send U.S. armed forces into an area for a period of sixty days but then must get the approval of Congress or terminate the use of armed forces. The president is also required to consult with Congress, if possible, before military intervention is ordered.

Every president since Nixon has taken the position that the War Powers Act is unconstitutional because a statute cannot take away powers that are traditionally the preserve of presidents in the conduct of foreign policy. But every president has complied with its provisions. If and when a time comes in which a president refuses to comply with the law, the Supreme Court will decide on the constitutionality of the act.

The wisdom of the War Powers Act continues to be a source of dispute. In June 1995, Representative Henry Hyde, a Republican from Illinois, offered amendments to a bill that would have repealed the act, replacing it with mandatory consultation between the president and Congress before and after the sending of troops and timely and comprehensive reports from the president to Congress within forty-eight hours.

The House defeated the Hyde amendments on June 7, 1995 by a vote of 217–201. In criticizing the War Powers Act, which he believes is unconstitutional, Hyde makes the following main points:

1. No president has ever used the War Powers Act or acknowledged that it is constitutional, and Congress itself has never used it to compel the withdrawal of U.S. troops from foreign deployments.
2. Congress already has the constitutional power to cut off funding, and this is sufficient authority to halt any commitment of troops.
3. The president is commander in chief and needs flexibility so that the nation's enemies will not be able to manipulate divisions between the president and Congress.

Representative Lee Hamilton, a Democrat from Indiana, argues against these amendments. He agrees, however, that the act has not worked well and recognizes its limitations. But he contends:

1. The Constitution absolutely requires that Congress share with the president the decision to send troops abroad for combat. The Hyde amendment would cede that power away.
2. The War Powers Act is a check on the mistakes of the president in sending troops abroad.
3. Because of the War Powers Act, presidents are much more careful about consulting with Congress. It gives Congress some leverage in this important decision.
4. The War Powers Act actually strengthens the president's hand because it puts Congress on record in support of the president.
5. The power of the purse is not a sufficient check on the president.

 YES

Should the War Powers Act Be Repealed?

HENRY HYDE

The Case for Repealing the War Powers Act

I am offering an amendment that repeals the War Powers Act and sets up a structure for consultation and reporting by the President.

This amendment that I am offering does three things: in addition to repealing the War Powers Resolution, it requires ongoing consultation between Congress and the President, the President to consult with Congress, before the introduction of troops, ongoing consultation while they are there and after the troops are introduced, and the third thing it does, it requires timely and comprehensive reports to Congress, within 48 hours of the engagement, and in detail. These also are ongoing.

Mr. Chairman, the War Powers Resolution was passed in 1973. In casting about for the best way to describe it, I came up with the inelegant phrase "wet noodle," but that is about what the War Powers Act has been. It has never been used. No President has ever acknowledged that it is there or that it is constitutional. The vice, the flaw, the fault with the War Powers resolution is that the President must withdraw troops within 60 days after he has committed them unless Congress acts specifically to endorse the deployment.

Congress can halt a deployment after 60 days by doing nothing, by dithering, by debating. If Congress is unsympathetic or opposed to the commitment of troops, Congress can pass a bill cutting off the funding. The ultimate weapon, the ultimate power of the purse under the Constitution, remains with Congress. Therefore, that is all the authority we need to halt, to bring to a screeching halt, any commitment of troops. But to have on the books a law that says by doing nothing, by inaction we can halt and reverse and turn around a military commitment of troops is really an absurdity. What it does is provide our enemies with a statutory timetable. They can wait it out to see if Congress and the President are not getting along.

There are a couple of things we ought to always bear in mind. First of all, the Constitution says that President is Commander in Chief. That is true whether Ronald Reagan, George Bush, or Bill Clinton is President. We are talking about the institution and constitutional powers that devolve on the President, whoever that may be.

The second unshakable, immutable, important point is we always have the purse strings clutched in our hand. We can pass a bill, and we have passed several to withhold funding for certain military operations. That is the effective way to work our will should we disagree with the President.

Congress alone can declare war but the President who is charged with the responsibility of defending this country needs flexibility, he needs to act quickly, . . . and the law should not provide our enemies, whether it is Saddam Hussein or Raoul Cedras or anybody else, with the hope, with the expectation that in 60 days they will all have to come home.

That is a disincentive to settle a dispute and to negotiate.

So, I think that is a mistake and I think it has been on the books too long and it ought to be taken off.

No President has ever considered the war powers resolutions as constitutional. I have letters from President Ford, President Jimmy Carter, President George Bush. Henry Kissinger said it should be repealed; it is misleading and ineffective. Howard Baker when he was the majority leader in the Senate said it is an attempt to write in the margins of the Constitution. It is confusing and gives comfort to our opponents.

Congress has used its power of the purse to limit and even halt military operations, many, many times, and I have a list here from the congressional reference service. During the Vietnam war in December of 1970 we prohibited the use of funds to finance the introduction of ground combat troops into Cambodia or to provide advisers to or for Cambodian military forces. In 1973 we cut off funds for combat activities in Indochina after August 15, 1973. . . .

We set a personnel ceiling of 4,000 Americans in Vietnam six months after the enactment and 3,000 within a year; in Somalia we did the same. In Rwanda we did the same. And interestingly enough, the congressional reference service says, and I quote, "With respect to your question regarding the number of instances when the Congress has utilized the War Powers Resolution, since its enactment in 1973, to compel the withdrawal of U.S. military forces from foreign deployments, we can cite no single specific instance when this has occurred."

So it is a useless anachronism and we ought not to have it on the books. No Supreme Court test is even possible. Several attempts have been made to test it. The courts have said they are not justifiable. It did not stop what we did in Somalia, it did not stop what we did in Haiti. We had a vote on Desert Storm but nobody conceded that was pursuant to the War Powers Resolutions.

It provides a false hope to our adversaries; it is confusing.

My amendment does not just wipe the books clean of the War Powers Resolution; it requires adequate, timely, prompt consultation with Congress, and notice of what the President is going to do, and reporting, comprehensive reporting. There is a Presidential waiver, but that is for the Entebbe sort of situation and we still hold the ultimate weapon which is the purse.

We cannot get, as I say, a constitutional test on it, but it emboldens our adversaries while hamstringing the President when he most urgently needs the authority and the flexibility to act.

Permit me just to read from George Bush's letter of April 17, this year. "Dear Henry, you are 100 percent correct in opposing the War Powers Resolution as an unconstitutional infringement on the authority of the President. I hope that you are successful in your effort to change the War Powers Resolution and restore proper balance between the Executive and Legislative Branches. George Bush."

Gerald Ford: "Dear Henry, I share your views that the War Powers Resolution is an impractical, unconstitutional infringement on the authority of the President. I opposed it as a Member of the House. As President I refused to recognize it as a constitutional limitation on the power of the commander in chief."

Jimmy Carter to Congressman Henry Hyde: "I fully support your effort to repeal the War Powers Resolution. Best wishes in this good work," et cetera.

So I just say to my colleagues, they are not yielding anything, they are retaining the power of the purse, which is the ultimate weapon. But my amendment requires notice, consultation, and reports, and with that in one hand and the power of the purse in the other, we are yielding no autonomy on the issue of committing troops, but are clearing off the books of unconstitutional infringement on the President's power, and are giving the President flexibility that the President may need over a weekend when something happens. And we are not giving hope and comfort to our adversaries that if they just wait it out, 60 days will elapse, we will be dithering, we will be debating, and nothing will happen and the military engagement will end.

Should the War Powers Act Be Repealed?

LEE HAMILTON

The Case against Repealing the War Powers Act

Let me say first of all that I think the gentleman from Illinois, Mr. Hyde, has performed a genuine service here in bringing this amendment forward. There just is not any doubt at all that the War Powers Act just has not worked well.

The gentleman from Illinois has a serious amendment. It needs to be and is being carefully discussed. He very well points out that there are serious flaws in the War Powers Resolution. He is correct when he says that no President accepts the War Powers Resolution in its current form. He is correct, I think, when he says that the 60-day clock provision means the Congress can control by inaction, and thereby play into the hands of an adversary.

He is correct, I think, when he says that the concurrent resolution mechanism does not work. Put aside constitutional questions, which are serious, but that mechanism does not work. The statute does not define hostilities, and that allows the executive branch to stretch the meaning of it beyond rationality. The consultative process could stand a lot of improvement. I concede all that. I acknowledge that.

On the constitutional level, although it has not been finally determined, the concurrent resolution mechanism has likely been rendered moot by the *Chadha* decision on legislative vetoes. The 60-day clock by which congressional silence or inaction requires a President to bring the troops home very likely steps over the line into the President's Commander-in-Chief powers.

Having said all of that, on the constitutionality of the core principle behind the War Powers Resolution, it is at that point that I think that the gentleman from Illinois [Mr. Hyde] and I disagree. I believe that the Constitution absolutely requires that Congress share with the President the decision to send troops abroad for combat. We do not always do it, we often do not like to do it, but I do not think that we should cede the power away. That is the way I read the gentleman's amendment.

Mr. Chairman, it is very important to recognize the advantages of the War Powers Resolution. Despite all of its deficiencies, there are some real advantages to it. The decision to commit American forces to combat is the gravest decision that a government makes. Presidents are not infallible. They do make mistakes. They are surrounded by aides, almost invariably aides who favor the executive power. When faced with a judgment about committing troops abroad, I believe that the President needs the balanced judgment from the legislative branch.

The core principle behind the War Powers Resolution is that sending troops abroad requires the sound collective judgment of the President and the Congress. I do not think that principle should be abandoned. The War Powers Act provides a framework for shared decision making. It gives the President strong incentive to consider the opinion of the Congress, and I think most of us who served in the Congress before the War Powers Act and after the War Powers Act understand that presidents now are much, much more careful about consulting with the Congress with the War Powers Resolution than without it. It provides a precedent process to get congressional advice to consult with the Congress, and it does, I think, give the Congress some leverage on this key decision of sending troops into combat.

Mr. Chairman, the argument is made that the War Powers Resolution weakens the President's hand. I believe I would argue just the opposite. When the Congress goes on record in support of the President's judgment to send combat troops abroad, that collective judgment strengthens the President's hand. I think it strengthens the role of the United States in the conflict, because it shows that the Congress and the American people support the President. Absent the clear indication of support that a congressional authorization provides, the President and his policies are vulnerable to every blink of public reaction when U.S. forces face hostilities. . . .

Mr. Chairman, we do a lot of signal sending in this body. I think the signal sending we do today is important. I have come down on the side that repealing the War Powers Act sends the wrong signal, because, as others have stated, it represents an abdication of our powers. It gives the President a kind of a green light for his action without the legislative branch, except consultation.

The argument is made, of course, that we have the power of the purse, and we certainly do, and that that is enough. I do not think I can agree with that. The power of the purse is not equivalent to Congress sharing the critical threshold decision, up front, about whether to send troops at all. The power of the purse is usually, not always, but usually exercised after the fact, weeks after the fact, sometimes months after the fact.

It is true that we can cut off funding any time for a given operation. It is very difficult to cut off funding before an operation starts, although we have done it on occasion, but it is difficult to do. Presidents are going to fight, as they should, to keep their options open. However, it is also difficult to cut funding after the troops are in the field. Senator Javits I think rightly pointed out that Congress can hardly cut off appropriations when we have American troops fighting for their lives in the field.

Mr. Chairman, I understand that the gentleman from Illinois has received a number of endorsements from former Presidents. However, I do not think that should surprise anyone. Former executives are not exactly disinterested parties in questions about war powers authority. This discussion goes to the very heart of what our institutional responsibilities are. Institutional prerogatives govern the war powers debate. It is not surprising that Presidents want fewer restrictions on their ability to take action.

However, I believe that the Congress should hold tenaciously to the power to share the tough decision about putting troops into battle. I look upon the act of repealing the War Powers Act as an act of abdication by the Congress of its power. . . .

Mr. Chairman, the Congress can stand against a President. The Congress can stand beside a President. What Congress must not do is to stand aside. Congress should not cede its constitutional responsibilities. We are a co-equal branch of government.

Of course, consultation is necessary and important, but it is not enough when it comes to the War Powers Resolution. This is an extraordinarily important debate that the gentleman from Illinois [Mr. Hyde], has opened up. I know him well enough to know, and I have visited with him about it, that this amendment is the beginning, and not the end, of a serious dialogue on the war powers. It is my hope that his amendment, if it is adopted, is not the final proposal, but I do think our vote today sends a signal. . . .

Mr. Chairman, if we are prepared to cede congressional power on this important decision, then the vote is yes. However, if Members believe, as I do, that Congress has a role to play when we send these troops into action, that we ought to be in on that decision, even though we reluctantly take that decision, or try to avoid it, then I think Members should vote against this amendment.

Questions for Discussion

1. How should the United States go about requiring and implementing "meaningful" consultation between the president and Congress, particularly in emergency situations?
2. Does the War Powers Act weaken the power of the president in foreign policy? What are the reasons for your answer?
3. If the War Powers Act is repealed, how would the president's willingness to commit U.S. troops to combat situations change?
4. Does Congress's constitutional power to declare war mean anything anymore? What are the reasons for your answer?
5. Can the War Powers Act be improved? What are the reasons for your answer?

Suggested Readings

Ely, John Hart. *War and Responsibility: Constitutional Lessons of Vietnam and Its Aftermath.* Princeton, N.J.: Princeton Univ. Press, 1993.

Fisher, Louis. *Presidential War Power.* Lawrence: Univ. Press of Kansas, 1995.

Franklin, Daniel P. *Extraordinary Measures: The Exercise of Prerogative Powers in the United States.* Pittsburgh: Univ. of Pittsburgh Press, 1991.

Keynes, Edward. *Undeclared War: Twilight Zone of Constitutional Power.* University Park: Pennsylvania State Univ. Press, 1991.

Lehman, John F. *Making War: The 200-Year-Old Battle between the President and Congress over How America Goes to War.* New York: Maxwell Macmillan International, 1992.

Rosner, Jeremy D. *Congress, the Executive Branch, and National Security: The New Tug-of-War.* Washington, D.C.: Carnegie Endowment for International Peace, 1995.

Rourke, John T. *Presidential Wars and American Democracy: Rally 'Round the Flag.* New York: Paragon Press, 1993.

Stern, Gary M., and Morton H. Halperin, eds. *The U.S. Constitution and the Power to Go to War.* Westport, Conn.: Greenwood Press, 1994.

Turner, Robert F. *Repealing the War Powers Resolution: Restoring the Rule of Law in U.S. Foreign Policy.* Washington, D.C.: Brassey's, 1991.

U.S. Cong., House of Representatives. *The War Powers Resolution: Relevant Documents, Reports, Correspondence.* Prepared by the Subcommittee on International Security, International Organizations and Human Rights, 103d Cong., 2d Sess., 1994.

———, Senate. *The Constitutional Roles of Congress and the President in Declaring and Waging War.* Hearing before the Committee on the Judiciary, 102d Cong., 1st Sess., 1991.

Westerfield, Donald L. *War Powers: The President, the Congress, and the Question of War.* Westport, Conn.: Praeger, 1996.

Chapter 15

Is the Federal Government Trying to Do Too Much, Too Often, for Too Many?

When the Constitution was adopted in the late eighteenth century, only a few hundred people were employed by government at the national level. Today, however, there are nearly 3 million civilian federal government employees. Millions of other public employees serve in the armed forces and the agencies of state and local governments.

Government has grown remarkably in this century because of its increased activities in foreign affairs, the domestic economy, and welfare. In the late eighteenth century the United States was a small power on the periphery of the world's major powers of Europe. For more than four decades after World War II, it became one of the two strongest military powers, challenged principally by the other superpower, the Soviet Union.

Even after the disintegration of the Soviet Union, the United States was the world's only superpower. The United States still requires the services of large numbers of people in the armed forces. Government, moreover, is engaged in dispensing foreign aid, gathering intelligence information, assisting individuals and groups abroad, and helping to promote international trade.

In addition to the growth of foreign policy activities, domestic factors are responsible for government expansion. Business asks for government assistance to build highways, improve railroads, construct dams, widen waterways, and administer tariffs. It also requests government support for research in energy, transportation, and military technology. The demands of labor also increase government involvement in the economy. Labor asks for government inspection involving safety at work sites, government supervision of minimum wage laws, and government employment of those who cannot find jobs in the private sector. Labor seeks government protection of unions against the power of business.

Finally, the welfare state contributes to government growth. Individuals and groups demand government help to provide health care, Social Security, housing, and education. All these goals require programs that are administered by government, and that administration is the bureaucracy.

Big government has long been criticized. In the election of 1976, for example, Jimmy Carter ran under a campaign promise to reduce the size of the federal government. Ronald Reagan became even more identified than Carter with such a reduction. He tried to reduce the size and budget of the federal government but failed to do so. Since then, antigovernment rhetoric has intensified. And while federal expenditures continued to grow in the Bush and Clinton administrations, the federal work force is now decreasing not only in real numbers but as a percentage of the American work force. In 1955, there were 10 federal workers per 1,000 Americans; today there are 7.3, the lowest ratio of federal employees to Americans since 1940.[1]

Perceptions of inefficient and wasteful federal programs continue to be widespread, however. The Republicans who seized control of both the House and Senate following the 1994 elections sought additional reductions in government spending and battled President Bill Clinton over the federal budget.

For his part, President Clinton sought to improve efficiency in the federal government. In his 1996 State of the Union Address, he acknowledged that "the era of big government is over." His next sentence added a qualifier, however: "But we cannot go back to the time when our citizens were left to fend for themselves."[2] Whether the scope of the federal government should be reduced is still a matter of debate, as many people are opposed to big government in the abstract but not to a reduction in services that benefit them as individuals. Polls show much support for Social Security, Medicare, and environmental protection, for example. And in the 1996 presidential campaign, Clinton's poll ratings were high as he supported these programs.

Critics of federal bureaucracy argue that government is now so unwieldy and unnecessary that it is a threat to citizens. Economist Thomas J. DiLorenzo argues that most of the federal government is unconstitutional and should be abolished. He observes:

1. Article I of the Constitution sets forth specific powers of Congress. But because of decisions by federal judges in the past sixty years, the federal government unconstitutionally controls and regulates in too many areas.
2. Federal, state, and local governments take far too much money in taxes and in so doing, harm middle-class economic advancement.
3. Government regulations are disastrous to the American economy.
4. Monetary and fiscal policy has been a failure.
5. If 90 percent of the federal government were eliminated, Americans immediately would experience an unprecedented boost in prosperity and freedom.

Democratic party consultant Victor Kamber defends the federal government. He argues:

1. While Americans may voice frustrations about government in the abstract, they strongly support most programs.

2. Specifically, Americans do not want broad cuts in welfare, Social Security, Medicare, and environmental protection. Nor do they favor eliminating key departments and government agencies, even the National Endowment for the Arts and the Corporation for Public Broadcasting.
3. Republican critics of the federal government seek, at the same time, to protect corporate welfare.
4. Antigovernment rhetoric is exploited by special interests, such as wealthy people, the Christian Coalition, and the militia movement.
5. The federal government serves noble interests, such as preserving the wilderness, maintaining safety and security, and protecting people through food- and workplace-safety regulations.
6. The federal government is all that stands between the American people and many giant, multinational corporations that could cause great harm.
7. The federal government is the most powerful force of social cohesion that Americans have.

NOTES

1. John M. Berry, "Any Way You Slice It, the Federal Work Force Is Dwindling," *Washington Post*, December 28, 1995, pp. D1, D11. Berry uses Bureau of Labor Statistics data that exclude U.S. Postal Service employees.
2. President Bill Clinton, State of the Union Address, January 23, 1996, transcript.

 ☑ *YES*

Is the Federal Government Trying to Do Too Much, Too Often, for Too Many?

THOMAS DiLORENZO

Most of the Federal Government Is Unconstitutional and Should Be Abolished

One can verify this statement by simply reading the U.S. Constitution. Article I, Section 8 gives Congress the power only to provide for national defense; borrowing; patents; declaration of war; calling forth the militia; the federal courts; the post office; coining money; administration of the District of Columbia; punishment of counterfeiting; regulating commerce with foreign nations; naturalization and bankruptcy laws; and punishing piracies and felonies committed on the high seas. That's it. There are no other constitutional powers. The powers not delegated to the federal government by the Constitution, the Tenth Amendment declares, are reserved to the states respectively, or to the people.

For the past 60 years, however, socialist ideologues dressed up in judges' robes have subverted the Constitution so that today the federal government unconstitutionally controls and regulates everything from the shape of toilet seats to where farmers may park their tractors to the permissible size of plums to knitting mittens in one's own home and smoking a pipe in the privacy of one's office. That former Surgeon General Joycelyn Elders even proposed a federal masturbation-education program shows how wildly out of control the federal leviathan — and the liberal mind-set — has become.

Federal, state and local governments take 47 percent of personal income, according to the *Statistical Abstract of the United States.* As economist Paul Craig Roberts has pointed out, even medieval serfs never were compelled to hand over more than 40 percent of their earnings to feudal lords. In the name of fairness, much of this money is used to support the lifestyles of other Americans who refuse to work, sometimes disobey the law and constantly demand more. "We just want what everyone else has," a welfare mother demanding better public-housing accommodations in the suburbs recently told the *Baltimore Sun* newspaper. American taxpayers pay through the teeth to support a welfare state that has destroyed families, perpetuated poverty and made crime rampant.

Americans are being strangled to death economically by the federal government and 87,000 state and local governmental units that impose Social Security taxes; income taxes; Medicare taxes; school taxes; property taxes; personal-property taxes; more than 70 different excise taxes; sales taxes; inheritance taxes; use taxes; capital-gains taxes, small-business taxes; license taxes; gross-receipts taxes; unincorporated-business taxes; fishing and hunting taxes; securities-trading taxes; intangible-wealth taxes; workers-compensation taxes; corporate-income taxes; luxury taxes; unemployment-insurance taxes; telephone and cable-television taxes; property-transfer taxes; parking taxes; airline, car-rental, hotel and restaurant taxes; wheel taxes; travel taxes; snack taxes; water and sewer taxes; marriage taxes; nanny taxes; environmental taxes; special-district taxes; bridge and highway taxes; and the ultimate tax — asset forfeiture.

Liberals are fond of blaming the economy — their code word for capitalism — for the failure of many middle-class families to improve their living standards, but the biggest roadblock to middle-class economic advancement is that governments confiscate nearly half of all family income. Out of 365 days in the calendar year, the average American taxpayer works 171 days — from January 1 until June 20 — just to pay taxes. In 1950, the average family sent to Washington $1 of every $20 earned; today, $1 of every $4 earned is taken to feed the federal leviathan.

This is why millions of married women who would rather stay home to raise their children are compelled to work outside the home. The real threat to middle-class families is not the capitalist economy; it's the IRS [Internal Revenue Service].

Since the federal government spends more than it takes in revenues, the real burden of government is even more than 47 percent of the economy. Government borrowing to finance the federal budget deficit annually diverts hundreds of billions of dollars of credit away from more productive, private-sector uses (such as business creation and expansion, home building and auto and appliance purchases). If the federal government monetizes the debt by expanding the money supply, inflationary pressures are created that reduce the real value of all privately held wealth. Thus, because government debt also constitutes an implicit tax, the real tax burden of government in America easily exceeds 50 percent of gross domestic product.

It gets worse. In addition to taxing and spending, the federal government controls hundreds of billions of dollars of credit allocation through its direct-loan, loan-guarantee and government-sponsored enterprise programs. For example, in 1993 there was $170 billion in government-sponsored enterprise borrowing for things such as the farm-credit banks and cooperatives administered by the Farmers Home Administration, or FmHA. This agency essentially is in the business of making bad loans to unsuccessful farm businesses not otherwise creditworthy.

In 1988 the General Accounting Office estimated that FmHA had made so many bad loans that it had an accumulated operating deficit of $36 billion. The agency admits that more than one-fourth of farm bankruptcies are the result of farmers having received too many FmHA loans. Congress and the FmHA thus have created tens of thousands of mini-Mexicos in rural America, according to journalist James Bovard.

Much of the remaining 35–40 percent of the economy still in private hands is only nominally private; 130,000 federal regulators, and tens of thousands more at the state and local levels, oversee everything from what color one may paint one's house to whom one may hire and fire to what prices one may charge for one's products. The enormous web of regulation is the American style of central planning and is premised on the same fatal conceit, as Friedrich Hayek called it, that a small bureaucratic elite can plan an economy better than the millions of consumers, producers and employees cooperating in the free market.

The effects of the American regulatory state are just as disastrous — and sometimes as ludicrous — as the stories that used to be told about central-planning debacles in the former Soviet Union:

- The Environmental Protection Agency forces Columbus, Ohio, to spend tens of thousands of dollars testing its water supply for pesticides that are used only on pineapples in Hawaii.
- Hundreds of billions of dollars are spent ripping asbestos out of school buildings despite there being no scientific evidence whatsoever that the asbestos poses a health threat.

- Fuel economy standards force automakers to make smaller, lighter and more dangerous cars, causing thousands of additional traffic deaths each year.
- Under the Americans with Disabilities Act, a Bellevue, Wash., strip club was fined because it didn't provide a ramp for handicapped strippers; a deaf woman sued Burger King for discriminating against her with its drive-in windows; and college students have sued their universities for not accommodating aversion to exams.

Thousands of additional regulatory absurdities could be used to illustrate what author Philip Howard calls the death of common sense with regard to regulation. Economists Michael Hazilla and Raymond Kopp estimate that the costs of regulation exceed $400 billion annually — about one-and-a-half times the defense budget. And it is getting more and more difficult to find any benefits from regulation. Much of the regulatory cost is simply unnecessary, concludes the Brookings Institution's Robert Crandall.

Communism's endless experiments with central planning proved one thing: It doesn't work. Unfortunately, America's central planners have not learned this and futilely attempt to plan the U.S. economy with what is euphemistically called stabilization policy, or fine-tuning.

So-called fine-tuning through monetary and fiscal policy has been a flop from the beginning. As economists Richard Vedder and Lowell Galloway show in their book, *Out of Work: Unemployment and Government in Twentieth-Century America,* when the Federal Reserve was created — ostensibly to stabilize the economy — there were wild swings in the money supply from negative 12 percent to positive 30 percent in the first 10 years. The result was catastrophic economic upheaval that was deviously blamed on the free market by socialist politicians and their intellectual supporters. Indeed, the Fed's decision from 1929 to 1932 to reduce the money supply by 30 percent was a major cause of the Great Depression. This, coupled with the Smoot-Hawley tariff and the largest tax increase in history up to that point in 1933, guaranteed economic disaster, but dishonest historians have misled generations of Americans into believing that market failure caused the Depression.

As a rule, the more activist the government's fine-tuning, the worse economic performance becomes. As Vedder and Galloway show, the periods in which governmental influence on macroeconomic events was the strongest are those marked by the poorest performance. The average unemployment rate today is 50 percent higher than it was before government fine-tuning was put into place. The government's ludicrously named stabilization policies have produced bouts of stagflation and a $5 trillion national debt.

Socialism is economic poison, and at least 60 percent of the U.S. economy is socialist. Much of the remaining 40 percent is affected negatively by government regulations that tend to provide little benefit, if any, at enormous cost. America's century-long experiment with statism has failed. If 90 percent of the federal government were to be eliminated tomorrow, Americans immediately would experience a boost in prosperity and freedom unprecedented in history.

The proper size and scope of government was defined by Thomas Jefferson more than two centuries ago when he wrote, "A wise and frugal government which shall restrain men from injuring one another, which shall leave them otherwise free to regulate their own pursuits of industry and improvement, and shall not take from the mouth of labor the bread it has earned — this is the sum of good government." Jefferson, a man who had the courage of his convictions, acted early in his presidency to abolish most federal taxes. Forget about the flat tax. What Americans need is a strong dose of Jeffersonian tax reform.

Is the Federal Government Trying to Do Too Much, Too Often, for Too Many?

VICTOR KAMBER

The American People Haven't Lost Faith in the Federal Government

They've lost faith in politicians who treat government not as an agent of the people, but as a political punching bag or, worse, as a giant purse to be plundered for the gain of their special-interest benefactors.

While Americans may voice frustrations about government in the abstract, they strongly support most specific programs. Sure, they say they want the budget trimmed, but when you start cutting the benefits they count on — and there are many more of these than right-wingers ever will admit — they get nervous.

While the Republicans use budget balancing as a ruse to take money from the elderly, working families and poor people and give it to the rich, the public wises up to the value of government. According to a variety of recent polls conducted by independent news organizations, 62 percent of Americans don't want broad cuts in welfare; 68 percent say, "Leave Social Security alone"; and 59 percent don't want Medicare touched. By a margin of 4-to-1, Americans would rather continue having budget deficits than alter Medicare, and by a margin of 3-to-1 they prefer unbalanced budgets to changes in Social Security, according to a *New York Times*/CBS poll in August [1995]. Despite the best efforts of the National Rifle Association and the militias, 69 percent support gun control, according to a *Newsweek* poll in September. Although House Majority Whip and former bug exterminator Tom DeLay of Texas calls the Environmental Protection Agency "a Gestapo," a vast majority of Americans favor tougher environmental laws. And 90 percent expect national parks to be protected, according to a Colorado State University poll.

Most Americans oppose eliminating the departments of Energy, Commerce, Transportation, Veterans Affairs and Housing and Urban Development, as well as the Small Business Administration — agencies targeted by Republicans. Even the National Endowment for the Arts and the Corporation for Public Broadcasting are supported by a majority — 76 percent think the Public Broadcasting Service shouldn't even be cut, much less killed. And there's a whole host of government programs whose popularity among the middle class is self-evident, such as education funding, student loans, worker training, workplace safety, anticrime efforts and interstate highways; the list goes on. And let's not forget Medicaid, which the GOP wants to emasculate as part of its "War on the Poor" but which Republicans forget is the middle-class safety net when an elderly parent or relative requires nursing-home care.

There are some parts of the federal government that most Americans favor cutting, but they're not the ones the GOP would slash. There's corporate welfare, which, according to the Cato Institute, will cost taxpayers $85 billion in 1995. We could cut the defense budget, since Pentagon officials themselves say they can't spend all the money that Congress is throwing at them. And we could make the wealthy and corporations give more to the society from which they've gotten rich.

The only political crisis of faith comes from a lack of leadership. The more politicians attack their opponents, the institutions they serve in and even politics itself, the less faith people have in their leaders and the government. I'd like to blame Newt Gingrich for everything. I'd like to blame him for bad weather, traffic jams, airline food — even the Chicago Cubs' failure to make the playoffs this year. Perhaps he's innocent of these last charges, but he is responsible — as the bomb-throwing, book-peddling leader of the Republican Party and speaker of the House — for the increasingly truculent and uncompromising nature of U.S. politics. Although he didn't invent the crude and nihilistic tactic of antipolitics, he has profited the most from it. But as Gingrich is finding out, it is impossible to run the government while constantly running against it. Pretty soon his bizarre contraption of antigovernment ranting, Scrooge economics, special-interest giveaways and high-tech palaver will sputter and stall. In fact, it's already happening.

Recent polls show that public approval of Gingrich's GOP is fading like a pair of cheap jeans. Overall, 65 percent of Americans disapprove of the Republican Congress' policies. More of them trust President Clinton to do a better job than the Gingrich gang. On specific issues, such as protecting social programs, Social Security, Medicare and Medicaid and helping the middle class, Clinton has a significant advantage over the disloyal opposition. Some 56 percent of Americans think Clinton is seeking the right changes. Only 44 percent think Gingrich is. Clinton could improve those numbers over the long haul if only he'd make a strong case for government action — especially to address America's No. 1 problem: declining wages and employment prospects for working families. But lately he hasn't, ceding the terms of the debate to the

GOP. He argues that he can cut government more fairly, compassionately and sensibly than the Republicans. That's true, and it may be a good tactical message, but it's God-awful strategy. If the middle class is ever going to have a fighting chance again, Clinton must argue forcefully that Americans need a strong federal government acting as an instrument of, by and for the people to strengthen the American standard of living and protect working families from corporate and special-interest greed.

The American people are wiser than their putative leaders. Whenever they give it serious thought, they understand how the federal government helps and protects them and they're willing to work together, even as politicians seek to drive them further apart. But instead of practicing politics, America's lawmakers engage in antipolitics. Candidates slander their opponents and insult the institutions they wish to serve. They slice and dice the electorate through polarizing rhetoric. The profit-driven media — which would rather entertain than inform — stirs fears and hatreds into a hurly-burly of racial antagonism and general paranoia.

The negative tenor of today's politics often is exploited by special interests with hidden agendas. The term-limits movement is but one example. Antigovernment wingnuts and their media cheerleaders point to term limits as an expression of discontent with incumbent politicians. But the term-limits movement was created by a handful of rich, well-connected zealots who used their wealth and power to build a political organization that appeared to be grassroots when it really often was astroturf.

If term limits show how the rich and powerful can turn their political fancies into a national movement, the Million Man March showed how disenfranchised members of society can become politically empowered, even if it means organizing under the sponsorship of the loathsome Louis Farrakhan. Jesse Jackson said it best: "Did Minister Farrakhan organize the march? No! Clarence Thomas and Gingrich organized the march — just like Bull Connor organized the march in 1963!" If African-American men, and women for that matter, weren't scapegoated by Republicans and ignored by too many Democrats, they might not feel they had to march on Washington in order to be heard and in order to strengthen their own bonds.

Some fringe elements have gained disproportionate attention, partly because they are willing to state antigovernment arguments with increasing vehemence and irresponsibility. The religious right, led by the Christian Coalition, pretends to speak for the nation's Christians when it merely represents an extremist sect whose goals are more profane than sacred. I was born to a Pentecostal minister and grew up among evangelical Christians. I know from personal experience that they include as many Democrats as Republicans; while they may be more conservative on social issues, saying that evangelicals are represented by the Christian right is like saying that Baptists are represented by snake handlers.

The militia movement is little more than kooky, sociopathic gun nuts and greed heads, nativist loners whose only bond is a revulsion for common society. And that's okay, because this is a big country and there's lots of room for these people to go off by themselves, drinking moonshine and eating roadkill.

But they can't opt out of citizenship altogether. The federal government they revile and even plot against also happens to be the institution that protects the wilderness they love from commercial development (which, if their Republican friends had their way, would quickly be strip-mined or strip-malled). The government maintains their safety and security and guarantees their right to privacy, free speech and assembly. And while they may be content to live off the land, the rest of us buy our food in supermarkets and live in houses with electricity and running water. We need government protections such as food- and workplace-safety regulations.

The federal government is all that stands between the American people and many giant, multinational corporations that would destroy the environment, force people to work in unsafe conditions, deny workers fair wages and benefits and produce shoddy products in pursuit of ever-higher profit margins if left unfettered. Those protections benefit all of us equally, militia members as well as normal citizens.

The Oklahoma City bombing revealed the abominable, inhuman immorality of some antigovernment extremists. But it also showed that the country can unite in sorrow, grief and anger when its people and institutions are threatened. If there is something to be gained from this tragedy, it is that a terrorist act taught us most Americans do respect their government and the hard-working federal employees who put their lives on the line to serve the people.

It's popular these days to refer to the federal government as if it were a malign entity, some omnivorous leviathan that washed up on the shores of the Potomac River. But as Teddy Roosevelt said, "The government is us; we are the government, you and I." The federal government is the most powerful source of social cohesion that America has, and now that the country is becoming increasingly divided, strong leadership is needed more than ever. If political leaders had the courage and the vision to unite Americans to meet our common challenges rather than exploiting differences, and if they used the federal government as a force for positive change, the United States could move ahead as a nation instead of slipping backward into the dark and ignominious realm of antipolitics.

If someone would lead, the people would follow.

Questions for Discussion

1. What effect would the dismantling of big government have on U.S. society?
2. What evidence can be used to determine whether the American people support big government?
3. How can waste in government be reduced?
4. What powers does the Congress have to control the bureaucracy?
5. What powers does the bureaucracy have to thwart the will of Congress?

Suggested Readings

Berry, John M. "Any Way You Slice It, the Federal Work Force Is Dwindling." *Washington Post*, December 28, 1995, pp. D1, D11.

Bovard, James. "Petty Dictatorships Are Proliferating in the Federal Government." *USA Today Magazine* 123, no. 2596 (January 1995): 18–21.

Browne, Harry. *Why Government Doesn't Work.* New York: St. Martin's Press, 1995.

Dionne, E. J. "The Era of 'Big' Government." *Commonweal* 123, no. 4 (February 23, 1996): 11–14.

Goodsell, Charles T. *The Case for Bureaucracy: A Public Administration Polemic,* 3d ed. Chatham, N.J.: Chatham House, 1994.

Handler, Joel F. *Down from Bureaucracy: The Ambiguity of Privatization and Empowerment.* Princeton, N.J.: Princeton Univ. Press, 1996.

Howard, Philip. *The Death of Common Sense: How Law Is Suffocating America.* New York: Random House, 1994.

Nasar, Sylvia. "The Bureaucracy: What's Left to Shrink?" *New York Times*, June 11, 1995, sec. IV, p. 1.

Pearlstein, Steven. "The Myths That Rule Us." *Washington Post*, March 5, 1995, pp. H1, H4.

Stein, Herbert. "Okay, Cut Back Government." *Washington Post*, February 26, 1995, p. C7.

Weisberg, Jacob. *In Defense of Government: The Fall and Rise of Public Trust.* New York: Scribner's, 1996.

Chapter 16

Is the Confirmation Process a Mess?

Article II, Section 2 of the Constitution provides that the president nominate candidates for Supreme Court justices. It also provides that for the nominees to be appointed to the Court, they must be confirmed by the Senate. The Constitution says nothing, however, about the professional and intellectual backgrounds of the nominees; nor does it say anything about the criteria that should be used by the president in nominating candidates or by the Senate in evaluating them for confirmation.

From George Washington's day to the present, presidents have nominated candidates to the Court from a variety of backgrounds, including lower court judges, cabinet members, senators, and governors. In making their choices, presidents have based their considerations on judicial background, legal philosophy, intellectual talent, personal honesty and integrity, party unity, political and ideological compatibility, and other factors.

The Senate has often confirmed the nominees. At times, however, it has rejected them. Senators, too, have used criteria similar to those of the president in voting on confirmation.

The results of the confirmation process have not always been happy for presidents. As early as 1795, the Senate rejected John Rutledge as George Washington's nominee to be chief justice of the Supreme Court. Rutledge, who had been one of the authors of the Constitution, seemed qualified. He had even served as a Supreme Court justice. But he had opposed the Jay Treaty, which would have improved relations between the United States and Great Britain. And the Federalists, who dominated the Senate, favored the treaty. The Senate, consequently, did not confirm Rutledge.

From George Washington to Bill Clinton, presidents have had to be careful in nominating candidates to the Supreme Court for fear that their nominations would not win confirmation. At times, presidents have been willing to engage in major battles with the Senate for their candidates. At other times, however, presidents have made cautious nominations that resulted in quick and favorable confirmation.

For most of the twentieth century, the Senate has confirmed presidential nominees to the Court. From 1900 to 1968 only one nominee — John J. Parker in 1930 — was rejected by the Senate. But since then, presidents have had a harder time getting their nominees confirmed. Lyndon Johnson could not get Abe Fortas confirmed as chief justice in 1968. Richard Nixon faced defeat with his nominees of Clement Haynsworth and

G. Harrold Carswell. Ronald Reagan's candidate Robert Bork went down to defeat, too. One of Reagan's nominees, Judge Douglas H. Ginsburg, was forced to withdraw from consideration after revelations about his personal life brought criticisms from conservative sources.

The Senate confirmation process has become increasingly acrimonious, too. Because the Supreme Court deals with some of the most controversial political issues of our times, such as abortion, affirmative action, criminal justice, and separation of church and state, groups concerned about the outcome of policy have good reason to be vitally involved with decisions dealing with appointments to the Supreme Court. Conservatives favor conservative justices, and liberals support liberal justices — although no one can be certain about how justices will decide cases once they are appointed to the Court. Since the stakes are so high, the fight over court nominations has on occasion become fierce.

Public attention to Supreme Court nomination has been reflected in procedural changes as well as media involvement in the subject. Until the nomination of Harlan Fiske Stone in 1925, Supreme Court nominees did not even personally appear before the Senate Judiciary Committee, the unit responsible for initiating the confirmation process in the Senate. Today, all Supreme Court nominees must personally appear before the committee. The hearings, which are now televised, have given the process even greater publicity.

Some of the stormiest controversies involving nominees occurred in the Reagan and Bush administrations. Although William Rehnquist, who was an associate justice of the Supreme Court, was confirmed as chief justice, he faced tough hearings. He won confirmation with fewer favorable Senate votes than any successful nominee for the post in the twentieth century. The Robert Bork hearings were stormy, and the Senate voted against him. And the nomination of Clarence Thomas to succeed Thurgood Marshall as associate justice produced extraordinary hearings centered on accusations of sexual harassment by a former associate, Anita Hill. Thomas won confirmation but at great cost to his reputation.

In addition to Supreme Court justices, the president nominates other key officials to posts, subject to Senate confirmation. In recent years, the confirmation proceedings for some candidates for these other posts have been acrimonious. President Bill Clinton's nomination of Lani Guinier, a professor at the University of Pennsylvania Law School, to be head of the Civil Rights Division of the Justice Department, was withdrawn when critics claimed that her academic articles were radical. And Clinton's first two nominees to head the Justice Department — Zoe Baird and Kimba Wood — were withdrawn as a result of revelations that they had hired illegal aliens as household help.

Yale Law School professor Stephen L. Carter looked at these high-profile confirmation cases and concludes that the confirmation process is "a mess." His book, from which an excerpt appears below, is titled *The Confirmation Mess: Cleaning Up the Federal Appointments Process.* Carter argues that the people who wrote and ratified the Constitution did not envision that the confirmation process would be so chaotic. Television, particularly, has made the confirmation hearings national events and transformed them into spectacles. The test for Supreme Court justices is not professional competence but rather a determination of whether their interpretations will be liberal or conservative. Carter calls for an approach to confirmation based more on *qualifications* rather than on *disqualifications.*

In reviewing Carter's book, Michael A. Kahn takes issue with Carter. He contends:

1. The confirmation process has not drastically changed and may not have even changed at all over the years.
2. The Supreme Court is a political body and as such does not require unique treatment in our political system.
3. Carter's remedies for change are wrong. The confirmation system is not broken and is not in need of repair.

 YES

Is the Confirmation Process a Mess?

STEPHEN L. CARTER
The Confirmation Mess

THE MEDIA CULTURE

Perhaps it is only our imagination that suggests, in this constantly televised age, that today's confirmation hearings are rougher than those of the past. Probably there has been no era in our history when trashing the candidate — digging up dirt — was anything other than the order of the day. Yet it is difficult to imagine that those who wrote and ratified the Constitution, when they designed the balance of power between executive and legislature in the appointment process, envisioned quite the mess into which we have worked ourselves.

To be sure, vicious confirmation battles have been around since the Founding. George Washington ran into them at least twice, once famously, when John Rutledge, his nominee for Chief Justice, was accused by political enemies of having taken leave of his senses — he later attempted suicide, making their attacks on him look prescient — and on another occasion, when his nominee for chief naval officer for Georgia was brushed aside for no other reason than that the state's two senators had a candidate of their own. Thomas Jefferson regretfully explained to a candidate for an ambassadorship that his was one of many nominations that the Senate was turning down because of a foreign policy dispute with the executive branch. Andrew Jackson's nomination of Roger Taney to serve as secretary of the treasury was rejected by an angry Senate over a policy dispute. And even before our modern era, lots of nominees have been the victims of vicious smears — in this century alone, one thinks of Louis Brandeis and Thurgood Marshall — but all of that was prior to the entry of television into the fray.

Television gave us the Bork hearings. Even without the cameras, there would have been hearings; but the presence of the cameras, the first ever for a full confirmation hearing, transformed an inside-the-Beltway ritual into a full-blown national extravaganza. Fans of the Block Bork Coalition, which combined some startling and uncomfortable truths about Bork's record with some even more startling and uncomfortable lies, have painted the hearings in romantic tones, referring to them as a national seminar on constitutional interpretation. To Bork supporters, however, the hearings were nothing but an effort to extract commitments that the nominee would vote the way that liberals preferred. Either way, it was television that brought the issue to the American people.

We watched television to learn about Zoe Baird's nanny and Roberta Achtenberg's homosexuality. To find out whether Robert Bork wanted to turn back the clock on civil liberties. To learn whether Lani Guinier was a dangerous radical. To discover whether Ruth Bader Ginsburg could possibly be as wonderful as everybody said and whether David Souter could possibly be as stealthy a candidate as everybody said. To see whether Joycelyn Elders could control her barbed wit. And, of course, to decide whether Clarence Thomas had sexually harassed Anita Hill.

A television network executive quoted in *The New Yorker* on the bizarre popularity of made-for-television movies about Amy Fisher echoed the words of any number of cultural critics in recent years: "People used to sit on the back fence and talk to each other. . . . [N]eighbors would talk. Television has replaced the back fence. Americans love to gossip. It's just something that's part of who we are. We get our gossip from television."

Well, of course! That is what television supplies for us in the confirmation hearings, too. You can call it "gossip" or you can call it "the opportunity for the American people to be informed on the character and fitness of those who would serve them in public office." But whatever you call it, you can see how it works, and how, in our neighborless society, it fulfills our need to be involved. Government, over the years, has receded from the citizens it theoretically serves; local governance, which the Founders thought would be more important than national governance, has fallen into desuetude. Not government — governance. A far higher proportion of voters turns out for national elections than for, say, elections for the school board.

The hearings on Anita Hill's charges of sexual harassment against Clarence Thomas made for riveting television as millions of viewers watched and chose up sides; in fact, the spectacle was so riveting that most Americans apparently forgot that there were other issues about the nomination to be debated. Instead, those who believed Thomas's testimony seemed to think he should be confirmed and those who believed Hill's seemed to think he should not. For just this reason, contrary to the conservative image of a left wing cackling with glee when Hill's charges were revealed, many liberal activists say they wish she had never come forward, for they believe to this day that they had a chance to beat Thomas on the issues.

"The issues" — there's the rest of it. At the cabinet level we scarcely care, but for Supreme Court nominees able to pass the media scrutiny evidently aimed at determining their moral fitness for judicial service, another test awaits. It has become part of our routine to press potential Justices to give us — the people — enough information to allow us to predict their likely votes on the cases we care about most. We take surveys on what voters think is the right outcome in cases few of them have read, based on interpretations of constitutional provisions few of them would recognize. All of this, it is said, in the name of a "democratic check" on the otherwise unaccountable judicial power. As for the old law school (and high school civics) image of judges who make up their minds after they hear arguments instead of before, well, it has been dumped into the ashcan of history by joint consent of left-wing and right-wing activists, few of whom seem actually to relish the idea of an independent judiciary.

True, judicial independence from the control of popular majorities is a threat to democracy. It is supposed to be. That is the distinction, as Simeon Baldwin pointed out in 1905 in a fine book entitled *The American Judiciary,* between the role of a plenary legislature and the role of a constitutional legislature. In a plenary legislature, the people, through their representatives, always get their way. In a constitutional legislature, however, the people, through their representatives, get their way only up to the limits that a prior agreement — a constitution — places upon their government. If temporary legislative majorities have the authority to control the directions of the courts, one moves away from the model of the constitutional legislature and toward the model of the plenary legislature. This was Thomas Jefferson's preference; he thought the federal courts so in need of a democratic check that he proposed that the judges face the voters every few years. . . . Each time another politician or scholar steps into the Jeffersonian tradition and calls for a democratic check on the Supreme Court, we take another step along that road — the last one, I would think, that either liberals (committed to equality and individual autonomy) or conservatives (committed to liberty, property, and tradition) would want to travel.

But a confirmation fight, like a nomination decision, is an opportunity for our elected representatives to signal us, the voters, on their own ideological bona fides. And presumably, since we are the ones who elect them, this is precisely what we want them to do.

CAN THE CONFIRMATION MESS BE CLEANED UP?

So what do we do? Finding the right answer . . . begins with understanding what the question is. And the question is why we focus so relentlessly on a nominee's *disqualifications* rather than *qualifications*. Once we know why we behave that way, we will be able to move forward toward a richer confirmation process.

With important exceptions, it is not my purpose in this book to rehash the charges and countercharges that arose in many recent confirmation cases (although I will try to let the reader know where I stand); certainly the book is not a brief on behalf of any particular nominee. Rather, it is my aim to use the controversies over several recent nominations, to both the executive and the judicial branches, to illuminate the notion that an aspect of an individual's past might disqualify her from public service or, at least, public service requiring Senate confirmation. In particular, I shall agrue that we must regain the ability to balance the wrongs that a candidate might have done against the strengths that she might bring to public service — an ability that has tended to atrophy in an age that allows the mass media to play the role of guardians of public morality.

The trend toward searching for disqualifying factors means that we have become less interested in how well a nominee for cabinet or Court will do the job than in whether the individual deserves it, as though the vital question is whether the candidate should get the chance to add the post to her resume, which simply reinforces public cynicism about motives for entering public life. We have come to treat public service as a reward rather than a calling, which takes us down a rather dangerous road, for it becomes impossible to bring any sense of proportionality to bear on the evaluation of potential officials.

Further, the search for disqualifying factors potentially leads to a rather freewheeling investigation into the backgrounds of nominees. The possibility of keeping one's private life private becomes virtually nil, as only the tissue-thin wall of news judgment stands between the nominee and the disclosure (and condemnation) of whatever the candidate might least wish to discuss. This might seem just fine, until one takes the time to consider some of the things that might be disclosed in later cases. (Again, one thinks of Bork's videotape rentals.) To be sure, there are some facts about an individual's background that *should* be disqualifying, but I fear that recent history has shown us to be a bit mixed up about what they are. . . .

In the case of Supreme Court nominees, the disqualification problem is particularly acute: in addition to the personal detritus through which all nominees must wade, the potential Justice also risks defeat if she has written or said things that will anger powerful constituencies who are wary of the way in which she will exercise her commission. In principle, there is nothing wrong with trying to get a full picture of nominees for the Court, especially given the awesome authority that the Justices wield in contemporary society; indeed, neither the President nor the Senate would be acting in accordance with the constitutional design were no weight given to the nominee's outlook. In practice, however, the effort too often deteriorates into a public relations campaign in which the would-be Justice is praised or excoriated for her likely votes in actual cases. At that point, . . . we are well on the way to electing our Justices, raising a serious question about why we do not just go ahead and do it explicitly. Indeed, . . . if we are not prepared to change the way we think about the Court, we probably should consider electing its members, as is done in most of the states, where the voters know what they want from their judges and how to get it.

I would prefer not to go that far; I would prefer that we make important changes in our national mood rather than tinker around with the Constitution. If, however, we are too set in our ways of envisioning the judicial role to rethink such matters as whether it really is wise to campaign for or against nominees according to their likely votes, then constitutional change might be our only way of avoiding the considerable blood that is too frequently spilled in our confirmation fights.

Is the Confirmation Process a Mess?

MICHAEL A. KAHN
Is There a Confirmation Mess?

ASSUMPTIONS RECONSIDERED

I have three basic disagreements with Professor Carter's analysis. First, I do not agree with his conclusion that the process whereby we elevate persons to the Supreme Court has drastically changed (if it has changed at all). Second, I disagree with Carter's assertions, implicit and explicit, that the Supreme Court is not a political body and that the need for judicial independence qualifies it for unique treatment in our political system. Third, though I am also repelled by the means that have been utilized in many confirmation fights, I am not ready to throw out this proverbial baby with the dirty bath water upon which Carter dwells. I will discuss these points seriatim.

Carter's Historical Conclusions Are Not Warranted

Carter identifies 1971 as the great divide after which he believes the confirmation process for Supreme Court Justices simply got out of hand. His thesis is that there is something new and different in the current process in that it has become a political free-for-all in which large-scale campaigns have been mounted for or against a candidate. Carter laments every aspect of these political activities but is especially offended by the unprincipled way the records of qualified candidates such as Lani Guinier and Robert Bork have been distorted. Carter goes to great lengths to demonstrate that the examples used to prove that Bork was a monstrous woman-hater — the so-called sterilization decision — and that Guinier was a radical reverse racist — the *Michigan Law Review* article — were unfairly represented by Bork's and Guinier's foes. According to Carter, "In both cases . . . activists opposed to confirmation could not content themselves with stating in reasoned, thoughtful terms the grounds for their disagreements."

There is no doubt that Guinier and Bork were the victims of mean-spirited, results-oriented political campaigns. However, in the heavenly queue of such victims, they will have to join many other similarly mistreated candidates. Take, for example, John Crittenden, whose main deficiency was that he was appointed by the lame duck President John Quincy Adams (who was, after all, only following a family tradition in doing so). Crittenden in 1828 and 1829 complained about the unfair and scurrilous treatment he received at the hands of the Senate and, though he remained a public figure until his death over thirty years later, the rest of his political career was haunted by this experience. But poor John Crittenden was not even the first victim of this type of treatment. George Washington's nomination of John Rutledge for Chief Justice in 1795 was rejected on purely political grounds, and Rutledge was so despondent over the event that he attempted suicide. In 1881, the Senate confirmed President Garfield's nominee to the Court, Stanley Matthews, by the narrowest margin (twenty-four to twenty-three), and only after two months of acrimonious debate. Thus, results-oriented campaigns and accompanying ugly Senate fights are not unique to the new generation. Indeed, they have occurred throughout our history.

There is no question that the means by which nominees are attacked today are more modern and perhaps more efficient. The use of mass mailings, television commercials, and other instruments of our current political battlefield may lead us to feel that contemporary struggles over appointments are more intense and overwhelming than those of the past. But the campaign against the Supreme Court and all appointees who refused to spout a racist line in the 1950s following the *Brown* decision, which included, among other things, billboards denouncing Earl Warren dotting the Southern landscape, was equally ugly. Moreover, there can be no doubt that the massive resistance of Southern society (and others) to the racial freedom movement of the 1950s and 1960s cast a pall over the deliberations of the Supreme Court and placed the appointment and confirmation of Supreme Court Justices in a confrontational environment. The disingenuous and truncated confirmation process endured by John Harlan in 1954 and 1955, and by Potter Stewart in 1959, including obvious and sustained grandstanding and race baiting by Southern senators, were reminders that the political stakes in Supreme Court appointments were high and political emotions deeply felt during that time period.

Moreover, Carter too easily dismisses the significance of the disgraceful process whereby Louis Brandeis was elevated to the Court. If we focus on Brandeis' list of legitimate qualifications it is easy to rank him right up there with Thurgood Marshall as one of history's most qualified candidates. Indeed, by the time of his appointment, Brandeis, who had excelled at Harvard Law School, had been a nationally renowned corporate lawyer, introduced sociological jurisprudence to the Court with his "Brandeis" brief, and achieved national prominence as "the people's lawyer." Yet, incredibly, seven former presidents of the American Bar Association, one of whom happened to be a former President of the United States, William Howard Taft, joined in statements to the Senate subcommittee holding hearings on the nomination that stated Brandeis was not qualified to sit on the Court. No doubt anti-semitism fueled this opposition, but it was substantially motivated by conservative and big business forces who feared Brandeis' liberal views. This incident is remarkable for its similarity to modern confirmation battles. No one could seriously contend that Brandeis was not qualified for the Court. Yet, that is exactly the way criticism of him, like that of Robert Bork and Thurgood Marshall, was framed. Moreover, twenty-two senators (out of sixty-nine voting) voted against him.

Judge John J. Parker is another person who was victimized by the Senate and a public out to get a scalp. Parker had the misfortune to be unsuccessfully nominated by an increasingly unpopular and out-of-touch President during a bleak period of our history (1930). After he was nominated by President Hoover, he was attacked in the most vicious and personal fashion. Though the attacks against Parker were couched as personal criticism, their underlying political motivation is clearly revealed by the fate of Charles Evans Hughes' nomination for Chief Justice just months before. Hughes had already served on the Court and was a former nominee of his party for President. (He lost the election by a whisker.) Nevertheless, in opposing him, Nebraska's progressive senator, George W. Norris, declaimed Hughes, stating that, "No man in public life so exemplifies the influence of powerful combinations in the political and financial world as does Mr. Hughes." Eventually, despite his many achievements and his national stature, twenty-six senators voted against Hughes and he was confirmed only after a bitter and distasteful fight.

I do not mean to suggest that Carter is unaware of this musty history. On the contrary, Carter has sufficient familiarity with some of these incidents to acknowledge them. However, Carter's sympathy for poorly treated nominees seems to be much more acute when he deals with his friends and acquaintances than when he thinks about past victims. The unvarnished truth is that for John Rutledge, John Crittenden, Louis Brandeis, Charles Evans Hughes, John Parker, and others, the confirmation process was as nasty and brutish (if not as short) as it was for Robert Bork and Lani Guinier.

Carter misses the mark when he complains that the most recent politically-motivated attacks on presidential nominees are unique. The seeming ubiquity and pervasiveness of media and interest groups spewing forth propaganda about candidates creates the perception that the message is more urgent and ugly. But the fact of the matter is that from its inception the process of nominating and confirming appointments to the Supreme Court has been sporadically, yet predictably, infested with ugly, mean-spirited, and unfair campaigns against virtually defenseless fodder for our political cannons.

Nevertheless, if Carter is correct that the system is a mess, it begs the question to observe that it has been flawed from the start. The issues that Carter joins, and to which I now turn, are whether the nature of the Court and the need for judicial independence are such that we continue to endure and utilize this problem-laden system at our peril.

Carter's Argument for Political Immunity for Court Nominees Must and Should Fail

Carter is genuinely disturbed at the institutional ramifications of our current system of selecting Supreme Court Justices. He believes that the logical consequence of validating a results-oriented series of campaigns for or against Supreme Court candidates is to undermine the cherished value of judicial independence. In this regard Carter seems to dispute, or at least to ignore, the enshrined wisdom of Mr. Dooley who observed that the Supreme Court follows the election returns. Indeed, similar wisdom of the colloquial variety ("a switch in time saves nine"), of the jurisprudential variety (the political question doctrine), and of the scholarly variety (myriad books pronouncing the good political judgment of the Supreme Court in its decisions) pervades our understanding of the historical activities of the Court. Yes, it is true that the Supreme Court has, in a seemingly undemocratic fashion, plowed new and important ground in race relations and other fields. However, the other branches of government have, in equally undemocratic fashion, arrogated power for purportedly higher motives. Franklin Roosevelt's policy toward England before our entry in World War II, Abraham Lincoln's usurpation of the right of habeas corpus in the name of saving the Union, and countless other acts committed by presidents in the face of public pressures and legal prohibitions to the contrary, give the Presidency a claim to the mantle of the nation's most undemocratic institution which Carter is quick to award the Court. Moreover, it is ironic to claim that the Court, which can act only by a vote of five of its members, is less democratic than the President, who may act alone.

In short, without belaboring the argument, I think it facile to label the Court undemocratic and to attempt to insulate it from politics because one wishes to preserve its undemocratic characteristics. In truth the Court is a highly political institution. Indeed, I would be surprised if any person has ever served on the Court without a profound sense of its political nature. It is obvious that the Court plays a vital counterbalancing role (which varies dramatically over time) within the democratic political system which governs us. Moreover, Supreme Court Justices are appointed by a politician and confirmed by one hundred other politicians. Each of these politicians has subjected his own career to the vicissitudes, perils, and degradations of political campaigns in order to attain the power to choose and vote upon Supreme Court Justices. Often, the act of appointing or voting on a justice is a visible and significant part of an ongoing political campaign to retain that power (to which phenomenon we gratefully owe the appointments of Cardozo and Brennan). It is not only naive and unfair, but it also defies the nature of political affairs, to urge that in this blizzard of political activity we should place as a tropical island a principled, qualification-oriented, nonpolitical confirmation process.

In sum, I think Carter is wrong when he argues that the Court is uniquely nonpolitical or that the appointments process can operate in a manner that is not susceptible to domination by results-oriented politics. The Supreme Court has always operated in this highly political environment. Indeed, one of the most remarkable achievements of the Court has been its ability to be such a vibrant, powerful force in this political context despite its lack of inherent resources.

Nevertheless, even if the evidence does not support Professor Carter's conclusion that the Court should be and historically has been uniquely nonpolitical, it does not necessarily follow that the Court's members must always be selected by a highly charged political process. The question remains: does the confirmation process need changing anyway?

If It Ain't Broke, Don't Fix It

Carter's book is in no small part a plea to instill civility into the process by which we appoint and confirm Supreme Court Justices and other presidential appointees. It is difficult to disagree with this sentiment. (One expects that the candidates would certainly agree.) Regardless of one's politics, the specter of Clarence Thomas writhing in pain on his bedroom floor over the unfairness of the process to him and his family, as described in Senator Danforth's new book, must evoke revulsion. Obviously, there is something wrong with a system that rewards public-minded candidates with relentless personal vilification and humiliation. President Clinton would no doubt agree with this senti-ment, though he may have a different perspective on who the main victim of unwarranted, unfair, and disgraceful personal attacks has been in recent years.

In evaluating the appointments process, this country's political process may serve as an apt comparison. It is difficult to mount an argument that somehow Bork, Thomas, Guinier, or Baird was treated more unfairly or harshly than the crop of candidates who ran for office in the 1994 mid-term elections. Indeed, the entire history of our political process (not to mention that of our fellow democracies) is riddled with the devastated bodies and souls of our citizens who entered the arena only to be pummelled in the process. Sometimes the victims of the most vicious attacks persevere and are able to respond philo-sophically like Abraham Lincoln who commented, "If I were to try to read, much less answer, all the attacks made on me, this shop might as well be closed for any other business. . . . [But] [i]f the end brings me out all right, what is said against me won't amount to anything." However, more often, it is the vanquisher, like Richard Nixon (whose victims like Jerry Voorhis and Helen Douglas remained scarred for life) who perseveres. Like it or not, mean, rotten, and nasty personal campaigns have always been the stuff of our democracy. Each generation believes that it has seen the worst of it and each generation works hard to prove that point.

It is tempting to argue that candidates for elected office ask for this treat-ment by deciding to run and have the tools to defend themselves in their own campaigns. One may wish to argue, as Carter does, that somehow our politi-cal appointees deserve special treatment. Upon closer inspection, however, such a distinction does not seem justified.

Why, after all, are political campaigns so hard fought? The simple answer is that it matters, from important policy and special (and not-so-special) interest perspectives, who is elected. To argue that Supreme Court nominees should be immune from such campaigns is to ignore fundamental realities. First, the cases that the Supreme Court decides are critically and fundamentally important to all of our lives. The Court's docket comprises issues, such as capital punishment and abortion, that are literally issues of life or death. Second, the undeniable re-ality is that who is deciding these issues makes a difference in terms of results.

Carter urges us to put aside the short-sighted focus on this second reality and simply to select the most qualified people and let them decide the cases as a matter of conscience, exercising their undemocratic judicial independence. This may be a good way to go about the process of selecting Justices, but Carter's implicit suggestion that it is the only legitimate way for our body politic to ap-proach the process is unconvincing. Take the choice of Robert Bork. Let us as-sume that he was unfairly maligned and mistreated. Let us further assume that employing all of Carter's criteria he was fully qualified to sit on the Court. Let us further assume that he was a sure fifth and deciding vote to reverse *Roe*. Why would it be less appropriate to engage in a full-scale, no-holds-barred campaign against him than it would be to engage in such a campaign against a president who might appoint him or a senator who might confirm him?

It is important in this discussion to distinguish personal behavior and principles from legitimate political behavior. I personally may be drawn to Carter's dispassionate, reason-oriented decision-making philosophy, but that does not mean that I do not acknowledge the legitimacy of other forms of political behavior within our system. This is where I believe Carter's argument breaks down. It is unrealistic, and even unfair, to urge that participants in an unrestrained political system refrain from political activity (however personally offensive) when faced with the lifetime anointment of a highly political officer who is to be endowed with vast power and discretion over their lives.

Finally, though on an individual basis the system surely produces many victims who are treated unfairly or even disgracefully, on a broader perspective it is not convincing to argue that the system is not working. I may not always agree with them, but I find it impossible to sanction the criticism that the current Supreme Court Justices are not honest, intelligent, thoughtful persons of the highest integrity. It is always easy to take pot shots at a system for its failures, but it seems to me that a process that has given us the services of the likes of both Marshalls, both Harlans, Holmes, Warren, Brennan, and Brandeis is significant for its remarkable successes, not for its failures.

Thus, I believe that Carter has it wrong on all accounts. The appointment and confirmation process has always worked pretty much as it operates now — as a highly political process within a democratic system — and it has always, in the main and viewed as a whole, served us well. In short, it ain't broke and it don't need fixing — even if we could use a little attitude adjustment.

CONCLUSION

We should not ignore Carter's aspirations. All of the foregoing notwithstanding, Carter has done us a service with his book. Carter's moral and philosophical message should be heeded. Obviously, the confirmation process is not always, or even usually, unacceptably indecent and dishonest. Moreover, as difficult as this is to believe, I think the process is always restrained, even in the cases of Thomas and Bork, by our own morality and views of appropriate restraint. Carter appeals to our better selves. He urges us to focus on the right things and to devalue the currency of disqualification. He urges us to be honest and decent in this process for the sake of the system and for ourselves. These are important messages and they clearly resonate. We do not need to deny the legitimacy and the success of our political system to aspire to be better actors within it. We do not need to reform our processes to be more decent and honest. We do not need to deny the importance of the immediate results of the Supreme Court's deliberations and our role in affecting those results to achieve the attitude adjustment that Carter counsels. And, thus, we do not have to accept Carter's historical or political analysis to adopt his moral and philosophical aspirations.

Questions for Discussion

1. How has the confirmation process changed in the past two centuries?
2. What criteria should be used in selecting a nominee to the Supreme Court? What are the reasons for your answer?
3. What can be done to remove the controversy surrounding Supreme Court nominations?
4. What effect does the nomination process have on the authority and respect of appointees once they are confirmed by the Senate?
5. What questions are appropriate to ask nominees? What are the reasons for your answer?

Suggested Readings

Abraham, Henry J. *Justices and Presidents: A Political History of Appointments to the Supreme Court*, 3d ed. New York: Oxford Univ. Press, 1992.

Ad Hoc Committee on the Senate Confirmation Process. "Report on the Senate Confirmation Process." *Record of the Association of the Bar of the City of New York* 47, no. 5 (June 1992): 543–566.

DeConcini, Dennis. "The Confirmation Process." *St. John's Journal of Legal Commentary* 7, no. 1 (Fall 1991): 1–13.

Gitenstein, Mark. *Matters of Principle: America's Rejection of the Bork Nomination*. New York: Simon & Schuster, 1992.

Kahn, Michael A. "The Appointment of a Supreme Court Justice: A Political Process from Beginning to End." *Presidential Studies Quarterly* 25, no. 1 (Winter 1995): 25–41.

Mackenzie, G. Calvin, and Robert Shogan. *Under the Microscope: The Report of the Twentieth Century Fund Task Force on Presidential Appointments*. New York: Twentieth Century Fund Press, 1996.

Maltese, John Anthony. *The Selling of Supreme Court Nominees*. Baltimore, Md.: Johns Hopkins Univ. Press, 1995.

Mikva, Abner J. "How Should We Select Judges in a Free Society?" *Southern Illinois Univ. Law Journal* 16 (Spring 1992): 547–556.

Simon, Paul. *Advice and Consent: Clarence Thomas, Robert Bork and the Intriguing History of the Supreme Court's Nomination Battle*. Washington, D.C.: National Press Books, 1992.

Watson, George, and John A. Stookey. *Shaping America: The Politics of Supreme Court Appointments*. New York: HarperCollins College Publishers, 1995.

Chapter 17

Should the Supreme Court Abide by a Strict Constructionist Philosophy?

Of the three branches of the federal government — president, Congress, and the Supreme Court — the last is the least democratic. Although representative democracy requires periodic elections, the members of the Supreme Court are appointed, never run for office in popular elections, and once on the Court, usually remain there for life or until they retire. Presidents, senators, and representatives may envy the justices' luxury of not having to run for public office.

The Supreme Court's power of judicial review is — at least on the surface — another undemocratic feature of this arm of government. Judicial review is the power of the Supreme Court to examine state and federal laws and the acts of state and federal public officials to determine whether they are in conflict with the Constitution. If these laws and acts are in conflict, then the court may declare them invalid. The fact that a majority of nine unelected members of the Court may declare null and void the laws enacted by the representatives of the majority of the people who vote seems to be a limitation on the principle of majority rule. The argument is often made, however, that the specific content of court decisions has strengthened rather than weakened democracy.

Judicial review is not the practice in all representative democracies. The British system of government, for example, permits the courts to interpret the laws but not to declare an act of Parliament void. Judicial review is not specifically mentioned in the Constitution of the United States. Debate surrounds the question of whether the Framers intended the Supreme Court to have this power over the laws of the federal government. There is general agreement, however, that the Framers understood that judicial review is applicable to acts of state legislatures in conflict with the Constitution. The Supreme Court first declared an act of Congress unconstitutional in *Marbury v. Madison* (1803). In this case the court found the Judiciary Act of 1789 to be in conflict with Article III of the Constitution.[1] Today the Supreme Court's authority to declare a statute unconstitutional is unchallenged.

Over the past century the Supreme Court has exercised its power of judicial review in a variety of cases. Those who have benefited from the Court's decisions have hailed the wisdom of the Court. The "losers" have called for a variety of responses, including limiting the jurisdiction of the Court, amending the Constitution, enlarging the size of the Court, or impeaching the chief justice.

Court decisions have not supported one group of people exclusively. In the early part of the twentieth century, for example, Court decisions were more favorable to big business, states' rights advocates, and segregationists. Since the days of the Warren Court (for former Chief Justice Earl Warren) in the mid-1950s, however, Court decisions have been more favorable to groups demanding extension of civil rights and civil liberties. The changing character of Supreme Court decisions is a reflection of such factors as the composition of the Court, legal precedents, and the political environment. One other factor that has received much attention, however, is the philosophical outlook of the judges.

Two principal philosophical outlooks have guided judicial decision making, and they are always in conflict. As we saw in Chapter 1, William Bradford Reynolds held the intentions of the Framers of the Constitution in the highest regard, while Thurgood Marshall argued that the wisdom of the Constitution lies in its adaptability to changing social needs. Strict constructionists, like Reynolds, believe that the Supreme Court should be bound by the intent of the Framers and the language in the document itself. Loose constructionists argue that strict constructionism is misconceived, impossible, or even fraudulent. At various times in U.S. history, conservatives have supported strict constructionism, but liberals, too, at times, have taken a similar philosophical approach.

The debate below elicits the main arguments of the contending schools. Federal appeals court judge J. Clifford Wallace makes a case for interpretivism — the principle that judges, in resolving constitutional questions, should rely on the express provisions of the Constitution or upon those norms that are clearly implicit in its text. He contends:

1. The Constitution itself envisions and requires interpretivist review.
2. Interpretivist review promotes the stability and predictability essential to the rule of law.
3. Judges are not particularly well suited to make judgments of broad social policy.
4. The argument put forward by noninterpretivists that certain constitutional provisions invite justices to use value judgments outside the Constitution is invalid.
5. Although the Framers' intent cannot be ascertained on every issue, interpretivism will exclude from consideration entire ranges of improper judicial responses.
6. The Fourteenth Amendment did not produce so fundamental a revision in the nature of U.S. government that the intentions of the Framers are scarcely relevant any longer.
7. The Constitution can still be changed by the only legitimate means for which it provides: formal amendment.

8. When noninterpretivists justify their actions on the basis of "doing justice," they act improperly because they are incapable of deciding what is just.
9. An activist judiciary undermines the very principles of democracy.
10. An interpretivist view shows respect for precedent.

Law professor Jeffrey M. Shaman takes the negative position on the issue. He contends:

1. History shows that whenever the Supreme Court makes a decision that someone does not like, the justices are accused of holding to their own personal views and not to the words of the Constitution or the intent of the Framers.
2. From its early history, the Supreme Court has had to go outside the written Constitution and the intent of the Framers in making some decisions.
3. The Court often must create meaning for the Constitution because the document is rife with general and abstract language.
4. There is no reason to pay greater attention to the intent of the Framers than to that of the people who ratified the Constitution or to the succeeding generations who retain it.
5. The intent of the Framers is difficult to discern.
6. The conditions that shaped the Framers' attitudes have changed in two centuries of constitutional experience.
7. The Constitution provides only the bare bones; its meaning must be augmented by the justices.
8. The Court is subject to popular constraints that keep its power limited.

NOTE

1. *Marbury v. Madison*, 1 Cranch 137 (1803).

Should the Supreme Court Abide by a Strict Constructionist Philosophy?

J. CLIFFORD WALLACE
The Case for Judicial Restraint

This year [1987] we celebrate the 200th anniversary of our Constitution. This remarkable document has structured our government and secured our liberty as we have developed from 13 fledgling colonies into a mature and strong democracy. Without doubt, the Constitution is one of the grandest political achievements of the modern world.

In spite of this marvelous record, we will celebrate our nation's charter in the midst of a hotly contested debate on the continuing role that it should have in our society. Two schools of constitutional jurisprudence are engaged in a long-running battle. Some contend that the outcome of this conflict may well determine whether the Constitution remains our vital organic document or whether it instead becomes a curious historical relic. The competing positions in this constitutional battle are often summarized by a variety of labels: judicial restraint versus judicial activism, strict construction versus loose construction, positivism versus natural law, conservative versus liberal, interpretivism versus noninterpretivism.

In large measure, these labels alone are of little assistance in analyzing a complex problem. Ultimately, what is at stake is what Constitution will govern this country. Will it be the written document drafted by the Framers, ratified by the people, and passed down, with amendments, to us? Or will it be an illusive parchment upon which modern-day judges may freely engrave their own political and sociological preferences?

In this article, I intend to outline and defend a constitutional jurisprudence of judicial restraint.[1] My primary thesis is that a key principle of judicial restraint — namely, interpretivism — is required by our constitutional plan. I will also explore how practitioners of judicial restraint should resolve the tension that can arise in our current state of constitutional law between interpretivism and a second important principle, respect for judicial precedent.

INTERPRETIVISM VERSUS NONINTERPRETIVISM

What is the difference between "interpretivism" and "noninterpretivism"? This question is important because I believe interpretivism to be the cornerstone of a constitutional jurisprudence of judicial restraint. By "interpretivism," I mean the principle that judges, in resolving constitutional questions, should rely on the express provisions of the Constitution or upon those norms that are clearly implicit in its text.[2] Under an interpretivist approach, the original intention of the Framers is the controlling guide for constitutional interpretation. This does not mean, of course, that judges may apply a constitutional provision only to situations specifically contemplated by the Framers. Rather, it simply requires that when considering whether to invalidate the work of the political branches, the judges do so from a starting point fairly discoverable in the Constitution.[3] By contrast, under noninterpretive review, judges may freely rest their decisions on value judgments that admittedly are not supported by, and may even contravene, the text of the Constitution and the intent of the Framers.[4]

Interpretivist Review

I believe that the Constitution itself envisions and requires interpretivist review. To explore this thesis, we should first examine the Constitution as a political and historical document.

As people read the Constitution, many are struck by how procedural and technical its provisions are. Perhaps on first reading it may be something of a disappointment. In contrast to the fiery eloquence of the Declaration of Independence, the Constitution may seem dry or even dull. This difference in style, of course, reflects the very different functions of the two documents. The Declaration of Independence is an indictment of the reign of King George III. In a flamboyant tone, it is brilliantly crafted to persuade the world of the justice of our fight for independence. The Constitution, by contrast, establishes the basic set of rules for the nation. Its genius lies deeper, in its skillful design of a government structure that would best ensure liberty and democracy.

The primary mechanism by which the Constitution aims to protect liberty and democracy is the dispersion of government power. Recognizing that concentrated power poses the threat of tyranny, the Framers divided authority between the states and the federal government. In addition, they created three separate and co-equal branches of the federal government in a system of checks and balances.

The Framers were also aware, of course, that liberty and democracy can come into conflict. The Constitution, therefore, strikes a careful balance between democratic rule and minority rights. Its republican, representative features are designed to channel and refine cruder majoritarian impulses. In addition, the Constitution's specific individual protections, particularly in the Bill of Rights, guarantee against certain majority intrusions. Beyond these guarantees, the Constitution places its trust in the democratic process — the voice of the people expressed through their freely elected representatives.

Raoul Berger argues persuasively in *Government by Judiciary* that the Constitution "was written against a background of interpretive presuppositions that assured the Framers their design would be effectuated."[5] The importance of that statement may escape us today, when it is easy to take for granted that the Constitution is a written document. But for the Framers, the fact that the Constitution was in writing was not merely incidental. They recognized that a written constitution provides the most stable basis for the rule of law, upon which liberty and justice ultimately depend.

As Thomas Jefferson observed, "Our peculiar security is in the possession of a written constitution. Let us not make it a blank paper by construction."[6] Chief Justice John Marshall, in *Marbury v. Madison,* the very case establishing the power of judicial review, emphasized the constraints imposed by the written text and the judicial duty to respect these constraints in all cases raising constitutional questions.[7]

Moreover, the Framers recognized the importance of interpreting the Constitution according to their original intent. In Madison's words, if "the sense in which the Constitution was accepted and ratified by the Nation . . . be not the guide in expounding it, there can be no security for a consistent and stable government, [nor] for a fruitful exercise of its powers."[8] Similarly, Jefferson as President acknowledged his duty to administer the Constitution "according to the safe and honest meaning contemplated by the plain understanding of the people at the time of its adoption — a meaning to be found in the explanations of those who advocated . . . it."[9] It seems clear, therefore, that the leading Framers were interpretivists and believed that constitutional questions should be reviewed by that approach.

Next, I would like to consider whether interpretivism is necessary to effectuate the constitutional plan. The essential starting point is that the Constitution established a separation of powers to protect our freedom. Because freedom is fundamental, so too is the separation of powers. But separation of powers becomes a meaningless slogan if judges may confer constitutional status on whichever rights they happen to deem important, regardless of textual basis. In effect, under noninterpretive review, the judiciary functions as a superlegislature beyond the check of the other two branches. Noninterpretivist review also disregards the Constitution's careful allocation of most decisions to the democratic process, allowing the legislature to make decisions deemed best for society. Ultimately, noninterpretivist review reduces our written Constitution to insignificance and threatens to impose a tyranny of the judiciary.

Prudential Considerations

Important prudential considerations also weigh heavily in favor of interpretivist review. The rule of law is fundamental in our society. To be effective, it cannot be tossed to and fro by each new sociological wind. Because it is rooted in written text, interpretivist review promotes the stability and predictability essential to the rule of the law. By contrast, noninterpretivist review presents an infinitely variable array of possibilities. The Constitution would vary with each judge's conception of what is important. To demonstrate the wide variety of tests that could be applied, let us briefly look at the writings of legal academics who advocate noninterpretivism.

Assume each is a judge deciding the same constitutional issue. One professor seeks to "cement a union between the distributional patterns of the modern welfare state and the federal constitution." Another "would guarantee a whole range of nontextually based rights against government to ensure 'the dignity of full membership in society.'" A third argues that the courts should give a "concrete meaning and application" to those values that "give our society an identity and inner coherence [and] its distinctive public morality." Yet another professor sees the court as having a "prophetic" role in developing moral standards in a "dialectical relationship" with Congress, from which he sees emerging a "more mature" political morality. One professor even urges that the court apply the contractarian moral theory of Professor Rawls' *A Theory of Justice* to constitutional questions.[10] One can easily see the fatal vagueness and subjectivity of this approach: each judge would apply his or her own separate and diverse personal values in interpreting the same constitutional question. Without anchor, we drift at sea.

Another prudential argument against noninterpretivism is that judges are not particularly well-suited to make judgments of broad social policy. We judges decide cases on the basis of a limited record that largely represents the efforts of the parties to the litigation. Legislators, with their committees, hearings, and more direct role in the political process, are much better equipped institutionally to decide what is best for society.

Noninterpretivist Arguments

But are there arguments in favor of noninterpretivism? Let us consider several assertions commonly put forth by proponents. One argument asserts that certain constitutional provisions invite judges to import into the constitutional decision process value judgments derived from outside the Constitution. Most commonly, advocates of this view rely on the due process clause of the Fifth and Fourteenth Amendments. It is true that courts have interpreted the due process clause to authorize broad review of the substantive merits of legislation. But is that what the draftsmen had in mind? Some constitutional scholars make a strong argument that the clause, consistent with its plain language, was intended to have a limited procedural meaning.[11]

A second argument asserts that the meaning of the constitutional text and the intention of the Framers cannot be ascertained with sufficient precision to guide constitutional decisionmaking. I readily acknowledge that interpretivism will not always provide easy answers to difficult constitutional questions. The judicial role will always involve the exercise of discretion. The strength of interpretivism is that it channels and constrains this discretion in a manner consistent with the Constitution. While it does not necessarily ensure a correct result, it does exclude from consideration entire ranges of improper judicial responses.

Third, some have suggested that the Fourteenth Amendment effected such a fundamental revision in the nature of our government that the intentions of the original Framers are scarcely relevant any longer. It is, of course, true that federal judges have seized upon the Fourteenth Amendment as a vehicle to restructure federal/state relations. The argument, however, is not one-sided. Berger, for example, persuasively demonstrates that the framers of the Fourteenth Amendment sought much more limited objectives.[12] In addition, one reasonable interpretation of the history of the amendment demonstrates that its framers, rather than intending an expanded role for the federal courts, meant for Congress (under section 5 of the amendment) to play the primary role in enforcing its provisions.[13] Thus, it can be argued that to the extent that the Fourteenth Amendment represented an innovation in the constitutional role of the judiciary, it was by limiting the courts' traditional role in enforcing constitutional rights and by providing added responsibility for the Congress.

Advocates of noninterpretivism also contend that we should have a "living Constitution" rather than be bound by "the dead hand of the Framers." These slogans prove nothing. An interpretivist approach would not constrict government processes; on the contrary, it would ensure that issues are freely subject to the workings of the democratic process. Moreover, to the extent that the Constitution might profit from revision, the amendment process of Article V provides the only constitutional means. Judicial amendment under a noninterpretivist approach is simply an unconstitutional usurpation.

Almost certainly, the greatest support for a noninterpretive approach derives from its perceived capacity to achieve just results. Why quibble over the Constitution, after all, if judges who disregard it nevertheless "do justice"? Such a view is dangerously shortsighted and naive. In the first place, one has no cause to believe that the results of noninterpretivism will generally be "right." Individual judges have widely varying conceptions of what values are important. Noninterpretivists spawned the "conservative" substantive economic due process of the 1930s as well as the "liberal" decisions of the Warren Court. There is no principle result in noninterpretivism.

But even if the judge would always be right, the process would be wrong. A benevolent judicial tyranny is nonetheless a tyranny. Our Constitution rests on the faith that democracy is intrinsically valuable. From an instrumental perspective, democracy might at times produce results that are not as desirable as platonic guardians might produce. But the democratic process — our participation in a system of self-government — has transcendental value. Moreover, one must consider the very real danger that an activist judiciary stunts the development of a responsible democracy by removing from it the duty to make difficult decisions. If we are to remain faithful to the values of democracy and liberty, we must insist that courts respect the Constitution's allocation of social decisionmaking to the political branches.

RESPECT FOR PRECEDENT

I emphasized earlier the importance of stability to the rule of law. I return to that theme now to consider a second principle of judicial restraint: respect for precedent. Respect for precedent is a principle widely accepted, even if not always faithfully followed. It requires simply that a judge follow prior case law in deciding legal questions. Respect for precedent promotes predictability and uniformity. It constrains a judge's discretion and satisfies the reasonable expectations of the parties. Through its application, citizens can have a better understanding of what the law is and act accordingly.

Unfortunately, in the present state of constitutional law, the two principles of judicial restraint that I have outlined can come into conflict. While much of constitutional law is consistent with the principle of interpretivism, a significant portion is not. This raises the question of how a practitioner of judicial restraint should act in circumstances where respecting precedent would require acceptance of law developed under a noninterpretivist approach.

The answer is easy for a judge in my position, and, indeed, for any judge below the United States Supreme Court. As a judge on the Ninth Circuit Court of Appeals, I am bound to follow Supreme Court and Ninth Circuit precedent even when I believe it to be wrong. There is a distinction, however, between following precedent and extending it. Where existing precedent does not fairly govern a legal question, the principle of interpretivism should guide a judge.

For Supreme Court justices, the issue is more complex. The Supreme Court obviously is not infallible. Throughout its history, the Court has at times rejected its own precedents. Because the Supreme Court has the ultimate judicial say on what the Constitution means, its justices have a special responsibility to ensure that they are properly expounding constitutional law as well as fostering stability and predictability.

Must Supreme Court advocates of judicial restraint passively accept the errors of activist predecessors? There is little rational basis for doing so. Periodic activist inroads could emasculate fundamental doctrines and undermine the separation of powers. Nevertheless, the values of predictability and uniformity that respect for precedent promotes demand caution in overturning precedent. In my view, a justice should consider overturning a prior decision only when the decision is clearly wrong, has significant effects, and would otherwise be difficult to remedy.

Significantly, constitutional decisions based on a noninterpretivist approach may satisfy these three criteria. When judges confer constitutional status on their own value judgments without support in the language of the Constitution and the original intention of the Framers, they commit clear error. Because constitutional errors frequently affect the institutional structure of government and the allocation of decisions to the democratic process, they are likely to have important effects. And because constitutional decisions, unlike statutory decisions, cannot be set aside through normal political channels, they will generally meet the third requirement. In sum, then, despite the prudential interests furthered by respect for precedent, advocates of judicial restraint may be justified in seeking to overturn noninterpretivist precedent.

CONCLUSION

It is obvious that courts employing interpretivist review cannot solve many of the social and political problems facing America, indeed, even some very important problems. The interpretivist would respond that the Constitution did not place the responsibility for solving those problems with the courts. The courts were not meant to govern the core of our political and social life — Article I gave that duty, for national issues, to the Congress. It is through our democratically elected representatives that we legitimately develop this fabric of our life. Interpretivism encourages that process. It is, therefore, closer to the constitutional plan of governance than is noninterpretivist review.

After two hundred years, the Constitution is not "broke" — we need not fix it — just apply it.

NOTES

This article is adapted from an address given at Hillsdale College, Hillsdale, Michigan, on March 5, 1986.

1. I have elsewhere presented various aspects of this jurisprudence. See, e.g., Wallace, "A Two Hundred Year Old Constitution in Modern Society," 61 *Texas Law Review*, 1575 (1983); Wallace, "The Jurisprudence of Judicial Restraint: A Return to the Moorings," *George Washington Law Review* 1 (1981).

2. Wallace, "A Two Hundred Year Old Constitution," *supra* n. 1; Ely, *Democracy and Distrust* 1 (Cambridge, Mass.: Harvard University Press, 1980).

3. Ely, *supra* n. 2, at 2.

4. See *id.* at 43–72.

5. Berger, *Government by Judiciary* 366 (Cambridge, Mass.: Harvard University Press, 1977).

6. *Id.* at 364, *quoting* Letter to Wilson Cary Nicholas (Sept. 7, 1803).

7. *Marbury v. Madison*, 5 U.S. (1 Cranch) 137, 176–180 (1803).

8. Berger, *supra* n. 5, at 364, quoting *The Writings of James Madison* 191 (G. Hunt ed. 1900–1910).

9. *Id.* at 366–367, citing 4 Elliot, *Debates in the Several State Conventions on the Adoption of the Federal Constitution* 446 (1836).

10. Monaghan, "Our Perfect Constitution," 56 *New York University Law Review*, 353, 358–360 (1981) (summarizing theories of noninterpretivists).

11. See, e.g., Berger, *supra* n. 5, at 193–220.

12. See *id.*

13. See *id.* at 220–229.

Should the Supreme Court Abide by a Strict Constructionist Philosophy?

JEFFREY M. SHAMAN

The Supreme Court's Proper and Historic Function

Considerable criticism, frequently quite sharp, has recently been directed at the Supreme Court for the way it has gone about its historic function of interpreting the Constitution. In particular, Edwin Meese, the current Attorney General of the United States [1987], has accused the Court of exceeding its lawful authority by failing to adhere strictly to the words of the Constitution and the intentions of the Framers who drafted those words.[1]

The Attorney General's attack upon the Court echoes a similar one made by Richard Nixon, who, campaigning for the Presidency in 1968, denounced Supreme Court Justices who, he claimed, twisted and bent the Constitution according to their personal predilections. If elected President, Nixon promised to appoint to the Court strict constructionists whose decisions would conform to the text of the Constitution and the intent of the Framers. (Ironically, it is some of the Nixon appointees to the Court that Meese now accuses of twisting and bending the Constitution.)

I hasten to add that it is not only politicians who sing the praises of strict constructionism; there are judges and lawyers, as well as some scholars, who join the song. Among legal scholars, though, the response to strict constructionism has been overwhelmingly negative. There are legal scholars, for instance, who describe strict constructionism as a "misconceived quest,"[2] an "impossibility,"[3] and even a "fraud."[4]

Those who criticize the Court point to rulings during the tenure of Chief Justice Burger, most notably the decision in *Roe v. Wade*[5] legalizing abortion, as examples of illegitimate revision or amendment of the Constitution based upon the personal beliefs of the justices. Some years ago, similar charges were leveled at the Warren Court for its ruling requiring reapportionment along the lines of one person–one vote,[6] its decision striking down school prayer,[7] and other rulings, even including the one in *Brown v. Board of Education* outlawing school segregation.[8]

It should not be supposed, however, that strict constructionism is always on the side of conservative political values. In the 1930s it was the liberals who claimed that the Supreme Court was not strictly construing the Constitution when the justices repeatedly held that minimum wage, maximum hour, and other protective legislation violated the Fourteenth Amendment.[9] As the liberals then saw it, the conservative justices on the Court were illegitimately incorporating their personal values into the Fourteenth Amendment, which had been meant to abolish racial discrimination, not to protect the prerogatives of employers.

HISTORY LESSONS

The lesson of this bit of history seems to be that, whether liberal or conservative or somewhere in between, whoever has an ox that is being gored at the time has a tendency to yell "foul." Whenever the Supreme Court renders a decision that someone doesn't like, apparently it is not enough to disagree with the decision; there also has to be an accusation that the Court's decision was illegitimate, being based upon the justice's personal views and not the words of the Constitution or the intent of the Framers.

We can go back much further in history than the 1930s to find the Supreme Court being accused of illegitimacy. In 1810, for instance, Thomas Jefferson condemned Chief Justice John Marshall for "twistifying" the Constitution according to his "personal biases."[10]

History also reveals something else extremely significant about the Court, which is that from its earliest days, the Court has found it necessary in interpreting the Constitution to look beyond the language of the document and the intent of the Framers. In the words of Stanford Law Professor Thomas Grey, it is "a matter of unarguable historical fact" that over the years the Court has developed a large body of constitutional law that derives neither from the text of the document nor the intent of the Framers.[11]

Moreover, this has been so from the Court's very beginning. Consider, for example, a case entitled *Hylton v. United States*,[12] which was decided in 1796 during the term of the Court's first Chief Justice, John Jay. The *Hylton* case involved a tax ranging from $1.00 to $10.00 that had been levied by Congress on carriages. Mr. Hylton, who was in the carriage trade and owned 125 carriages, understandably was unhappy about the tax, and went to court to challenge it. He claimed that the tax violated section 2 of Article I of the Constitution, which provides that direct taxes shall be apportioned among the several states according to their populations. Hylton argued that this tax was a direct one, and therefore unconstitutional because it had not been apportioned among the states by population. This, of course, was years before the enactment of the Sixteenth Amendment in 1913, authorizing a federal income tax. Prior to that, Article I prohibited a federal income tax, but what about a tax on the use or ownership of carriages — was that the sort of "direct" tax that was only permissible under Article I if apportioned among the states by population?

The Supreme Court, with several justices filing separate opinions in the case (which was customary at that time), upheld the tax as constitutional on the ground that it was not direct, and therefore not required to be apportioned. What is most significant about the *Hylton* case is how the Court went about making its decision. As described by Professor David Currie of the University of Chicago Law School, the Court in *Hylton* "paid little heed to the Constitution's words," and "policy considerations dominated all three opinions" filed by the Justices.[13] In fact, each of the opinions asserted that apportioning a carriage tax among the states would be unfair, because a person in a state with fewer carriages would have to pay a higher tax. While this may or may not be unfair, the justices pointed to nothing in the Constitution itself or the intent of the Framers to support their personal views of fairness. Moreover, one of the justices, Justice Patterson, went so far in his opinion as to assert that the constitutional requirement of apportioning direct taxes was "radically wrong," and therefore should not be extended to this case. In other words, he based his decision, at least in part, upon his antipathy to a constitutional provision.

While Justice Patterson went too far in that respect, he and his colleagues on the court could hardly have made a decision in the case by looking to the text of the Constitution or the intent of the Framers. The language of the document simply does not provide an answer to the constitutional issue raised by the situation in *Hylton.* The text of the document merely refers to "direct" taxes and provides no definition of what is meant by a direct tax. Furthermore, as Professor Currie points out, the records of the debates at the Constitutional Convention show that "the Framers had no clear idea of what they meant by direct taxes."[14] Thus, to fulfill their responsibility to decide the case and interpret the law, the justices found it necessary to create meaning for the Constitution.

CREATING MEANING

Indeed, it is often necessary for the Supreme Court to create meaning for the Constitution. This is so because the Constitution, being a document designed (in the words of John Marshall) to "endure for ages,"[15] is rife with general and abstract language. Those two great sources of liberty in the Constitution, the due process and equal protection clauses, are obviously examples of abstract constitutional language that must be invested with meaning. The Fourth Amendment uses extremely general language in prohibiting "unreasonable" searches and seizures, and the Eighth Amendment is similarly general in disallowing "cruel and unusual" punishment.

Even many of the more specific provisions of the Constitution need to be supplied with meaning that simply cannot be found within the four corners of the document. The First Amendment, for instance, states that Congress shall not abridge freedom of speech — but does that mean that the government may not regulate obscene, slanderous, or deceptive speech? The First Amendment also says that Congress shall not abridge the free exercise of religion — does that mean that the government may not prohibit polygamy or child labor when dictated by religious belief? These questions — which, by the way, all arose in actual cases — and, in fact, the vast majority of constitutional questions presented to the Supreme Court, cannot be resolved by mere linguistic analysis of the Constitution. In reality there is no choice but to look beyond the text of the document to provide meaning for the Constitution.

There are those, such as Attorney General Meese, who would hope to find meaning for the Constitution from its authors, the beloved and hallowed Framers of the sacred text. By reputation, these fellows are considered saints and geniuses; in actuality, they were politicians motivated significantly by self-interest.

THEORETICAL DRAWBACKS

But even if the Framers do deserve the awe that they inspire, reliance on their intentions to find meaning for the Constitution still has serious theoretical drawbacks. In the first place, why should we be concerned only with the intentions of the 55 individuals who drafted the Constitution and not the intentions of the people throughout the nation who ratified it, not to mention the intentions of the succeeding generations who retain the Constitution? After all, even when finally framed, the Constitution remained a legal nullity until ratified by the people, and would be a legal nullity again if revoked by the people. The Framers wrote the Constitution, but it is the people who enacted and retain the Constitution; so if anything, it is the people's intent about the document that would seem to be the relevant inquiry.

Moreover, there are considerable difficulties in discerning what in fact the Framers intended. The journal of the Constitutional Convention, which is the primary record of the Framer's intent, is neither complete nor entirely accurate. The notes for the journal were carelessly kept, and have been shown to contain several mistakes.[16]

Even when the record cannot be faulted, it is not always possible to ascertain the Framers' intent. As might be expected, the Framers did not express an intention about every constitutional issue that would arise after the document was drafted and adopted. No group of people, regardless of its members' ability, enjoys that sort of prescience. When the Framers did address particular problems, often only a few of them spoke out. What frequently is taken to be the intent of the Framers as a group turns out to be the intent of merely a few or even only one of the Framers.

There are also constitutional issues about which the Framers expressed conflicting intentions. A collective body of 55 individuals, the Framers embraced a widely diverse and frequently inconsistent set of views. The two principal architects of the Constitution, James Madison and Alexander Hamilton, for instance, had extremely divergent political views. Madison also on occasion differed with George Washington over the meaning of the Constitution. When Washington, who had presided over the Constitutional Convention, became President, he claimed that the underlying intent of the Constitution gave him the sole authority as President to proclaim neutrality and to withhold treaty papers from Congress. Madison, who had been a leader at the Constitutional Convention, disagreed vehemently. And so, the man who would come to be known as the father of this nation and the man who would come to be known as the father of the Constitution had opposing views of what the Framers intended.[17]

These examples demonstrate that it simply makes no sense to suppose that a multi-member group of human beings such as the Framers shared a unitary intent about the kind of controversial political issues addressed in our Constitution. We can see, then, that, at best, the so-called Framers' intent is inadequately documented, ambiguous, and inconclusive; at worst, it is nonexistent, an illusion.

Even if these insurmountable obstacles could be surmounted, there are other serious problems with trying to follow the path laid down by the Framers. The Framers formed their intentions in the context of a past reality and in accordance with past attitudes, both of which have changed considerably since the days when the Constitution was drafted. To transfer those intentions, fashioned as they were under past conditions and views, to contemporary situations may produce sorry consequences that even the Framers would have abhorred had they been able to foresee them. Blindly following intentions formulated in response to past conditions and attitudes is not likely to be an effective means of dealing with the needs of contemporary society.

LOCKED TO THE PAST

Some scholars take this line of reasoning one step further by maintaining that the Framers' intent is inextricably locked to the past and has no meaning at all for the present.[18] In other words, because the Framers formed their intentions with reference to a reality and attitudes that no longer exist, their intentions cannot be transplanted to the present day. What the Framers intended for their times is not what they may have intended for ours. Life constantly changes, and the reality and ideas that surrounded the Framers are long since gone.

The futility of looking to the Framers' intent to resolve modern constitutional issues can be illustrated by several cases that have arisen under the Fourth and Fifth Amendments. The Fourth Amendment prohibits unreasonable searches and seizures, and further requires that no search warrants be issued unless there is probable cause that a crime has been committed. Are bugging and other electronic surveillance devices "unreasonable searches"? May they be used by the police without a warrant based on probable cause? What about the current practice of some law enforcement agencies of using airplanes to fly over a suspect's property to take pictures with a telescopic camera — is that an "unreasonable search"? The Fifth Amendment states that no person shall be compelled to be a witness against himself. What about forcing a suspect to take a breathalyzer test, or a blood test, or to have his or her stomach pumped — do those procedures amount to self-incrimination that violates the Fifth Amendment?

Whatever you may think should be the answers to these questions, you cannot find the answers by looking to the Framers' intent. The Framers had no intent at all about electronic surveillance, airplanes, telescopic cameras, breathalyzer tests, blood tests, or stomach pumping, for the simple reason that none of those things existed until well after the days of the Framers. Not even Benjamin Franklin, for all his inventiveness, was able to foresee that in the twentieth century constables would zip around in flying machines taking snapshots of criminal suspects through a telescopic lens.

Many of the difficulties in attempting to resolve constitutional issues by turning to the Framers are illustrated by the school prayer cases.[19] The religious beliefs of the Framers ranged from theism to atheism, and among even the more devout Framers there was a wide diversity of opinion concerning the proper relationship between church and state. Moreover, as often happens when human beings ponder complex issues, the views of individual Framers about church and state did not remain the same over time. As a member of Congress, James Madison, for example, once voted to approve a chaplain for the House of Representatives, but later decided that the appointment of the chaplain had been unconstitutional.[20] Insofar as school prayer specifically was concerned, the Framers expressed virtually no opinion on the matter, for the simple reason that at the time public schools were extremely rare. Thus, the Framers had no intention, either pro or con, about prayer in public schools.

Given the theoretical deficiencies of trying to decide constitutional questions by looking to the Framers' intent, it should come as no surprise that this approach has been a failure when attempted by the Supreme Court. Scholars who have closely studied the Court's use of this approach commonly agree that it has not been a satisfactory method of constitutional decisionmaking, because the Court ends up manipulating, revising, or even creating history under the guise of following the Framers' intent.[21] The fact of the matter is that neither the Framers' intent nor the words of the document are capable of providing much constitutional meaning.

BARE BONES

What we are left with, then, are the bare bones of a Constitution, the meaning of which must be augmented by the justices of the Supreme Court. And that is exactly what the justices have been doing since the Court was first established. The overwhelming evidence of history shows that the meaning of the Constitution has undergone constant change and evolution at the hands of the Supreme Court. Through the continual interpretation and reinterpretation of the text of the document, the Court perpetually creates new meaning for the document. Although it is formally correct that we, unlike the citizens of Great Britain, have a written Constitution, its words have been defined and redefined to the extent that for the most part we, like the citizens of Great Britain, have an unwritten Constitution, the meaning of which originates with the Supreme Court.

Strict constructionists argue that it is undemocratic for Supreme Court Justices — unelected officials who are unaccountable to the populace — to create meaning for the Constitution. Of course, using the Framers' intent to interpret the Constitution also is undemocratic; following the will of the 55 persons who supposedly framed the Constitution or the smaller group of them who actually participated in the framing is hardly an exercise in democracy.

When strict constructionists cry that the Court is undemocratic, they are ignoring that our government is not (and was not intended by the Framers) to be a pure democracy. Rather, it is a limited or constitutional democracy. What this means is that there are constitutional limits to what the majority may do. The majority may not, for example, engage in racial discrimination, even if it votes to do so in overwhelming numbers. The majority may not abridge freedom of speech or the free exercise of religion or other constitutional rights guaranteed to every individual.

Article III of the Constitution states that there shall be a Supreme Court, and in combination with Article II, decrees the Court's independence from the electorate. By its very terms, the Constitution establishes a counter-majoritarian branch of government, the Supreme Court, in juxtaposition to the more democratic executive and legislative branches. This scheme reflects one of the guiding principles that underlies the Constitution — the principle of separate powers that check and balance one another. The Supreme Court's constitutionally mandated independence functions as a check and balance upon the more majoritarian branches of federal and state governments. It thereby provides a means of maintaining constitutional boundaries on majoritarian rule.

The role of the Supreme Court is to enforce constitutional requirements upon the majoritarian branches of government, which otherwise would be completely unbridled. As dictated by the Constitution, majority control should be the predominant feature of our government, but subject to constitutional limits.

Moreover, the Supreme Court is not quite as undemocratic as the strict constructionists sometimes like to portray it to be. While it is true that the justices who sit on the Court are appointed rather than elected and that they may be removed from office only for improper behavior, it is also true that they are appointed by a popularly elected president, and their appointment must be confirmed by a popularly elected Senate. Turnover of the Court's personnel, which sometimes occurs frequently, enhances popular control of the Court. Additionally, the Court's constitutional rulings may be overruled by the people through constitutional amendment, which, though a difficult procedure, has been accomplished on four occasions.[22] Thus, while the court is not directly answerable to the public, it is not entirely immune from popular control.

THE ULTIMATE AUTHORITY

The people also have the ultimate authority to abolish the Supreme Court. That they have not done so during our two centuries of experience indicates popular acceptance of the Court's role. Admittedly, there are particular decisions rendered by the Court that have aroused considerable public outcry, but given the many controversial issues that the Court must decide, this is inevitable. More telling about the public attitude toward the Court is that the people have taken no action to curtail the Court's authority to interpret the Constitution. Indeed, the public has shown little, if any, inclination toward abolishing the Court or even restricting its powers. Despite Franklin Delano Roosevelt's overwhelming popularity, his "court-packing plan" was a dismal failure;[23] the proposal to establish a "Court of the Union" composed of state court justices which would have the power to overrule the Supreme Court evoked such widespread public disapproval that it was quickly abandoned;[24] the campaigns to impeach Justices Earl Warren and William O. Douglas never got off the ground;[25] and although various members of Congress often propose bills threatening to restrict the Court's jurisdiction, the full Congress always rebuffs those threats.[26] These experiences suggest that even in the face of controversial constitutional decisions, there has been abiding public consent to the role of the Supreme Court in our scheme of government.

The Court's role, when all is said and done, is to create meaning for a Constitution that otherwise would be a hollow document. It is perfectly appropriate for anyone to disagree with Supreme Court decisions, and to criticize the Court on that basis. But it is not appropriate to attack the Court's decisions as illegitimate on the ground that they do not follow the Framers' intent. Pretending to use the Framers' intent to impugn the legitimacy of the Supreme Court is a spurious enterprise. The Court's legitimate function is, and always has been, to provide meaning for the Constitution.

NOTES

1. Address by Attorney General Edwin Meese, III, before the American Bar Association, Washington, D.C. (July 9, 1985); "Q and A with the Attorney General," *American Bar Association Journal* 81, no. 44 (July 1985).

2. Brest, "The Misconceived Quest for the Original Understanding," *Boston University Law Review* 60, no. 204 (1980).

3. Ely, "Constitutional Interpretation: Its Allure and Impossibility," *Indiana Law Journal* 53, no. 399 (1978).

4. Nowak, "Realism, Nihilism, and the Supreme Court: Do the Emperors Have Nothing But Robes?" 22 *Washburn Law Journal* 246, 257 (1983).

5. 410 U.S. 113 (1973).

6. *Reynolds v. Sims*, 377 U.S. 533 (1964).

7. *Engle v. Vitale*, 370 U.S. 421 (1962); *Abington School Dist. v. Schempp*, 374 U.S. 203 (1963).

8. 347 U.S. 483 (1954).

9. See, e.g., Boudin, *Government by Judiciary* 433–43 (New York: W. Goodwin, 1932); Haines, *The American Doctrine of Judicial Supremacy* (Berkeley, Calif.: University of California Press, 1932).

10. Ford (ed.) 9 *Writings of Thomas Jefferson* 275–76 (1902).

11. Grey, "Origins of the Unwritten Constitution: Fundamental Law in American Revolutionary Thought," 30 *Stanford Law Review* 843, 844 (1978).

12. 3 U.S. (3 Dall.) 171 (1796).

13. Currie, *The Constitution in the Supreme Court,* 1789–1888 34 (Chicago: University of Chicago Press, 1985).

14. *Id.* at 36.

15. *McCulloch v. Maryland,* 17 U.S. (4 Wheat.) 316, 414 (1819).

16. See, Rohde & Spaeth, *Supreme Court Decision Making* 41 (1976); 1 *The Records of the Federal Convention of 1787* xii–xiv (Farrand ed. San Francisco: W. H. Freeman, 1937).

17. Burns, *The Vineyard of Liberty* 101–104 (New York: Knopf, 1982).

18. Wofford, "The Blinding Light: The Uses of History in Constitutional Interpretation," 21 *University of Chicago Law Review* 502 (1964).

19. *Supra* n. 7.

20. Strokes & Pfeffer, *Church and State in the United States* 181–82 (Colorado Springs: Shepard's, 1975).

21. See, e.g., tenBroek, "Uses by the United States Supreme Court of Extrinsic Aids in Constitutional Construction," 27 *California Law Review* 399, 404 (1939); Kelly, "Clio and the Court: An Illicit Love Affair," 1965 *Supreme Court Review* 119, 122–25; Alfange, "On Judicial Policymaking and Constitutional Change: Another Look at the 'Original Intent' Theory of Constitutional Interpretation," 5 *Hastings Constitutional Law Quarterly* 603, 617 (1978).

22. The Eleventh Amendment overruled the holding of *Chisholm v. Georgia,* 2 U.S. (2 Dall.) 419 (1793); the Fourteenth Amendment nullified, in part, the decision in *Dred Scott v. Sandford,* 60 U.S. (19 How.) 393 (1857); the Sixteenth Amendment nullified the holding of *Pollack v. Farmers' Loan and Trust, Co.,* 157 U.S. 429 (1895); the Twenty-sixth Amendment neutralized *Oregon v. Mitchell,* 400 U.S. 112 (1970).

23. "Not all the influence of a master politician in the prime of his popularity was quite enough to carry a program that would impair judicial review," McCloskey, *The American Supreme Court* 177 (Chicago: University of Chicago Press, 1960). The plan was rejected vehemently by the Senate Judiciary Committee. See *Senate Comm. on the Judiciary, Reorganization of the Fed. Judiciary Adverse Report,* S. Rep. No. 711, 75th Cong., 1st Sess. 23 (1937).

24. Pfeffer, *This Honorable Court* 424–25 (Boston: Beacon Press, 1965).

25. Those who campaigned for Chief Justice Warren's impeachment were unable to have impeachment proceedings initiated against him. While impeachment proceedings were instituted against Justice Douglas, they never got beyond the subcommittee stage and were eventually forsaken. See *Special Subcomm. on H. Res., 920 of the House Comm. on the Judiciary,* 91 Cong., 2d Sess., Final Report, Associate Justice William O. Douglas (Comm. Print 1970).

26. "In the fifteen year between 1953 and 1968, over sixty bills were introduced in Congress to eliminate the jurisdiction of the federal courts over a variety of specific subjects; none of these became law." Bator, Mishkin, Shapiro & Wechsler, *Hart & Wechsler's the Federal Courts and the Federal System* 360 (Mineola, N.Y.: Foundation Press, 2d ed. 1973).

Questions for Discussion

1. What kinds of contemporary issues would the Framers have never contemplated?
2. What consequences about strict interpretivism can be drawn from your answer to Question 1?
3. How would you evaluate the qualifications of a person nominated to the Supreme Court who accepts the strict constructionist viewpoint?
4. Can the noninterpretivist view be reconciled with the U.S. system of democratic rule? What are the reasons for your answer?
5. Does the Constitution as written require the judiciary to follow the principle of judicial restraint? What are the reasons for your answer?

Suggested Readings

Barnum, David G. *The Supreme Court and American Democracy*. New York: St. Martin's Press, 1993.

Bryden, David P. "A Conservative Case for Judicial Review." *Public Interest*, no. 111 (Spring 1993): 72–85.

Clegg, Roger. "Curbing Our Imperial Courts." *American Enterprise* 6, no. 3 (May/June 1995): 61–63.

Farber, Daniel A. "The Originalism Debate: A Guide for the Perplexed." *Ohio State Law Journal* 49, no. 4 (1989): 1085–1106.

Franck, Matthew. *Against the Imperial Judiciary: The Supreme Court vs. the Sovereignty of the People*. Lawrence: Univ. Press of Kansas, 1996.

Gangi, William. *Saving the Constitution from the Courts*. Norman: Univ. of Oklahoma Press, 1995.

McKeever, Robert J. *Raw Judicial Power? The Supreme Court and American Society*. Manchester, Eng.: Manchester Univ. Press, 1993.

O'Brien, David M. *Storm Center: The Supreme Court in American Politics*, 6th ed. New York: W. W. Norton, 1996.

Quirk, William J., and R. Randall Bridwell. *Judicial Dictatorship*. New Brunswick, N.J.: Transaction Publishers, 1995.

Wolfe, Christopher. *Judicial Activism: Bulwark of Freedom or Precarious Security?* Pacific Grove, Calif.: Brooks/Cole, 1991.

Chapter 18

Is Criminal Misconduct the Only Justification for Removing a Federal Judge?

At 5 AM on April 21, 1995, undercover police observed a car bearing Michigan license plates slowly driving along the streets of Washington Heights, a drug-ridden area in uptown Manhattan. When the car, which was driven by a woman alone, stopped, four men loaded two duffel bags into the woman's trunk as she remained behind the steering wheel. The men spotted the police and fled quickly. The police stopped the woman, Carol Bayless. Believing that they had "reasonable suspicion" that drugs were in the duffel bags, they searched the items and found 80 pounds of cocaine and heroin. They arrested Ms. Bayless.

Federal district judge Harold Baer, Jr. held a hearing in the matter of *United States v. Carol Bayless.* In January 1996, he ruled that the police should not have searched the car. He said: "The mere presence of an individual in a neighborhood known for its drug activity . . . fails to raise a reasonable suspicion that the person observed is there to purchase drugs. . . ." He also said that the particular hour of the day in which the incident occurred should not give rise to a reasonable suspicion that a person is involved in criminal activity although it "may constitute an articulable fact to consider."

Judge Baer then commented on police behavior. He said that although one or more of the males ran from the corner once they were aware of the officers' presence, "it is hard to characterize this as evasive conduct." The judge alluded to the fact that an investigatory commission found that residents in the neighborhood "tended to regard police officers as corrupt, abusive and violent. After the attendant publicity surrounding the above event [the hearings and final report of the commission], had the men not run when the cops began to stare at them, it would have been unusual."[1]

The Baer decision provoked a political outburst of criticism. Bob Dole, Senate Majority leader, called for Baer's impeachment, and 150 members of Congress, mostly Republicans, wrote a letter to President Clinton asking the president to seek Baer's resignation. House Speaker Newt Gingrich commented: "This is the kind of pro–drug dealer, pro–crime, anti–police and anti–law enforcement attitude that makes it so hard for us to win the war on drugs."[2] New York City Mayor Rudolph Giuliani also criticized the ruling but did not call for the judge to be removed.

Reporters inquired about the views of President Clinton, who had appointed Baer to his judgeship. At first White House spokesman Michael McCurry indicated that the Clinton administration was critical of the decision and that the president might ask the judge to resign. But later, Jack Quinn, counsel to the president, clarified the president's position. Quinn observed that the president felt that the decision was grievously wrong but that the best way to contest judicial decisions was to challenge them in the courts. The president supported the independence of the judiciary, Quinn noted.[3]

The judge did not resign. On March 15, 1996, Judge Baer held a rehearing of the case. In a decision released on April 1, he reversed his earlier decision, and reinstated the evidence. He noted that the police testimony was more credible than that of Bayless. In May, Judge Baer removed himself from hearing the case.

The decision of the judge brought to national attention the issue of the independence of judges in making unpopular decisions. Federal judges are appointed for life. Article III, Section 1 of the Constitution stipulates that federal judges may continue in office during good behavior and prohibits the diminution of their compensation. Under Article I, federal judges, like other civil officers, may be removed from office against their will if they are impeached and convicted for "high crimes and misdemeanors." But if they do not commit a crime, should they be dismissed when making a decision that is regarded as wrong?

Speaking at the Washington College of Law Centennial Celebration at American University in Washington, D.C., Chief Justice William Rehnquist championed judicial independence as vital to the functioning of the federal court system. Although he made no direct reference to Judge Baer, his comments were believed to be directed at the Baer controversy. His speech notes that Congress has taken actions over the years to clarify the constitutional provisions dealing with removal from office. In Thomas Jefferson's presidency, the House of Representatives impeached Samuel Chase, an associate justice of the Supreme Court, for delivering a partisan charge to a grand jury and for other offenses based on his conduct during another trial. The Senate, however, did not garner the two-thirds majority necessary to convict, and Chase, consequently, was acquitted. This move, along with the decision of the Supreme Court in *Marbury v. Madison* recognizing the authority of the federal courts to declare legislative acts unconstitutional, signified that federal judges would not be removed from office by impeachment and conviction for their rulings from the bench. The principle has been established that only criminal conduct is the basis for removal, and this principle is a good one.

Columnist Jeff Jacoby takes issue with Rehnquist. He indicates that criminal misconduct should not be the only basis for removal of a judge. Otherwise a judge who is incompetent can remain on the court "if he exercises unsound judgment or perverts justice or endangers the public with scandalous rulings." The Constitution does not say that judges are exempt from the system of checks and balances. It is for Congress to decide the meaning of "good behavior." When judges make "abominable" rulings, the people have a right to remove them.

NOTES

1. "Excerpts from Ruling on Search," *New York Times*, January 28, 1996, p. 27.
2. Ian Fisher, "Gingrich Asks Judge's Ouster for Ruling Out Drug Evidence," *New York Times*, March 7, 1996, p. B4.
3. See Linda Greenhouse, "Judges as Political Issues," *New York Times*, March 23, 1996, pp. 1, 11.

☑ *YES*

Is Criminal Misconduct the Only Justification for Removing a Federal Judge?

WILLIAM REHNQUIST
On Judicial Independence

I have said that the judiciary must change with the changing times. But there are a very few essentials that are vital to the functioning of the federal court system as we know it. Surely one of these essentials is the independence of the judges who sit on these courts.

Article III of the Constitution guarantees to federal judges the right to continue in office during good behavior, and prohibits the diminution of their compensation. But these two constitutional provisions did not settle every question about the independence of the judiciary. As a result, there have been several actions by Congress over the years which have fleshed out the constitutional provision in a manner akin to the development of an "unwritten constitution" in Great Britain.

Article I of the Constitution provides that civil officers — including judges — may be impeached by the House of Representatives for "high crimes and misdemeanors," and if convicted by the Senate may be thereupon removed from office. The term "high crimes and misdemeanors" was sufficiently amorphous to leave open the possibility that a federal judge could be removed from office, not only for conduct that was criminal, but for rulings from the bench that seemed flagrantly wrong.

An important episode early in our nation's history in effect resolved this question. This was the impeachment trial of Samuel Chase, then an Associate Justice of the Supreme Court, in 1805. Chase had been appointed to the Supreme Court by George Washington in 1796, but in those days the

Supreme Court docket was even lighter than it is today; Supreme Court justices spent most of their judicial time riding circuit trying lawsuits in tandem with the resident judge. Chase was a striking figure physically — over six feet tall, with a ruddy complexion which earned him the sobriquet (behind his back, of course) of "Old Bacon Face." He was able but imperious, and totally lacking in the patience necessary for a trial judge.

Two years after Thomas Jefferson took office as President, in 1803, Chase delivered a partisan charge to a grand jury in Baltimore. Jefferson, learning of this, wrote to his lieutenants in the House of Representatives suggesting that they do something about it. The House proceeded to impeach Chase on a number of counts. The first count was the charge to the Baltimore grand jury. Other counts were based on his conduct of the trial of John Fries for treason in Philadelphia in 1800, and still others were based on his conduct in the trial of James Callender in Richmond for violation of the Sedition Act in the same year. The trial before the Senate began in February, 1805, presided over by the Vice President, Aaron Burr. Burr himself was a fugitive from justice at the time, having killed Alexander Hamilton in a duel at Weehawken, New Jersey, the preceding summer. Criminal indictments were out for him in both New Jersey and New York, which caused one wag to remark that whereas in most courts the criminal was arraigned before the judge, in this court the judge was arraigned before the criminal.

More than fifty witnesses testified before the Senate. The charges pertaining to the Fries trial did not amount to much — at the most they showed him to be headstrong and somewhat domineering, a trait not unknown in other federal judges. The charges in connection with the Callender trial were a good deal more serious. Callender was charged under the Sedition Act with bringing President John Adams into disrepute, inasmuch as he called him a toady to British interests in a long and incredibly turgid book entitled *The Prospect Before Us.* The evidence showed that Chase had actually taken the book with him from Baltimore to Richmond in order to allow the grand jury to consider it, and that during the stagecoach trip from Baltimore to Richmond he referred to Callender as a "scoundrel" to another passenger.

On March 1, 1805, the Senate convened to vote on the articles of impeachment against Chase. At that time there were thirty-four senators, twenty-five of whom were Jeffersonian Republicans. If these senators voted a party line, there would be the necessary two-thirds majority to convict Chase and remove him from office. Happily, they broke ranks. On the articles based on the Fries trial, the vote was sixteen to convict, and eighteen to acquit. The vote on the articles relating to the Callender trial was eighteen to convict, and sixteen for acquittal. On the count based on the charge to the Baltimore grand jury, the House managers came closest to prevailing — nineteen senators voted guilty, and fifteen voted not guilty. But even this number fell four votes short of the two-thirds majority required, and Chase was therefore acquitted on all of the counts against him.

This decision by the Senate was enormously important in securing the kind of judicial independence contemplated by Article III. Coming only two years after the seminal decision of the Court in *Marbury v. Madison,* it coupled with the authority of the federal courts to declare legislative acts unconstitutional the assurance to federal judges that their judicial acts — their rulings from the bench — would not be a basis for removal from office by impeachment and conviction. And that has been the guiding principle of the House of Representatives and the Senate from that day to this; federal judges have been impeached and convicted — happily, only a very few — but it has been for criminal conduct such as tax evasion, perjury, and the like.

This principle only goes so far. It obviously does not mean that federal judges should not be criticized for the decisions which they make; they are frequently so criticized by the media and by law review, and there is certainly no reason why other citizens should not engage in the same practice. And the doctrine of judicial independence does not mean that the country will be forever in sway to groups of non-elected judges. When vacancies occur through death or retirement on any of the federal courts, replacements are nominated by the President, who has been elected by the people of the entire nation, subject to confirmation by the Senate, whose members have been elected by the people of their respective states. Both the President and the Senate have felt free to take into consideration the likely judicial philosophy of any nominee to the federal courts. Thus there is indirect popular input into the selection of federal judges.

This principle is perhaps best illustrated by the experience of President Franklin Roosevelt with appointments to the Supreme Court. Dissatisfied with decisions of that court which invalidated some provisions of his New Deal program, he asked Congress to enact what soon became known as a "court-packing plan," which would allow him to replace any Justice over seventy who did not retire with an additional Justice, up to the number of fifteen. This rather bald effort to change the philosophy of the Court was rejected by the United States Senate in 1937. But although Roosevelt lost that battle, he eventually won the war by serving three full terms as President and appointing eight of the nine members of the Court. This simply shows that there is a wrong way and a right way to go about putting a popular imprint on the judiciary.

The framers of the United States Constitution came up with two quite original ideas — the first was the idea of a chief executive who was not responsible to the legislature, as Chief Executives are under the parliamentary system. The second was the idea of an independent judiciary with the authority to declare laws passed by Congress unconstitutional. The first idea — a President not responsible to Congress — has not been widely copied by other nations in the Western world when they have come to review their systems of government. But the second idea — that of an independent judiciary with the authority to finally interpret a written constitution — has caught on with many other nations, particularly since the end of the Second World War. It is one of the crown jewels of our system of government today.

Change is the law of life, and the judiciary will have to change to meet the challenges which will face it in the future. But the independence of the federal judiciary is essential to its proper functioning and must be retained.

☑ *NO*

Is Criminal Misconduct the Only Justification for Removing a Federal Judge?

JEFF JACOBY

Judges Aren't Untouchable — Incompetent Ones Should Be Impeached

In the matter of William Rehnquist vs. Bill Clinton, Bob Dole, Newt Gingrich, et al., I'll take my stand with the politicians.

Speaking at American University last week, the chief justice delivered a sermon on the subject of judicial independence. His remarks were meant as a rebuke to the president, the Senate majority leader and the speaker of the House, all of whom had gone so far in criticizing a federal judge — the Hon. Harold Baer Jr. of New York — as to suggest that he be expelled from the bench. Since federal judges enjoy lifetime appointments, the only way to remove Baer would be to impeach him or to pressure him to resign. Dole proposed the former; Clinton and Gingrich (along with 150 House members), the latter.

For shame, scolded Rehnquist. Such threats amount to an assault on "one of the crown jewels of our system of government," namely, the confidence of federal judges "that their judicial acts — their rulings from the bench — would not be a basis for removal from office by impeachment and conviction." In Rehnquist's view, the only justification for forcing a judge to step down is "criminal conduct such as tax evasion, perjury and the like."

In other words, if a judge lies or steals, he can be stripped of his robe. But if a judge is *incompetent* — if he exercises unsound judgment or perverts justice or endangers the public with scandalous rulings — he should be immune from discipline.

This is "one of the crown jewels of our system"?

Recall what Judge Baer did to ignite this firestorm: He ruled that $4 million worth of cocaine and heroin seized from a woman's rented car in a high-crime section of New York was inadmissible as evidence against her, since the police had searched her car without reasonable suspicion. And why was their suspicion not reasonable? Because all they saw were four men stuffing duffel bags into the trunk of her car — and running away when they spotted the police. Nothing suspicious about that, said Baer — boys in the 'hood don't like cops. "Had the men *not* run when the cops began to stare at them," he wrote, "it would have been unusual."

That wasn't all. If the search was illegal, the woman's subsequent arrest was illegal, too. So Baer also threw out her videotaped confession that she was an experienced drug courier who regularly made the run between Detroit and Manhattan and was being paid $20,000 for this trip. Bottom line: Evidence suppressed, charges dropped, professional criminal given a pass.

There followed an eruption of criticism, complete with the impeachment rumbles; in due course, Judge Baer saw the light (read: felt the heat) and reversed himself. But the question remains: Does this man belong on the federal bench?

And if the consensus is that he — or any other judge — does not, how do we get rid of him?

You don't, say Rehnquist and the judicial fraternity. Judges may be impeached only for "high crimes and misdemeanors." Absent that, the only remedy for an intolerable judge is to await his death or retirement. This, in Rehnquist's words, is the sacred "doctrine of judicial independence."

It is also nonsense.

Nowhere does the Constitution decree that judges shall be untouchable gods, exempt from the checks and balances that bridle the other branches of government. In the system the Framers devised, the people — not the judges — are sovereign. Just as the executive and legislative branches are controllable by the people, so is the judicial branch. And the tool for dislodging judges who have lost the public's confidence or abused its trust is impeachment.

Not only for "high crimes and misdemeanors," either. That phrase comes from Article II of the Constitution, which deals with the presidency; it is the standard set forth for removing "the President, Vice President and all civil Officers of the United States." But Article III, which covers the judicial branch, expresses a far more flexible standard: "The Judges, both of the supreme and inferior Courts, shall hold their Offices during good Behavior." What is "good behavior"? That is for the House and Senate to decide.

Were there political motives in the attack on Baer's ruling? Sure there were. The Republicans wanted to score points against Clinton, who appointed him; the president wanted to deflect their criticism by coopting it. Moreover, Baer is widely reported to be a conscientious man; I've no doubt he firmly believed in the rightness of his ruling.

Nevertheless. If a Democratic president, the Republican leaders of Congress, 150 members of the House, numerous local officials, and a great swath of the public all agree that a judge's ruling was an abomination, that's a fairly good indication that it *was* an abomination. A judge who issues abominable rulings, however sincerely, breaches his constitutional obligation of "good behavior" — and the people have the right to get rid of him.

The impeachment tool has grown rusty with disuse. It ought to be resorted to more frequently. When judges make blunders that shock the conscience, calls for their removal aren't cheap shots. They are healthy and honest, and just what the Framers intended.

Questions for Discussion

1. Should considerations of removal for office be different for judges than for other federal officials? What are the reasons for your answer?
2. How would you interpret the provisions of the Constitution dealing with removal of federal officials?
3. What criteria should be used to determine the kinds of noncriminal behavior of a judge in court that make the judge's rulings "abominable"?
4. Who should decide whether a judge's rulings are abominable? What are the reasons for your answer?
5. What would be the consequences to judicial behavior if federal judges may be removed for conduct that is legal but unpopular?

Suggested Readings

Cutler, Lloyd N. "Unfair to Judge Baer." *Washington Post*, March 27, 1996, p. A15.

Fisher, Ian. "Gingrich Asks Judge's Ouster for Ruling Out Drug Evidence." *New York Times*, March 7, 1996, p. B4.

Goshko, John M. "Accusations of Coddling Criminals Aimed at Two Judges in New York." *Washington Post*, March 14, 1996, p. A3.

———— and Nancy Reckler. "Controversial Drug Ruling Is Reversed." *Washington Post*, April 2, 1996, pp. A1, A5.

Greenhouse, Linda. "Judges As Political Issues." *New York Times*, March 23, 1996, pp. 1, 11.

Lewis, Anthony. "Where Should You Hide?" *New York Times*, April 8, 1996, p. A15.

"Perspectives on Court-Congress Relations: The View from the Hill and the Federal Bench." *Judicature* 79, no. 6 (May/June 1996): 303–309.

Pollak, Louis H. "Criticizing Judges." *Judicature* 79, no. 6 (May/June 1996): 299–302.

Roberts, Paul Craig. "Bench Mark for Impeachment." *Wall Street Journal*, February 12, 1996, p. A15.

Van Natta, Don, Jr. "Dismissing Defense Effort, Judge Stays on Drug Case." *New York Times*, April 13, 1996, p. 25.

————. "Judge Baer Takes Himself Off Drug Case." *New York Times*, May 17, 1996, p. B1.

————. "Judge's Ruling Likely to Stand." *New York Times*, January 28, 1996, p. 27.

————. "Judge to Hear Bid to Reverse a Drug Ruling." *New York Times*, February 3, 1996, pp. 25, 27.

————. "Officer's Credibility Is Key for Judge Rehearing Case." *New York Times*, March 16, 1996, p. A26.

Public Policy

P olitical democracy involves a contest over public policy. An element of that contest includes convincing individuals, private groups, and political leaders that particular policies are wise and just. An underlying theme of democratic rule is that conflicts should be resolved peacefully through discussion, freedom of association, and agreed-upon procedures for determining policy outcomes.

People who choose sides on different issues of public policy do so for many reasons. Sometimes, the choice is based on self-interest, as when a manufacturer or trade union favors protectionism so as to reduce competition from abroad. At other times, the choice is based on a perception of justice, as in issues relating to the elimination of racism or the protection of the environment. Often, choices derive from a combination of self-interested and altruistic impulses.

Part V deals with some contemporary issues in domestic and foreign policy matters of concern to the people of the United States. Specifically, the debate questions consider gun control, drug decriminalization, global warming, and the United Nations.

Chapter 19

Will Gun Control Laws Reduce Violence?

Firearms take a heavy toll of life and limb in the United States. According to the Federal Bureau of Investigation, firearms were responsible for 15,456 murders in the United States in 1994. Of this number 12,769 were committed with handguns.[1] Handguns are also responsible for suicides and accidental deaths, and they are used in a multitude of crimes, including theft, assault, and rape.

Young people live in a world of guns. Particularly in the inner cities, children of all ages hear gunshots on their streets; know people who have been threatened, wounded, or killed by guns; and even have guns of their own. Metal detectors have been installed in schools to prevent youngsters from carrying weapons into the classrooms.

National interest has focused on guns as responsible for much violent crime not only from personal experience but also because of incidents that have attracted national attention. To cite a few:

- In 1968, Robert Kennedy, a U.S. senator from New York, and brother of the slain president, was assassinated with a firearm.
- In 1981, John Hinckley used a handgun in attempting to assassinate President Ronald Reagan. He wounded the president and caused serious and permanent injury to James Brady, the president's press secretary.
- In January 1991, Patrick Purdy opened fire with a Kalashnikov-type semiautomatic rifle in a Stockton California, schoolyard. He killed five children and wounded nearly thirty others.
- On December 7, 1993, Colin Furguson opened fire on a crowded Long Island Railroad commuter train. He declared war on "whites, Asians, and 'Uncle Tom Negroes." He killed six people and wounded nineteen.

The high number of killings by firearms has led to calls for laws that would regulate their possession or use or even ban them. Already on the books is a 1934 statute, the National Firearms Act, which makes it difficult to obtain types of firearms perceived to be especially lethal or to be the chosen weapons of gangsters. Among these weapons are machine guns and sawed-off shotguns. The 1934 law also provides for a firearm registration system.

Passed in 1968, the Gun Control Act requires all persons dealing in firearms to be federally licensed. It also tightens federal licensing procedures, prohibits the interstate sale of handguns generally, prescribes categories of individuals to whom firearms and ammunition cannot be sold, prohibits the importation of nonsporting firearms or ammunition, requires that dealers maintain records of all commercial gun sales, and contains other regulatory provisions. In 1986, the McClure-Volkmer Amendments (named for Senator James A. McClure, a Republican from Idaho, and Representative Harold L. Volkmer, a Democrat from Missouri) to the Gun Control Act banned the further manufacture of machine guns. They also tightened enforcement of gun control laws at the same time that they modified or eliminated provisions of the existing law that were opposed by gun owners and the gun industry.

On November 30, 1993, President Bill Clinton signed into law the Brady Bill (named after James Brady). The law, which went into effect in 1994, requires a five-day waiting period during which local police are required to conduct a criminal background check of prospective handgun buyers. Some states and localities, moreover, have enacted laws that are more stringent than federal laws, including the banning of all handguns (except for law enforcement officers).

In 1994, President Clinton signed into law an anticrime bill. One of its provisions banned for ten years the manufacture, sale, and possession of nineteen types of assault weapons and "copycat" versions of those guns. Assault weapons are military-style or police-style weapons with large clips holding twenty to thirty bullets. The law also banned some guns with two or more features associated with assault weapons. But it specifically excluded 650 types of semiautomatic weapons.

The debate over gun control is a continuing one, involving such matters as social science research and legal issues. Advocates and opponents of gun control differ in their assessment of the facts, especially whether social science data prove that gun control deters violent crime. They also disagree in their interpretations of the Second Amendment to the Constitution, which reads: "A well regulated Militia, being necessary to the security of a free State, the right of the people to keep and bear Arms, shall not be infringed."

The debate on gun control and violence is joined in the two articles below that are written by organizations that are key players in the politics of gun control: the Coalition to Stop Gun Violence (CSGV) and the National Rifle Association (NRA). CSGV, an organization committed to eliminating the private sale of handguns and assault weapons in the United States, makes a case for gun control. It contends:

1. Firearm violence is increasing in the United States. It is currently the second leading cause of injury-related death in the United States.
2. The murder rate in the United States surpasses that of every other industrialized country in the world. One reason is that

many other industrialized countries virtually ban handguns and assault weapons.

3. Gun control would reduce the number of suicides and accidental deaths.
4. The primary purpose of a handgun is to kill human beings.
5. Assault weapons are the most commonly traced firearms for organized crime and drug trafficking offenses.
6. The cost to treat victims of firearm violence is overwhelming. Much of the cost of health care expenses due to gunshot injuries and fatalities is paid at taxpayer expense.
7. Gun control will reduce violence.
8. Firearm ownership is not an absolute individual right, assured to citizens by the Second Amendment to the Constitution.
9. Keeping a handgun in the home for self-defense places a gun owner and his or her family in great jeopardy.
10. Every major law enforcement organization and the majority of the American citizenry approve legislation that makes handguns more difficult to acquire.

For its part, the NRA Institute for Legislative Action, the legislative arm of the NRA, opposes gun control. It argues:

1. The majority of Americans generally, and law-enforcement officials specifically, are opposed to gun control.
2. The most commonly cited reason for owning a handgun is protection against criminals.
3. Americans use guns for protection from criminals. It is not true that a gun in a home is many times more likely to kill a family member than to stop a criminal.
4. The registration and licensing of guns have no effect on crime, as criminals, by definition, do not obey laws.
5. Differences in a nation's collection of crime data and disparities in political, cultural, racial, religious, and economic conditions explain why some countries have high crime rates and others do not. Gun control does not deserve credit for low crime rates in Britain, Japan, or other nations.
6. Most murders are not argument-related "crimes of passion" against a relative, neighbor, friend, or acquaintance. On the contrary, the vast majority of murders are committed by persons with long-established patterns of violent criminal behavior.
7. Semiautomatic military and military-style rifles have a legitimate sporting purpose.
8. The Second Amendment to the Constitution gives citizens an individual right to bear arms.

9. Carry laws that prevent law-abiding citizens from carrying weapons result in more deaths and injuries than permissive carry laws.
10. Gun laws have a negative effect on crime.

NOTE

1. *Uniform Crime Reports for the United States, 1994* (Washington, D.C.: Government Printing Office, 1995), table 2.10, p. 18.

☑ *YES*

Will Gun Control Laws Reduce Violence?

COALITION TO STOP GUN VIOLENCE
Gun Violence in America

THE EXTENT OF GUN VIOLENCE

Firearm violence is currently the second leading cause of injury-related death, behind automobile-related fatalities, in the United States, and this violence is increasing at an alarming rate. By the year 2003, firearm fatalities are projected to become the United States' leading cause of injury-related death, unless the violence is curbed.[1] In 1991, Texas and Louisiana, two of the states leading the nation in gun ownership per capita, saw firearm fatalities surpass automobile fatalities. The District of Columbia, New York, Virginia, Nevada, and California also have followed this trend. In fact, the firearm death rate is increasing faster than any other cause of death except AIDS [acquired immune deficiency syndrome]-related fatalities.[2]

Firearms claimed the lives of 39,595 people in the United States in 1993. Of these deaths, 18,940 were suicides, 18,571 were firearm homicides, 1,521 were unintentional shootings, and 563 were of undetermined cause.[3] This marks a 25.4 percent increase in firearm fatalities since 1985.

In 1993, the firearm fatality rate averaged 15.4 per 100,000 persons in the United States. Males have a firearm fatality rate (26.8 per 100,000) six times that of females (4.5). The rate for blacks (36.6) was nearly three times that for whites (12.5). Black males between the ages of 15 and 24 years are the group most at risk. They were killed by firearms at the rate of 179.0 per 100,000.[4] If the rest of the American population were being killed at the same rate as that of young black men, over 460,000 people would die of gunshots each year.[5]

HOMICIDE

In 1994, there were 23,305 homicides in the U.S. according to the Federal Bureau of Investigation (FBI). Of these, 15,456 involved firearms and 13,483 involved handguns alone. From 1985 to 1994, the nation's murder rate increased 22.8 percent, the firearm murder rate increased over 45.8 percent, and the handgun murder rate increased 65.2 percent. Handguns have fueled the increase in total homicides. While handguns represent only one-third of all firearms privately owned in the United States, they were responsible for 58 percent of all homicides and 82.6 percent of all firearm homicides. Since 1985, murder by handguns has risen steadily as instances of murder with all other weapons actually have declined.[6] Over the last five decades, the increasing rate of firearm deaths in the United States has paralleled the rate of firearms production.[7]

The notion that gun violence is solely related to gang and drug violence is a myth. In 1994, the most common reason leading to a homicide was an "argument," representing 28 percent of all homicides. Most incidents of gun violence occur in the home, not on the streets in gang warfare. The FBI reports that drug crimes and gang killings account for only 7.0 percent and 0.6 percent, respectively, of gun-related homicides in 1994.[8]

INTERNATIONAL COMPARISONS

The murder rate in the United States surpasses that of every other industrialized country in the world. The murder rate in Washington, D.C., is fifteen times greater than that in Northern Ireland, a nation plagued by terrorism.[9] This level of handgun violence does not occur in other developed nations. In 1990, handguns were used to murder 22 people in Great Britain, 68 in Canada, 87 in Japan, and 11,719 in the U.S.[10]

The number of young men killed in the U.S. versus the rest of the world also is staggering. In 1990, the homicide rate per 100,000 population for males ages 15–24 was as follows.[11]

United States	37.2
Italy	4.3
Germany	1.1
Canada	0.9
United Kingdom	0.6
Japan	0.5

Why is there such a large discrepancy between these nations? One reason is that in Germany, France, Canada, Britain, and Japan, handguns and assault weapons are virtually banned from the general public.

A study by Arthur Kellermann comparing the rates of firearm violence in Seattle, Washington, and Vancouver, Canada, demonstrates how a ban on handguns in the United States would decrease violence. These two cities are less than three hours apart by car and are culturally similar in many ways. However, Vancouver regulates handguns strictly. The two cities have similar rates of burglary, robbery, and assault, but in Seattle there is an almost five times greater risk of being murdered with a handgun than in Vancouver.[12]

SUICIDE

Approximately 60 percent of all suicides in the United States involve guns.[13] Research indicates as many as 69 percent of firearm suicides involve handguns.[14] In 1993, the last year for which figures are available, there were 18,940 firearm-related suicides, outnumbering firearm homicides that year by 369.[15] The rate of firearm suicide has risen for the last several decades while suicide by all other means has remained unchanged.[16] The increases among women and young people in particular are alarming.

Firearms are the method of suicide used most frequently by both males and females and by all age groups.[17] Perhaps the most alarming fact regarding firearm suicide is that over 92 percent of attempts are fatal. Firearms do not allow time for intervention or a change of heart and, therefore, rarely give a suicide victim a second chance for life.[18]

Historically, males complete suicide two[19] to five[20] times more often than females because males tend to use more lethal methods such as guns. However, females attempt suicide two[21] to nine[22] times more often than males. The increase in the use of firearms as a method of suicide among women has resulted in a dramatic increase in female suicide fatalities. In 1960, the method of suicide most frequently employed by females was poison. That year, only 25.3 percent of female suicide victims used a gun. By 1989, the percentage of female suicide fatalities involving firearms increased to 41 percent.[23]

Firearm suicide also has increased among the young. In fact, since 1980, the majority of suicide victims have been 40 years or younger.[24] From 1980 to 1992, the suicide rate for persons 15 to 19 years of age increased 28.3 percent, and the rate for persons 10 to 14 increased by 120 percent.[25] Suicides using firearms account for most of this increase.

UNINTENTIONAL SHOOTINGS

People who keep guns in the home for self-protection place themselves and their families at risk, particularly when the firearm is kept loaded and in an unsecured area. In 1991, there were 1,441 unintentional shooting fatalities. Of these, 551 fatalities were children 19 years of age and younger.[26] Research shows that many gun owners do not take safety precautions. For instance, half of all gun owners keep their firearms in an unlocked area. One-fourth keep their firearms unlocked and loaded, leaving their guns vulnerable to theft, accidental shootings, suicide, and homicide.[27] A 1995 survey found that 59 percent of parents who admitted to having a gun in the home did not lock the gun away from their children.[28]

FIREARM INJURIES

The murder rate is only one way to measure violence in the United States. While 39,595 people died in 1993 from firearm-related injuries, the total number of people injured by firearms is not known. No accurate means of data collection exists to count the number of incidents of firearm-related injuries each year. Researchers estimate there are from four to twelve nonfatal gun-related injuries for every gun-related death.[29] This means between 198,000 and 515,000 people were victims of firearm violence in 1993. Most researchers accept 7.5 as the best estimated ratio of nonfatal firearm injuries to firearm fatalities. If firearm violence remains at its current level, researchers predict nearly 3 million firearm shootings, fatal and nonfatal, will occur between the years 1993 and 2000.[30]

The Sporting Arms and Ammunition Manufacturers' Institute, Inc. (SAAMI), a gun industry trade association, admits that 1 of every 100 firearms "purchased lawfully from licensed dealers at retail are ever involved with any human gunshot wounds."[31] Imagine any other industry publicly admitting that 1 of every 100 of its products will cause an injury and 1 of every 750 will cause death.

KIDS & GUNS

Perhaps the greatest tragedy of gun violence is the tremendous numbers of children and youth killed or injured each year by firearms — and these numbers are increasing at an alarming rate. In 1985, the number of firearm homicides for youth 19 years and younger was 1,339.[32] In 1993, it was 2,928. That year, guns accounted for 85.9 percent of homicides of persons 15 to 18 years of age.[33] Gun violence is the leading cause of death for black males ages 5 to 19.[34]

Youth suicide also has increased. In 1985, there were 1,256 firearm suicides for youths 10 to 19 years of age.[35] In 1991, this number increased to 1,436. Unintentional firearm deaths among children 19 years of age and under totaled 551 in 1991.

In the same year, a total of 5,356 children 19 years of age and younger died by firearm homicide, suicide, unintentional shootings, and unknown circumstances.[36] On average, more than 14 kids each day are killed by gunshots.

More and more young people are in possession of firearms. A national survey in 1990 by the Centers for Disease Control revealed that 1 in 20 high school students reported carrying a firearm, usually a handgun, in the past month.[37] In 1992, 54,200 juveniles were arrested for weapons violations.[38] In 1976, 59 percent of murders committed by juveniles involved a gun. In 1991, that number had increased to 78 percent.[39]

GUNS IN SCHOOLS

Gun violence in our nation's schools is becoming more prevalent. A 1994 Gallup poll of Americans shows that for the first time, "fighting, violence, and gangs" moved to the top of the list to tie with "lack of discipline" as the biggest problem facing schools.[40] No longer a safe haven for learning, schools have come to reflect the violence found on the streets.

Many students fear violent attacks traveling to and from school as well as within school itself. This fear leads many young people to conclude mistakenly that a gun is their best means of defense. It is difficult to determine what effect the threat of violence has upon the learning of each student, but clearly education takes a back seat to one's own sense of security and well-being.

How violent have our schools become, and how do today's students cope with this violence?

- A 1990 survey conducted by the Centers for Disease Control found that 1 in 20 high school students carried a gun in the past month.[41]
- A 1994 poll conducted by Lou Harris found that only 1 in 5 students would tell a teacher if he or she knew of another student carrying weapons to school.[42]

Theories differ about where young people get their guns. School security experts and law enforcement officials estimate that 80 percent of the firearms students bring to school come from home, while students estimate that 40 percent of their peers who bring guns to school buy them on the street.[43] The Chicago-based Joyce Foundation conducted a poll which found that only 43 percent of parents with children under 18 years of age who own a gun keep that gun safely locked.[44] An estimated 1.2 million elementary-aged, latchkey children have access to guns in their homes.[45] Parents must take more responsibility for their children's actions and their children's safety.

The measures taken by schools to curb the flow of guns into schools have been largely ineffective. Metal detectors, both hand-held and walk-through, provide little resistance to students determined to bring a gun to school. Most schools lack sufficient funds to purchase or enact adequate security measures.

Moreover, metal-detector searches are time-consuming, especially considering that to be entirely effective, hundreds and even thousands of students must be processed through a single checkpoint. In short, metal detectors are both inefficient and ineffective, but little else has been proposed to prevent guns from entering schools.

As of October 1995, 47 states adopted policies of mandatory suspension for students who bring a gun to school, and preliminary findings reveal there has been a decrease in the incidence of guns in schools since such policies were established.[46] While the zero-tolerance policy may reduce school violence, it does not address guns outside of school, where violence against youth is most likely to occur.[47]

Since it is impossible to separate the problem of kids of guns from the more general societal problem of gun violence, we should enact measures that more strictly regulate the sale, manufacture, transfer, and possession of handguns by all Americans and therefore kids' access to handguns as well. Although possession of handguns by minors is illegal, it is important to remember that every handgun a child obtains, through whatever means, was at one time produced, bought and sold legally. In order to cut off the flow of handguns to youths, we must do a better job in regulating the flow of handguns to adults.

HOW MANY GUNS ARE THERE IN THE U.S.?

The Bureau of Alcohol, Tobacco and Firearms (ATF) reports there were over 211,000,000 firearms privately owned in the United States in 1991, of which approximately 70,666,000 were handguns.[48] Since 1989, manufacturers and importers introduced an average of 3.5 million new guns into the U.S. market each year.[49] These statistics indicate there is approximately one gun for each adult and half the children in America.[50] Every ten seconds a gun is manufactured in the United States. Every eleven seconds, a gun is imported.[51] In 1992, firearm sales reached $2.1 billion.

Since 1980, domestic production of pistols has doubled, while domestic production of rifles and shotguns has been cut 40 percent and 14 percent respectively. In 1980, pistols made up less than 15 percent of the total firearms produced in the U.S. In 1993, they represented more than 40 percent of total firearm production.[52]

HANDGUNS

The primary function of the handgun is to kill a human being. Unlike rifles or shotguns, they serve no practical sporting purpose. Moreover, the handgun can be concealed easily, making it the weapon of choice for criminals. It is the concealable handgun which threatens and intimidates the citizens of the U.S. — not the rifle or shotgun. Rifles and shotguns make up nearly two-thirds of the firearms in the U.S.,[53] but account for only one-third of all firearm crime. Handguns comprise only one-third of all firearms, but account for two-thirds of firearm crime and over 80 percent of all firearm homicide.[54] The Department of Justice reported that handguns were used in a record 931,000 violent crimes in 1992, accounting for 13 percent of all violent crimes.[55]

SATURDAY NIGHT SPECIALS

"Saturday Night Special" is a term that refers to handguns that are extremely small and typically poorly made. Due to their concealability and price, these guns are ideal crime guns. Typically, Saturday Night Specials have a barrel length of less than four inches[56] and they retail for as little as $69.[57] Their low price also brings these guns within the economic reach of children. Also, Saturday Night Specials frequently are poorly made, thus posing a danger to users as well as victims.

Under the 1968 Gun Control Act, the Congress delegated the Bureau of Alcohol, Tobacco and Firearms (ATF) the authority to set standards for imported firearms, including Saturday Night Specials. ATF's specific mission is to reject imported firearms that are not "generally recognized as particularly suitable for or readily adaptable to sporting purposes."[58] Basically, ATF considers four characteristics: size, caliber, safety, and quality of materials. These standards are required of imported guns, but not mandated for those manufactured domestically. Thus, Saturday Night Specials cannot be imported into the United States. However, domestic manufacturers continue to make these dangerous guns with no limitations.

Statistics from the FBI indicate that small, cheap handguns (i.e., Saturday Night Specials) frequently are used for crime. Of the seventeen guns most frequently traced by ATF from 1991 to 1994, nine sell for under $115, and seven would not meet the ATF's import standards for minimum size.[59] Clearly, Saturday Night Specials pose a great risk to public safety. It is time the standards required of imported firearms also are applied to domestically manufactured guns. Another approach would be increase the excise tax on Saturday Night Specials, making them less appealing and accessible to criminals and young people.

ASSAULT WEAPONS

The "Violent Crime Control and Law Enforcement Act of 1994," commonly known as the Crime Bill, includes provisions that ban the future manufacture and sale of 19 specific assault weapons models and their copycats, as well as ammunition magazines with more than ten rounds. Weapons manufactured before the ban are still legal for sale and ownership. Although assault weapons make up less than 1 percent of privately owned firearms in the U.S., they are traced to as many as 10 percent of firearm crimes, according to the ATF. Even more alarming is that assault weapons were the firearms most commonly traced for organized crime and drug trafficking offenses.[60] Between 1986 and 1993, assault weapons made up 9 percent of the guns used to kill police officers. A 1995 study found that assault weapons were used in 1 out of 10 homicides of police officers.[61]

Assault weapons are based on firearms designed by the military to kill people as efficiently as possible, not for recreational or hunting purposes. Many forms of assault weapons are concealed easily, thus making them even more deadly. Unlike hunting rifles and shotguns, they are not designed for accuracy. Large capacity magazines, like those banned by the 1994 Crime Bill, make it possible to spray areas with large quantities of bullets in a short amount of time. Many assault weapons come equipped with folding stocks, tripods, and other devices to help reduce recoil, thus allowing rapid firing from the hip. Typical semiautomatic assault weapons are able to fire up to 100 rounds of ammunition per minute, and, if illegally converted to an automatic, may fire between 600 and 1,100 rounds per minute.[62] None of these devices is necessary for sporting or hunting purposes.

The gun lobby contends that gun control advocates invented the term "assault weapons" for political purposes, and that there is no such thing as an assault weapon. The truth is that *Gun Digest* and other firearm publications, as well as the gun lobby itself, described these same weapons as "assault-type weapons" as early as 1984, well before banning assault weapons became a political issue. *Gun Digest* even published an entire book entitled *Assault Weapons* in 1986, which discusses fully automatic and semiautomatic "assault weapons."[63] Contrary to the gun lobby's claims, the term "assault weapon" was introduced by gun proponents themselves for marketing purposes, not gun control advocates for political need.

State and community bans on assault weapons have achieved considerable success in deterring gun violence. According to the Oakland, California, Police Department, since California banned assault weapons in 1989, instances in which an assault weapon was used in commission of a crime have decreased by half.[64] Clearly, the federal ban on assault weapons is a good first step toward ending our nation's gun violence epidemic.

DEALERS

The "Violent Crime Control and Law Enforcement Act of 1994," enacted on September 13, 1994, increased the fee for a three-year federal firearms dealer license from $30 to $200 and required that firearms dealers follow federal, state, and local regulations governing them. When the law was enacted, there were 218,411 federally licensed firearms dealers in the United States. Since then, the number has decreased by an average of 150 each day. As of August 1995, there were 163,815 firearms dealers.[65]

A 1993 ATF report, "Operation Snapshot," investigating 400 randomly selected federally licensed firearms dealers, found that only 18 percent conducted business from commercial premises and 74 percent operated out of their home. Another 8 percent did business on a commercial site, such as an auto repair shop or real estate office, whose primary purpose was not the sale of goods to the public. Many of these dealers acquired their licenses not to operate as legitimate dealers, but to purchase firearms at wholesale prices and through gun catalogues across state lines. In 1994, more than half of the crime guns traced by the ATF came from federally licensed firearms dealers.[66] Even at $200, the current cost of a federal firearms dealer's license is modest. An increase in the fee would do little harm to legitimate businesses but would have a dramatic effect in driving out illegitimate dealers.

ECONOMIC COSTS OF GUN VIOLENCE

The cost to treat victims of firearm violence is overwhelming. Firearm-related injuries make up 0.5 percent of all injuries, yet they represent 9 percent of total cost of injury over a lifetime. Almost 85 percent of all health-care expenses due to gunshot injuries and fatalities is charged to taxpayers.[67]

Estimates of the total cost of gun violence vary. Researchers Max and Rice estimate that the 1990 costs of direct medical spending and lost productivity in the United States totaled $20.4 billion. Other researchers, Miller and Cohen, concluded that the total 1992 cost of firearm violence was $112 billion when taking into consideration direct medical costs, lost productivity, and lost quality of life. This study also reported that each of the estimated 4.91 billion bullets sold in 1992 represented $23 in costs due to firearm violence, including $0.60 in medical and emergency services, $7.20 in lost productivity, and $15.10 in pain, suffering, and lost quality of life.[68] A study by Gannet, Inc., estimates that the average expense of each incidence of gun violence totals well over $300,000.[69] This study estimates that the total cost of gun violence is $135 billion each year.[70]

Gun violence's financial costs particularly burdens trauma care centers. Between 1986 and 1991, 92 of the 549 trauma care centers in the United States closed. Many more have or are expected to close in the next few years.[71] Because many gunshot victims are uninsured, almost 85 percent of medical charges due to gunshots are paid by taxpayers through public health care and public debt.[72]

Hospital fees are structured so that insured patients cover the losses due to uninsured patients. This means that private health insurance plans compensate most of the medical costs caused by guns, even though they pay for only one-fourth of the actual injuries. The costs of treating uninsured gunshot victims that aren't picked up through public health care are passed on to those privately insured through higher premiums. This means non-gun-owners who are taxpayers and privately insured are paying for the problems created by widespread gun ownership and availability.

THE THREE MYTHS USED AGAINST GUN CONTROL

Myth 1: "Gun control won't stop gun violence," or "Crime control, not gun control."

The gun lobby uses this false statement incessantly to justify unlimited availability of firearms. The fact is that most criminals acquire their handguns through legal channels. A Criminal Justice Research Center survey of prison inmates reports that most obtained handguns from family members and friends. Only 27 percent of the adult inmates surveyed reported buying a handgun on the black market, while 69 percent acquired their handgun(s) from family, friends, private owners, or retail outlets.[73] A survey of juvenile inmates revealed that 43 percent obtained their most recent gun from the black market, but 55 percent obtained it from friends, family, or a gun shop.[74]

Each and every firearm sold on the black market was, at one time, manufactured and sold legally. In effect, legal gun owners and dealers are the suppliers of the black market. Between 1985 and 1994, an average of 274,000 guns were reported stolen to the FBI each year.[75] Gun owners and dealers are the gatekeepers of the guns used in crime, homicide, suicide, and unintentional shootings. Their guns pose a risk to all of us.

Myth 2: "Firearm ownership is a constitutional right."

A well regulated Militia being necessary to the security of a free State, the right of the people to keep and bear Arms, shall not be infringed. — Second Amendment to the United States Constitution

---

The Supreme Court decided in the 1939 case, *United States v. Miller,* 307 U.S. 174, that possession of a firearm is not protected by the Second Amendment unless it has "some reasonable relationship to the preservation or efficiency of a well regulated militia." The Supreme Court has stated that today's militia is the National Guard.[76]

No gun control law brought before the Supreme Court or other federal courts ever has been overturned on Second Amendment grounds, including several local statutes outlawing handguns.[77] Lower federal courts consistently follow the *Miller* decision that the Second Amendment does not protect an absolute individual right to keep and bear arms.[78] In *United States v. Toner,* 728 F.2d 115, 128 (2d Cir. 1984), the court states that gun possession is "clearly not a fundamental right." In *United States v. Swinton,* 521 F.2d 1255, 1259, *cert. denied,* 424 U.S. 918 (1976), the court states there is "no absolute constitutional right to possess a firearm." This case's appeal was denied a hearing by the Supreme Court. Since the *Miller* decision, the Supreme Court has declined to hear any case brought on Second Amendment grounds, leading many legal authorities such as retired Chief Justice Warren Burger, Justice David Souter, and the American Bar Association to declare this legal issue settled law.

Myth 3: "Handguns are a good means of self-defense."

Keeping a handgun in the home for self-defense places a gun owner and his/her family in great jeopardy. Research indicates that residents of homes where a gun is present are five times more likely to experience a suicide[79] and three times more likely to experience a homicide[80] than residents of homes without guns. Additionally, a gun kept in the home is 43 times more likely to kill a member of the household, or friend, than an intruder.[81] In fact, research indicates that the use of a firearm to resist a violent assault actually increases the victim's risk of injury and death.[82]

A study of 743 gunshot deaths by Dr. Arthur Kellermann and Dr. Donald Reay published in *The New England Journal of Medicine* found the majority of these deaths (398) occurred in the home where the handgun was kept. Residents most often were shot by a relative or family member, their spouse, a roommate, or themselves — not a "criminal" stranger. In fact, 84 percent of these homicides occurred during altercations in the home. Only 2 of the 743 gunshot deaths occurring in the home involved an intruder killed during an attempted entry, and only 9 of the deaths were determined by police/courts to be "justified."[83]

Justifiable homicide is narrowly defined as the use of deadly force in defense of one's life or against serious bodily harm. In legal terms, this means that the person committing a justifiable homicide must reasonably believe his/her life is in danger. For example, shooting someone who is stealing one's car would not be considered a justifiable homicide. Many states also require that persons use deadly force in self-defense only after all other options have been exhausted. This means that, if there is a back door one is able to run out, legally one is obligated to do so instead of shooting a perpetrator.

The evidence revealed in the Kellermann study is consistent with data reported by the FBI. In 1993, there were 24,526 people murdered, 13,980 with handguns, yet only 251 justifiable homicides by civilians using handguns.[84]

SUPPORT FOR GUN CONTROL

Every major law enforcement organization and the majority of the American citizenry approve the creation of legislation which makes handguns more difficult to acquire. Consider the following:

- 81 percent of the public see the availability of guns and the increase in the number of guns as the root cause of increasing gun violence.[85]
- 52 percent of the public support a ban on the sale of handguns.[86]
- 62 percent support a special tax on handguns.[87]
- 81 percent favor the registration of all handguns.[88]
- 70 percent of gun owners support more strict gun control.[89]
- 73 percent favor bans on "Saturday Night Specials" and "cheap, poor-quality handguns."[90]
- 73 percent of the public and 72 percent of gun owners support a ban on semiautomatic assault weapons.[91]

NOTES

1. Centers for Disease Control (CDC), "Deaths Resulting from Firearm- and Motor-Vehicle-Related Injuries: United States, 1968–1991," *Mortality and Morbidity Weekly Report,* vol. 4, 1994, pp. 37–42; and L.A. Fingerhut, C. Jones, D. Makuo, "Firearm and Motor Vehicle Injury Mortality — Variation by State and Race and Ethnicity: United States, 1990–1991," *Advance Data from Vital and Health Statistics,* no. 242, National Center for Health Statistics (NCHS), Hyattsville, Md., 1994.

2. CDC, "Deaths Resulting from Firearm- and Motor-Vehicle-Related Injuries: United States, 1968–1991," pp. 37–42.

3. NCHS.

4. NCHS.

5. NCHS.

6. Federal Bureau of Investigation, *Uniform Crime Reports 1994,* 1995.

7. Garen Wintemute, "Firearms As a Cause of Death in the United States, 1920–1982," *Journal of Trauma,* vol. 27, 1987, p. 532.

8. FBI, *Uniform Crime Reports 1993,* 1994.

9. "Harper's Index," *Harper's Magazine,* January 1994, p. 15.

10. NCHS.

11. NCHS.

12. John Henry Sloan, et al., "A Tale of Two Cities," *New England Journal of Medicine,* vol. 319, November 10, 1988, p. 1256.

13. NCHS.

14. Garen Wintemute, MD, MPH, Stephen P. Teret, JD, MPH, Jess F. Kraus, MPH, PhD, and Mona W. Wright, BS, "The Choice of Weapons in Firearm Suicides," *American Journal of Public Health,* vol. 78, no. 7, July 1988, p. 825.

15. NCHS.

16. Susan P. Baker, Brian O'Neill, Marvin J. Ginsburg, and Guohua Li, *The Injury Prevention Notebook,* 2d ed., 1992, p. 75.

17. Ibid.

18. American Association of Suicidology.

19. Linda G. Peterson, MD, McKim Peterson, MD, Gregory J. O'Shanick, MD, and Alan Swann, "Self Inflicted Gunshot Wounds: Lethality of Method Versus Intent," *American Journal of Psychiatry,* vol. 142, no. 2, February 1985, p. 230.

20. Mark L. Rosenberg and M.A. Fenley, Eds., *Violence in America: A Public Health Approach,* Oxford University Press, New York, 1991, p. 136.

21. Peterson, et al., p. 230.

22. Susan J. Blumenthal, MD, MPA, and David J. Kupfer, MD, Eds., *Suicide Over the Life Cycle: Risk Factors, Assessment, and Treatment of Suicidal Patients,* American Psychiatric Press, Washington, D.C., 1990, p. 261.

23. Susan Glick, MHS, *Female Persuasion: A Study of How the Firearms Industry Markets to Women and the Reality of Women and Guns, Violence Policy Resource Center,* Washington, D.C., 1994, p. 43.

24. Rosenberg and Fenley, *Violence in America,* p. 4.

25. "Suicide Among Children, Adolescents, and Young Adults: United States, 1980–1992," *Morbidity and Mortality Weekly Report,* vol. 44, no. 15, April 21, 1995, p. 289.

26. NCHS.

27. Douglas S. Weil and David Hemenway, "Loaded Guns in the Home: Analysis of a National Random Survey of Gun Owners," *Journal of the American Medical Association,* vol. 267, June 10, 1992, pp. 3033–3037; and David Hemenway, PhD, Sara J. Solnick, MS, Deborah R. Azrael, MS, "Firearm Training and Storage," *Journal of the American Medical Association,* vol. 273, no. 1, January 4, 1995, pp. 47, 49.

28. Talmey Drake Research & Strategy, Inc., *The Family Safety Survey: A National Survey of Parents' Compliances with the Family Safety Check,* National SAFE KIDS Campaign, Washington, D.C., May 9, 1995, p. 11.

29. Linda E. Saltzman, et al., "Weapon Involvement and Injury Outcomes in Family and Intimate Assaults," *Journal of the American Medical Association,* June 10, 1992, pp. 3043–3047; D.R. Rice and E.L. MacKenzie, *Cost of Injury in the United States: A Report to Congress,* Injury Prevention Center, the Johns Hopkins University and Institute for Health and Aging, University of California, San Francisco, Calif., 1989; and Joseph L. Annest, PhD, James A. Mercy, PhD, Delinda R. Gibson, and George W. Ryan, PhD, "National Estimates of Nonfatal Firearm-Related Injuries," *Journal of the American Medical Association,* vol. 273, no. 2, June 14, 1995, pp. 1749–1754.

30. Garen Wintemute, MD, MPH, "Trauma in Transition: Trends in Deaths from Firearm and Motor Vehicle Injuries," Violence Prevention Research Program, University of California, Davis, Calif., January 1995, p. 5.

31. Sporting Arms and Ammunition Manufacturers' Institute, Inc., *Excise Taxes on Firearms and Ammunition,* Background Paper 4.

32. L. A. Fingerhut, "Firearm Mortality among Children, Youth, and Young Adults 1–34 Years of Age, Trends and Current Status: United States, 1985–90," *Advance Data from Vital and Health Statistics,* National Center for Health Statistics, no. 231, Hyattsville, Md., 1993.

33. FBI, *Crime in the United States: Uniform Crime Reports 1994,* 1995.

34. Kenneth D. Kochanek, MA, and Bettie L. Hudson, "Advance Report of Final Mortality Statistics, 1992," *Monthly Vital Statistics Report,* National Center for Health Statistics, Hyattsville, Md., vol. 43, no. 6(S), March 22, 1995, pp. 30, 56.

35. Fingerhut, "Firearm Mortality among Children, Youth, and Young Adults," Table I.

36. NCHS.

37. Office of Juvenile Justice and Delinquency Prevention, U.S. Department of Justice, *Juvenile Offenders and Victims: A National Report,* Washington, D.C., p. 52.

38. Ibid., p. 100.

39. Ibid., p. 58.

40. Gallup Organization and Phi Delta Kappa, "26th Annual Gallup Poll of the Public's Attitude Toward the Public Schools," 1994.

41. CDC, "Weapon Carrying among High School Students," *Morbidity and Mortality Weekly Report,* vol. 40, no. 40, October 11, 1991.

42. Louis Harris and Associates, Inc., "Violence in America's Schools: The Family Perspective," *The Metropolitan Life Survey of the American Teacher,* 1994.

43. Donna Harrington-Leuker, "Blown Away," *The American School Board Journal,* May 1992, p. 22.

44. Louis Harris Research, Inc., "A Survey of the American People on Guns as a Children's Health Issue," p. 20.

45. R. K. Lee and J. J. Sacks, "Latchkey Children and Guns at Home," *Journal of the American Medical Association,* vol. 264, November 7, 1990, p. 2210.

46. Maria Newman, "Some Progress Is Seen on Federal Initiative for Gun-Free Schools," *New York Times,* October 27, 1995, p. A27.

47. Office of Juvenile Justice and Delinquency Prevention, U.S. Department of Justice, *Juvenile Offenders and Victims: A National Report,* Washington, D.C., p. 30.

48. Bureau of Alcohol, Tobacco and Firearms (ATF), "How Many Guns?" *ATF News Release* FY-91-36, GPO, Washington, D.C., 1991.

49. ATF, June 29, 1994; "U.S. Firearms Production," *American Firearms Industry,* March 1994, p. 41; ATF, February 23, 1993; and "U.S. Firearms Production 1993," *American Firearms Industry,* January 1995, p. 74.

50. U.S. Department of Commerce. Bureau of the Census.

51. ATF, *Annual Firearms Manufacturing and Exportation Report,* 1993, cited in *Mother Jones,* pullout, January/February 1994.

52. "U.S. Firearms Production 1993," *American Fireams Industry,* March 1994, p. 41; and "U.S. Firearms Production," *American Firearms Industry,* January 1995, p. 74.

53. ATF, cited in "How Many Guns?" *ATF News Release* FY-91-36, 1991.

54. FBI, *Crime in the United States: Uniform Crime Reports 1994,* 1995.

55. Michael R. Rand, "Guns and Crime," *Crime Data Brief, U.S.* Department of Justice NCI-14703, April 1994.

56. §§ 18 USC 921 *et sec.*

57. *Gun Digest 1995,* 49th Annual Edition, Northbrook, Ill., DBI Books, Inc., 1994, p. 288.

58. §§ 18 USC 921 *et sec.*

59. ATF, 1994.

60. ATF, cited in Robert O'Harrow, Jr., "Power Price and Availability Make Assault Weapons Popular," *Washington, Post,* January 28, 1993, p. B4.

61. Violence Policy Center, *Cop Killers: Assault Weapon Attacks on America's Police,* Washington, D.C., September 1995.

62. "Machine Gun U.S.A.," *Newsweek,* October 14, 1985.

63. Jack Lewis, Ed., *The Gun Digest Book of Assault Weapons,* Northbrook, Ill. DBI Books, 1986.

64. Oakland Police Department Weapons Unit.

65. ATF.

66. Philip P. Pan, "Trail of Violence Keeps Leading to Md. Gun Shop," *Washington Post,* November 1, 1995, pp. A1, A14.

67. Michael Martin, Thomas Hunt, and Stephen Hulley, "The Cost of Hospitalization for Firearm Injuries," *Journal of the American Medical Association,* vol. 260, November 25, 1988, p. 3048.

68. Ted R. Miller and Mark A. Cohen, "Costs of Penetrating Injury," p. 8, for publication in *Textbook of Penetrating Trauma,* Rao Ivatury and C. Gene Cayten, Eds., Leq and Febinger, Malvern, Pa. 1995.

69. Lori Sharn, "Shootings, Killings, Cost the USA Untold Billions," *USA Today,* December 29, 1993, p. 4A.

70. National Public Services Research Institute.

71. "Congress Acts to Resuscitate Nation's Financially Ailing Trauma Care Systems," *Journal of the American Medical Association,* vol. 267, June 10, 1992, p. 2996.

72. M. Martin, K. Hunt, and S. Hulley, "Cost of Hospitalization for Firearm Injuries," p. 3050; and Garen Wintemute, MD, MPH, and Mona A. Wright, BS, "Initial and Subsequent Hospital Costs of Firearm Injuries," *Journal of Trauma,* vol. 33, no. 4, October 1992, p. 558.

73. Criminal Justice Research Center.

74. J. F. Sheley and J. Wright, "Gun Acquisition and Possession in Selected Juvenile Samples," *Research in Brief,* National Institute of Justice, U.S. Department of Justice, Washington, D.C., 1993.

75. Marianne W. Zawitz, "Firearms Crime, and Criminal Justice: Guns Used in Crime," Bureau of Justice Statistics, U.S. Department of Justice, Washington, D.C., July 1995, p. 3.

76. *Burton v. Sills,* 248 A.2d 521 (N.J. 1968) *appeal dismissed* 394 U.S. 812 (1969).

77. *Quilici v. Village of Morton Grove,* 532 F Supp 1169 (ND III 1981), *aff'd,* 695 F2d 261 (7th Cir 1982), *cert denied,* 464 US 863 (1983).

78. *United States v. Cruikshank,* 92 United States 542 (1876); *Presser v. Illinois,* 116 US 252 (1886); *United States v. Miller,* 307 US 174 (1939); *Lewis v. United States,* 445 US 55 (1980); and *Quilici v. Village of Morton Grove,* 532 F Supp 1169 (ND III 1981), *aff'd,* 695 F2d 261 (7th Cir 1982), *cert denied,* 464 US 863 (1983).

79. Arthur L. Kellermann, MD, MPH, Frederick P. Rivara, MD, MPH, Grant Somes, PhD, Donald T. Reay, MD, Jerry Francisco, MD, Joyce Gillentine Banton, MS, Janice Prodzinski, BA, Corinne Fligner, MD, and Bela B. Hackman, MD, "Suicide in the Home in Relation to Gun Ownership," *New England Journal of Medicine,* vol. 327, no. 7, August 13, 1992, pp. 467–472.

80. Arthur L. Kellermann, MD, MPH, Frederick P. Rivara, MD, MPH, Norman B. Rushforth, PhD, Joyce G. Banton, MS, Donald T. Reay, MD, Jerry T. Francisco, MD, Ana B. Locci, PhD, Janice Prodzinski, BA, Bela B. Hackman, MD, and Grant Somes, PhD, "Gun Ownership as a Risk Factor for Homicide in the Home," *New England Journal of Medicine,* vol. 329, no. 15, October 7, 1993, pp. 1084–1091.

81. Arthur Kellermann and Donald Reay, "Protection of Peril? An Analysis of Firearm-Related Deaths in the Home," *New England Journal of Medicine,* vol. 314, no. 24, June 1986, pp. 1557–1560.

82. F. E. Zimring, "Firearms, Violence, and Public Policy," *Scientific American,* vol. 265, 1991, p. 48.

83. Ibid.

84. FBI, *Crime in the United States: Uniform Crime Reports 1994,* 1995.

85. Louis Harris, "A Survey of the American People on Guns as a Children's Health Issue," A Study Conducted by L. H. Research, Inc. for The Harvard School of Public Health, June 1993, p. 14.

86. Ibid., p. xi.

87. Ibid., p. 14.

88. "Opinion Outlook," *National Journal,* December 22, 1989, p. 3109.

89. *USA Today*/CNN/Gallup poll, 1992.

90. *Time*/CNN poll, December 15, 1989.

91. *Time*/CNN poll, December 15, 1989.

Will Gun Control Laws Reduce Violence?

NATIONAL RIFLE ASSOCIATION INSTITUTE
FOR LEGISLATIVE ACTION
Ten Myths about Gun Control

We will never fully solve our nation's horrific problem of gun violence unless we ban the manufacture and sale of handguns and semiautomatic assault weapons.
—*USA Today*, December 29, 1993

Why should America adopt a policy of near-zero tolerance for private gun ownership? . . . [W]ho can still argue compellingly that Americans can be trusted to handle guns safely? We think the time has come for Americans to tell the truth about guns. They are not for us, we cannot handle them.
—*Los Angeles Times*, December 28, 1993

These editorial opinions expressed by two of the nation's most widely read newspapers represent the absolute extreme in the firearms controversy: that no citizen can be trusted to own a firearm. It is the product of a series of myths which — through incessant repetition — have been mistaken for truth. These myths are being exploited to generate fear and mistrust of the 60–65 million decent and responsible Americans who own firearms. Yet, as this brochure proves, none of these myths will stand up under the cold light of fact.

Myth: "The majority of Americans favor strict new additional federal gun controls."

Polls can be slanted by carefully worded questions to achieve any desired outcome. It is a fact that most people do not know what laws currently exist; thus, it is meaningless to assert that people favor "stricter" laws when they do not know how "strict" the laws are in the first place. Asking about a waiting period for a police background check presumes, incorrectly, that police can and will actually conduct a check during the wait. Similarly, it is meaningless to infer anything from support of a 7- or 5-day waiting period when respondents live in a state with a 15-day wait or a 1–6 month permit scheme in place. Asked whether they favor making any particular law "stricter," however, most people do not. Unbiased, scientific polls have consistently shown that most people:

- Oppose costly registration of firearms.
- Oppose giving police power to decide who should own guns.
- Do not believe that stricter gun laws would prevent criminals from illegally obtaining guns.

In 1993, Luntz Weber Research and Strategic Services found that only 9 percent of the American people believe "gun control" to be the most important thing that could be done to reduce crime. By a margin of almost 3–1, respondents said mandatory prison would reduce crime more than "gun control." This poll, unlike many others, allowed respondents to answer more honestly by using open ended questions without leading introductions. The result was an honest appraisal of the attitude of the American people: *"gun control" is not crime control.*

One clear example of a poll done which used biased questions and flawed procedures was conducted by Louis Harris Research Inc. (LHRI) in the summer of 1993. The poll reported unprecedented levels of gun abuse by high school students. However, after examining the poll, Professor Gary Kleck of Florida State University, the nation's leading scholar on crime and firearms, called the findings ". . . implausible, being inconsistent with more sophisticated prior research." Prof. Kleck found the Harris findings of students who had been shot at or who had actually shot at someone to be insupportable by crime and victimization statistics as reported by the Department of Justice: "Even if the percent of handgun crime victimization had doubled from the average for the 1979–1987 period, the LHRI results would still be overstated by a factor of 100." In the end, he labeled the LHRI poll "advocacy polling."[1]

A more direct measure of the public's attitude of "gun control" comes when the electorate has a chance to speak on the issue. Public opinion polls do not form public policy, but individual actions by hundreds of thousands of citizens do. For example, in 1993, the voters of Madison, Wisconsin, were presented with a referendum calling for a ban on handgun ownership in that city. Pollsters predicted an overwhelming win for the gun banners. When Second Amendment rights activists rallied opposition and educated the electorate on the facts about gun ownership, the referendum was defeated.

In the 1993 gubernatorial elections, the incumbent governor in New Jersey and the front-runner in Virginia made "gun control" a central theme of their campaigns. Both candidates lost to opponents who stressed real criminal justice reforms, not "gun control."

In November 1982, Californians rejected, by a 63–37 percent margin, a statewide handgun initiative that called for the registration of all handguns and a "freeze" on the number of handguns allowed in the state. Again, pre-election pollsters reported support for the measure. That initiative was also opposed by the majority of California's law enforcement community. Fifty-one of the state's 58 working sheriffs opposed Proposition 15, as did 101 chiefs of police. Nine law enforcement organizations, speaking for rank-and-file police, went on record against the initiative.

Increasingly, the American people are voicing support for reform of the criminal justice system. The NRA [National Rifle Association] also actively supports initiatives calling for mandatory jail time for violent criminals. In 1982, the residents of Washington, D.C., enacted an NRA-endorsed mandatory penalty bill, actively opposed by the anti-gun D.C. City Council, that severely punishes those who use firearms to commit violent crimes. In 1988, the residents of Oregon approved, by a 78–22 percent margin, an NRA-supported initiative mandating prison sentences for repeat offenders after the state legislature and governor failed to act on the issue. In 1993, the residents of Washington state overwhelmingly approved the "three strikes you're out" initiative calling for life sentences without parole for anyone convicted of a third serious crime. NRA's CrimeStrike program was instrumental in collecting the needed signatures to put that question on the ballot.

In 1993, the Southern States Police Benevolent Association conducted a scientific poll of its members. Sixty-five percent of the respondents identified "gun control" as the least effective method of combating violent crime. Only 1 percent identified guns as a cause of violent crime, while 48 percent selected drug abuse, and 21 percent said the failure of the criminal justice system was the most pressing cause. The officers also revealed that 97 percent support the right of the people to own firearms, and 90 percent said they believed the Constitution guarantees that right.

The SSPBA findings affirmed a series of polls conducted by the National Association of Chiefs of Police of every chief and sheriff in the country, representing over 15,000 departments. In 1991 the poll discovered for the third year in a row that law enforcement officers overwhelmingly agree that "gun control" measures have no effect on crime. A clear majority of 93 percent of the respondents said that banning firearms would not reduce a criminal's ability to get firearms, while 89 percent said that the banning of semi-automatic firearms would not reduce criminal access to such firearms. Ninety-two percent felt that criminals obtain their firearms from illegal sources; 90 percent agreed that the banning of private ownership of firearms would not result in fewer crimes. Seventy-three percent felt that a national waiting period would have no effect on criminals getting firearms. An overwhelming 90 percent felt that such a scheme would instead make agencies less effective against crime by reducing their manpower and only serve to open them up to liability lawsuits.

These are the only national polls of law enforcement officers in the country, with the leadership of most other major groups adamantly refusing to poll their membership on firearms issues.

Myth: "The only purpose of a handgun is to kill people."

This often repeated statement is patently untrue, but to those Americans whose only knowledge of firearms comes from the nightly violence on television, it might seem believable. When antigun researcher James Wright, then of the University of Massachusetts, studied all the available literature on firearms, he concluded: "Even the most casual and passing familiarity with this literature is therefore sufficient to belie the contention that handguns have 'no legitimate sport or recreational use.' "

There are an estimated 75–80 million privately owned handguns in the United States that are used for hunting, target shooting, protection of families and businesses, and other legitimate and lawful purposes. By comparison, handguns were used in an estimated 13,000 homicides in 1994 — less than 0.02 percent (two hundredths of 1 percent) of the handguns in America. Many of these reported homicides (1,500–2,800) were self-defense or justifiable and, therefore, not criminal. That fact alone renders the myth about the "only purpose" of handguns absurd, for more than 99 percent of all handguns are used for no criminal purpose.

By far the most commonly cited reason for owning a handgun is protection against criminals. At least one-half of handgun owners in America own handguns for protection and security. A handgun's function is one of insurance as well as defense. A handgun in the home is a contingency, based on the knowledge that if there ever comes a time when it is needed, no substitute will do. Certainly no violent intent is implied, any more than a purchaser of life insurance intends to die soon.

Myth: "Since a gun in a home is many times more likely to kill a family member than to stop a criminal, armed citizens are not a deterrent to crime."

This myth, stemming from a superficial "study" of firearm accidents in the Cleveland, Ohio, area, represents a comparison of 148 accidental deaths (including suicides) to the deaths of 23 intruders killed by home owners over a 16-year period.[2]

Gross errors in this and similar "studies" — with even greater claimed ratios of harm to good — include: the assumption that a gun hasn't been used for protection unless an assailant dies; no distinction is made between handgun and long gun deaths; all accidental firearm fatalities were counted whether the deceased was part of the "family" or not; all accidents were counted whether they occurred in the home or not, while self-defense outside the home was excluded; almost half the self-defense uses of guns in the home were excluded on the grounds that the criminal intruder killed may not have been a total stranger to the home defender; suicides were sometimes counted and some self-defense shootings misclassified. Cleveland's experience with crime and accidents during the study period was atypical of the nation as a whole and of Cleveland since the mid-1970s. Moreover, in a later study, the same researchers noted that roughly 10 percent of killings by civilians are justifiable homicides.[3]

The "guns in the home" myth has been repeated time and again by the media, and anti-gun academics continue to build on it. In 1993, Dr. Arthur Kellermann of Emory University and a number of colleagues presented a study that claimed to show that a home with a gun was much more likely to experience a homicide.[4] However, Dr. Kellermann selected for his study only homes where homicides had taken place — ignoring the millions of homes with firearms where no harm is done — and a control group that was not representative of American households. By only looking at homes where homicides had occurred and failing to control for more pertinent variables, such as prior criminal record or histories of violence, Kellermann et al. skewed the results of this study. Prof. Kleck wrote that with the methodology used by Kellermann, one could prove that since diabetics are much more likely to possess insulin than non-diabetics, possession of insulin is a risk factor for diabetes. Even Dr. Kellermann admitted this in his study: "It is possible that reverse causation accounted for some of the association we observed between gun ownership and homicide." Law Professor Daniel D. Polsby went further, "Indeed the point is stronger than that: 'reverse causation' may account for *most* of the association between gun ownership and homicide. Kellermann's data simply do not allow one to draw any conclusion."[5]

Research conducted by Professors James Wright and Peter Rossi,[6] for a landmark study funded by the U.S. Department of Justice, points to the armed citizen as possibly the most effective deterrent to crime in the nation. Wright and Rossi questioned over 1,800 felons serving time in prisons across the nation and found:

- 81 percent agreed the "smart criminal" will try to find out if a potential victim is armed.
- 74 percent felt that burglars avoided occupied dwellings for fear of being shot.
- 80 percent of "handgun predators" had encountered armed citizens.
- 40 percent did not commit a specific crime for fear that the victim was armed.
- 34 percent of "handgun predators" were scared off or shot at by armed victims.
- 57 percent felt that the typical criminal feared being shot by citizens more than he feared being shot by police.

Professor Kleck estimates that annually 1,500–2,800 felons are legally killed in "excusable self-defense" or "justifiable" shootings by civilians, and 8,000–16,000 criminals are wounded. This compares to 300–600 justifiable homicides by police. Yet, in most instances, civilians used firearms to threaten, apprehend, shoot at criminals, or to fire warning shots without injuring anyone.

Based on his extensive independent survey research, Kleck estimates that each year Americans used guns for protection from criminals at least 2.5 million times annually.[7] U.S. Department of Justice victimization surveys show that protective use of a gun lessens the chance that robberies, rapes, and assaults will be successfully completed while also reducing the likelihood of victim injury. Clearly, criminals fear armed citizens.

Myth: "Honest citizens have nothing to fear from gun registration and licensing which will curb crime by disarming criminals."

"Gun control" proponents tout automobile registration and licensing as model schemes for firearm ownership. Yet driving an automobile on city or state roads is a *privilege* and, as such, can be regulated, while the individual *right* to possess firearms is constitutionally protected from infringement. Registration and licensing do not prevent criminal misuse or accidental fatalities involving motor vehicles in America, where more than 40,000 people die on the nation's highways each year. By contrast, about 1,400 persons are involved in fatal firearm accidents each year.

Registration and licensing have no effect on crime, as criminals, by definition, do not obey laws. A national survey of prisoners conducted by Wright and Rossi for the Department of Justice found that 82 percent agreed that "gun laws only affect law-abiding citizens; criminals will always be able to get guns."

Further, felons are constitutionally exempt from a gun registration requirement. According to the U.S. Supreme Court's decision in *Haynes v. United States,* since felons are prohibited by law from possessing a firearm, compelling them to register firearms would violate the Fifth Amendment protection against self-incrimination.[8] Only law-abiding citizens would be required to comply with registration — citizens who have neither committed crimes nor have any intention of doing so.

Registration and licensing of America's 60–65 million gun owners and their 230 million firearms would require the creation of a huge bureaucracy at tremendous cost to the taxpayer, with absolutely no tangible anti-crime return. Indeed, New Zealand authorities repealed registration in the 1980s after police acknowledged its worthlessness, and a similar recommendation was made by Australian law enforcement. Law enforcement would be diverted from its primary responsibility, apprehending and arresting criminals, to investigating and processing paperwork on law-abiding citizens.

In the United States, after President Clinton, Attorney General Reno, and others announced support for registration and licensing, police response was immediate and non-supportive. Dewey Stokes, President of the Fraternal Order of Police said, ". . . I don't want to get into a situation where we have gun registration." Other law enforcement officers responded even more strongly. Charles Canterbury, President of the South Carolina FOP said, "On behalf of the South Carolina law enforcement, I can say we are adamantly opposed to registration of guns." Dennis Martin, President of the National Association of Chiefs of Police reported, "I have had a lot of calls from police chiefs and sheriffs who are worried about this. They are afraid that we're going to create a lot of criminals out of law-abiding people who don't want to get a license for their gun."

Finally, a national registration/licensing scheme would violate an individual's right to privacy protected by the Fourth Amendment and establish a basis upon which gun confiscation could be implemented. More than 60,000 rifles and shotguns were confiscated in April, 1989 from honest citizens who had dutifully registered their guns with the authorities in Soviet Georgia *(Chicago Sun-Times,* April 12, 1989, *The Atlanta Journal and Constitution,* May 21, 1989). Could that happen in America? Gun prohibitionists in Massachusetts, Ohio, and Washington, D.C., have already proposed using registration lists for such purposes. And, since 1991, New York City authorities have used registration lists to enforce a ban on semi-automatic rifles and shotguns. Avowed handgun prohibitionist Charles Morgan, as director of the American Civil Liberties Union's Washington office, in a 1975 hearing before the House Subcommittee on Crime stated: "I have not one doubt, even if I am in agreement with the National Rifle Association, that that kind of a record-keeping procedure is the first step to eventual confiscation under one administration or another."

Reasonable fears of such confiscation leads otherwise law-abiding citizens to ignore such laws, creating a disrespect for law and a lessened support for government. In states and cities which recently required registration of semi-automatic firearms, estimates of compliance range from 5 to 10 percent.

Myth: "Stiff 'gun control' laws work as shown by the low crime rates in England and Japan, while U.S. crime rates continue to soar."

All criminologists studying the firearms issue reject simple comparisons of violent crime among foreign countries. It is impossible to draw valid conclusions without taking into account differences in each nation's collection of crime data, and their political, cultural, racial, religious, and economic disparities. Such factors are not only hard to compare, they are rarely, if ever, taken into account by "gun control" proponents.[9]

Only one scholar, attorney David Kopel, has attempted to evaluate the impact of "gun control" on crime in several foreign countries. In his book *The Samurai, the Mountie and the Cowboy: Should America Adopt the Gun Controls of Other Democracies?,* named a 1992 Book of the Year by the American Society of Criminology, Kopel examined numerous nations with varying gun laws, and concluded: "Contrary to the claims of the American gun control movement, gun control does not deserve credit for the low crime rates in Britain, Japan, or other nations." He noted that Israel and Switzerland, with more widespread rates of gun ownership, have crime rates comparable to or lower than the usual foreign examples. And he stated: "Foreign style gun control is doomed to failure in America. Foreign gun control comes along with searches and seizures, and with many other restrictions on civil liberties too intrusive for America. Foreign gun control . . . postulates an authoritarian philosophy of government fundamentally at odds with the individualist and egalitarian American ethos."[10]

America's high crime rates can be attributed to revolving-door justice. In a typical year in the U.S., there are 8.1 million serious crimes like homicide, assault, and burglary. Only 724,000 adults are arrested and fewer still (193,000) are convicted. Less than 150,000 are sentenced to prison, with 36,000 serving less than a year (*U.S. News and World Report,* July 31, 1989). A 1987 National Institute of Justice study found that the average felon released due to prison overcrowding commits upwards of 187 crimes per year, costing society approximately $430,000.

Foreign countries are two to six times more effective in solving crimes and punishing criminals than the U.S. In London, about 20 percent of reported robberies end in conviction; in New York City, less than 5 percent result in conviction, and in those cases imprisonment is frequently not imposed. Nonetheless, England annually has twice as many homicides with firearms as it did before adopting its tough laws. Despite tight licensing procedures, the handgun-related robbery rate in Britain rose about 200 percent during the past dozen years, five times as fast as in the United States.

Part of Japan's low crime rate is explained by the efficiency of its criminal justice system, fewer protections of the right to privacy, and fewer rights for criminal suspects than exist in the United States. Japanese police routinely search citizens at will and twice a year pay "home visits" to citizens' residences. Suspect confession rate is 95 percent and trial conviction rate is over 99.9 percent. The Tokyo Bar Association has said that the Japanese police routinely ". . . engage in torture or illegal treatment. Even in cases where suspects claimed to have been tortured and their bodies bore the physical traces to back their claims, courts have still accepted their confessions." Neither the powers and secrecy of the police nor the docility of defense counsel would be acceptable to most Americans. In addition, the Japanese police understate the amount of crime, particularly covering up the problem of organized crime, in order to appear more efficient and worthy of the respect the citizens have for the police.

Widespread respect for law and order is deeply ingrained in the Japanese citizenry. This cultural trait has been passed along to their descendants in the United States where the murder rate for Japanese-Americans (who have access to firearms) is similar to that in Japan itself.

If gun availability were a factor in crime rates, one would expect European crime rates to be related to firearms availability in those countries, but crime rates are similar in European countries with high or relatively high gun ownership, such as Switzerland, Israel, and Norway, and in low availability countries like England and Germany. Furthermore, one would expect American violent crime rates to be more similar to European rates in crime where guns are rarely used, such as rape, than in crimes where guns are often used, such as homicide. But the reverse is true: American non-gun violent crime rates exceed those of European countries.

Myth: "Most murders are argument-related 'crimes of passion' against a relative, neighbor, friend or acquaintance."

The vast majority of murders are committed by persons with long established patterns of violent criminal behavior. According to analyses by the U.S. Senate Subcommittee on Juvenile Delinquency, the FBI [Federal Bureau of Investigation], and the Chicago, New York City, and other police departments, about 70 percent of suspected murderers have criminal careers of long standing — as do nearly half their victims. FBI data show that roughly 47 percent of murderers are known to their victims.

The waiting period, or "cooling-off" period, as some in the "gun control" community call it, is the most often cited solution to "crimes of passion." However, state crime records show that in 1992, states with waiting periods and other laws delaying or denying gun purchases had an overall violent crime rate more than 47 percent higher and a homicide rate 19 percent higher than other states. In the five states that had some jurisdictions with waiting periods (Georgia, Kansas, Nevada, Ohio and Virginia), the non-waiting period portions of all five states had far lower violent crime and homicide rates.

Recent studies by the Justice Department suggest that persons who live violent lives exhibit those violent tendencies "both within their home and among their family and friends and outside their home among strangers in society." A National Institute of Justice study reveals that the victims of family violence often suffer repeated problems from the same person for months or even years, and if not successfully resolved, such incidents can eventually result in serious injury or death. A study conducted by the Police Foundation showed that 90 percent of all homicides, by whatever means committed, involving family members, had been preceded by some other violent incident serious enough that the police were summoned, with five or more such calls in half the cases.

Circumstances which might suggest "crimes of passion" or "spontaneous" arguments, such as a lover's triangle, arguments over money or property, and alcohol-related brawls, comprise 29 percent of criminal homicides, according to FBI data.

Professor James Wright of the University of Massachusetts describes the typical incident of family violence as "that mythical crime of passion" and rejects the notion that it is an isolated incident by otherwise normally placid and loving individuals. His research shows that it is in fact "the culminating event in a long history of interpersonal violence between the parties."

Wright also speaks to the protective use of handguns. "Firearms equalize the means of physical terror between men and women. In denying the wife of an abusive man the right to have a firearm, we may only be guaranteeing her husband the right to beat her at his pleasure," says Wright.[11]

Myth: "Semi-automatic firearms have no legitimate sporting purpose, are the preferred weapon of choice of criminals, and should be banned."

Use of this myth by gun prohibitionists is predicated purely on pragmatism: whichever "buzzword" can produce the most anti-gun emotionalism — "Saturday Night Special," "assault weapons," and "plastic guns" — will be utilized in efforts to generate support for a ban on entire classes of firearms.

Examples of this anti-gun legislative history abound. A "Saturday Night Special" ban bill enacted in Maryland establishes a politically appointed "Handgun Roster Board" with complete authority to decide which handguns will be permitted in the so-called "Free State" — any handgun could therefore be banned. Federal legislation aimed at the non-existent "plastic gun" would have banned millions of metal handguns suitable for personal protection. In the 1994 crime bill, Congress did ban semi-automatic "assault weapons," based on their cosmetic appearance. After passage, however, not even the virulently anti-gun Washington Post pretended the ban would have a crime fighting effect, labeling it "mainly symbolic."

Criminals and law-abiding citizens both follow the lead of police and military in choosing a gun. Criminals generally pick as handguns .38 Spl. and .357 Mag. revolvers, with barrels about 4¢ long and retailing (an unimportant matter for criminals) at over $200. Only about one-sixth fit the classic description of the so-called "Saturday Night Special" — small caliber, short barrel and inexpensive. While criminals are unconcerned with the cost of a firearm, the law-abiding certainly are. A ban on inexpensive handguns will have a disproportionate impact on low income Americans, effectively disarming them. This is particularly unfair, since it is the poor who more often must live and work in high crime areas.

As more and more police departments, following the lead of the military, switch from revolvers to 9 mm semi-auto pistols, criminals and honest citizens will both follow suit. Indeed, semi-auto pistols have risen from one-fourth of American handgun manufacturing in the 1970s to three-fourths today.

Criminals rarely use long guns and, when they do, are more apt to use a sawed-off shotgun than a semi-automatic rifle, whether military style or not. In America's largest and most crime ravaged cities, only about 1/2–3 percent of "crime guns" are military-style semi-autos. As military establishments adopted medium-velocity rifles with straight-stock configuration, target shooters, hunters, and collectors have acquired the semi-automatic models of these firearms.

While not all guns incorrectly attacked as "preferred by criminals" are popular for hunting, many are, but hunting is not the only valid purpose for owning a firearm. Small handguns, which may be ill-suited for hunting or long-range target shooting, are useful for personal protection, where the accuracy range rarely needs to exceed ten feet. Semi-automatic rifles and shotguns are suitable for hunting a variety of game. Semi-automatic military and military-style rifles, including the M1 Garand, Springfield M1A and the Colt Sporter, are used in thousands of sanctioned Highpower Tournaments each year and the National Matches at Camp Perry, Ohio. Hundreds of thousands of individuals use these rifles for recreational target shooting and plinking.

The Second Amendment clearly protects ownership of firearms which are useful "for the security of a free state" and semi-automatic versions of military arms are clearly appropriate for that purpose. It was the clear intention of the Framers of our Constitution that the citizenry possess arms equal or superior to those held by the government. That was viewed as the best deterrent to tyranny, and it has worked for over 200 years. It was also the intention of the Founding Fathers that citizens be able to protect themselves from criminals, and that doesn't necessarily require a gun suitable for hunting, target shooting, or plinking. All modern firearms may be used for such protective purposes.

Myth: "The right guaranteed under the Second Amendment is limited specifically to the arming of a 'well-regulated Militia' that can be compared today to the National Guard."

The Second Amendment reads: "A well regulated Militia, being necessary to the security of a free State, the right of the people to keep and bear Arms, shall not be infringed." In contrast to other portions of the Constitution, this Amendment contains no qualifiers, no "buts" or "excepts." It is a straightforward statement affirming the people's right to possess firearms.

The perception that the Second Amendment guarantees a "collective right" or a "right of states to form militias" rather than an individual right is a wholly inaccurate twentieth-century invention. Historically, the term "militia" refers to the people at large, armed and ready to defend their homeland and their freedom with arms supplied by themselves (*United States v. Miller*, 1939). Federal law (Title 10, Section 311 of the U.S. Code) states: "The Militia of the United States consists of all able-bodied males at least 17 years of age. . . ." Moreover, historical records, including Constitutional Convention debates and the *Federalist Papers,* clearly indicate that the purpose of the Second Amendment was to guard against the tyranny that the Framers of the Constitution feared could be perpetrated by any professional armed body of government. The arms, records and ultimate control of the National Guard today lie with the Federal Government, so that it clearly is not the "militia" protected from the federal government.

The Supreme Court recently affirmed this virtually unlimited control of the Guard by the federal government in the case of *Perpich v. Department of Defense* (1990). The Court held that the power of Congress over the National Guard is plenary (entire, absolute, unlimited) and such power is not restricted by the Constitution's Militia Clause. The Second Amendment was not even mentioned by the Court, undoubtedly because it does not serve as a source of power for a state to have a National Guard.

In *The Federalist No. 29,* Alexander Hamilton argued that the army would always be a "select corps of moderate size" and that the "people at large (were) properly armed" to serve as a fundamental check against the standing army, the most dreaded of institutions. James Madison, in *The Federalist No. 46,* noted that unlike the governments of Europe which were "afraid to trust the people with arms," the American people would continue under the new Constitution to possess "the advantage of being armed," and thereby would continually be able to form the militia when needed as a "barrier against the enterprises of despotic ambition."

A 1990 Supreme Court decision regarding searches and seizures confirmed that the right to keep and bear arms was an individual right, held by "the people" — a term of art employed in the Preamble and the First, Second, Fourth, Ninth and Tenth Amendments referring to all "persons who are part of a national community" (*United States v. Verdugo-Urquidez,* 1990).

The case of *United States v. Miller* (1939) is frequently though erroneously, cited as the definitive ruling that the right to keep and bear arms is a "collective" right, protecting the right of states to keep a militia rather than the individual right to possess arms. But that was not the issue in *Miller,* and no such ruling was made; the word "collective" is not used any place in the court's decision.

While such a decision was sought by the Justice Department, the Court decided only that the National Firearms Act of 1934 was constitutional in the absence of evidence to the contrary. The case hinged on the narrow question of whether a sawed-off shotgun was suitable for militia use, and its ownership by individuals thus protected by the Second Amendment.

The Court ruled that:

> In the absence of (the presentation of) any evidence tending to show that possession or use of a "shotgun having a barrel of less than eighteen inches in length" at this time has some reasonable relationship to the preservation or efficiency of a well-regulated militia, we cannot say that the Second Amendment guarantees the right to keep and bear such an instrument. Certainly it is not within judicial notice — common knowledge, that need not be proven in court — that this weapon is any part of the military equipment or that its use could contribute to the common defense.

Because no evidence or argument was presented except by the federal government, the Court was not made aware that some 30,000 short-barreled shotguns were used as "trench guns" during World War I.

The Supreme Court has ruled on only three other cases relating to the Second Amendment — all during the last half of the nineteenth century. In each of these cases, the Court held that the Second Amendment only restricted actions of the federal government, not of private individuals (*United States v. Cruikshank,* 1876) or state governments (*Presser v. Illinois,* 1886, and *Miller v. Texas,* 1984). The Court also held, in *Presser,* that the First Amendment guarantee of freedom of assembly did not apply to the states; and in *Miller v. Texas,* it held that the Fourth Amendment guarantee against unreasonable search and seizure did not apply to the states, since the Court believed that all the amendments comprising the Bill of Rights were limitations solely on the powers of Congress, not upon the powers of the states.

It was not until two generations later that the Court began to rule, through the Fourteenth Amendment, that the First, Fourth, and other provisions of the Bill of Rights limited both Congress and state legislatures. No similar decision concerning the Second Amendment has ever been made in spite of contemporary scholarship proving that the purpose of the Fourteenth Amendment was to apply all of the rights in the Bill of Rights to the states. That research proves that the Fourteenth Amendment was made a part of the Constitution to prevent states from depriving the newly freed slaves of the rights guaranteed in the Bill of Rights, including what the Supreme Court's *Dred Scott* decision referred to as one of the rights of citizens, the right "to keep and carry arms wherever they went."[12]

The only significance of the Supreme Court's refusal to hear a challenge to the handgun ban imposed by Morton Grove, Illinois, is that the Court will still not rush to apply the Second Amendment to the states. The refusal to hear the case has no legal significance and, indeed, it would have been very unusual for the Court to make a decision involving the U.S. Constitution when the Illinois courts had not yet decided if Morton Grove's ban conflicted with the state's constitution.

Myth: "A person in a public place with a gun is looking for trouble."

Gun prohibitionists use this myth to oppose legislative proposals to allow law-abiding citizens to obtain permits to carry concealed firearms. In spite of this opposition, numerous states have adopted favorable concealed carry laws over the past few years. In each case, anti-gun activists and politicians predicted that allowing law-abiding people to carry firearms would result in more deaths and injuries as people would resort to gunfire to settle minor disputes. Shoot-outs over fender-benders and Wild-West lawlessness were predicted in an effort to stir up public fear of reasonable laws.

This tactic — seeking to frighten people into supporting desired positions — is employed more and more frequently by gun prohibitionists. Prof. Gary Kleck explains the reasoning thusly: "Battered by a decade of research contradicting the central factual premises underlying gun control, advocates have apparently decided to fight more exclusively on an emotional battlefield, where one terrorizes one's targets into submission rather than honestly persuading them with credible evidence."[13]

When the concealed carry laws were passed and put into practice, the result was completely different from the hysterical claims of the gun prohibitionists. In Florida, since the concealed carry law was changed in 1987, the homicide rate has dropped 21 percent, while the national rate has risen 12 percent. Across the nation, states with favorable concealed carry laws have a 33 percent lower homicide rate overall and 37 percent lower robbery rate than states that allow little or no concealed carry.

Gun prohibitionists have also acted to penalize and discourage gun ownership by imposing mandatory prison terms on persons carrying or possessing firearms without a license or permit, a license or permit they have also made impossible or very difficult to obtain. Massachusett's Bartley-Fox Law and New York's Koch-Carey Law are premier examples of this "gun control" strategy. Such legislation is detrimental only to peaceful citizens, not to criminals.

By the terms of such a mandatory or increased sentence proposal, the unlicensed carrying of a firearm — no matter how innocent the circumstances — is penalized by a six-to-twelve month jail sentence. It is imposed on otherwise law-abiding citizens although in many areas it is virtually impossible for persons to obtain a carry permit. It is easy to see circumstances in which an otherwise law-abiding person would run afoul of this law: fear of crime, arbitrary denial of authorization, red-tape delay in obtaining official permission to carry a firearm, or misunderstanding of the numerous and vague laws governing the transportation of firearms.

The potential for unknowingly or unwittingly committing a technical violation of a licensing law is enormous. Myriad legal definitions of "carrying" vary from state to state and city to city, including most transportation of firearms — accessible or not, loaded or not, in a trunk or case. And out-of-state travelers are exceedingly vulnerable because of these various definitions.

One need only examine the first persons arrested under the Massachusetts and New York City "mandatory penalty" laws for proof that such laws are misdirected: an elderly woman passing out religious pamphlets in a dangerous section of Boston and an Ohio truck driver coming to the aid of a woman apparently being kidnapped in New York City.

In New York City — prior to the enactment of the Koch-Carey mandatory sentence for possession law — the bureaucratic logjam in the licensing division, combined with a soaring crime rate, forced law-abiding citizens to obtain guns illegally for self-protection. In effect, citizens admitted that they would rather risk a mandatory penalty for illegally owning a firearm than risk their lives and property at the hands of New York's violent, uncontrolled criminals. Honest citizens feared the streets more than the courtrooms.

By contrast, the city's criminal element faces no similar threat of punishment. A report carried in the March 1, 1984, issue of the *New York Times* says it all: "Conviction on felony charges is rare. Because of plea-bargaining, the vast majority of those arrested on felony charges are tried on lesser, misdemeanor charges." In one year, according to the *Times,* there were 106,171 felony arrests in New York City, but only 25,987 cases received felony indictments and only 20,641 resulted in convictions, with imprisonment a rarity. This condition persists, the *New York Times* reported again on June 23, 1991: in 1990 felony indictments were resolved by plea bargains in over 83 percent of cases. Only 5.7 percent of cases ended with a trial verdict, with only 3.8 percent ending in conviction. Not surprisingly, with just 3 percent of the nation's population, in 1992 New York City accounted for 12 percent of the nation's homicides.

In championing New York's tough Koch-Carey Law, then Mayor Ed Koch said contemptuously of gun owners, "Nice guys who own guns aren't nice guys." No such rancor was expressed about the city's revolving-door criminal justice system where the chances of hardened criminals being arrested on felony charges are one in one hundred. Later, the Police Foundation study of New York's Koch-Carey Law found that it failed to reduce the number of guns on the street and did not reduce gun use in rape, robbery or assault.

Such legislation invites police to routinely stop and frisk people randomly on the street on suspicion of firearms possession. In fact, the Police Foundation has called for the random use of metal detectors on the streets to apprehend people carrying firearms without authorization. In disregarding the constitutionally guaranteed right to privacy and against unreasonable searches and seizures, police would be empowered under the Police Foundation's blueprint for disarmament to "systematically stop a certain percentage of people on the streets . . . in business neighborhoods and run the detectors by them, just as you do at the airport. If the detectors produce some noise then that might establish probable cause for a search."

While admitting that such "police state" tactics would require" methods . . . that liberals instinctively dislike," government researchers James Q. Wilson and Mark H. Moore called for more aggressive police patrolling in public places, saying: "To inhibit the carrying of handguns, the police should become more aggressive in stopping suspicious people and, where they have reasonable grounds for their suspicions, frisking (i.e., patting down) those stopped to obtain guns. Hand-held magnetometers, of the sort used by airport security guards, might make the street frisks easier and less obtrusive. All this can be done without changing the law." (*The Washington Post,* April 1, 1981) Note, they said "people," not criminals.

Myth: "Gun control reduces crime."

This is perhaps, the greatest myth that is perpetrated today by national gun ban groups.

No empirical study of the effectiveness of gun laws has shown any positive effect on crime. To the dismay of the prohibitionists, such studies have shown a negative effect. That is, in areas having greatest restrictions on private firearms ownership, crime rates are typically higher, because criminals are aware that their intended victims are less likely to have the means with which to defend themselves.

If gun laws worked, the proponents of such laws would gleefully cite examples of reduced crime. Instead, they uniformly blame the absence of tougher or wider spread measures for the failures of the laws they advocated. Or they cite denials of applications for permission to buy a firearm as evidence the law is doing something beyond preventing honest citizens from being able legally to acquire firearms. They cite Washington, D.C., as a jurisdiction where gun laws are "working." Yet crime in Washington has risen dramatically since 1976, the year before its handgun ban took effect. Washington, D.C., now has outrageously higher crime rates than any of the states (D.C. 1992 violent crime rate: 2832.8 per 100,000 residents; U.S. rate: 757.5), with a homicide rate eight times the national rate (1992 rate: 75.4 per 100,000 for D.C., 9.3 nationally).

No wonder former D.C. Police Chief Maurice Turner said, "What has the gun control law done to keep criminals from getting guns? Absolutely nothing. . . . [City residents] ought to have the opportunity to have a handgun."

Criminals in Washington have no trouble getting either prohibited drugs or prohibited handguns, resulting in a skyrocketing of the city's murder rate. D.C.'s 1991 homicide rate of 80.6 per 100,000 population was the highest ever recorded by an American big city, and marked a 200 percent rise in homicide since banning handguns, while the nation's homicide rate rose just 11 percent. Since 1991, the homicide rate has remained near 75 per 100,000, while the national rate hovers around 9.5.

Clearly, criminals do not bother with the niceties of obeying laws — for a criminal is, by definition, someone who disobeys laws. Those who enforce the law agree.

In addition, restrictive gun laws create a "Catch-22" for victims of violent crime. Under court decisions, *the police have no legal obligation to protect any particular individual.* This concept has been tested numerous times including cases as recent as 1993. In each case the courts have ruled that the police are responsible for protecting society as a whole, not any individual. This means that under restrictive gun laws, people may be unable to protect themselves or their family from violent criminals.

The evidence that restrictive gun laws create scofflaws is evident to anyone willing to look. In New York City, there are only about 70,000 legally-owned handguns, yet survey research suggests that there are at least 750,000 handguns in the city, mostly in the hands of otherwise law-abiding citizens. In Chicago, a recent mandatory registration law has resulted in compliance by only a fraction of those who had previously registered their guns. The rate of compliance with the registration requirement of California's and New Jersey's semi-automatic bans have been very low. The same massive noncompliance — not by criminals, whom no one expects will comply, but by people fearful of repression — is evident wherever stringent gun laws are enacted.

FACTS WE CAN ALL LIVE WITH

Laws aimed at criminal misuse of firearms are proven crime deterrents. After adopting a mandatory penalty for using a firearm in the commission of a violent crime in 1975, Virginia's murder rate dropped 23 percent and robbery 11 percent in fifteen years. South Carolina recorded a 24 percent murder rate decline between 1975 and 1990 with a similar law. Other impressive declines were recorded in other states using mandatory penalties, such as Florida (homicide rate down 33 percent in 17 years), Delaware (homicide rate down 33 percent in 19 years), Montana (down 42 percent 1976–1992) and New Hampshire (homicide rate down 50 percent 1977–1992).

The solution to violent crime lies in the promise, not the mere threat, of swift, certain punishment.

Our challenge: To reform and strengthen our federal and state criminal justice systems. We must bring about a sharp reversal in the trend toward undue leniency and "revolving door justice." We must insist upon speedier trials and upon punishments which are commensurate with crimes. Rehabilitation should be tempered with a realization that not all can be rehabilitated, and that prisons cost society less than the crime of active predatory criminals.

NRA is meeting that challenge with its CrimeStrike division, established to advance real solutions to the crime problem while protecting the rights of all honest citizens. Working in states across the nation, CrimeStrike has worked for passage of "truth in sentencing laws" which require that criminals actually serve at least 85 percent of time sentenced, "Victim's Bill of Rights" constitutional amendments, and "Three Strikes You're Out" laws.

The job ahead will not be an easy one. The longer "gun control" advocates distract the nation from this task by embracing that single siren song, the longer it will take and the more difficult our job will be. Beginning is the hardest step, and the NRA's Institute for Legislative Action has taken it. Join NRA. Support ILA. Work with us. We need your help.

NOTES

1. Gary Kleck, "Reasons for Skepticism on the Results from a New Poll on: The Incidence of Gun Violence among Young People," *Public Perspective,* September/October 1993, pp. 3–6.

2. Rushforth, et al., "Accidental Firearm Fatalities in a Metropolitan County," 100 *American Journal of Epidemiology* 499 (1975).

3. Norman B. Rushforth, et al., "Violent Death in a Metropolitan County," 297 *New England Journal of Medicine* 1531, 533 (1977).

4. Arthur Kellermann, et al., "Gun Ownership as a Risk Factor for Homicide in the Home," *New England Journal of Medicine* 467 (1993).

5. Daniel D. Polsby, "The False Promise of Gun Control," *The Atlantic Monthly,* March 1994.

6. James Wright and Peter Rossi, *Armed and Considered Dangerous: A Survey of Felons and Their Firearms* (New York: Aldine de Gruyter, 1986).

7. Gary Kleck and Marc Gertz, "Armed Resistance to Crime: The Prevalence and Nature of Self-Defense with a Handgun," *Journal of Criminal Law and Criminology,* 86 (1995): 150.

8. *Haynes v. United States,* 309 U.S. 85 (1968).

9. James D. Wright et al., *Under the Gun: Weapons, Crime and Violence in America* (New York: Aldine, 1983).

10. David Kopel, *The Samurai, the Mountie, and the Cowboy: Should America Adopt the Gun Controls of Other Democracies?* (Buffalo, N.Y.: Prometheus Books, 1992), 431–32.

11. James Wright, "Second Thoughts about Gun Control," 91 *Public Interest,* 23 (Spring 1988).

12. Stephen P. Halbrook, *That Every Man Be Armed: The Evolution of a Constitutional Right* (Albuquerque: University of New Mexico Press, 1984).

13. Kleck, "Reasons for Skepticism."

Questions for Discussion

1. What would be the consequences of a law banning the possession of hand-guns to (a) criminal violence, (b) accidental injury, and (c) self-defense?
2. How would a ban on handguns be enforced?
3. Would a ban on handguns be more or less effective than the ban on illegal drugs? What are the reasons for your answer?
4. How do you account for differences in homicide rates among nations?
5. Have gun-control laws been effective in reducing violence? What are the reasons for your answer?
6. Does the large number of guns available to Americans cause violence, or does violence cause the possession of large numbers of guns? What are the reasons for your answer?

Suggested Readings

Cottrol, Robert J., ed. *Gun Control and the Constitution: Sources and Explorations on the Second Amendment.* 3 vols. New York: Garland Publishing, 1993.

Hofstadter, Richard. "America as a Gun Culture." *American Heritage* 21 (October 1970): 4–11, 82–85.

Kleck, Gary. *Point Blank: Guns and Violence in America.* New York: Aldine de Gruyter, 1991.

Kopel, David B. *The Samurai, the Mountie, and the Cowboy: Should America Adopt the Gun Controls of Other Democracies?* Buffalo, N.Y.: Prometheus Books, 1992.

Larson, Erik. *Lethal Passage: How the Travels of a Single Handgun Expose the Roots of America's Gun Crisis.* New York: Crown, 1994.

Levine, Herbert M. *Gun Control.* Austin, Tex.: Raintree Steck-Vaughn, 1998.

Nisbet, Lee, ed. *The Gun Control Debate: You Decide.* Buffalo, N.Y.: Prometheus Books, 1990.

Quigley, Paxton. *Armed and Female.* New York: E. P. Dutton, 1989.

Spitzer, Robert J. *The Politics of Gun Control.* Chatham, N.J.: Chatham House, 1995.

Sugarmann, Josh. *National Rifle Association: Money, Firepower and Fear.* Washington, D.C.: National Press Books, 1992.

"Violence." *JAMA: Journal of the American Medical Association* 267 (June 10, 1992): entire issue.

Weil, Douglas S., and David Hemenway. "Loaded Guns in the Home." *Journal of the American Medical Association* 267 (June 10, 1992): 3033–3037.

Wilson, James Q. "Just Take Away Their Guns." *New York Times Magazine,* March 20, 1994, p. 47.

Wright, James D. "Ten Essential Observations on Guns in America." *Society* 36 (March/April 1995): 63–68.

———, and Peter H. Rossi. *Armed and Considered Dangerous: A Survey of Felons and Their Firearms,* expanded ed. New York: Aldine de Gruyter, 1994.

Zimring, Franklin E., and Gordon Hawkins. *The Citizen's Guide to Gun Control.* New York: Macmillan, 1992.

Chapter 20

Should Drugs Be Decriminalized?

In the 1960s the culture of drugs won some popular approval — particularly among the young. In the minds of some advocates of drugs at that time, rational decision making had brought the United States involvement in the Vietnam War, a high military budget when other national priorities were neglected, and the rigidities of a conformist society. Timothy Leary, a former Harvard instructor, supplied the drug culture with its motto: Turn on, tune in, drop out.

The drug culture of the 1960s was in the spotlight with Haight-Asbury, a section of San Francisco where "hippies" pursued their way of life, and Woodstock, a small town in New York State that hosted a huge rock concert, with much drug use. But drugs began to take their toll. Many performers, including some who performed at Woodstock, died of overdoses and addictions: John Belushi, Jimi Hendrix, Janis Joplin, Elvis Presley. Hundreds of thousands of men and women from all social strata suffered death and physical and mental disabilities.

By the 1980s drug use was no longer a subject of comic quips by entertainment figures anxious to get quick laughs, and Americans were overwhelmingly hostile to drug abuse and drug pushers — the people who sold drugs. Elected public officials declared wars on drugs, and funding to fight against drug use was provided at all levels of government.

Although the term "drugs" is used here to mean illegal drugs, it is important to remember that not all drugs are illegal. People who are ill use drugs prescribed by physicians that otherwise would be illegal, although these are also sometimes given to abuse. Alcohol and tobacco are drugs that are legal and available to most adults. But the major drugs of most concern are cocaine (and its derivative "crack") and heroin. Marijuana, too, has been increasingly considered to be unsafe because today's variety of that substance is many times more powerful than the "grass" hippies smoked in the 1960s.

As public awareness and government action have increased, actual drug use declined in the 1980s. Even use of alcohol and tobacco declined as Americans became increasingly concerned about good health and physical fitness. From a health point of view, tobacco and alcohol take a greater toll on the lives and health of American people than do the major illegal drugs.

Still, the problem of drug use remains serious. The total number of illicit drug users in the United States reached a high of 25.4 million people in 1979 but declined until 1992 when it remained steady.[1] But drug studies in the 1990s showed that drug abuse among young people had increased sharply in the first half of the 1990s. For example, in 1996, the National Household Survey on Drug Abuse showed that the percentage of adolescents between the age of twelve and seventeen who admitted to using illicit drugs in the month preceding the survey increased from 5.3 percent in 1992 to 10.9 percent in 1995 — a doubling of the use of such drugs for this age group.[2]

Criminal activities and street deaths that drug abuse spawns remain a serious problem also. And there is no agreement on a solution to reducing illicit drug use. One approach is to intensify criminal punishment. Some would do so by increasing police budgets, working harder with governments of foreign countries where drugs are produced, and imposing the death penalty on drug dealers. Another approach is to provide increased public awareness for treatment.

Since the 1980s, a number of observers have argued in favor of legalization or decriminalization of hard drugs. This approach has won the support of some eminent public figures, including Kurt Schmoke, the mayor of Baltimore; William F. Buckley Jr., the conservative columnist; and George Shultz, secretary of state in the Reagan administration.

The debate below pits David Boaz, executive vice-president of the Cato Institute, against former New York City Mayor Edward I. Koch. Boaz favors decriminalization. He contends:

1. Drug prohibition causes high crime rates.
2. It encourages corruption.
3. It brings users into contact with criminals and gets them involved in a criminal culture.
4. It results in the creation of more potent drugs.
5. It destroys civil liberties.
6. It is futile.

Boaz calls for decriminalization of all recreational drugs, including marijuana, cocaine, and heroin.

Koch opposes legalization. He contends:

1. Drug legalization would mean that we have surrendered in the war on drugs.
2. More than 90 percent of the American public reject decriminalizing all illegal drugs.
3. Legalization would not reduce drug abuse and crime but increase them.
4. The cost of legalization would be higher than the cost of retaining the present system.
5. Greater resources for the war on drugs will help to solve the problem.

NOTES

   1. Robert Suro, "Teens' Use of Drugs Still Rising," *Washington Post*, August 21, 1996, p. A10.
   2. Ibid., p. A1.

☑ YES

Should Drugs Be Decriminalized?

DAVID BOAZ
The Case for Decriminalizing Drugs

Let me start my discussion of drug prohibition with the following quotation:

> For thirteen years federal law enforcement officials fought the illegal traffic. State and local reinforcements were called up to help. The fight was always frustrating and too often futile. The enemy used guerrilla tactics, seldom came into the open to fight, blended easily into the general population, and when finally subdued turned to the United States Constitution for protection. His numbers were legion, his resources unlimited, his tactics imaginative. Men of high resolve and determination were summoned to Washington to direct the federal forces. The enemy was pursued relentlessly on land and sea and in the air. There were an alarming number of casualties on both sides, and, as in all wars, innocent bystanders fell in the crossfire.

That passage wasn't written recently. It was written about the prohibition of alcohol in the 1920s, and it illustrates a very simple point: Alcohol didn't cause the high crime rates of the 1920s, prohibition did. Drugs don't cause today's alarming crime rates, drug prohibition does.

What are the effects of prohibition? (Specifically I'm considering drug prohibition here, but the analysis applies to almost any prohibition of a substance or activity people want.) The first effect is crime. This is a very simple matter of economics. Drug laws reduce the number of suppliers and therefore reduce the supply of the substance, driving up the price. The danger of arrest for the seller adds a risk premium to the price. The higher price means that users often have to commit crimes to pay for a habit that would be easily affordable if it was legal. Heroin, cocaine, and other drugs would cost much less if they were legal. Experts estimate that at least half of the violent crime in major U.S. cities is a result of drug prohibition.

Crime also results from another factor, the fact that dealers have no way to settle disputes with each other except by shooting each other. We don't see shoot-outs in the automobile business or even in the liquor or the tobacco business. But if a drug dealer has a dispute with another dealer, he can't sue, he can't go to court, he can't do anything except use violence.

And then the very illegality of the drug business draws in criminals. As conservatives always say about guns, if drugs are outlawed, only outlaws will sell drugs. The decent people who would like to be selling drugs the way they might otherwise sell liquor will get squeezed out of an increasingly violent business.

The second effect of prohibition is corruption. Prohibition raises prices, which leads to extraordinary profits, which are an irresistible temptation to policemen, customs officers, Latin American officials, and so on. We should be shocked not that there are Miami policemen on the take, but that there are some Miami policemen not on the take. Policemen make $35,000 a year and have to arrest people who are driving cars worth several times that. Should we be surprised that some of this money trickles down into the pockets of these policemen?

A third effect, and one that is often underestimated, is bringing buyers into contact with criminals. If you buy alcohol you don't have to deal with criminals. If a student buys marijuana on a college campus, he may not have to deal with criminals, but the person he buys it from probably does deal with criminals. And if a high school student buys drugs, there is a very good chance that the people he's buying drugs from — the people who are bringing drugs right to his doorstep, to his housing project, to his schoolyard — are really criminals; not just in the sense that they are selling drugs, but people who have gone into the drug business precisely because it's illegal. One of the strongest arguments for legalization is to divorce the process of using drugs from the process of getting involved in a criminal culture.

A fourth effect is the creation of stronger drugs. Richard Cowan in *National Review* has promulgated what he calls the iron law of prohibition: The more intense the law enforcement, the more potent the drugs will become. If a dealer can only smuggle one suitcase full of drugs into the United States or if he can only drive one car full of drugs into Baltimore, which would he rather be carrying — marijuana, coca leaves, cocaine, or crack? He gets more dollars for the bulk if he carries more potent drugs. An early example of that is that a lot of people turned to marijuana when alcohol became more difficult to get during Prohibition. A few years after Prohibition began in the 1920s there began to be pressures for laws against marijuana. When one advocates drug legalization, one of the standard questions is, "Well, marijuana is one thing, maybe even cocaine, but are you seriously saying you would legalize crack?" And the answer is that crack is almost entirely a product of prohibition. It probably would not have existed if drugs had been legal for the past 20 years.

The fifth effect of prohibition is civil liberties abuses. We have heard a lot recently about Zero Tolerance and the seizure of cars and boats because a small amount of marijuana or cocaine is allegedly found. I recall a time in this country when the government was only allowed to punish someone after he got convicted in a court of law. It now appears that the drug authorities can punish an American citizen by seizing his car or his boat, not even after an in-dictment — much less a conviction — but after a mere allegation by a police officer. Whatever happened to the presumption of innocence?

There is an inherent problem of civil liberties abuses in victimless crimes. Randy Barnett wrote about this in the Pacific Research Institute book *Dealing with Drugs;* the problem is that with victimless crimes, such as buying drugs, there is no complaining witness. In most crimes, say robbery or rape, there is a person who in our legal system is called the complaining witness: the person who was robbed or raped, who goes to the police and complains that some-body has done something to him or her. In a drug purchase, neither party to the transaction complains. Now what does this mean? It means there are no eyewitnesses complaining about the problem so the police have to get the evi-dence some other way. The policemen have to start going undercover, and that leads to entrapment, wiretapping, and all sorts of things that border on civil liberties abuses — and usually end up crossing the border.

The sixth effect of prohibition is futility. The drug war simply isn't working. Some say that much of today's support for legalization that we're seeing from politicians and others is merely a sign of frustration. Well, frustration is a ratio-nal response to futility. It's quite understandable why people have gotten frus-trated with the continuing failure of new enforcement policies.

If a government is involved in a war and it isn't winning, it has two basic choices. The first is escalation, and we've seen a lot of proposals for that.

New York Mayor Ed Koch has proposed to strip-search every person entering the United States from South America or Southeast Asia. Members of the D.C. City Council have called for the National Guard to occupy the capital city of the United States. Congress has bravely called for the death penalty for drug sellers.

Jesse Jackson wants to bring the troops home from Europe and use them to ring our southern border. The police chief of Los Angeles wants to invade Colombia.

The White House drug adviser and the usually sensible *Wall Street Journal* ed-itorial page have called for arresting small-time users. The *Journal,* with its usual spirit, urged the government to "crush the users"; that's 23 million Americans.

The Justice Department wants to double our prison capacity even though we already have far more people in prison as a percentage of our population than any other industrialized country except South Africa. Former attorney general Edwin Meese III and others want to drug test all workers.

The Customs Service has asked for authorization to "use appropriate force" to compel planes suspected of carrying drugs to land. It has clarified, in case there was any doubt, that yes, it means that if it can't find out what a plane is up to, it wants the authority to shoot the plane down and then find out if it's carrying drugs.

These rather frightening ideas represent one response to the futility of the drug war.

The more sensible response, it seems to me, is to decriminalize — to de-escalate, to realize that trying to wage war on 23 million Americans who are obviously very committed to certain recreational activities is not going to be any more successful than Prohibition was. A lot of people use drugs recreationally and peacefully and safely and are not going to go along with Zero Tolerance. They're going to keep trying to get drugs. The problems caused by prohibition are not going to be solved by stepped-up enforcement.

So how exactly would we legalize drugs? Defenders of drug prohibition apparently consider that a devastating question, but it doesn't strike me as being particularly difficult. Our society has had a lot of experience with legal dangerous drugs, particularly alcohol and tobacco, and we can draw on that experience when we legalize marijuana, cocaine, and heroin — as we will, fairly soon, when more Americans come to understand the cost of prohibiting them.

Some critics of prohibition would legalize only "soft" drugs — just marijuana in many cases. That policy would not eliminate the tremendous problems that prohibition has created. As long as drugs that people very much want remain illegal, a black market will exist. If our goal is to rid our cities of crime and corruption, it would make more sense to legalize cocaine and heroin while leaving marijuana illegal than vice versa. The lesson of alcohol prohibition in the 1920s and the prohibition of other drugs today is that prohibition creates more problems than it solves. We should legalize all recreational drugs.

Then what? When we legalize drugs, we will likely apply the alcohol model. That is, marijuana, cocaine, and heroin would be sold only in specially licensed stores — perhaps in liquor stores, perhaps in a new kind of drugstore. Warning labels would be posted in the stores and on the packages. It would be illegal to sell drugs to minors, now defined as anyone under 21. It would be illegal to advertise drugs on television and possibly even in print. Committing a crime or driving under the influence of drugs would be illegal, as with alcohol.

It is quite possible that such a system would be *less* effective in attracting young people to drug use than the current system of schoolyard pushers offering free samples. Teenagers today can get liquor if they try, and we shouldn't assume that a minimum purchasing age would keep other drugs out of their hands. But we don't see many liquor pushers peddling their wares on playgrounds. Getting the drug business out of our schoolyards and streets is an important benefit of legalization.

It is likely that drug use would initially increase. Prices would be much lower, and drugs would be more readily available to adults who prefer not to break the law. But those drugs would be safer — when's the last time you heard of a liquor store selling gin cut with formaldehyde? — and people would be able to regulate their intake more carefully.

In the long run, however, I foresee declining drug use and weaker drugs. Consider the divergent trends in legal and illegal drugs today. Illegal drugs keep getting stronger — crack, PCP, ecstasy, designer drugs — as a result of the Iron Law of Prohibition. But legal drugs are getting weaker — low-tar cigarettes, light beer, wine coolers. About 41 million Americans have quit smoking, and sales of spirits are declining; beer and wine keep the alcohol industry stable. As Americans become more health-conscious, they are turning away from drugs. Drug education could do more to encourage this trend if it was separated from law enforcement.

By reducing crime, drug legalization would greatly increase our sense of safety in our neighborhoods. It would take the astronomical profits out of the drug trade, and the Colombian cartel would collapse like a punctured balloon. Drugs would be sold by Fortune 500 companies and friendly corner merchants, not by Mafiosi and 16-year-olds with BMWs and guns. Legalization would put an end to the corruption that has engulfed so many Latin American countries and tainted the Miami police and U.S. soldiers in Central America.

Legalization would not solve all of America's drug problems, but it would make our cities safer, make drug use healthier, eliminate a major source of revenue for organized crime, reduce corruption here and abroad, and make honest work more attractive to inner-city youth — pretty good results for any reform.

☑ NO

Should Drugs Be Decriminalized?

EDWARD I. KOCH

The Case against Decriminalizing Drugs

I would normally preface my remarks by saying that I'm glad to be here, but today that is not the case. Given the devastation that drugs have wrought on our communities and nation, particularly over the last few years, I find it astounding that I am here to discuss a notion that seems to me to be the equivalent of extinguishing a raging fire with napalm — a fire that at this very moment is frying the brains of thousands of Americans.

Mr. Chairman, this committee, along with the very active support of the vast majority of America's mayors, has made valiant efforts in the past few years to devise ways to combat the drug scourge that continues to tear at our nation. Today, a small, small, number in these ranks are unwittingly impeding our progress by suggesting that we wave the white flag in the war on drugs and succumb to the enemy. Is their vision for the future of this country nothing better than one of its becoming a banana republic?! I hope not, but surely that is where their proposition would lead us.

I am far from alone in feeling this way. The September 15th [1988] *New York Times* reported that an ABC news poll found that more than 90 percent of the American public *reject* decriminalizing all illicit drugs. They also believe, by a 2 to 1 ratio, that the legalization of drugs would lead to an increase in crime.

And yet, in part because of the frustration some have had with the difficult task of addressing the drug problem, the idea of legalization has been elevated, undeservedly, to a place within the realm of debatable, if not potential, policy alternatives. Now that it is there, it may in fact be necessary to put the question of legalization on the table, but only to put it to rest, so that we can move forward with the strategies that *will* have an impact.

Before I continue, let me cite some statistics which reveal the dimension and impact of the drug problem.

There are over 500,000 heroin abusers in this country and 6 million people who have a serious cocaine or crack abuse problem. Even more troubling is the increasing numbers of our youth who are abusing certain drugs. Although no one knows for certain the number of juveniles using drugs, surveys of high school students have shown dramatic increases in their use of cocaine over the last ten years.

The devastating effects of drug abuse and the drug trafficking that supplies the abusers with their poison are quite clear. Reliable studies have concluded that drug abuse and drug traffickers are responsible for much of the violent crime in our nation.

These assertions are supported by data from the National Institute of Justice's drug forecasting survey, which recently showed that in New York City, 79 percent of the surveyed arrestees tested positive for at least one drug (including marijuana), 63 percent tested positive for cocaine, including crack, and 25 percent tested positive for heroin.

Indeed, the New York City Police Department has arrested almost 150,000 people for drug related crime over the last two years—up 17 percent from 1986 to 1987 and 11 percent in the first five months of 1988. These data clearly underscore the relationship between drug abuse and crime.

It is undeniable that, if we do not reduce drug abuse, its resulting crime and other destructive physiological consequences will continue to escalate and will result in a national tragedy of much greater proportions than it is today.

The suggestion that we should legalize drugs is therefore all the more shocking. How would legalization reduce drug abuse and its resulting devastation and crime? Let's analyze the legalization arguments.

To start with, some would have us believe that the laws against drug use and drug trafficking are prohibitions against a manner of personal conduct or style and that they are the imposition of society's moral values on the individual. This is just not the case. Rather, they are laws that prohibit conduct which destroys not only the individual users, but their families, the innocent victims of their crimes and the very foundation of a productive society.

The proponents of legalization are weak on the specifics of the implementation of a policy of "drugs for all." Some suggest that government should play a "big brother" role, providing fixed doses to addicts, and thereby limiting drug use. Their lack of understanding of drug abuse is startling, since there is no such thing as a fixed dose that will satisfy a drug addict's appetite for greater and greater quantities. Accordingly, the black market that legalizers say will be eliminated, would, of necessity, exist to provide an additional avenue of obtaining that which is not available from "legitimate" sources.

Piggy-backing on the assertion that legalization will eliminate the high profit margins on drug sales and therefore the black market, proponents say that crime associated with drug trafficking will diminish once drugs become an acceptable commodity. They ignore history and the facts.

Cheap drugs won't reduce crime and they never have.

In fact, given England's desperate failure to relieve its heroin addiction problem through heroin distribution programs during the 1960s and 1970s, the opposite is closer to the truth.

Until 1970, heroin was freely prescribed in Britain by private doctors. But over-prescription led to a doubling of the addicted population between 1970 and 1980. Then it took off.

Cheap heroin from Pakistan, which sold for $5 a fix on the street, began flooding the black market. Not only was it super cheap, it was more potent than what the government was handing out and came without bureaucratic restrictions. Cheap, potent and hassle free, the new street heroin *quadrupled the number of addicts in five years.* By 1986 the British Home Office estimated that there were 50,000 to 60,000 heroin addicts in the country. Some unofficial estimates were three times greater.

How was crime in Britain affected by legalization? In one 1978 study, 50 percent of the addicts in government programs were convicted of crimes in their first year of participation. Unemployment among addicts remained chronic too, as did other kinds of drug use — 84 percent of the addicts registered with the government were found to use other illicit drugs as well. All told, the government program was a disaster.

Another facet of the crime problem associated with drugs that is frequently overlooked is that a number of drugs, and crack in particular, have been shown to have behavioral effects that result in violent criminal conduct not limited to theft to obtain money to purchase drugs. I don't think that we would be too far from the mark by assuming that the emerging "designer" drugs would have similar effects as the drug sellers search for a product that gives quicker and more intense highs. Should the government distribute or condone these crime-inducing drugs too?

Permitting drug use and encouraging even greater drug use by legalization would perpetuate and *expand* the devastating effects of drug abuse and its resulting crime.

Another erroneous argument for legalization is based on the economic rationale that it would be cheaper to provide drugs to addicts than it is to enforce the laws and pursue anti-drug strategies. It would not be cheaper. As the drug using population increases, the costs to society for the crime and other detrimental health effects of drug abuse would be far greater than they are now. We would still require the police, courts, prosecutors and jails to deal with drug related crime. We would need to dramatically increase treatment programs for those who, once on drugs, want to get off. And we would still have the economic impact on business, not only in terms of lost productivity, but in terms of increased health care insurance, worker safety and unemployment benefits.

Even if it is more expensive to do what we are doing to eradicate this problem, can government's obligation to protect the public safety be abdicated because it is expensive? Clearly not.

Two weeks ago on a nationwide television broadcast on this same topic, it was suggested that anti-drug law enforcement efforts, now estimated at $8 billion nationwide, could be cut to $2 billion if drugs were legalized. How can we say that $8 billion is too much to spend? How much is too much? Earlier this year I read in the *Washington Post* that leaders of the infamous Medellin drug cartel offered to pay off Colombia's estimated $15 *billion* national debt in return for immunity from prosecution and the scrapping of the country's extradition treaty with the U.S. This handful of individuals were willing to spend almost twice as much to stay in the game than we, at 240 million strong, are to keep them out. I think that it is all too painfully obvious that $8 billion is not nearly enough and we need to commit more — in the right places.

Part of our problem has been a lack of national commitment — not on the part of the average American, but by those who are representing them. The tough choices that have to be made are not being made. While the 1986 Omnibus Drug Bill authorized $230 million for drug law enforcement, only $70 million was actually appropriated. Why? The most common excuse is that there's no more money for anything since Gramm-Rudman. Let's face it, unless we find a new revenue stream for funding anti-narcotics efforts, we may never be able to adequately address our needs.

On a number of occasions over the past year I have suggested a three year federal income tax surcharge dedicated *solely* to eliminating the drug problem. I believe that the American public would support such a tax if it were proposed in this context. However, in this election year [1988], everyone in Washington is loath to mention that "T" word for any purpose. I believe that that is terribly shortsighted.

Now I'm not throwing the entire burden in the lap of the federal government, but I think you'll agree that whether it's Los Angeles, New York, Utica or Topeka, on its own, a city can't win the war on drugs. Washington must do its job too.

The cities are already doing their part. New York City, in particular, is dedicated to do whatever it can in terms of fighting the drug war. With 1,400 officers dedicated solely to narcotics interdiction, we are spending *nearly half a billion dollars* in city money to address all aspects of drug control.

But I plan to do more. Building on the success of a special police unit we organized last spring, the "Tactical Narcotics Team" (TNT), which was used to clean up a particularly drug infested area of Queens, I am in the process of expanding its efforts citywide with close to 650 additional officers.

This huge expansion of our drug enforcement efforts will obviously put pressure on our criminal justice system. It will necessitate an increase in jail beds over and above the 3,800 in my current capital plan and the 4,700 added in the last two years. It will increase the caseloads of district attorneys and the Legal Aid Society who will receive $9.5 million more than previously planned over the next two years.

The total price tag for this expansion: $110 million. How will I fund it? By making some tough decisions — raise taxes on cigarettes and alcohol, temporarily increase local property taxes or, if neither of these alternatives are successful, cut some city services. However we do it, it must be done.

The reaction of some people to my proposal has been that perhaps I should wait and hope the next president and the new Congress will be able to do more to fight drugs. But those of us out there on the front lines, those who deal on a daily basis with the ravages of this war simply can't afford to wait.

Mr. Chairman, what it comes down to is this. When people say that we should legalize drugs because law enforcement efforts have failed, they ignore the fact that a truly effective war has yet to be launched against drugs. What we really need to do is more, not less. A real war on drugs must include interdiction of illicit drugs by the armed forces at the borders, in the air and on the high seas. It must include more federal funding for education and treatment on demand. It must include "federalization" of drug prosecution and incarceration. These are all ideas I've laid out in detail in previous forums. I will continue to strive to see that they become part of the arsenal in the war on drugs.

It is time to raise the battle flag, not wave the white one.

Questions for Discussion

1. What effect would decriminalization of drugs have on crime?
2. What effect would decriminalization of drugs have on solving the drug problem?
3. What relevance does U.S. experience with the prohibition of alcohol between 1920 and 1933 have on the issue of decriminalizing drugs today?
4. What is the best method to reduce the use of illegal drugs?
5. Is drug abuse a victimless crime? What are the reasons for your answer?

Suggested Readings

Baum, Dan. *Smoke and Mirrors: The War on Drugs and the Politics of Failure.* Boston: Little, Brown, 1996.

Bowman, Frank O., III. "Playing '21' with Narcotics Enforcement: A Response to Professor Carrington." *Washington and Lee Law Review* 52, no. 3 (1995): 937–986.

Califano, Joseph. "Don't Stop This War." *Washington Post*, May 26, 1996, p. C7.

Carrington, Paul D. "The Twenty-First Wisdom." *Washington and Lee Law Review* 52, no. 1 (1995): 333–356.

Committee on Drugs and the Law of the Association of the Bar of the City of New York. "A Wiser Course: Ending Drug Prohibition." *Record of the Association of the Bar of the City of New York* 49, no. 5 (June 1994): 521–577.

Inciardi, James A., and Christine A. Saum. "Legalization Madness." *Public Interest*, no. 123 (Spring 1996): 72–82.

Jonnes, Jill. *Hep-Cats, Narcs, and Pipe Dreams: A History of America's Romance with Illegal Drugs.* New York: Scribner's, 1996.

Levine, Herbert M. *The Drug Problem.* Austin, Tex.: Raintree Steck-Vaughn, 1998.

Schmoke, Kurt L. "An Argument in Favor of Decriminalization." *Hofstra Law Review* 18, no. 3 (Spring 1990): 501–525.

Shenk, Joshua Wolf. "Why You Can Hate Drugs and Still Want to Legalize Them." *Washington Monthly* 27, no. 10 (October 1995): 32–40.

Stares, Paul B. "Drug Legalization?" *Brookings Review* 14, no. 2 (Spring 1996): 18–20.

"The War on Drugs Is Lost." *National Review* 48, no. 2 (February 12, 1996): 34–48. (Articles by William F. Buckley, Jr., Ethan A. Nadelmann, Kurt Schmoke, Joseph D. McNamara, Robert W. Sweet, Thomas Szasz, and Steven R. Duke.) *See also* "400 Readers Give Their Views." *National Review* 48, no. 12 (July 1, 1996): 32–37.

U.S. Cong., House of Representatives. *Effectiveness of the National Drug Control Strategy and the Status of the Drug War.* Hearings before the National Security, International Affairs, and Criminal Justice Subcommittee of the Committee on Government Reform and Oversight, 104th Cong., 1st Sess., 1995.

Wilson, James Q. "Against the Legalization of Drugs." *Commentary* 89, no. 2 (February 1990): 21–28.

Chapter 21

Is Human-Made Global Warming a Proven Environmental Threat?

Economic development in the United States, other advanced industrial societies, and developing nations has been responsible for much that is good for humanity, such as a high standard of living, long life expectancy, new inventions, and good health. But this development has also produced negative consequences, such as air and water pollution and soil erosion, that are dangerous to health and prosperity.

To respond to these environmental dangers, the United States and other nations have adopted legislation to regulate the activities of industry and ordinary citizens. Laws restrict the dumping of chemical wastes, prohibit the use of lead in gasoline, control the fuels used in industry, and require the recycling of waste material. These laws have produced a cleaner and healthier environment than would have existed without them. Not only have individuals benefited, but some businesses have profited, too. Manufacturers of energy-efficient technology make new products, and people who fish for their livelihood appreciate that fish harvests are not diminished by waste materials and poisonous chemicals.

But environmental laws can also have economic consequences that harm business and worker interests. Some companies must close down because they cannot afford to purchase mandated equipment or because the government bans items they were producing. Workers have lost jobs. According to Eugene M. Trisco, an attorney who represents the United Mine Workers of America on environmental issues, "We lost thousands of jobs as a result of the [1990] amendments to the Clean Air Act."[1]

One of the most important environmental issues of the 1990s deals with global warming—the rising temperature of the world. Scientists have observed that the temperature of the Earth has increased by 1 degree Fahrenheit since the beginning of the twentieth century. Some scientists foresee further increases of the magnitude of 2 to 7 degrees Fahrenheit in the twenty-first century unless steps are taken to reduce the amount of carbon dioxide and other gases that affect the Earth's temperature. The consequences of a "greenhouse effect," a process whereby heat is trapped by the atmosphere at the surface of the Earth and warms the Earth, are often cited in the discussion of this issue. Some of the heat is human-made, caused by "greenhouse gases" such as carbon dioxide, methane, nitrous oxide, and chlorofluorocarbons.

Scientists differ about the accuracy of the predictions. Forecasting accurate climate changes requires data about past climate conditions that are not available. Attempts to use computer modeling have produced much controversy about the utility of the models. Climate change is also difficult to predict because it involves many interacting processes. Small-scale processes can influence large-scale processes, thus confounding an accurate prediction.

In addition, scientists do not agree among themselves about the consequences of global warming to society. Some say that warming may destroy crops; but others say that it will benefit other crops. Some say it will spread tropical diseases to temperate zones. Others predict the rise of sea levels so great as to produce disasters for certain low-lying regions, such as Bangladesh in Asia and southern Louisiana in the United States. Still others say the temperature increase will be minimal or even nonexistent, as there is also evidence of global cooling.

The prospect of global warming is particularly important to the United States because it is the biggest producer of greenhouse gases in the world. Its economy depends heavily on the use of energy resources, such as oil and coal, that produce greenhouse gases. Some industries have attempted to respond to environmental concerns by making more energy-efficient products and by operating environmentally sound industrial activities. To some extent, companies and consumers have saved money from this approach. But if the United States is required to reduce a large amount of its energy resources, then that reduction could have an adverse impact on the economy. And so some economic groups, such as utilities and automobile manufacturers, find themselves at odds with environmentalists and some government representatives over the dangers of global warming.

The U.S. government has taken steps to deal with global warming. In 1992, it joined with 142 other countries at the Earth Summit in Rio de Janeiro to sign the U.N. Framework Convention on Climate Change. The pact called upon all countries to design plans to limit greenhouse-gas emissions to 1990 levels by the year 2000. In 1993, President Bill Clinton announced his Climate Change Action Plan, which asked businesses and industries to reduce emissions of gases thought to be linked to global warming. The plan involved more than 50 energy-saving projects. Environmentalists complained that it was based on voluntary compliance.

At a follow-up conference to the 1992 Rio Summit in Berlin in 1995, delegates from more than 120 nations backed a plan that became known as the Berlin mandate. It recognized that the 1992 framework convention was inadequate for achieving the goals it had adopted. The Berlin conference established a two-year negotiation process designed to set specific targets and timetables for reducing emissions of carbon dioxide and other greenhouse gases after the year 2000. A conference is planned in Kyoto, Japan, for the end of 1997 to complete the work of the Berlin conference. In 1996, U.S. Undersecretary of State for Global Affairs Timothy E. Worth announced that at the Kyoto conference the United States will call for establishing legally binding targets and timetables on the release of greenhouse gases after 2000.

Scientific research about global warming continues, and it is likely that the subject will be debated for a long time. Science will no doubt develop better tools for analyzing climate, and the continuing industrialization of the world may pose new challenges. In the following debate, Robert T. Watson, an associate director for environment in the White House Office of Science and Technology Policy, argues that global warming is a major environmental threat to health, agriculture, and biodiversity. He contends:

1. The overwhelming majority of scientific experts believe human-induced climate change is inevitable. This view is shared by 130 nations, including the United States.
2. Dramatic reductions in greenhouse-gas emissions are technically feasible at little or no cost to society due to an array of energy technologies and policy measures.
3. Human activities undoubtedly are increasing atmospheric concentrations of greenhouse gases, which tend to warm the atmosphere.
4. There is no doubt that Earth's climate has changed during the last hundred years.
5. While there has been, as yet, no definitive detection of a human-induced global-warming signal in the climate record, the evidence increasingly points in that direction.
6. Assuming no climate-change policies, emissions of carbon dioxide and other greenhouses gases are bound to increase.
7. Projected temperature changes would be accompanied by changes in the patterns and intensity of rainfall, with an increased tendency for floods and droughts and increase in sea level of 10 to 120 centimeters by 2100.
8. A warmer climate will be accompanied by changes in precipitation, floods, droughts, heat waves, and rises in sea level. In addition, some scientists worry about changes in the frequency and intensity of tornadoes, cyclones, and hurricanes.
9. Climate change could adversely affect human health, food and water supplies, economic growth, and national security.
10. Timely, prudent actions will allow us to slow global warming and develop mitigation and adaptation options without serious economic dislocation.

Atmospheric physicist S. Fred Singer argues that global warming is not a proven threat to humankind. He contends:

1. The environmental disasters predicted by scientists are not grounded in fact but spring from the feverish imagination of activists and their ideological desire to impose controls on energy use and micromanage economic growth.

2. An Intergovernmental Panel on Climate Change shows considerable skepticism about man-made global warming. The report admits that there are scientific dissenting views to the "scientific consensus."

3. Because the U.S. government spends $2.1 billion a year for global-change research, a wide constituency — made up of UN bureaucrats, assorted politicians, environmental activists, and compliant scientists — support policies to overcome what is a phantom threat.

4. There is not, nor ever was, a "scientific consensus" in support of climate catastrophes, as is so often claimed.

5. Skeptical scientists recognize that climate forecasts are simply the result of quite primitive "models" of the real atmosphere that are fed into giant computers. The models of climate change have failed miserably in accounting for past temperature changes, cannot explain the highly accurate global record from weather satellites, and are internally inconsistent.

6. Many experts believe that there will be a modest but barely detectable average warming in the next century. The result of the modest increase will lead to higher nighttime and winter temperatures with consequences that are on the whole beneficial, especially for agriculture.

7. It's climate cooling we should be afraid of — how to hold off the soon-expected ice age.

8. We need to reexamine the Global Climate Treaty's goal of greenhouse-gas stabilization: its need, timing, and feasibility.

9. One can question the feasibility of the Global Climate Treaty by noting that one cannot reconcile economic development with cutting back on energy use in less-developed nations.

10. Before the world causes mischief and economic disasters by insisting on mandatory cutbacks of carbon-dioxide emissions and energy use, we should (a) find out what is wrong with the models, (b) take prudent steps that are necessary without the global warming scare, such as conserving energy, increasing efficiency, and adding forest mass by cutting fewer trees and planting more, and (c) encourage nuclear energy.

NOTES

1. Quoted in Dan Morgan, "Strengthened U.S. Commitment Lights a Fire under Global Warming Debate," *Washington Post*, September 13, 1996, p. A4.

Is Human-Made Global Warming a Proven Environmental Threat?

ROBERT T. WATSON

Global Warming Bodes Ill for Health, Agriculture, and Biodiversity

A small, vocal minority of skeptics claims there is no scientific evidence to support the theory that man-made emissions of greenhouse gases will alter the Earth's climate. They claim that global warming is liberal, left-wing, claptrap science and a ploy by the scientific community to ensure funding for yet another "Chicken Little" scare. Others suggest that attempts to reduce greenhouse-gas emissions by changing energy- or land-use policies would needlessly cost the American taxpayer tens to hundreds of billions of dollars annually and that it is really part of an international conspiracy to undermine America's competitiveness in the global marketplace.

The truth, however, is quite different. The overwhelming majority of scientific experts believes human-induced climate change is inevitable. The question is not *whether* climate will change in response to human activities, but rather *where* (regional patterns), *when* (the rate of change) and by *how much* (magnitude). This is the fundamental conclusion of a careful and objective analysis of all relevant scientific, technical and economic information by thousands of experts from academia, governments, industry and environmental organizations under the auspices of the UN [United Nations] Intergovernmental Panel on Climate Change.

The view of the majority of scientists is shared by 130 nations, including the United States, that signed and ratified the UN Convention on Climate Change. At a meeting in Berlin in March 1995, all parties to the treaty agreed that current actions to mitigate climate change are inadequate to protect society from the threat of human-induced global warming.

The good news is that the majority of energy experts, and energy organizations such as the World Energy Council, believe that dramatic reductions in greenhouse-gas emissions are technically feasible at little or no cost to society due to an array of energy technologies and policy measures. Many of these will have other benefits for society. For example, the use of more energy-efficient buildings and motor vehicles would reduce dependence on the importation of foreign oil and reduce air pollution at the same time. Although significant progress can be made with current technologies, a commitment to further research and development is essential.

However, we must keep in mind the following points about current scientific understanding of the climate system:

First, human activities undoubtedly are increasing atmospheric concentrations of greenhouse gases, which tend to warm the atmosphere. The most important greenhouse gas directly affected by human activities is carbon dioxide, which has increased by nearly 30 percent since 1700, primarily because of changes in land use (deforestation) and the burning of coal, oil and gas. In some regions of the world, human activities also have increased the atmospheric concentrations of aerosols (tiny airborne particles), which tend to cool the atmosphere.

Second, there is no doubt that the Earth's climate has changed during the last 100 years. The global mean air-surface temperature over the land and ocean has warmed between 0.6 and 1.1 degrees Fahrenheit, glaciers have retreated globally and sea level has risen 10 to 25 centimeters. Since the late 1970s there has been a decrease in Arctic Ocean ice and an unusual persistence of the El Niño conditions in the Pacific Ocean that affect severe weather patterns globally. In addition, the nine warmest years this century have occurred since 1980.

Third, while there has been, as yet, no definitive detection of a human-induced global-warming signal in the climate record, the evidence increasingly points in that direction. Comparing the observed changes in global mean temperature with model simulations that incorporate the effect of increases in greenhouse gases and aerosols suggests that the observed changes during the last century are unlikely to be due entirely to natural causes. This conclusion is strengthened further when the observed regional and vertical patterns of temperature changes are compared to those expected from human activities. This similarity in patterns suggests that the temperature record is reflecting human activities. In addition, the increase in the frequency of heavy rains in the United States is yet another signal consistent with human-induced global warming.

Fourth, assuming no climate-change policies, emissions of carbon dioxide and other greenhouse gases are bound to increase. For example, emissions of carbon dioxide in the year 2100 could range from about 6 billion tons per year, similar to current emissions, to as high as 36 billion tons per year. Such emissions would lead to carbon-dioxide concentrations ranging from three to eight times the preindustrial levels and still increasing rapidly. Climate models suggest that these projected emissions in greenhouse gases and aerosols would lead to an increase in the global mean temperature of 2 to 7 degrees Fahrenheit by 2100, the swiftest such rise in the last 10,000 years.

Fifth, these projected temperature changes would be accompanied by changes in the patterns and intensity of rainfall, with an increased tendency for floods and droughts and an increase in sea level of 10 to 120 centimeters by 2100.

Many people, especially those who live in colder climes, question whether we should care if the climate becomes warmer. The answer is quite simple: A warmer climate will be accompanied by changes in precipitation, floods, droughts, heat waves and rises in sea level. Some scientists also worry about changes in the frequency and intensity of tornadoes, cyclones and hurricanes, but their concern is much more speculative.

Granted, modern societies have evolved to coexist with today's climate and its natural variability. But even technologically sophisticated nations fall victim to unusual weather woes. Every year throughout the world, thousands die, hundreds of thousands are made homeless and billions of dollars are lost because of floods, droughts, tornadoes, cyclones and hurricanes. Every year during the last decade, the United States has faced a major weather-related disaster, costing lives and an average loss of $1 billion per week. Recall the drought of 1988, Hurricane Andrew of 1992 and the Mississippi River and California floods of 1993 and 1995. Chicago and other American cities still are recovering from July's [1995] deadly heat wave, which claimed hundreds of lives — mostly the young and the elderly.

True, climate change would be a boon to some regions of the world, but it could adversely affect those things we care about most: human health, food and water supplies, economic growth and national security.

For example, a warmer world could lead to an increase in vector-borne diseases such as malaria and yellow fever in tropical countries. Add to this an increase in the incidence of heat-stress mortality similar to the effects of the July heat wave. Agricultural production would suffer in some regions, particularly in developing countries in the tropics and subtropics, even though the effect of climate change on global food production might be small. A rise in sea level would wash away human habitat for millions of people, triggering floods of environmental refugees. Without a doubt the United States will hear calls for increased defense and foreign-aid expenditures to cope with massive displacements of peoples in certain developing countries. Plants and animals will be hit too: A shift in the boundaries of many ecosystems (forests and grasslands, for example) likely will diminish biological diversity, an important source of food, fibre and medicines.

While it is important that society treat human-induced global warming as a serious global-scale environmental threat requiring concerted global action, there is no reason to panic or take draconian measures. Timely, prudent actions will allow us to slow global warming and develop mitigation and adaptation options without serious economic dislocation. So the question is: How do we rationally deal with the threat of human-induced global warming?

We began when President Bush signed (and the Senate ratified) the Climate Convention, the primary goal of which is the "stabilization of greenhouse-gas concentrations in the atmosphere at a level that would prevent dangerous human-induced interference with the climate system." The treaty specifies that such a stabilization should be achieved within a period sufficient to allow ecosystems to adapt naturally to climate change without endangering food production or economic development.

The United States can pursue this goal without sacrificing our economic competitiveness, or even destroying it, as some have suggested. This would require utilizing better energy-efficiency technologies (both supply and demand), initiating a switch to modern renewable energies such as wind, solar power and biofuels, improving the fuel efficiency of vehicles and improving management of agricultural lands, rangelands and forests. Such actions would reduce our energy bills, dependence upon foreign oil and congestion in our streets. The same steps would enhance rural development, improve air quality and reduce soil erosion. These actions would make sense even if there were no threat of global warming.

This is a global problem, hence it requires global solutions. These solutions provide American industry with opportunities to provide low-emission greenhouse-gas technologies to the rest of the world and become the market leader. If U.S. industry fails to invest in the required research and development of these technologies, we will end up importing them from Germany and Japan.

Policymakers are faced with responding to the risks posed by human-induced emissions of greenhouse gases in the face of scientific uncertainties, particularly with respect to accurate predictions of the magnitude, rate and regional patterns of climate change, but this is no excuse to ignore the problem. Decisions made during the next few years are particularly important because climate-induced environmental changes cannot be reversed for decades, if not millennia.

☑ NO

Is Human-Made Global Warming a Proven Environmental Threat?

S. FRED SINGER

Doomsayers Are Just Trying to Scare Money Out of the Government

Political scientist Aaron Wildavsky termed global warming the "mother of all environmental scares." A phenomenon that may not even exist has been linked to all sorts of calamities: collapse of the Antarctic ice sheet, worldwide flooding as ocean levels rise, disastrous hurricanes, droughts and agricultural disasters, mass starvation and the spread of tropical diseases putting 3 billion people at risk. These disasters are not grounded in fact but spring from the feverish imagination of activists and their ideological desire to impose controls on energy use and micromanage economic growth.

The fearmongers beating the drums have a spokesman high in the ranks of government—none other than Vice President Al Gore, who sought to give credence to the cataclysmic scenarios in his 1992 best-seller, *Earth in the Balance.* To convince the public, the fearmongers claim that a "scientific consensus" supports their nightmarish extrapolations. The many who disagree are labeled a "tiny minority" of skeptics and naysayers in an obvious attempt to avoid public debate on the scientific evidence.

The activists invoke the UN [United Nations]-sponsored Intergovernmental Panel on Climate Change, or IPCC, involving some 300 scientists. Not mentioned, however, is that the widely touted IPCC report in full — as opposed to the 1990 "policymakers' summary" prepared by the IPCC leadership — shows considerable skepticism about the reality of man-made global warming. The foreword of the IPCC report admits to dissenting views that "could not be accommodated" by the editors. Evidently, "consensus" means simply disregarding or discrediting scientists who disagree.

Given the huge amount of U.S. government funding for global-change research — $2.1 billion per year, topping the budget of the National Cancer Institute — it is surprising that so many scientists openly express their skepticism. Thanks to generous spending of taxpayers' money, a wide constituency — made up chiefly of UN bureaucrats, assorted politicians, environmental activists and compliant scientists — has been created in support of policies to overcome this phantom threat.

In 1992, at the Rio de Janeiro UN Conference on Environment and Development, or UNCED, then-President Bush reluctantly initialed the Global Climate Treaty. In view of what we have learned since, we should exercise Article 25 and withdraw from the Climate Treaty without delay. The American Legislative Exchange Council, a bipartisan organization of more than 3,000 state legislators, already has passed a resolution recommending such a withdrawal.

The treaty's ultimate objective is "stabilization of greenhouse-gas concentration in the atmosphere," not, as some might imagine, the same as stabilization of global emissions — which would be a less daunting goal. Keeping emission rates level, if achievable on a global scale, merely would delay a doubling of greenhouse gases — and an alleged catastrophic warming. The IPCC report makes clear that avoiding a further increase in the concentration of carbon dioxide requires an emission reduction — globally — of 60 to 80 percent! And that translates into a reduction of energy use from fossil fuels by about the same percentage.

The statesmen assembled at the Rio "Earth Summit" were led to accept three propositions — all of them false: There will be a major warming soon; it will be catastrophic for the world; and something can and should be done to stop it. Their doubts were swept away by the IPCC's claim that a scientific "consensus" backed these propositions.

But the scientific basis for climate warming has come under attack in the world's leading scientific journals. An editorial in the September 22, 1994, issue of *Nature* chastises IPCC leaders for recommending deep cuts in the emission of carbon dioxide supported by little more than press releases, executive summaries and "sound-bites directed at those who do not read." The editorial also notes that "argument persists in the scientific community about the effects of CO_2 on climate."

Nature is right on the mark. There is not, nor ever was, a "scientific consensus" in support of climate catastrophes — as is so often claimed. Skeptical scientists recognize that climate forecasts are simply the result of quite primitive "models" of the real atmosphere that are fed into giant computers. But the models don't agree with one another. Their forecasts depend on the detailed way in which they are set up. In the September 9, 1994, issue of *Science,* reporter Richard Kerr reveals the "fudging" in which modelers engage to come up with the "correct" numbers.

For a model to predict future climate with any credibility, it first must be able to reproduce the current climate. But to do this, Kerr reports, "nearly everybody cheats a little." In other words, modelers are forced to manipulate their models to make them agree with today's climate. Some do this by "adjusting" the transfer of energy between ocean and atmosphere. Others "tune" their models by changing the strength of the solar radiation until they get just the right answer. The old cliché still applies: garbage in, garbage out.

Nevertheless, the IPCC claim that the global-warming theory explains the temperature record of the past century — that the two are "broadly consistent" — has become the mantra of activists pushing to control the emission of carbon dioxide by curtailing energy use. This artfully worded phrase covers up the fact that the models have failed miserably in accounting for past temperature changes, cannot explain the highly accurate global record from weather satellites — and are internally inconsistent to boot. Model predictions of future global warming vary by 300 percent — from 1.5 to 4.5 degrees Celsius.

As is widely recognized from global-climate data, a major temperature increase — evidently a natural fluctuation — occurred before 1940, well before much carbon dioxide had been added to the atmosphere. Since 1940, there may have been a slight warming or even a slight cooling, depending upon which data compilation one accepts, but nothing like the temperature increase predicted. Certainly, the high-quality global data from weather satellites, available since 1979, show no warming whatsoever — and are in no way "broadly consistent" with the predicted increase of 0.3 degrees Celsius per decade.

How can there be more than one climate record? Simple. It all depends how the record from hundreds of observing stations is "glued" together, how one combines the temperatures from land stations in the northern and southern hemispheres and how one corrects and adjusts the sparse and not always accurate sea-surface data. (The ocean covers 70 percent of the earth's surface.) Of the many observed temperature records during the past century, three are worth mentioning to illustrate the problem — one by the IPCC, one by NASA [National Aeronautics and Space Administration] modeler James Hansen and one by University of Wisconsin climatologist Reid Bryson. Without making any prejudgment about which is the most accurate, let's just note that all three show a temperature increase before 1940 that exceeds what the models would have predicted. And none of the three shows a post-1940 increase compatible with even the lowest predicted value. What's more: The IPCC record shows a slight increase since 1940, the Hansen record shows none and the Bryson global record shows a definite decrease, a cooling that is consistent with surface data for the United States analyzed independently by climatologist Tom Karl of the National Oceanographic and Atmospheric Administration. The weather satellite data, available only since 1979, also show a slight global cooling.

Still, most atmospheric scientists do expect a modest average warming in the next century as greenhouse gases accumulate in the atmosphere. Many experts believe it barely will be detectable, leading to higher nighttime and winter temperatures with consequences that are on the whole beneficial, especially for agriculture. Increased atmospheric carbon dioxide will stimulate more rapid plant growth. Increased ocean evaporation and rainfall will lead to more soil moisture. The higher temperatures will usher in a longer growing season and fewer frosts. Not for nothing is the temperature "high" around 1000 A.D. called the "medieval climate optimum." It's climate cooling we should be afraid of — how to hold off the soon-expected ice age.

In light of these more sober appraisals we need to reexamine the treaty's goal of greenhouse-gas stabilization: its need, timing and feasibility. The need is rapidly disappearing in light of better science. The timing can be delayed safely by a decade or more, as indicated by the IPCC's own analyses. By then we also will have 25 years' worth of satellite data and perhaps a better scientific understanding of what's wrong with the theory.

The feasibility of the treaty's prescriptions should concern politicians the most. How on earth can one reconcile economic development — the other aim of the UNCED Earth Summit — with cutting back on energy use in less-developed nations? It is hard to believe that the statesmen assembled in Rio were blind to this obvious contradiction.

Before entrenched constituencies create more mischief and economic disasters by insisting on mandatory cutbacks of carbon-dioxide emissions — and energy use — we should first do the following:

On the scientific side, find out what is wrong with the models — whether it's their inadequate treatment of clouds or mishandling of water vapor, the most important of the greenhouse gases.

Beyond research, society should take all the prudent steps that make sense even without the global-warming scare: conserving energy, increasing efficiency and adding forest mass by cutting fewer trees and planting more. Finally — dare we mention it? — we should encourage nuclear energy. These are the steps recommended in 1991 by geophysicist Roger Revelle, "father" of greenhouse warming and Gore's one-time Harvard mentor.

Revelle also recommended that we "look before we leap" and cautioned against taking "drastic steps" — even before it was recognized that the theoretical warming predictions were not validated by the climate observations. In letters written in July 1988, at the height of the warming scare, to then-Rep. Jim Bates of California and then-Sen. Tim Wirth of Colorado, Revelle advised, "My own personal belief is that we should wait another ten or twenty years to really be convinced that the greenhouse is going to be important for human beings, in both positive and negative ways."

This is still good advice.

Questions for Discussion

1. What criteria should be used in evaluating the policy goals of scientists who differ about the likelihood of global warming?
2. What policies should the United States pursue to deal with global warming? What are the reasons for your answer?
3. Who would benefit from a massive program to reduce greenhouse gases?
4. Who would be hurt from a massive program to reduce greenhouse gases?
5. What effect should the policy of other nations on global warming have on the U.S. policy on this issue? What are the reasons for your answer?

Suggested Readings

Bailey, Ronald. "Fevers, Fires, Floods, oh my! . . . ." *Weekly Standard* 1, no. 20 (February 5, 1996): 12–13.

Gore, Albert. *Earth in the Balance: Ecology and the Human Spirit.* Boston: Houghton Mifflin, 1992.

Gribbin, John, and Mary Gribbin. "The Greenhouse Effect." *New Scientist* 151, no. 2037 (July 6, 1996): SS1–SS4.

Hertsgaard, Mark. "Who's Afraid of Global Warming?" *Washington Post*, January 21, 1996, pp. C1, C4.

Lempert, Robert. "A Global Warming Middle Ground." *Los Angeles Times*, November 16, 1995, p. B9.

Mathews, Jessica. "Global Warming No Longer in Doubt." *Washington Post*, December 26, 1995, p. A23.

Mitchell, George. *World on Fire: Saving an Endangered Earth.* New York: Charles Scribner's Sons, 1991.

Moore, Thomas Gale. *Global Warming: A Boon to Humans and Other Animals.* Stanford, Calif.: Hoover Institution on War, Revolution and Peace, 1995.

Parsons, Michael L. *Global Warming: The Truth behind the Myth.* New York: Insight Books, 1995.

Turekian, Karl K. *Environmental Change: Past, Present, and Future.* Upper Saddle River, N.J.: Prentice Hall, 1996.

Vogel, Shawna. "Has Global Warming Begun?" *Earth* 4, no. 6 (December 1995): 24–34.

Wildavsky, Aaron B. *But Is It True? A Citizen's Guide to Health and Safety Issues.* Cambridge, Mass.: Harvard University Press, 1995.

Chapter 22

Does the United Nations Serve U.S. Interests?

As a new country in the late eighteenth century, the United States sought to avoid foreign entanglements. Fearing that alliances would get the nation involved in overseas wars, it preferred to focus on continental expansion and economic development. Throughout most of the nineteenth century the United States could maintain a policy of isolationism because the major powers of the world were often more concerned about security threats from their neighboring rivals than they were about conflicts with the United States. Geography — protection from two oceans — was also a factor.

Beginning in the late nineteenth century, the United States became increasingly involved in world politics. As a result of war with Spain in 1898, the United States acquired the Philippines and became a Pacific power. In 1917 it joined Great Britain, France, and their allies in World War I and helped defeat Germany. After the war, President Woodrow Wilson hoped to involve the United States in a permanent international organization, the League of Nations. But he was unable to persuade the Senate to approve U.S. membership. The League continued without U.S. membership but failed to avoid World War II.

During World War II, President Franklin Roosevelt recommended the establishment of a new international organization and urged the United States to join. In 1945, the United States became a founding member of the United Nations (UN). The birth of this international organization coming at the end of a devastating world war brought hope to many Americans that a new world order would usher in an era of peace. Shortly after the organization was born, however, the United States and the Soviet Union, two superpowers, began a period of intense conflict known as the cold war marked by political, economic, and ideological competition. The United Nations became in part a vehicle for the conflict of the two superpowers. That conflict ended when the Soviet Union fragmented into many independent countries by the early 1990s, and the character of the United Nations changed.

In its more than half century, the United Nations has been involved in many matters dealing with international security and peace. It has played a role in mediating disputes among nations, generating support for the independence of new nations, and promoting arms control treaties. On a few occasions, it has deployed the armed forces of member countries to fight under its auspices, such as in the Korean War in the 1950s and in the Persian Gulf War against Iraq in 1991. It has also engaged in peacekeeping operations in which conflicting parties accepted UN observers or forces to keep the peace. Up to mid-1995, the United Nations had sent more than 750,000 peacekeepers on thirty-eight missions around the world at a total cost of $14 billion. And in 1995, it had 67,000 peacekeepers deployed in many countries, including the former Yugoslavia, Rwanda, and Cyprus.

To perform the goals set forth in the Charter, the United Nations is composed of several organs, the best known of which are the Security Council, the General Assembly, and the Secretariat. The Security Council consists of five permanent members and ten nonpermanent members. The permanent members are the United States, Russia, Great Britain, France, and China. Nonpermanent members serve for terms of five years. The Security Council has the power to take military and economic action. But the permanent members have a power to veto a proposal and prevent even a majority of the Security Council from deciding that matter.

The General Assembly is the principal deliberative body of the United Nations. All members of the organization are members of the General Assembly, and each member state has one vote. The General Assembly makes recommendations on issues. And the Secretariat performs all UN administrative functions. It is headed by the secretary general, who serves for a five-year term. The United Nations also consists of specialized agencies that deal with a variety of matters, including peaceful uses of atomic energy, economic development of poor countries, monetary cooperation, telecommunications, world health, world trade, and refugees.

The United Nations depends primarily on the financial support of member nations to fund its operations. An assessment is made on each nation based on national and per capita income. When the organization was established, the United States paid nearly half of its budget, but that rate was lowered to 25 percent as other nations grew more prosperous. The United States, however, is still the largest contributor. UN peacekeeping operations come out of a separate budget. The United States was paying 32 percent of peacekeeping operations but reduced that amount to 25 percent.

Starting in the 1980s, the United States began to withhold contributions to the United Nations in response to the organization's anti-Israel measures and its criticism of Western capitalism. By October 1996, it owed $1.7 billion.

Although the United States was a principal sponsor of the United Nations in 1945, some Americans have been critical of it. From its earliest days, some Americans feared that the organization was undermining U.S. sovereignty. In the years of the cold war, some Americans complained about the undue influence of communist countries in the organization. And criticism has also been made about the views of developing nations.

Both Republican and Democratic presidents have supported continuing American participation in the United Nations. But both Republican and Democratic presidents and members of Congress have expressed criticism of some UN policies and procedures. President Bill Clinton has called for reforms in the size and management of the UN bureaucracy. House Republicans in the 104th Congress called for reducing U.S. contributions to UN peacekeeping operations and restricting U.S. troop participation under UN command.

One of the enduring issues is whether the United Nations serves U.S. interests; this is the issue considered in the debate below. Madeleine K. Albright, former U.S. permanent representative to the United Nations and now secretary of state, argues that the United Nations serves U.S. interests. Speaking before the Women's Fund of the North Carolina Community Foundation, she notes:

1. The UN Charter protects American interests.
2. The United Nations is no threat to the Constitution and has no authority to entangle the United States in foreign conflicts.
3. The United Nations has made the world safer by helping to prevent outbreaks of violence in strategic regions, working to prevent nuclear weapons from falling into the hands of outlaw states, invoking sanctions against countries that support terrorism, establishing war crimes trials, promoting freedom, and strengthening democracy and peace.
4. The United Nations has made the world more humane by caring for refugees, providing food for children, and preventing the spread of epidemic disease.
5. UN specialized agencies perform a variety of useful functions.
6. The United Nations helps build a global consensus about the difference between right and wrong.
7. The United Nations does have weaknesses, such as an unnecessarily large bureaucracy and poor management, that require change. But these weaknesses can be corrected through reforming the United Nations rather than through abandoning it. The United States should pay up the money it owes to the organization so that its credibility to influence change will be strengthened.

Former Member of Congress Andrea Seastrand argues that the United Nations does not serve U.S. interests and that it is time for the United States to consider withdrawing from the international organization. She contends:

1. Because of U.S. involvement in the United Nations, the United States has become involved in one foreign quarrel after another, including Korea, Vietnam, and Bosnia.
2. Recent UN policy in trouble spots as Rwanda, Somalia, and Bosnia have served to increase conflict and human suffering.
3. The United Nations is one of the least representative political entities in the world, a situation that weakens the influence of the United States in the United Nations.

4. The United Nations is marked by waste and an excessively large bureaucracy.
5. The United States could withdraw from the United Nations and at the same time support those specialized UN agencies that are doing good work.
6. The United Nations does not support basic principles of human rights that are part of the Bill of Rights.
7. The United Nations is no friend to the free enterprise system.

 YES

Does the United Nations Serve U.S. Interests?

MADELEINE K. ALBRIGHT

The United Nations: What's in It for the United States?

Today . . . I thought I would talk about the United Nations and about America's role in it. I will outline why I believe our interests are served by our participation in and leadership at the UN. I will summarize our effort to reform that organization so that it works better and costs less. And I will describe the Administration's plan for meeting our obligations to it.

The UN was designed primarily by Americans — of both genders. But despite that, we have always been of two minds about it. We recognize the need for an institution that helps countries work together, but . . . we do not accept — and will never submit to — the idea of world government.

Fortunately, President Truman understood that, and, in signing the UN Charter, he was careful to protect American interests. As a result, the only part of the UN with the authority to compel anyone to do anything is the Security Council, of which we are a permanent member, with the right to veto any proposal we don't like.

So do not worry. The UN is no threat to our Constitution. It has no power to tax us. It has no authority to entangle us in foreign conflicts. And despite the fantasies of some, it is not going to descend upon us in black helicopters in the middle of the night and steal our lawn furniture.

As Republican Senator Arthur Vandenberg said a half-century ago, under the UN Charter, "America retains every basic attribute of its sovereignty. . . . In a word . . . the flag stays on the [Capitol] dome." For the past fifty years, that is where the flag has stayed, while administrations from both parties have found value to the United States in a UN that works. Over time, the UN system has made our world safer by helping to prevent outbreaks of violence in strategic regions such as Cyprus and the Middle East and by working to prevent nuclear weapons from falling into the hands of outlaw states. It has made

our world more just by invoking sanctions against countries that support terrorism, such as Libya and Iraq; by establishing war crimes tribunals for
Rwanda and the Balkans; and by denouncing Cuba's criminal shootdown of
civilian aircraft nine days ago [February 24, 1996]. It has made our world
more free by helping nations such as South Africa, El Salvador, Cambodia,
and Haiti make the great leap from division or war toward democracy and
peace. And it has made our world more humane by caring for refugees, providing food for children, and preventing the spread of epidemic disease.

The UN's specialized agencies also perform indispensable services. You
may think you have never benefited personally from the UN, but if you have
ever traveled on an international airline or shipping line, placed a phone call
overseas, or received mail from outside the country, you have been served directly or indirectly by the UN system.

In addition to all this, the UN provides a means for building a global consensus about the difference between right and wrong. In the UN's early days,
a great American First Lady, Eleanor Roosevelt, helped draft the Universal Declaration of Human Rights. This past fall, at the Fourth World Conference on
Women, another great First Lady reaffirmed America's commitment to that declaration in eloquent and memorable terms.

All Americans can take pride in the message Mrs. Clinton brought to Beijing
— a message that applies both in the United States and overseas — a message
that says that the physical abuse of women must stop; that the life of a girl
should be valued equally with that of a boy; that there should be equal access
to education, health care, and the levers of economic and political power;
and that women's rights are neither separable nor different from those of men.

Our goal now, in following up the women's conference, is to make this
message a reality. And let no one doubt what is at stake. Today, around the
world, appalling abuses are being committed against women, including coerced abortions and sterilizations, children sold into prostitution, ritual mutila-
tions, dowry murders, and official indifference to violence. Some say this is all
cultural and that there is nothing we can do about it. I say it's criminal and
that it is the responsibility of each and every one of us to stop it.

Despite recent gains, women remain an undervalued and underdeveloped
human resource. This is not to say that women have trouble finding work. In many
societies, in addition to bearing the children, women do most of the work. But
often they are barred from owning land, excluded from schools, denied financial
credit, provided less nourishment, and permitted little or no voice in government.

The Women's Conference could not solve these problems overnight, but it
could — and did — outline a plan for addressing them. This matters not only
to women but to all of us, for when women are empowered, families are
strengthened, socially constructive values are taught, sexually transmitted disease is slowed, and the global economy — upon which so many American
jobs depend — expands.

In summary, the UN system and the services it provides allow us to accomplish many things that matter to our families and to our country but which we

could not do or could not afford to do on our own. That is why former President Reagan urged the U.S. to "rely more on multilateral institutions." It is why President Bush called the UN a key instrument in enforcing international security and peace. And it is what President Truman meant when he said:

> We have tried to write into the Charter of the United Nations the essence of religion. The end of aggression, the maintenance of peace, the promotion of social justice and [the defense of] individual rights and freedoms — by these principles, the UN . . . laid the groundwork of the Charter on the sound rock of religious principles.

So the UN has accomplished much. Its goals are the right ones. Its success matters to America. But . . . the UN of today does not work as well as it should.

Here in North Carolina and throughout our country, citizens are demanding a dollar's worth of value for every tax dollar we spend. Our contributions to the UN should be no exception. Unfortunately, the UN developed wasteful habits during the Cold War that have yet to be fully cured.

Part of the problem is that the UN, because it has so many members, is inherently hard to manage. I have often compared it to a business with 185 members of the board — each from a different culture, each with a different philosophy of management, each with unshakable confidence in his or her own opinions, and each with a brother-in-law who is unemployed. As a result, the UN bureaucracy has grown to elephantine proportions. Now that the Cold War is over, we are asking that elephant to do gymnastics. That is why the Clinton Administration, with strong support from both parties in Congress, has been pushing so hard for UN reform.

That effort has already produced results: To make peacekeeping missions more effective, the Security Council has improved planning and has established rigorous guidelines to be considered before new missions are approved. A UN Inspector General has been appointed to crack down on fraud and waste. The UN's Undersecretary General for Management is an American — a former CEO of Price-Waterhouse — who is applying fiscal discipline learned in the corporate world. Last December [1995], the General Assembly approved a "no-growth" budget that will result in a 10 percent reduction in the number of UN Secretariat staff. A new efficiency board has been created, and a high-level group on reform has been charged with developing a blueprint for the UN for the twenty-first century.

In recent weeks, the U.S. has proposed a host of additional steps to make the UN smaller, better organized, and more productive. It is becoming clear, however, that the U.S. will not be able to gain support from other countries to make the kind of far-reaching changes wanted unless we are able to pay the UN what we owe it for past bills. Currently, we are almost $900 million behind in our payments.

Now, I get very indignant at the UN when other countries fail to meet their legal obligations. If anyone doubts that, they can ask the Cubans or Saddam Hussein. But in recent months, when I have tried to focus my colleagues on the reform agenda, I have found instead that the United States has become the agenda. Whenever I talk about how we can make the UN work better, I am told by friendly and not-so-friendly nations alike: If you care about making the UN work better than it does, why doesn't the U.S. pay its bills? The situation is so bad that the British Foreign Secretary, in a soundbite his countrymen have been waiting 200 years to use, has accused us of seeking "representation without taxation."

At the same time, we face skeptics in the Congress who doubt that the UN can be reformed enough to be worth continuing U.S. support. We have launched a bipartisan dialogue with both the House and Senate to try to come up with a plan that links UN reform to a reliable commitment by the U.S. to meet its obligations.

While it is possible that there are some in Congress who will never support funding for the UN, I am convinced that the majority would like to see us pay what we owe. As one Senate committee chairman told me, "the sanctity of contracts is fundamental to Republican philosophy. It's only those liberals who think you can have something for nothing."

Accordingly, we will be asking Congress to approve this year a five-year plan for paying our arrears to the UN. As we expect Congress will insist, the actual payment of those funds would occur as the UN reforms, keeps its budget down, and cuts unnecessary staff. We also will be asking UN members to reduce from 25 percent to 20 percent the U.S. share of the UN's regular budget. The way the UN works, this would have the effect of reducing our peacekeeping rate to no more than 25 percent.

The result of all this for the UN would be a more equitable and reliable system of financing. And for the American people, it would assure our continued leadership within a more effective UN at a reduced cost consistent with our effort to balance the budget. In other words, this is a true "win-win" proposition.

I believe that, with strong American leadership, the UN can become a powerful instrument for expanding freedom, human rights, and open markets around the globe. Although the outlook today is cloudy, I am confident that — in the end — we will have bipartisan support for providing that leadership. The nature of the world today demands it. Most Members of Congress understand it. The American people expect that kind of burden-sharing. And our participation in the UN has always had strong support from both parties.

We should never forget that the UN emerged not from a dream but from a nightmare. In the 1920s and 1930s, the world squandered an opportunity to organize the peace. The result was the invasion of Manchuria, the conquest of Ethiopia, the betrayal of Munich, the depravity of the Holocaust, and the devastation of world war.

It was not enough to say, after World War II, that the enemy had been vanquished — that what we were against had failed. We had to build the foundation of a lasting peace. And together, the generation of Truman, Marshall, Eisenhower, and Vandenberg designed a framework of principle and power that would one day defeat communism and promote democratic values and respect for human rights around the world.

Today, under President Clinton, we are called upon to develop a new framework for protecting our territory, our citizens, and our interests. In devising that framework, we will make necessary use of our own military and economic power. We will invite help from old friends and new. We will strengthen and reform the UN. And, because we are Americans, we will not shy from the responsibilities of global leadership.

My own family came to these shores as refugees. Because of this nation's generosity and commitment, we were granted asylum after the communist takeover of Czechoslovakia. The story of my family has been repeated in millions of variations over two centuries in the lives not only of immigrants, but of those overseas who have been liberated or sheltered by American soldiers, empowered by American assistance, or inspired by American ideals.

I will never forget something the then-Foreign Minister of Israel, Shimon Peres, said during the Middle East peace signing ceremony on the White House lawn two years ago — when the history books are written, he said,

> . . . nobody really will understand the United States. You have so much force and you didn't conquer the land of anyone. You have so much power and you didn't dominate another people. You have problems of your own and you have never turned your back on the problems of others.

This generation — our generation — of Americans has a proud legacy to fulfill. We have been given an opportunity at the threshold of a new century to build a world in which totalitarianism and fascism are absent, in which human liberty is expanded, in which human rights are respected, and in which our people are as secure as we can ever expect them to be. Let us, together, welcome that opportunity — not as Republicans or Democrats, not as men or women, but as Americans. And if we are together, you may be sure that we will succeed.

☑ NO

Does the United Nations Serve U.S. Interests?

ANDREA SEASTRAND

U.S. Security and World Peace Would Benefit from a Pullback

For nearly 50 years the United Nations has been the hub around which U.S. foreign policy has revolved. This entangling alliance with the world body and its web of specialized agencies and institutions has resulted in our involvement in one foreign quarrel after another, from Korea to Vietnam to Bosnia. We have paid dearly, in terms of blood, treasure and potential loss of sovereignty, for ignoring the sound advice of our first president who stated in his farewell address: "The great rule of conduct for us, in regard to foreign nations, is, in extending our commercial relations, to have with them as little political connection as possible."

In such recent trouble spots as Rwanda, Somalia and Bosnia, the UN has not merely proved inept in reducing conflict and human suffering; its efforts have served to increase both. In Bosnia, UN policy from the beginning has bolstered the Serbians at the expense of the Bosnian Muslims. The arms embargo, which effectively hamstrung only the Muslims, is merely one indication of that effect. Sadly, U.S. policy under the previous Republican and current Democrat administrations has let the deplorable UN policy lead us by the nose.

A recent political cartoon showed the Bosnian Serbs and the Muslims in a boxing ring. As the Serbs repeatedly delivered punishing left hooks, jabs and right crosses to the head of the Muslims, Uncle Sam stood behind the Muslims and held their arms back. That is what we have done with this dreadful UN's policy. Not only can the Muslims not launch an offensive combination of punches to regain a fair position in the fight, they cannot even bring their arms up to defend against the barrage launched against them.

Congress is working quickly to undo the damage caused by the Bosnian arms embargo. The Senate, by a veto-proof margin, voted to lift the arms embargo to allow the Muslims to defend themselves and the House voted August 1 [1995] to do the same. If this president will not lead in foreign policy, Congress will serve as a means to make basic, sound decisions regarding our world leadership.

Virtually everyone appears to agree that the UN is plagued with serious defects. The question is whether such flaws can be mended through reform or are so deeply embedded that the time has come for the United States to withdraw rather than waste time in a futile attempt to make a proverbial silk purse out of what from its inception was a sow's ear. For instance, while professing adoration for "democracy," the UN is one of the least-representative political entities in the world. The concept of one-nation, one-vote has sanctified minority rule within the organization, and there is no realistic way to change it under the supermajority requirements for amending the UN charter.

In the 185-member U.N. General Assembly, the United States, with nearly 262 million citizens, has the same vote as Palau, the UN's most recent member, with a 1990 population of slightly more than 15,000. Ten other nations have populations less than 75,000. One hundred two countries, with a combined population less than that of the United States, compose a 55 percent majority in the General Assembly, while 166 nations (90 percent) have a combined gross domestic product that is less than that of the United States.

This imbalance has its most serious impact when the vast majority of small and poor nations join together to approve policies related to war, economic expenditures, wealth redistribution and regulatory restrictions that only the minority of prosperous countries can finance and conduct.

There appears to be a built-in orientation toward waste and extravagance, as there is with most large government bureaucracies. For instance, in response to the man-made famine and resulting human suffering inflicted on Ethiopia by dictator Mengistu Maile Mariam in the 1980s, the General Assembly's Fifth (Administrative and Budget) Committee voted to designate $73.5 million in UN funds for Ethiopia. But the money was earmarked not to feed the starving but to embellish conference facilities of the UN's Economic Commission for Africa in Addis Ababa. In response to criticism, a UN spokesman vigorously argued that the upgraded facilities were sorely needed because "the support facilities at Africa Hall are wholly inadequate for the needs of the ECA." The diet of the average Ethiopian also was wholly inadequate at the time. The American taxpayers' share of the UN's facelift was $18.4 million.

It may come as a surprise to the average American taxpayer that U.S. citizens employed by the UN do not, in essence, pay income tax. Their tax burden is reimbursed in full by the UN. The reason, as explained by the State Department, is to assure that all UN employees "have equal take-home pay for equal work." Since the United States picks up a quarter of the UN tab, it means that most taxpayers are subsidizing the lucky few who work for the world body. For 50 years the UN has depended largely on "contributions" from member states to finance its activities, but now there are increasing calls for imposition of a tax (or taxes) that would provide reliable and substantially increased funds.

One can only cringe at the prospect of a United Nations empowered with legislative, executive and judicial powers backed by a global military, regulatory and taxing apparatus. Such power would be the most absolute that the world has ever seen.

At the UN's founding 50 years ago and for a few years thereafter, it was claimed that the organization was "mankind's last, best hope for peace." Today, Americans increasingly recognize that the UN has sponsored wars, passed one-sided resolutions (the arms embargo against Bosnia) and imposed a selective standard of justice.

There are those who maintain that despite the many drawbacks associated with our involvement in the UN, we should stay in the organization to promote the good accomplished by some of its specialized agencies. Actually, if we were to withdraw from (and stop financing) the General Assembly and Security Council, we still could support whatever specialized agencies we wish. The first order of business is to decide whether we should dissolve our financial and political ties to the Security Council and General Assembly, a move largely unrelated to what we then do about the specialized UN agencies.

The matter of human rights is another issue on which the United Nations' view is intrinsically at odds with the traditional American view. The first article of our Bill of Rights, for instance, states that "Congress shall make no law respecting an establishment of religion, or prohibiting the free exercise thereof; or abridging the freedom of speech, or of the press, or the right of the people peaceably to assemble, and to petition the Government for a redress of grievances." That wording clearly protects speech, reporting and petitioning that criticizes government. But consider the Universal Declaration of Human Rights, the UN's basic human-rights standard the General Assembly approved unanimously in 1948. The declaration espouses numerous rights in its early articles, then neuters them with this startling proclamation in Article 29, paragraph 3: "These rights and freedoms may in no case be exercised contrary to the purposes and principles of the United Nations." Which would seem to

mean that the article you are reading could be banned, as could any other effort critical of the alleged purposes and principles of the United Nations.

If the UN were to be dismantled, with what would it be replaced? Author G.
Edward Griffin, who has written extensively on UN-related issues, suggests that
we try freedom, by which he means "freedom for all people, everywhere, to live
as they please with no super-government directing them; freedom to succeed or
to fail and to try again; freedom to make mistakes and even to be foolish in the
eyes of others." Griffin contends that "until all nations follow the concept of limited government, it is unlikely that universal peace will ever be attained."

Someone once speculated that peace on Earth would come when its peoples
had as much as possible to do with each other, and their governments had as little as possible to do with the lives of the people. Most Americans likely would
support a federation of nations that was honestly intended to increase the freedom of individuals, goods and cultures legally to cross national boundaries and
to decrease government restrictions on individuals. But the United Nations has,
since its founding, been a powerful force pushing in the opposite direction.

There has never been a friend of the free-enterprise economic system at the
UN's helm. Those who have held the post of secretary-general since the UN
was conceived have favored big, rather than limited, government. The list includes the current secretary-general, Boutros Boutros-Ghali of Egypt, who has
sought dramatically to strengthen the UN militarily while emphasizing wealth
redistribution as an economic solution to the plight of poor nations.

The UN's heavy emphasis on wealth redistribution appears to be immune
to meaningful reform. If the UN and its specialized agencies were allowed to
confiscate everything from the "have" countries and distribute it to peoples in
the "have not" nations, the overall misery of the latter would scarcely be affected. There are simply too many of the latter, thanks in large part to the oppressive collectivist governments under which they live. If those countries
could break free of the shackles of socialism that weight them and adopt the
basic economic principles that were largely responsible for our own abun-
dance, the contribution to world stability and well-being would be unprecedented. The United Nations, sadly, stands as a roadblock to such a change. It
must be removed before there will be a real chance to cope effectively with
the problems of world hunger and poverty.

Former U.S. Ambassador to NATO [North Atlantic Treaty Organization]
Harlan Cleveland observed 30 years ago that "it is almost impossible even to
think about a durable world peace without the United Nations." Today, it
seems even more inconceivable to contemplate a durable world peace while
the UN meddles. As the noted American journalist Henry J. Taylor once
wrote, UN diplomacy "is like a man walking in the woods who stopped when
he saw a snake. It turned out to be a stick. But the stick he picked up to kill it
with turned out to be a snake." Throughout its 50-year existence the UN has
proved to be more serpent than savior. Twenty years ago former New Hampshire Gov. Meldrom Thomson concluded his overview of the UN in his book,
Live Free or Die, with these words: "Let us withdraw from the United Nations
and insist that the United Nations withdraw from the United States." Today,

that conclusion needs to be seriously discussed, debated and then acted upon in this country whose role as world leader is in question when we defer to the often ludicrous decisions of the United Nations.

In the words of Margaret Thatcher, "Consensus is the negation of leadership." If we continue to make our foreign policy subservient to the will of the UN, we will risk forfeiting our position as moral world leader.

Questions for Discussion

1. If the United States withdraws from the United Nations, what changes will occur in international politics? What are the reasons for your answer?
2. If the United States withdraws from the United Nations, what changes will occur in U.S. foreign policy? What are the reasons for your answer?
3. Why does the United States remain a member of the United Nations?
4. How can the United Nations be forced to make reforms?
5. What role should the United States play in peacekeeping operations?

Suggested Readings

Allen, James H. *Peacekeeping: Outspoken Observations by a Field Officer.* Westport, Conn.: Praeger, 1996.

Boutros-Ghali, Boutros. *An Agenda for Peace, 1995.* New York: United Nations, 1995.

Childers, Erskine. *Challenges to the United Nations: Building a Safer World.* New York: St. Martin's Press, 1995.

Helms, Jesse. "An Ultimatum to the U.N.: Reform or Die." *Wall Street Journal,* August 20, 1996, p. A10.

Maynes, Charles William, and Richard S. Williamson. *U.S. Foreign Policy and the United Nations System.* New York: W. W. Norton, 1996.

Meisler, Stanley. *The United Nations: The First Fifty Years.* New York: Atlantic Monthly Press, 1995.

Muravchik, Joshua. "What Use Is the UN?" *Commentary* 101, no. 4 (April 1996): 51–54.

Rieff, David. *Slaughterhouse: Bosnia and the Failure of the West.* New York: Simon & Schuster, 1996.

Simons, G. L. *UN Malaise: Power, Problems, and Realpolitik.* New York: St. Martin's Press, 1995.

U.S. Cong., House of Representatives. *The United Nations at 50: Prospects for Reform.* Hearing before the Committee on International Relations, 104th Cong., 1st Sess., 1995.

Zacarias, Agostinho. *The United Nations and International Peacekeeping.* New York: St. Martin's Press, 1996.

Acknowledgements (continued from page ii)

Theodore M. Shaw, prepared statement for U.S. Congress, House of Representatives. *Hearings on Affirmative Action in Employment*. Hearings before the Subcommittee on Employer-Employee Relations of the Committee on Economic and Educational Opportunities, 104 Cong., 1st Sess., 1995, pp. 167–186. Citations appear as endnotes.

Brian W. Jones, prepared statement for U.S. Congress, Senate. *Affirmative Action and the Office of Federal Contract Compliance*. Hearing of the Committee on Labor and Human Resources, 104th Cong., 1st Sess., 1995, pp. 77–82.

S. I. Hayakawa, "Bilingualism in America: English Should Be the *Only* Language." Reprinted from *USA Today Magazine* 118, no. 2530 (July 1989): 32–34. © July 1989 by Society for the Advancement of Education, Inc.

James C. Stalker, "Official English or English Only," *English Journal* 77, no. 3 (March 1988): 18–23. Copyright © 1988 by the National Council of Teachers of English. Reprinted with permission.

Gerald M. Pomper and Susan S. Lederman, "Elections and Democratic Politics." Reprinted by permission of the authors from Gerald I.M. Pomper and Susan S. Lederman, *Elections in America: Control and Influence in Democratic Politics*, 2d ed. (New York: Longman, 1980), pp. 210–227. Tables have been renumbered.

Howard L. Reiter, *Parties and Elections in Corporate America*, 2d ed. (New York: Longman, 1992), pp. 1–9. Copyright © 1993 by Longman Publishers. Reprinted by permission. Further Reading has been omitted.

Ann McBride, testimony before the Senate Committee on Rules and Administration, February 1, 1996. News release from Common Cause, February 1, 1996.

Bradley A. Smith, "Campaign Finance Regulation: Faulty Assumptions and Undemocratic Consequences." *Policy Analysis*, no. 238 (Washington, D.C.: Cato Institute, September 13, 1995). Executive summary and footnotes have been omitted.

Lawrence D. Longley, prepared statement for U.S. Congress, Senate. *The Electoral College and the Direct Election of the President*. Hearing before the Subcommittee on the Constitution of the Committee on the Judiciary, 102d Cong., 2d Sess., 1992, pp. 29–37.

Judith A. Best, prepared statement for U.S. Congress, Senate. *The Electoral College and the Direct Election of the President*. Hearing before the Subcommittee on the Constitution of the Committee on the Judiciary, 102d Cong., 2d Sess., 1992, pp. 88–101.

Robert Novak, "Political Correctness Has No Place in the Newsroom." *USA Today Magazine* 123, no. 2958 (March 1995): 44–45. © 1995 by Society for the Advancement of Education, Inc.

William H. Rentschler, "Resisting Pressures on a Free Press." *USA Today Magazine* 124, no. 2602 (July 1995): 68–70. © 1995 by Society for the Advancement of Education, Inc.

David M. Mason, testimony before U.S. Congress, House of Representatives. *Term Limits for Members of the U.S. Senate and House of Representatives*. Hearings before the Subcommittee on Civil and Constitutional Rights of the Committee on the Judiciary, 101st Cong., 1st and 2d Sess., 1993–1994, pp. 37–47.

Thomas E. Mann, prepared statement for U.S. Congress, House of Representatives. *Term Limits for Members of the U.S. Senate and House of Representatives*. Hearings before the Subcommittee on Civil and Constitutional Rights of the Committee on the Judiciary, 103d Cong., 1st and 2d Sess., 1993–1994, pp. 14–30.

Henry Hyde, "The Case for Repealing the War Powers Act." From *Congressional Record* 141, no. 92 (June 7, 1995): H5655–5656.

Lee Hamilton, "The Case against Repealing the War Powers Act." From *Congressional Record* 141, no. 92 (June 7, 1995): H5664–5665.

Thomas J. DiLorenzo, "Most of the Federal Government Is Unconstitutional and Should Be Abolished." *Insight on the News* 11, no. 46 (December 4, 1995): 18, 20–21. Reprinted with permission from *Insight*. Copyright 1995 *Insight*. All rights reserved.

Victor Kamber, "The American People Haven't Lost Faith in the Federal Government." *Insight on the News* 11, no. 46 (December 4, 1995): 19, 21. Reprinted with permission from *Insight*. Copyright 1995 *Insight*. All rights reserved.

Stephen L. Carter, *The Confirmation Mess: Cleaning Up the Federal Appointments Process* (New York: Basic Books, 1994), pp. 16–22. Copyright © 1994 by Stephen L. Carter. Footnotes have been omitted.

Michael A. Kahn, "Is There a Confirmation Mess? An Analysis of Professor Stephen Carter's Critique of the Federal Appointments Process." *California Law Review* 83, no. 1 (January 1995): 477–484. Copyright © 1995 California Law Review, Inc. Footnotes have been omitted.

Jeffrey M. Shaman and J. Clifford Wallace, "Interpreting the Constitution." *Judicature: The Journal of the American Judicature Society* 71, no. 2 (August/September, 1987), pp. 80–87, 122. Reprinted with permission of the authors.

Pamphlet published by Coalition to Stop Gun Violence, Washington, D.C., 1996. Copyright © 1996 by the Coalition to Stop Gun Violence. National Rifle Association, "Ten Myths About Gun Control," published by the National Rifle Association Institute for Legislative Action. March 1996.

David Boaz, prepared statement for U.S. Congress, House of Representatives. *Legalization of Illicit Drugs Part II*, Hearing before the Select Committee on Narcotics Abuse and Control, 100th Cong., 2d Sess., 1988, pp. 144–153.

Edward I. Koch, testimony before U.S. Cong., House of Representatives. *Legalization of Illicit Drugs: Impact and Possibility, Part I*, Hearing before the Select Committee on Narcotics Abuse and Control, 100th Cong., 2d Sess., 1988, pp. 231–239.

Robert T. Watson and S. Fred Singer, "Q: Is Man-Made Global Warming a Proven Environmental Threat?" *Insight on the News* 11, no. 34 (September 4, 1995): 18–21. Reprinted with permission from *Insight*. Copyright 1995 *Insight*. All rights reserved.

Madeleine K. Albright, "The UN: What's in It for the U.S.?" *U.S. Department of State Dispatch* 7, no. 11 (March 11, 1996): 104–106.

Andrea Seastrand, "U.S. Security and World Peace Would Benefit from a Pullback." *Insight on the News* 11, no. 33 (August 2, 1995): 18, 20–21. Reprinted with permission from *Insight*. Copyright 1995 *Insight*. All rights reserved.

Contributors

HERBERT M. LEVINE *taught political science at the University of Southwestern Louisiana for twenty years. He has written and edited several political science textbooks. He is currently a writer who lives in Chevy Chase, Maryland. He is coauthor most recently of* More than a Uniform: A Navy Woman in a Navy Man's World *(University of North Texas Press, 1997) and author of four books in the American Issues Debated series published by Raintree Steck-Vaughn in 1998.*

MADELEINE K. ALBRIGHT served as the U.S. permanent representative to the United Nations in the first administration of President Bill Clinton. She is currently secretary of state.

JAMES C. ANDERS is an attorney in the law firm of Fedor, Anders, Massey, and Whitlark in Columbia, South Carolina.

JUDITH A. BEST is Distinguished Teaching Professor of Political Science at the State University of New York at Cortland. She is author of *The Choice of the People? Debating the Electoral College* (Rowman & Littlefield).

DAVID BOAZ is executive vice-president of the Cato Institute in Washington, D.C. He is editor of *The Crisis in Drug Prohibition* (Cato Institute).

STEPHEN L. CARTER is William Nelson Cromwell Professor of Law at Yale University. He is author of *The Confirmation Mess: Cleaning Up the Federal Appointments Process* (Basic Books) and *Integrity* (Basic Books).

The **COALITION TO STOP GUN VIOLENCE**, a coalition of more than forty religious, professional, labor, medical, education, and civic organizations, has as its goal the orderly elimination of the private sale of handguns and assault weapons in the United States.

KIRK COX is a member of the House of Delegates, Commonwealth of Virginia.

THOMAS J. DILORENZO is professor of economics at Loyola College of Maryland in Baltimore and co-author of *Underground Government: The Off-Budget Public Sector* (Cato Institute).

J. MICHAEL ECHEVARRIA is associate professor of law, Southwestern University School of Law in Los Angeles.

LEE HAMILTON is a Democratic member of the House of Representatives from Indiana.

S. I. HAYAKAWA (1906–1992) was a U.S. senator from California. He was honorary chairman of U.S. English, a public interest organization in Washington, D.C., working to establish English as the official language of the United States.

HENRY HYDE is a Republican member of the House of Representatives from Illinois.

JEFF JACOBY is a columnist for the *Boston Globe*.

BRIAN W. JONES is president of the Center for New Black Leadership, a think tank in Washington, D.C.

MICHAEL A. KAHN is a practicing attorney with Folger, Levin, and Kahn and a member of the Board of Trustees of the Center for the Study of the Presidency.

VICTOR KAMBER, author of *Giving Up on Democracy: Why Term Limits Are Bad for America* (Regnery), is a Democratic consultant and president of the Kamber Group.

JOHN G. KESTER is a Washington attorney. He was once a law clerk to Justice Hugo Black.

EDWARD I. KOCH was mayor of New York City from 1978 to 1989. He was a member of the House of Representatives from 1969 to 1972.

SUSAN S. LEDERMAN is professor of public administration at Kean College in Union, New Jersey.

LAWRENCE D. LONGLEY is professor of government at Lawrence University in Appleton, Wisconsin. He is coauthor of both *The Politics of Electoral College Reform* (Yale University Press) and *The People's President: The Electoral College in American History and the Direct Vote Alternative* (Yale Univ. Press).

BARRY W. LYNN is executive director of Americans United for Separation of Church and State and coauthor of *The Right to Religious Liberty: The Basic ACLU Guide to Religious Rights* (Southern Illinois Univ. Press).

389

THOMAS E. MANN is director of government studies, Brookings Institution, Washington, D.C.

THURGOOD MARSHALL (1908–1993) served as associate justice of the U.S. Supreme Court from 1967 to 1991. As chief counsel for the National Association for the Advancement of Colored People Legal Defense and Educational Fund, he argued and won the 1954 landmark school desegregation case, *Brown v. Board of Education of Topeka, Kansas.*

DAVID M. MASON is director of the U.S. Congress Assessment Project of the Heritage Foundation, Washington, D.C.

ANN MCBRIDE is president of Common Cause, a public interest organization in Washington, D.C.

WILLIAM J. MURRAY is head of Citizens to Restore Voluntary School Prayer, based in Washington, D.C.

The **NATIONAL RIFLE ASSOCIATION INSTITUTE FOR LEGISLATIVE ACTION** is the legislative arm of the National Rifle Association, an organization that supports the right of Americans to have guns.

ROBERT NOVAK is a nationally syndicated columnist and co-host of the CNN interview program *Evans and Novak.*

WILLIAM T. PIZZI is professor of law at the University of Colorado.

GERALD M. POMPER is Board of Governors Professor at Rutgers University in New Brunswick, New Jersey, and author of *Passions and Interests* (Univ. Press of Kansas).

WILLIAM REHNQUIST is chief justice of the U.S. Supreme Court.

HOWARD L. REITER is a professor in the Department of Political Science at the University of Connecticut, Storrs. He is author of *Selecting the President: The Nominating Process in Transition* (Univ. of Pennsylvania Press).

WILLIAM H. RENTSCHLER, publisher of *The Rentschler Report,* a national journal of independent opinion, is a three-time winner of the Peter Lisagor Award by the Chicago Headline Club and a five-time Pulitzer Prize nominee.

WILLIAM BRADFORD REYNOLDS served as counselor to the attorney general and assistant attorney general in the Civil Rights Division of the Justice Department in the Reagan administration. He is an attorney in the law firm of Collier, Shannon, Rill, and Scott in Washington, D.C.

RABBI A. JAMES RUDIN is national interreligious affairs director of the American Jewish Committee (AJC). Before joining the professional staff of the AJC, he served Reform Jewish congregations in Kansas City, Missouri, and Champaign-Urbana, Illinois.

ANDREA SEASTRAND, a former Republican congresswoman from California, has been a state legislator and a public school teacher and is a longtime conservative activist.

LOUIS MICHAEL SEIDMAN is professor of law at Georgetown University Law Center in Washington D.C.

JEFFREY M. SHAMAN is Wicklander Professor of Law, DePaul College of Law in Chicago. He is also a senior fellow at the American Judicature Society.

THEODORE M. SHAW is associate director-counsel of the NAACP Legal Defense and Educational Fund, Inc.

S. FRED SINGER, an atmospheric physicist and former federal official, directs the Science and Environment Policy Project in Fairfax, Virginia.

BRADLEY A. SMITH is assistant professor at Capital State University Law School in Columbus, Ohio.

JAMES C. STALKER is a professor in the Department of English at Michigan State University in East Lansing.

ERNEST VAN DEN HAAG is the former John M. Olin Professor of Jurisprudence and Public Policy at Fordham University in New York City.

J. CLIFFORD WALLACE is chief judge, U.S. Court of Appeals for the Ninth Circuit.

ROBERT T. WATSON served as associate director for environment in the White House Office of Science and Technology Policy in the Clinton administration.